Boatowner's Illustrated Electrical Handbook

Second Edition

Charlie Wing

International Marine / McGraw-Hill

CAMDEN, MAINE • NEW YORK • CHICAGO • SAN FRANCISCO
LISBON • LONDON • MADRID • MEXICO CITY • MILAN
NEW DELHI • SAN JUAN • SEOUL • SINGAPORE • SYDNEY • TORONTO

1 2 3 4 5 6 7 8 9 10 QBC QBC 9 8 7 6

Library of Congress Cataloging-in-Publication Data
Wing, Charles, 1939–
   Boatowner's illustrated electrical handbook / Charlie Wing.—2nd ed.
      p. cm.
   Includes index.
   Rev. ed.: Boatowner's illustrated handbook of wiring, 1993.
   ISBN 978-1-265-62744-7 (pbk.)   ISBN 1-26-562744-4
   1. Boats and boating—Electric equipment. I. Wing, Charles, 1939–
Boatowner's illustrated handbook of wiring. II. Title.
   VM325.W56 2006
   623.8'503—dc22   2006000752

Questions regarding the content of this book should be addressed to
   International Marine
   P.O. Box 220
   Camden, ME 04843
   www.internationalmarine.com

Questions regarding the ordering of this book should be addressed to
   The McGraw-Hill Companies
   Customer Service Department
   P.O. Box 547
   Blacklick, OH 43004
   Retail customers: 1-800-262-4729
   Bookstores: 1-800-722-4726

Contents

Foreword

Since I have used Charlie Wing's first edition of the *Boatowner's Illustrated Electrical Handbook* as a text for some of my electrical courses over the years, I am quite familiar with its contents. I've just finished reviewing the second edition and can say without reservation that it is more than just an update. The diagrams are dramatically improved and the topics covered are really comprehensive, just what's needed in today's world of ever increasing complexity on newer boats.

This second edition is perfect for learning how your boat's electrical system and much of its equipment works, and it will be an invaluable guide when adding equipment as well. Further, Charlie Wing has remained faithful to the recommendation and application of the standards for installation and equipment as set forth by the American Boat and Yacht Council (ABYC). As the senior technical instructor for the ABYC and its curriculum designer I really appreciate the effort throughout the book to advise the reader on how to make repairs and modifications to his or her boat and remain compliant with the most recognized design and repair standards for recreational boats in the world. We at the ABYC know full well that adherence to these standards make a better, safer boat.

I have already begun recommending this second edition to my students and seminar participants, and will continue to do so. This book needs to be in every boater's library as a ready reference on how to make effective repairs and modifications that comply with ABYC standards.

Ed Sherman
ABYC Senior Instructor and Curriculum Designer

Many of us have, at the least, a passing familiarity with electrical wiring. When a switch or receptacle in our home fails, we replace it. Some of us feel secure in extending a circuit, adding a new circuit, even wiring an entire house. We are able to do so because of the *National Electric Code* (NEC) and because many excellent books, based on the NEC, have been written for both the novice and the professional.

Unfortunately, a boat is not a house—a fact that still escapes all too many boatyards.

I'll never forget the time I was working in a boatyard rigging masts. I had spent an hour trying to determine why a mast-top anchor light was not working. The blue anchor-light supply conductor disappeared into the base of the 60-foot mast, yet no blue conductor appeared at the other end. I commented on the mystery to a co-worker who I knew had worked as an electrician at one the country's premier boatbuilders.

"Sure," he said. "We'd grab a spool of #14 whatever, and when that ran out, we just spliced in another. The color of the wire doesn't matter."

Or ask a random sampling of boatbuilders whether bronze through-hulls should be bonded. Chances are good you will get an even split of opinions. No wonder boatowners are confused!

In fact, there is a voluntary standard for the construction and repair of boats, including the topics of AC and DC wiring, lightning protection, and bonding for corrosion control. It is the American Boat and Yacht Council (ABYC) *Standards for Small Craft*. The standards are the marine equivalent of the residential *National Building Code* and *National Electric Code*.

Twelve years ago, when the first edition of this book was written, few boat manufacturers and fewer boatyards paid much attention to the fledgling ABYC. Today, nearly all manufacturers and many boatyards have joined the organization and have sent employees to the excellent technical courses offered by the ABYC's Westlawn Institute of Marine Technology. In the words of the ABYC, the standards are: " . . . believed to represent, as of the date of publication, the consensus of knowledgeable persons, currently active in the field of small craft, on performance objectives that contribute to small boat safety."

This book is my attempt at interpretation and illumination of the several wiring-related ABYC standards and much more.

My joy in life derives from explaining and illustrating how things work—first as a physics teacher at Bowdoin College, then as founder of the first two owner-builder schools in the country, and later as author of thirteen books on home building and repair and six books on marine topics.

I have always felt that knowledge is of limited utility unless based upon an understanding of the basic principles—simply put, how things work. In this book you will find that each subject begins with a simple exploration and explanation of the hows and whys.

I also feel that books—even those of a technical nature—should be fun. We boatowners have no need for Miss Grundy to rap our knuckles to command our attention. Discovery of how your boat works should be fun and exciting. To this end you will find dozens of simple experiments and projects designed to make the light in your mind come on, perhaps even add to the comfort and convenience of your boat.

I hope you will come away from this book with the feeling that (to paraphrase Ratty in *Wind in the Willows*) "There is nothing half so much worth doing as messing about in your boat's electrical system."

I have invented nothing. You will find here no new law of physics, nor any previously unreported electrical or magnetic phenomena. I have simply attempted to bring to you, the reader, a lucid and clearly illustrated account of how the best minds in the business think a small boat should be wired.

To this end, in this second edition I have redrawn many of the original illustrations, added illustrations, and added color to the ABYC-recommended wiring for AC shore-power systems. Also new is the ABYC procedure for testing and sizing protective zinc anodes, material on absorbed-glass mat (AGM) batteries, specific recommendations for charging most marine batteries, descriptions of "smart" alternator regulators, and troubleshooting charts for engine-starting and battery-charging circuits.

May your boat never corrode, your engine never fail to start, and your batteries last forever!

CHAPTER 1

Basic DC Circuits

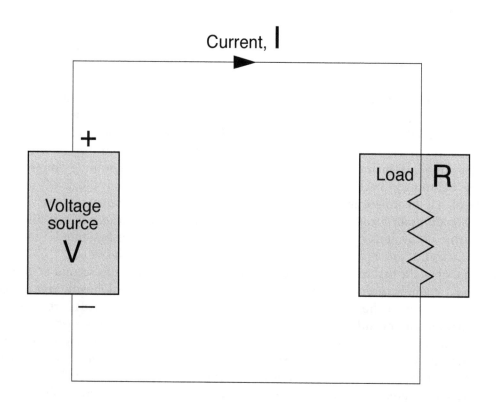

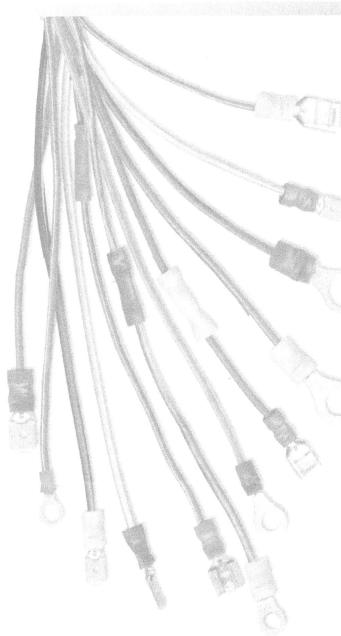

Basic to the ability to work with electrical wiring—be it residential or marine—is an understanding of what electricity is. You'll find that the discovery of electricity, as we now understand it, was fairly recent.

The key that unlocks the wiring puzzle is the concept of the electrical circuit. With this simple concept and a single formula—Ohm's Law—you can understand and predict the behavior of 99% of the wiring on your boat. You will be able to deal with circuits containing loads in series, loads in parallel, even loads in series/parallel combinations. Similarly, you will be able to predict the behavior of voltage sources in series and voltage sources in parallel. You will also discover the differences between voltage, current, energy, and power.

Finally I have provided a set of 18 practice problems on which you can cut your electrical teeth.

What Electricity Is

We live in the age of electricity. Without electricity we couldn't watch television, drive automobiles, make frozen margaritas, microwave popcorn, read at night, or talk to our friends on the phone.

Many people think electricity is difficult to understand. They are wrong. Because you are surrounded by and unconsciously use electrical devices every day, little lights will go on in your head as you discover the concepts. You'll probably say, "Oooh—so that's why my boat battery is dead every morning!"

I believe you will find electricity to be fun. I am absolutely sure that, having grasped the very simple concepts behind boat wiring, you will feel more confident both in your boat and in yourself.

Electricity consists of electrons. An electron is the smallest quantity of electricity that exists. It is such a small quantity, however, that we use the unit coulomb (1 coulomb = 6.24×10^{18} electrons) in calculations.

The flow of electrons is often compared to the flow of water, so it is natural that we call electron flow "electric current." The basic unit of electric current is the ampere (1 ampere = 1 coulomb per second of electrons moving past a point).

What we usually refer to as electricity is the control of electrons for useful purposes. Our understanding of electron behavior allows us to predict the flow of electrons through electrical circuits. The instruments on your boat contain circuits. Indeed, a boat's wiring is no more than a collection of circuits. When we understand circuits, we will understand the behavior of electricity on a boat.

A Circuit

Electrons can be neither created nor destroyed, but can move through conductive materials. An electric current requires a continuous path of electrically conductive material, through which the electrons can return to their source.

If this were not so, electrons would dribble from the end of a wire like water from a leaky faucet, and batteries would soon sit like empty water glasses with all their electrons lying around them in a pool.

We call a continuous electrical path a *circuit*. If a circuit is unbroken, we call it a closed circuit. If it is interrupted, preventing the flow of electricity, we say the circuit is open.

All materials present a degree of resistance to electron flow, but the variation is so great that some mate-

The Discovery of Electricity

Democritus (460?–370? BC) proposes an "atomic theory" wherein all matter is made up of indivisible particles, or atoms.

Charles de Coulomb (1736–1806) discovers that the force of attraction between electric charges is proportional to the product of the two charges and inversely proportional to the distance between them.

Luigi Galvani (1737–1798) discovers that two unlike metals immersed in blood cause the muscles of a frog's legs to twitch.

Alessandro Volta (1745–1827) discovers that a current flows between two connected unlike metals in a salt solution and, thus, invents the battery.

John Dalton (1766–1844) proposes the first table of atomic weights of elements.

André Ampere (1775–1836) develops the theory of magnetic lines of force and quantifies electric current for the first time.

Hans Oersted (1777–1851) discovers a connection between electric current and magnetism and a way to measure electric current by the deflection of a magnet.

Georg Ohm (1787–1854) discovers the relationship (Ohm's Law) between voltage, current, and resistance in a circuit.

Michael Faraday (1791–1867) analyzes the chemical reactions in batteries and defines the terms "electrode," "anode," "cathode," and "electrolyte."

James Clerk Maxwell (1831–1879) develops the mathematical equations relating electricity and magnetism.

Joseph Thomson (1856–1940) proves that electricity consists of electrons.

rials are termed conductors and others insulators.

The best conductors are gold, silver, mercury, copper, and aluminum. Copper is most often the best compromise between cost and conductivity. The best insulators are glass, ceramics, mica, and plastics. Plastic is the material most often used due to its low cost, durability, and ease of manufacture.

Unfortunately for boaters, salt solutions, such as seawater, are also good conductors.

Electrical current is expressed as a rate of electron flow. In a circuit, two factors control the current (I): the electrical driving force, or voltage (V), and the resistance (R) to flow of the circuit materials.

To see just how simple electricity is, we are going to consider the basic equation of current flow in an electrical circuit. With this equation you will be able to understand, predict, and troubleshoot more than 90% of all the electrical problems on a boat.

Question 1. Does current, I, increase or decrease as we increase the driving force (voltage, V)?

Answer 1. Current most likely increases with increasing voltage.

Question 2. Does current, I, increase or decrease as we increase the resistance to electron flow (resistance, R)?

Answer 2. Current most likely decreases with increasing resistance.

Question 3. Considering the answers to questions 1 and 2, what would be the simplest and, therefore, most likely, relationship between current (I), voltage (V), and resistance (R)?

Answer 3. There are four possible "simplest" equations:

$$I = V + R, I = V - R, I = V \times R, \text{ and } I = V/R$$

If you play with the values for a minute, you'll agree that the first three equations are unlikely. For example, if we make resistance, R, infinite, current, I, becomes ∞, $-\infty$, ∞, and 0. Only the last value is reasonable, so the relationship is most likely

$$I = V/R$$

Congratulations! You have just discovered Ohm's Law. If Georg Ohm hadn't beaten you to it in 1827, you might be up for a Nobel Prize.

Using Ohm's Law

This is such an important relationship, we must be precise in its definition and the ways in which it can be used. First, if we wish to calculate electrical quantities, we must define the units in which these quantities are measured.

$$I = V/R$$
where:
I = amperes, abbreviated as A
V = volts, abbreviated as V
R = ohms, abbreviated as Ω

Let's see how Ohm's Law is used. Ohm's Law applies to all situations, but it is useful only in circuits where electricity is flowing.

Fig. 1.1 Simple Electric Circuit

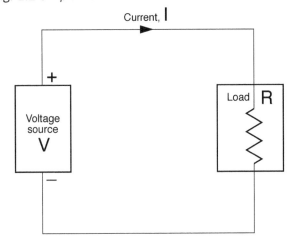

The voltage source in Figure 1.1 is a device that produces a voltage difference. Examples are batteries and power supplies. Unless otherwise noted, assume voltage sources are batteries. The load is any device or component that consumes electrical energy and, in so doing, results in a voltage drop. Examples are resistors, lamps, and motors. Unless otherwise stated, assume loads are resistances (the zigzag symbol). For a table of electrical symbols used in this book, see Figure 6-1.

Example: If the load is a resistance of 2 ohms, and the voltage source is a 12-volt battery, then by Ohm's Law

$$I = V/R = 12 \text{ V}/2 \text{ } \Omega = 6 \text{ A}$$

We can also rearrange Ohm's Law so that we can calculate either V or I, given the other two values. The alternate forms of Ohm's Law are:

$$V = I \times R$$
$$R = V/I$$

There is more good news. Ohm's Law applies to more complex circuits as well. We can combine loads and sources in series (end-to-end), parallel (side-by-side), and series/parallel, and the equations remain the simplest possible, as you will see in the figures and examples that follow.

Loads

Loads in Series

Resistive loads in series act like one continuous load of a total resistance equal to the sum of the individual resistances:

$$R = R_1 + R_2 + R_3, \text{etc.}$$
$$I = V/(R_1 + R_2 + R_3, \text{etc.})$$

Fig. 1.2 Series Loads

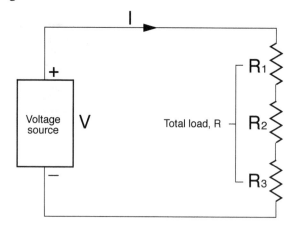

Example:
$$R_1 = 2\ \Omega, R_2 = 3\ \Omega, R_3 = 5\ \Omega, V = 12\ V$$
$$R = 2 + 3 + 5 = 10\ \Omega$$

Loads in Parallel

The same voltage, V, exists across each of the loads. Ohm's Law predicts the currents through the loads:
$$I_1 = V/R_1, I_2 = V/R_2, I_3 = V/R_3, \text{etc.}$$
Total current, I, is the sum of currents:
$$I = I_1 + I_2 + I_3, \text{etc.}$$
$$= V(1/R_1 + 1/R_2 + 1/R_3, \text{etc.})$$
In other words,
$$1/R = 1/R_1 + 1/R_2 + 1/R_3, \text{etc.}$$

Fig. 1.3 Parallel Loads

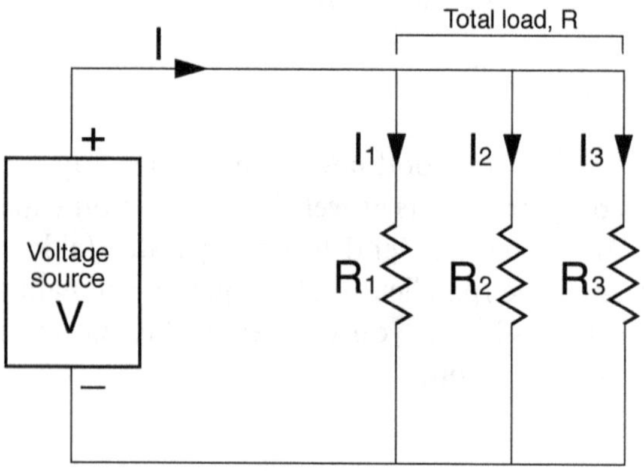

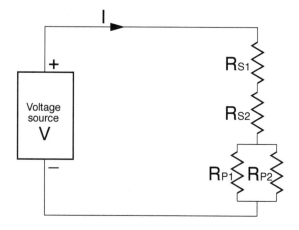

Example: $R_1 = 20\ \Omega, R_2 = 30\ \Omega, R_3 = 50\ \Omega, V = 12\ V.$
$$1/R = 1/R_1 + 1/R_2 + 1/R_3$$
$$= 1/20 + 1/30 + 1/50$$
$$= 0.050 + 0.033 + 0.020$$
$$= 0.103$$

$$R = 1/0.103 = 9.68\ \Omega$$

$$I = V/R$$
$$= 12\ V/9.68\ \Omega$$
$$= 1.24\ A$$

Loads in Series/Parallel

Observe that the parallel group of loads can be considered a single resistor in series with other series loads. We first calculate the equivalent value of the parallel loads, as in the previous example, and then add the result of the other series loads:

Fig. 1.4 Series/Parallel Loads

Example: $R_{S1} = 2\ \Omega, R_{S2} = 3\ \Omega, R_{P1} = 5\ \Omega, R_{P2} = 10\ \Omega, V = 12\ V$
$$1/R_P = 1/R_{P1} + 1/R_{P2}$$
$$= 1/5 + 1/10$$
$$= 0.20 + 0.10$$
$$= 0.30$$
$$R_P = 3.33\ \Omega$$

$$R = R_{S1} + R_{S2} + R_P$$
$$= 2\ \Omega + 3\ \Omega + 3.33\ \Omega$$
$$= 8.33\ \Omega$$

$$I = 12\ V/8.33\ \Omega$$
$$= 1.44\ A$$

Sources in Series

Fig. 1.5 Series Sources

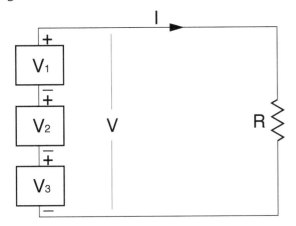

One example of a voltage source is a battery. If you've ever replaced the batteries in a flashlight, you know that batteries can be stacked end to end. When you do that the total voltage equals the sum of the individual voltages. In general, voltages in series add.

$$V = V_I + V_2 + V_3, \text{ etc.}$$
$$\text{Therefore, } I = (V_I + V_2 + V_3)/R$$

Example: $V_I = 1.5\,V, V_2 = 1.5\,V, V_3 = 3\,V, R = 4\,\Omega$
$$I = (1.5 + 1.5 + 3.0)V/4\,\Omega$$
$$= 1.5\,A$$

A caution is in order, however. If batteries are added in series, they must have the same ampere-hour capacities and start with the same states of charge. If not, the battery with the greatest capacity for supplying current may drive the voltage of the weakest battery negative, which usually destroys the weaker battery.

Fig. 1.6 Parallel Sources

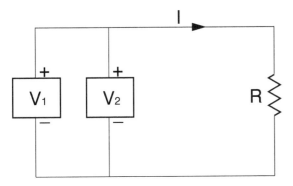

Sources in Parallel

Your boat probably has a battery selector switch. On its face it says:

OFF—1—2—BOTH

In the BOTH position, both of your batteries are connected in parallel; i.e., + terminal to + terminal, and – terminal to – terminal. Provided the batteries are of the same voltage, the net result is simply a single battery of capacity equal to the sum of the individual capacities. If they are not of the same voltage, the higher voltage battery will discharge into the lower voltage battery, possibly overcharging and destroying it.

There is much controversy over charging and discharging marine batteries in parallel. Some experts are dead set against it, saying that the batteries will eventually destroy each other. Other experts claim it is the only way to go when charging. Both arguments and the reasoning behind them will be presented in Chapter 4.

Energy and Power

Energy is defined as the *ability to do work. Power* is defined as the *rate of doing work.* Power is, therefore, the rate at which energy is used in doing work.

Two Olympic runners exemplify the difference between energy and power. The first runner holds the record in the marathon. He is a lean, efficient running machine. He burns nearly all of his stored energy resources steadily over a 2-hour period. The second runner holds the record in the 100-meter dash. He uses less total energy, but consumes it in an intense 10-second burst. The first runner uses more energy, but the second uses energy at a higher rate, or power.

Except in nuclear reactions, energy can be neither created nor destroyed. What it can do, however, is change between its many forms.

As an example, the water at the top of a hydroelectric dam possesses *potential energy* due to its height. As it falls and gains speed, its potential energy is converted into *kinetic (motion) energy.* When the water hits the blades of a turbine, the kinetic energy of the water is transferred to the spinning turbine. The turbine turns a generator where the kinetic energy is converted to *electrical energy.* The electricity flows into your home, where a lightbulb changes the electrical energy into *light energy* and *heat energy.* Ultimately, the heat escapes from your home into the atmosphere, where it causes water to evaporate into water vapor, which then turns into clouds, which then drop rain into the reservoir. And so it goes.

Practice Problems

For the moment, we will concern ourselves only with the energy transformations occurring between your boat's batteries and its loads. The battery, as we will see in detail later, is just a box full of chemicals. When it is connected to a closed electrical circuit, the chemicals react, sending a stream of electrons (amps) around the circuit under electrical pressure (volts). In flowing through the load (resistance), the electrons lose their pressure (the voltage drops), and the load produces heat, light, or some form of mechanical work. Chemical energy changes to electrical energy, which then changes to heat, light, or mechanical energy. You'll see later that recharging the battery involves the same steps, but in reverse order.

Power is calculated as easily as volts, amps, and ohms:

$$P = V \times I$$
where: P = power consumption in watts
V = volts across the load
I = amps through the load

Example: What is the power of a lightbulb that draws 1.25 amps at 12 volts?

$$P = V \times I$$
$$= 12 \text{ volts} \times 1.25 \text{ amps}$$
$$= 15 \text{ watts}$$

Example: How many amps would a 20-watt lamp draw in a 12-volt circuit?

$$P = V \times I$$
$$I = P/V$$
$$= 20 \text{ watts}/12 \text{ volts}$$
$$= 1.67 \text{ amps}$$

Electrical equipment is usually labeled with its power consumption. If you look at the back or bottom of equipment, or at the base of a bulb, you will generally find either (X) volts and (Y) amps, or (X) watts at (Y) volts.

Using Ohm's Law and the power equation, you should have no problem deducing either amps or watts, given two of the three variables in the equations.

The problems below are designed to sharpen your skills in the application of Ohm's Law. They range from the simplest possible to the most complex you'll ever encounter on your boat. All you need to solve them is a simple four-function calculator, scratch paper, and a pencil.

You can make solving them a parlor game. Get your mate to play with you. Take turns making up more problems and trying to stump the other person. Once you have mastered these examples, you are ready for real components and real circuits. The answers to the problems are listed at the end of this chapter.

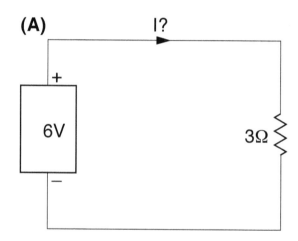

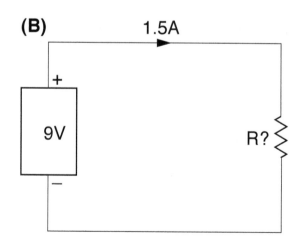

(C)

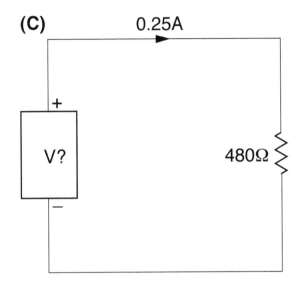

0.25A

V?

480Ω

(E)

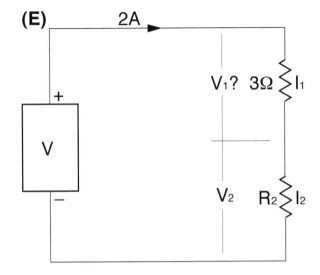

2A

V

V_1? 3Ω I_1

V_2 R_2 I_2

(D)

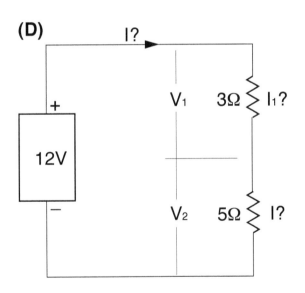

I?

12V

V_1 3Ω I_1?

V_2 5Ω I?

(F)

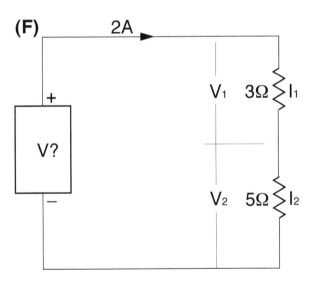

2A

V?

V_1 3Ω I_1

V_2 5Ω I_2

Practice Problems

(G)

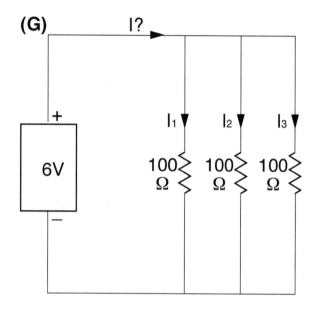

(I)

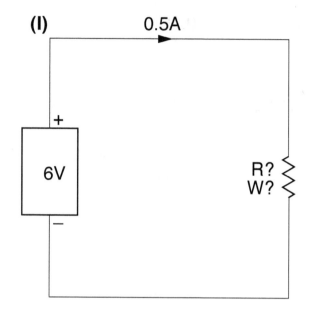

(H)

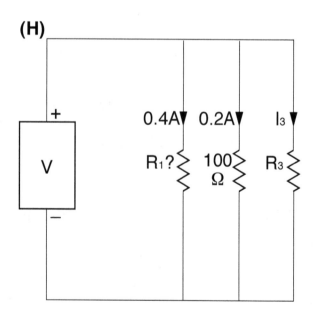

(J)

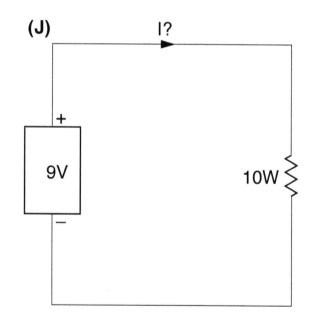

(K)

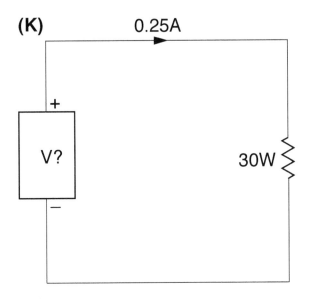

0.25A

V?

30W

(M)

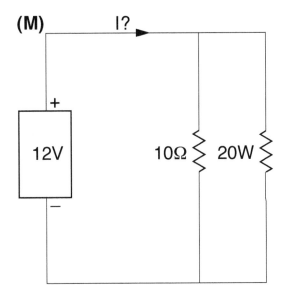

I?

12V

10Ω 20W

(L)

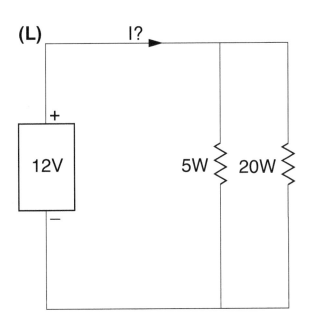

I?

12V

5W 20W

(N)

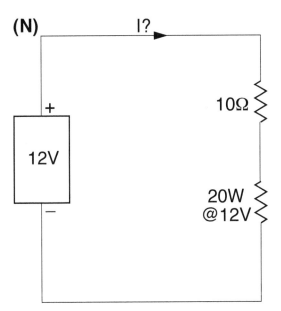

I?

12V

10Ω

20W
@12V

Practice Problems

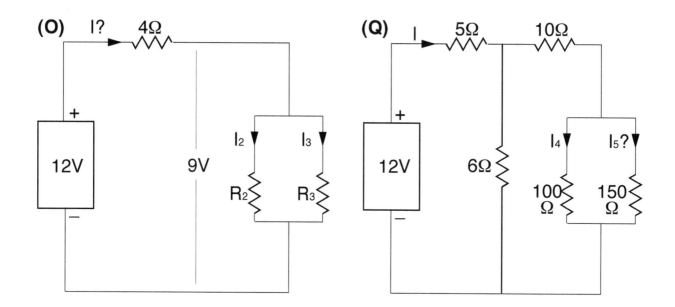

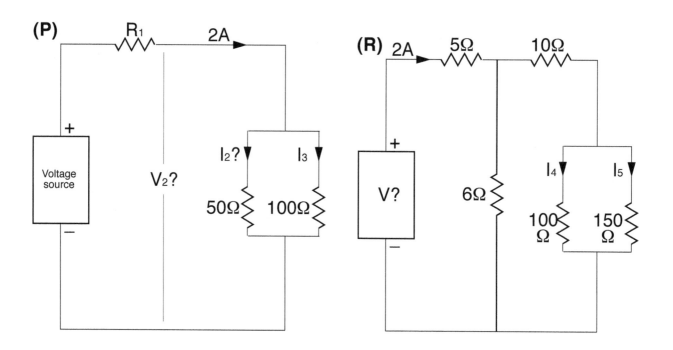

Answers to Problems:

a. I = 2 A	e. $V_1 = 6$ V	j. I = 1.11 A	o. I = 0.75 A
b. R = 6 Ω	f. V = 16 V	k. V = 120 V	p. $V_2 = 66.7$ V, $I_2 = 1.33$ A
c. V = 120 V	g. I = 0.18 A	l. I = 2.08 A	q. $I_5 = 0.036$ A
d. $I_1 = I_2 = I = 1.5$ A	h. $R_1 = 50$ Ω	m. I = 2.87 A	r. V = 21.05 V
	i. R = 12 Ω, W = 3 W	n. I = 0.7 A	

CHAPTER 2

DC Measurements

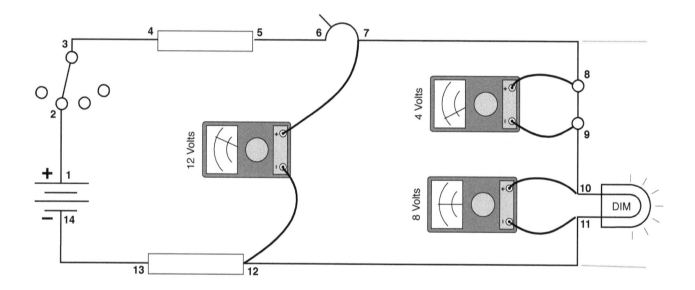

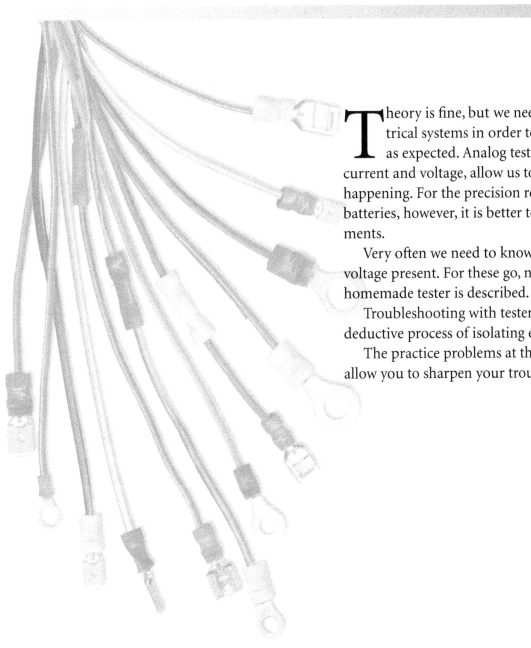

Theory is fine, but we need a way to monitor electrical systems in order to see if they are working as expected. Analog test instruments, displaying current and voltage, allow us to see, at a glance, what is happening. For the precision required to monitor batteries, however, it is better to use digital test instruments.

Very often we need to know only whether there is voltage present. For these go, no-go tests, a simple homemade tester is described.

Troubleshooting with testers leads you through the deductive process of isolating electrical problems.

The practice problems at the end of the chapter will allow you to sharpen your troubleshooting skills.

Analog Test Instruments

In Chapter 1, I asserted, " . . . with Ohm's Law, you will be able to understand, predict, and troubleshoot 90% of the electrical problems on a boat." Let me amend that figure to 99%.

You will recall that Ohm's Law allows us to calculate the theoretical relationships between the voltages, currents, and resistances in a circuit. What if there were instruments we could plug into a circuit that would show us the actual values of voltage, current, and resistance? By comparing the theoretical and actual values, we would find that either: (1) reality agreed with theory and all was well in the circuit, or (2) reality disagreed with theory and there was something wrong in the circuit.

There *are* instruments that measure volts, amps, and ohms, and using them to compare reality with theory is what we call troubleshooting. This chapter describes the instruments and their use.

Analog Ammeter (Current Meter)

The ammeter hasn't changed much since it was developed by Jacques d'Arsonval in 1811. In Figure 2.1, current flows into terminal 1, through the spring, around the moving coil, through a second spring on the backside, and out through terminal 2. The current in the coil produces a magnetic field that interacts with the field of the permanent magnet, forcing the coil to rotate about its bearing. The needle attached to the coil displays the rotation against the scale in the background.

In order that the ammeter be able to measure small currents, the meter movement is very delicate. The moving coil consists of many turns of fine wire, the springs are "hair springs" similar to those in a wind-up watch, and the coil pivots on jewel bearings. Typically, 50 µA (50×10^{-6} A or 0.000050 amp) deflects the needle full scale.

But the currents we are interested in typically range from 0.1 to 100 amps—about one million times 50 µA. You can imagine what would happen if we tried to measure the 50-amp charging current in our battery leads with the 50 µA meter of Figure 2.1.

How can we modify our 50 µA ammeter to measure 50 amps? Ohm's Law to the rescue! Although a perfect ammeter would offer zero resistance to the current flowing through it, real ammeters are made of real wire and so have a finite resistance.

Figure 2.2 shows the resistance, R_C, of our ammeter coil with full-scale current of 50 µA flowing through it. In parallel with the meter we place a *shunt* whose resistance, R_S, is 10^{-6} (one-millionth) of R_C. Since the voltage across both R_S and R_C is the same, Ohm's Law predicts that $I_S = 10^6$ (one million) $\times I_C$, or 50 amps.

Fig. 2.2 Ammeter Symbol and Internal Resistances

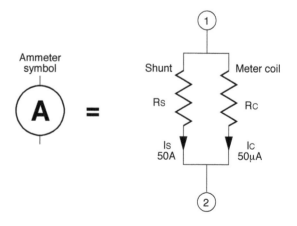

Using this principle, the same 50 µA ammeter can be made to measure 100 µA, 500 µA, 30 mA, 10 A, 100 A, or any other current merely by inserting the appropriate shunt across the terminals, as shown.

Fig. 2.1 D'Arsonval Ammeter

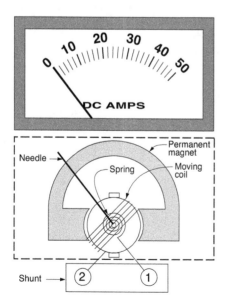

Analog Voltmeter

Might we use our little 50 µA d'Arsonval meter to measure voltage as well? Ideally, a voltmeter should measure the voltage across a circuit without disturbing the circuit. That means it should look like a very high resistance—much higher than any of the other resistances in the circuit.

Fig. 2.3 Using the Ammeter to Measure Voltage

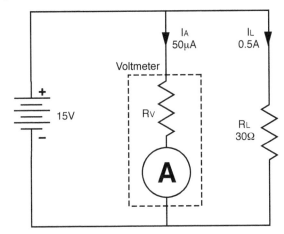

Figure 2.3 shows a circuit consisting of a 15-volt battery and 30-ohm load, resulting in a current of:

$$I = V/R_L$$
$$= 15 \text{ volts}/30 \text{ ohms}$$
$$= 0.5 \text{ amp}$$

We have placed a series resistor, R_V, inside the case of our 50 µA ammeter. If we want the ammeter to deflect full scale when the voltage is 15 volts, then Ohm's Law says that the series resistor that limits the current to 50 µA must be:

$$I_V = V/R_V$$
$$R_V = V/I_V$$
$$= 15 \text{ volts}/0.00005 \text{ amp}$$
$$= 300,000 \text{ ohms}$$

The load imposed on the circuit by our voltmeter—one ten-thousandth of the 30-ohm circuit load—is clearly negligible. If the circuit load, R_L, had been 30,000 ohms instead of 30 ohms, then our voltmeter would have siphoned off 10% of the current, giving a result 10% in error, as well as altering the performance of the circuit.

Voltmeters are simply ammeters with internal series resistors of 5,000 to 100,000 ohms per volt of full scale.

Analog Ohmmeter (Resistance Meter)

By now you are probably expecting me to tell you that our 50 µA ammeter can be modified to measure resistance as well. You are correct.

To measure the resistance of a resistor or other circuit load, we must isolate that component from the rest of the circuit. (Review the practice problems in Chapter 1 if you don't remember why.)

Sometimes we can open a switch; sometimes we can disconnect a terminal; sometimes we have to unsolder one end of the component. Regardless of how we isolate the item, we measure its resistance indirectly by applying a test voltage and measuring the resulting current. Because zero resistance (a possibility in case of a short circuit inside the component) would draw a possibly destructive high current, we place a known current-limiting resistor in series with the meter.

Figure 2.4 shows our ohmmeter. Inside its case are our same 50 µA ammeter, a 1.5-volt battery, and a series resistor, R_R. Maximum current will flow, and the meter will deflect full scale, when the resistance being tested, R_L, is zero. From Ohm's Law:

$$I = V/R_R$$
$$R_R = V/I$$
$$= 1.5 \text{ volts}/0.00005 \text{ amp}$$
$$= 30,000 \text{ ohms}$$

Fig. 2.4 Using the Ammeter to Measure Resistance

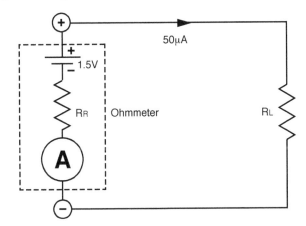

At the other end of the scale, the current approaches zero, and the needle shows essentially no deflection. Thus, we have a meter representing 0 ohms on the right, ∞ ohms on the left, and all other values on a logarithmic scale in between. Near 0 ohms the meter will be very sensitive and, as R_L approaches ∞, the meter will be less sensitive.

Digital Test Instruments

Analog Volt-Ohm Meter (VOM)

To troubleshoot a circuit, you may need an ammeter, a voltmeter, an ohmmeter, or all three. You may also need a variety of ranges. Conveniently, it is a simple matter to combine all of these functions into a single meter called a volt-ohm meter (VOM), as in Figure 2.5.

To the 50 µA ammeter, we add a 1.5- or 9-volt battery, assorted precision resistors and shunts, and a multipole, multiposition switch. More expensive VOMs incorporate input amplifiers that increase the input resistance and decrease the current drawn by the VOM. In this way, the VOM intrudes less on the tested circuit.

Fig. 2.5. Volt-Ohm Meter (VOM)

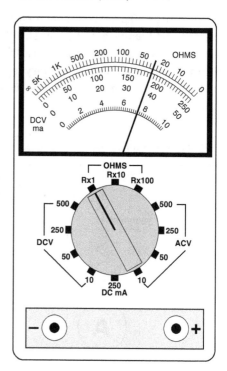

Digital Volt-Ohm Meter (DVM)

One of the very first clocks was a "water clock": Water dripped into a cup. When the cup was full, it tipped over, spilled its contents, and started over. In tipping, it advanced a counter mechanism that indicated the number of times it had tripped and thus the passage of time.

A digital ammeter is exactly the same, except that it counts electrons instead of water drops. The cup is an electrical capacitor. As the capacitor collects electrons, the voltage across its terminals increases. When the voltage of the capacitor reaches a predetermined level, the capacitor is discharged, and the charging begins again.

The greater the current (flow of electrons), the more rapidly the capacitor charges and discharges. The charge/discharge cycles are electronically counted, and the number of cycles per second are directly proportional to current.

The analogy between analog and digital ammeters, voltmeters, ohmmeters, and multimeters is similar. Given a digital ammeter, we just add shunts, resistors, batteries, and rotary switches. Figure 2.6 shows a typical digital volt-ohm meter.

Fig. 2.6. Digital Volt-Ohm Meter (DVM)

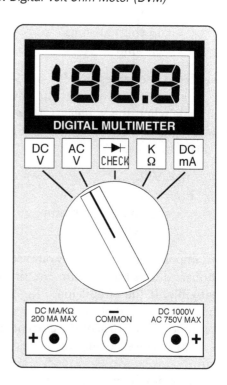

Digital vs. Analog Multimeters

So which is better—the analog or digital multimeter? Both are available in a range of sizes, from shirt pocket to benchtop, and both can be had for as little as $10 to as much as $400. To help you decide which is better for you, Table 2.1 lists the specifications of two typical midpriced units.

The specifications use several prefixes:

$$\mu \text{ (micro)} = 10^{-6} \text{ —multiply by 0.000001}$$
$$m \text{ (milli)} = 10^{-3} \text{ —multiply by 0.001}$$
$$k \text{ (kilo)} = 10^{3} \text{ —multiply by 1,000}$$
$$M \text{ (mega)} = 10^{6} \text{ —multiply by 1,000,000}$$

Table 2.1
Typical Analog and Digital Multimeter Specifications

Specification		Analog Multimeter	Digital Multimeter
DC volts	lowest range	250 mV	300 mV
	highest range	1,000 V	1,000 V
	accuracy[1]	±4%	±0.2%
AC volts	lowest range	5 V	3 V
	highest range	1,000 V	750 V
	accuracy[1]	±4%	±0.5%
DC amps	lowest range	50 µA	300 mA
	highest range	10 A	10 A
	accuracy[1]	±3%	±0.5%
Resistance	lowest range	2 kΩ	300 Ω
	highest range	20 MΩ	30 MΩ
	accuracy[1]	±3%	±0.2%

[1] Accuracy as percent of full scale

A glance at an old-fashioned watch gives you a sense of the approximate time very quickly. A digital watch, however, first requires recognition of the numbers displayed, then an interpretation of the significance of the numbers. The same is true of analog and digital multimeter displays.

If you wish to know simply whether your battery is charging or discharging (roughly 14 versus 12 volts), the analog meter with ±4% accuracy (±0.6 volt on a 15-volt scale) will do the job. But if you want to know the percentage of charge remaining in your battery, where the same ±0.6 volt represents ±50% of battery capacity, you'd better use a digital meter with its ±0.2% (±0.03 volt on a 15-volt scale) accuracy.

Digital vs. Analog Panel Meters

Ammeters and voltmeters (Figures 2.7 and 2.8) are used in distribution and circuit breaker panels to monitor battery voltage and rate of charge/discharge. An analog "battery charge indicator" is simply a voltmeter with its needle pegged at the left until the voltage reaches approximately 8 to 10 volts, thus expanding the scale over the useful voltage of a 12-volt battery.

Digital panel meters are slowly replacing analog meters. They cost no more to produce than the analog variety and are far more accurate, so one hopes their prices will soon drop.

Fig. 2.7 Analog Panel Meters

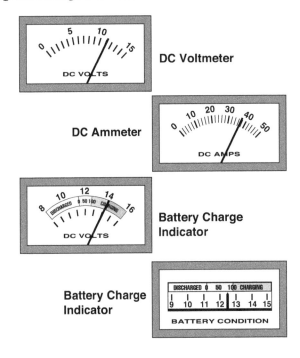

Fig. 2.8 Digital Panel Meters

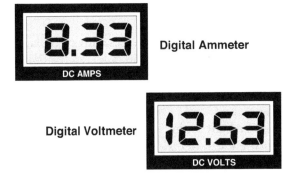

Homemade Testers

Most of the wiring problems on a boat are of the go, no-go variety. All DC circuits start at the boat's 12-volt battery. As you check a suspect circuit farther and farther from the battery, there either is or isn't voltage present. At the first point you find no voltage present, you can be sure the problem lies between this point and the last point where voltage was present.

The most common marine wiring problems are due to corrosion of connections and contacts. When copper corrodes, it forms green copper oxide—an excellent electrical insulator. As corrosion progresses, more and more of the contact surface through which current flows is eliminated. Eventually, there is so much resistance and voltage drop across the contact that the reduced voltage affects the load. If the load is a lamp, for example, the lamp will dim. If the load is a motor, the motor will slow down or not start at all.

There are two simple, do-it-yourself, troubleshooting devices you may end up using more than your fancy multimeter. The first is nothing more than an automotive bulb with attached test leads; the second is a Piezo electric alarm buzzer with test leads.

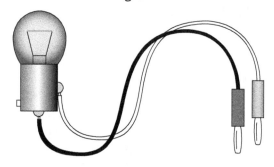

Fig. 2.9 Homemade Test Light

Figure 2.9 shows a typical 12-volt DC automotive bulb you can purchase at any Wal-Mart or auto parts store. Get a pair of high-quality "test leads" at Radio-Shack. These will be rubber-insulated, very fine-stranded #14 to #18 wire with alligator clips, banana plugs, or minitest tips attached. Solder the test leads to the side and base of the bulb, as shown, or to a lamp socket. Don't worry about ever having to replace the bulb. It is rated 5,000 hours at 13.5 V, so the only way it should fail is if you step on it or try to test a 110-volt circuit with it.

The second tool is similar but produces a noise instead of a light. As in Figure 2.10, solder test leads to a 3 V–16 V Piezo electric buzzer, which can be found at an electronics store for under $5.

If you want to get fancy, assemble both the light and

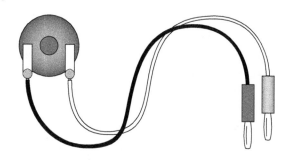

Fig. 2.10 Homemade Test Buzzer

the buzzer in a small box with a switch that allows you to use either the light, the buzzer, or both simultaneously.

When connected to 12 volts, the bulb will glow brightly. If the voltage is low, the bulb will glow, but dimly. If there is no voltage, the bulb will not glow. Similarly, at 12 to 16 volts, the buzzer will screech; at 3 to 12 volts, the buzzer will sound fainter; at less than 3 volts, the buzzer will not sound at all. In a noisy environment, the light works best. In bright sunlight, the buzzer is best.

Next pick your tips. I find a set of interchangeable tips, as shown in Figure 2.11, very useful. Permanently attached to the test leads are banana plugs. These can be plugged into banana-to-alligator adapters, banana-to-minipin adapters, and banana-to-miniprobe adapters. I choose the adapters based on wire size and whether I'm using one hand or two. Also handy is a single 50-foot extension lead with male and female banana plugs, so that I can extend one of the test leads the length of a boat or a mast.

Fig. 2.11 Interchangeable Test-Lead Tips

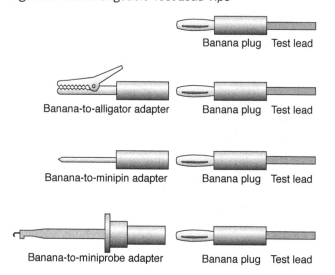

Multimeters, test lights, and test buzzers are all useful in troubleshooting circuits. Only where a precise voltage or a precise resistance is needed will the multimeter be more useful than the simpler light or buzzer, however. For simplicity, the examples and illustrations that follow will show only the simple test light. Just remember that where the test light is on, the buzzer would sound, and the multimeter would show a voltage, but where the test light is off, the buzzer would be silent, and the multimeter would show no or low voltage.

Figure 2.12 shows a simple cabin light circuit. The positive side of battery 1 is connected to terminal 1 of the battery-select switch by a wire. The common terminal of the battery switch feeds the positive bus bar in the distribution panel. The cabin light circuit originates at the "cabin lights" circuit breaker (or fuse) connected to the positive bus and then runs out of the panel to the cabin lights, which are connected as parallel loads.

At the light fixture, the positive wire feeds the on/off switch, which then controls the bulb. The other terminal of the bulb connects to the negative wire, which runs back to the negative bus in the distribution panel and the negative terminal of the battery, completing the circuit.

Fig. 2.12 Typical Cabin Light Circuit

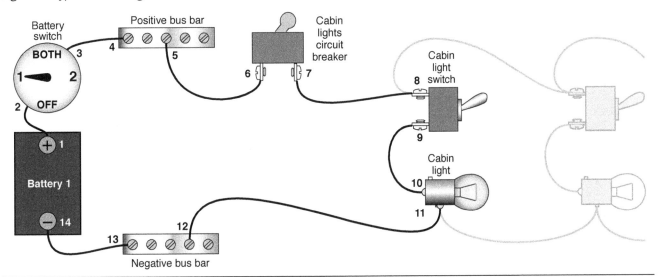

Figure 2.13 shows the same cabin light circuit in the form of a wiring diagram, using the standard component symbols listed in Figure 6-1. Note that the circuit load consists of lamps, which are nothing more than resistances that glow white hot. We could equally well have shown the load as parallel resistances, as in previous examples. In both Figures 2.12 and 2.13, fourteen points to which we could connect test leads are numbered. As we troubleshoot the circuit, we will connect our test light to pairs of these points to see whether voltage is present.

Fig. 2.13 Typical Cabin Light Wiring Diagram

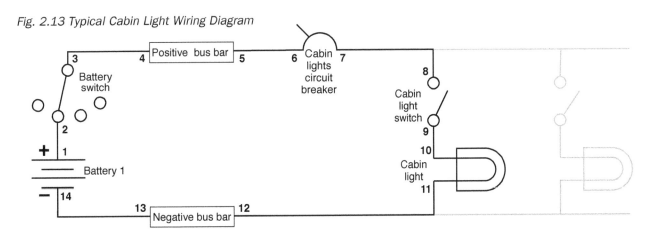

Troubleshooting

Turn all circuit switches to their on positions (Figure 2.14). The cabin lamps light up, meaning there is nothing wrong with the circuit. Since the wire and switches are designed to have near-zero resistance, we expect there to be no voltage drop between points 1 and 10. There should also be no voltage change from points 11 to 14. With one test lead on any of points 1 to 10 and the other lead on points 11 to 14, the test light should light, but with both leads on either the positive or negative side, the test light should not light.

Fig. 2.14 Properly Working Cabin Light Circuit

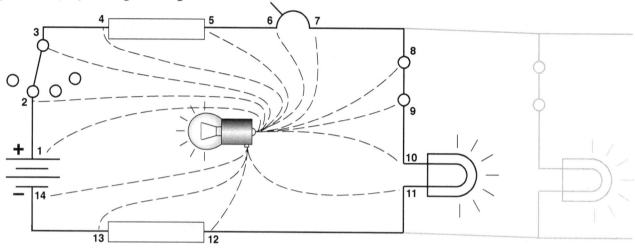

In Figure 2.15 we investigate a cabin lamp that will not light. All of the switches in the circuit are on, yet the light remains off. Furthermore, all of the other cabin lights in the same circuit do work.

We could start testing at points 1 and 14 and work our way toward the light. If we do, we'll find that the test lamp lights at every point, just as it did with the previous example of a normal circuit. If we suspect a burned-out bulb, however, we can save a lot of time by applying the test leads to points 10 and 11 immediately and discover that the circuit is OK all the way to the bulb holder.

At this point I'd simply replace the bulb. If you want to be sure it's the bulb and not the bulb holder, however, get out your multimeter and measure the resistance between the bulb contacts. If the multimeter reads infinite ohms, you know you have the culprit—a burned-out filament.

Fig. 2.15 Defective Cabin Light Circuit

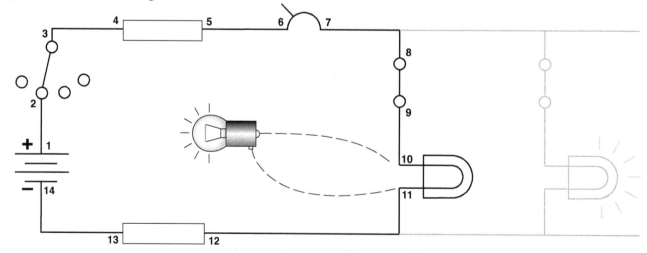

In Figure 2.16, we uncover a broken switch in the cabin light. We start as in the previous example with a cabin light that will not light up with all switches in the on position.

We suspect that the bulb filament has burned out, so we place our test lamp leads between points 10 and 11. The test lamp does not light. We therefore know that 12 volts is not reaching point 10. Next we place the test leads between 8 and 11. Now the test lamp lights up. The problem must be either in the switch or the short wire between the switch and the bulb holder.

We place the test leads across 8 and 9. Now both the test lamp and the cabin light glow dimly. What's going on? Our test lamp has bridged the broken switch, but acts like a load in series with the cabin light. This reduces the current and brightness of both bulbs. The bulb is OK, but the light switch must be replaced.

Fig. 2.16 Uncovering a Defective Switch

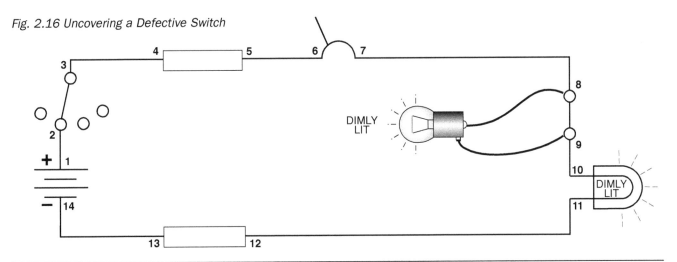

In the previous two examples, a component in the circuit had failed, resulting in an open circuit and zero current.

In Figure 2.17, we know the circuit is closed because the lamp is lit. But the lamp is dim. This is a very familiar phenomenon with flashlights—the light dims, but when we shake or hit the case the light becomes bright again.

The problem is due to poor contact. In a boat, poor contact is usually caused by corrosion of switch contacts or connectors. We will use this example to demonstrate the use of the multimeter.

Fig. 2.17 Troubleshooting with the Multimeter

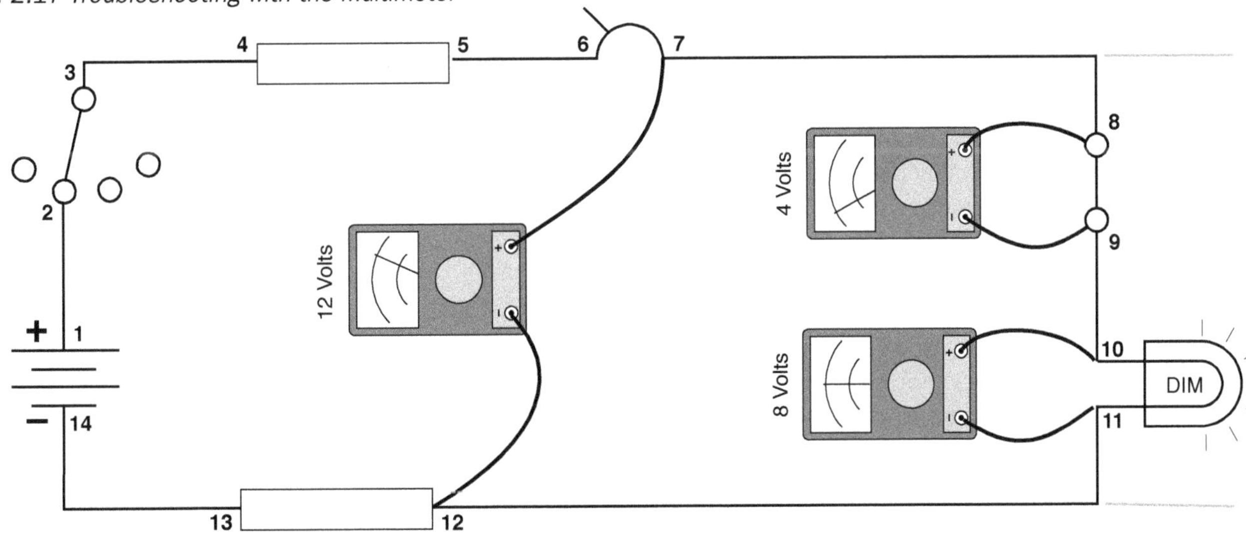

Troubleshooting

Just to be sure our battery isn't low, we measure between points 7 and 12, accessed behind the distribution panel. The meter reads 12 volts, so we know the battery is charged, and the circuit is OK up to the point where it leaves the panel for its run to the cabin lights.

Next, we try the other cabin lights in the circuit. They light normally, so we know our problem lies inside the dimmed light fixture. We remove the fixture base, exposing the internal switch and bulb holder wiring. We measure the voltage across the lamp itself, points 10 and 11, and the meter reads only 8 volts. Next, we measure the voltage across the switch, points 8 and 9. The meter reads 4 volts.

We have found the missing volts! Bad switch contacts are providing a resistance in series with the lamp, resulting in a voltage drop. In fact, one-third of the power in the circuit is being consumed within the switch, which we note is hot to the touch.

If we suspected internal resistance in the switch, why didn't we simply place the multimeter in the ohms mode and measure the resistance of the switch directly between points 8 and 9?

We could have, provided (and this is an extremely important "provided") we first opened the circuit by turning off either the battery switch or the circuit breaker.

If we tried measuring the resistance without opening the circuit, the 12-volt battery would still be in the circuit. Figure 2.4 showed that an ohmmeter consisted of a delicate 50 µA ammeter in series with an internal resistor and 1.5-volt battery. By placing the ohmmeter circuit in series with the cabin light circuit, we have effectively added or subtracted (depending on polarity) the 12-volt battery from the 1.5-volt battery. In the best case, the resistance reading will be grossly in error. At worst, we will burn out the 50 µA ammeter.

In general, to measure the resistance of a circuit component, you must first remove the component from the circuit by disconnecting one of its leads. Never try to measure resistance within a circuit with a live voltage.

A similar caution applies to measuring current in a circuit directly with a multimeter. Many inexpensive multimeters are designed to measure currents of up to 250 mA (0.25 amp). Others contain an internal shunt that allows measurements up to 10 amps. Make sure the current in a circuit is less than the maximum your meter can handle. Otherwise, you may blow the fuse or, worse, the meter itself.

A common mistake is to think you are measuring a voltage when, in fact, the multimeter is in the Amps position. The result is the same—something will blow.

Practice Problems

Table 2.2 below is intended to give you practice in troubleshooting a circuit. First, cover up column 3, then, referring to Figure 2.12, see if you can guess the cause of the problem, given the symptoms listed in columns 1 and 2. Column 3 lists the most likely causes.

Table 2.2 Symptoms and Causes

Test Light ON Between	Test Light OFF Between	Most Likely Cause
—	1 and 14	Dead battery
1 and 14	2 and 14	Positive battery cable
2 and 14	3 and 14	Battery switch off or defective
3 and 14	4 and 14	Bad connection or broken cable between battery switch and positive bus
6 and 14	7 and 14	Breaker off, defective breaker, or blown fuse
7 and 14	8 and 14	Broken wire from breaker to light switch
8 and 14	9 and 14	Switch off or defective
9 and 14	10 and 14	Broken wire between light switch and bulb holder
10 and 14	11 and 14	Burned-out lamp or poor contact between bulb and holder
10 and 14	10 and 13	Negative battery cable
10 and 13	10 and 11	Bad connection at negative bus or broken wire from bus to bulb holder

CHAPTER 3

Batteries

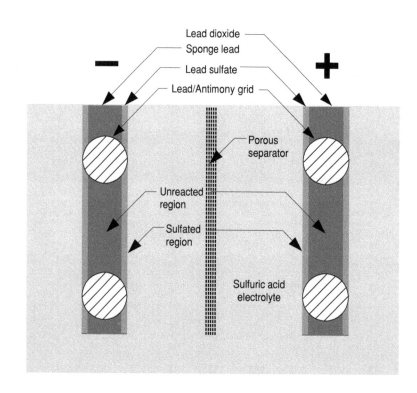

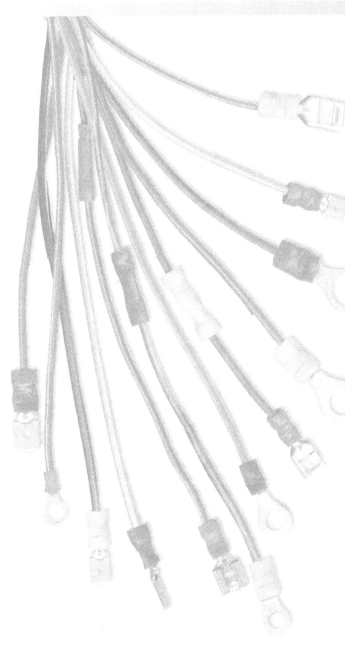

Except for the diesel engine, the greatest mystery to most boaters is the black box called the ship's battery.

What is a battery? Exactly what is going on inside that black box? In this chapter, you will find the simple answers and a few messy details as well.

Although it is more complex than simple conductors and resistors, it is useful to have an electrical model of the battery.

Monitoring batteries is the key to their performance. Monitoring the discharge/charge cycle requires an understanding of discharge characteristics, battery discharge ratings, and charging characteristics. You'll discover that charging recommendations vary between battery types.

In selecting batteries for your boat, you have several choices. In addition, you have to size the batteries to your load and decide whether to install multiple batteries in series or in parallel.

Safe installation involves electrical and mechanical considerations, both of which are covered by ABYC standards.

What Is a Battery?

Probably no aspect of a boat is less well understood by its owner than its batteries. Our "knowledge" of batteries often consists of a few remembered facts from a high school chemistry course, experience with our own boats and automobiles, and, unfortunately, a barrage of advertising hype.

As with most of today's mass-marketed products, engineering takes a backseat to marketing. Meaningful specifications and instructions have been replaced by technical-sounding words such as "heavy-duty," "marine-grade," "deep-cycle," and "Die-Hard." Some manufacturers have gone so far as to promise boating nirvana—a battery you can stick anywhere in your boat and never give it another thought.

This is most unfortunate because: (1) it is not true, and (2) nothing is more important to the cruising boat than an adequate and reliable 12-volt system. Without a reliable source of 12 volts, most of us would have no lighting, refrigeration, navigation, or communication. In fact, we couldn't even start our engines.

This chapter explains what you need to know in order to select and then maintain the batteries that are the heart of your boat's electrical system.

To read battery manufacturers' literature, you would think that today's batteries represent recent technological breakthroughs. The truth is that the chemistry of Thomas Edison's batteries of 100 years ago is identical to the chemistry of today's batteries. But what about the new, sealed, gel-cell batteries you can store under your bunk? You are right—they are newer. They were patented in 1933.

Most of what you need to know about lead-acid batteries can be observed in a galley experiment using a glass containing a cup of battery acid (siphon some from your battery, or buy a quart at the auto parts store), two lengths of lead solder, two D-cells, a battery holder, and a voltmeter. *Warning: battery acid is strong so wear rubber gloves and be very careful.*

Place the D-cells in the battery holder as in Figure 3.1. Connect one length of solder to the negative end, the other length to the positive end of the battery holder, and dip their ends into the acid.

Bubbles will form and rise in the acid. Soon you'll notice one of the lengths of solder turning brown. Remove the batteries and connect the voltmeter to the solder, as shown in Figure 3.2. The voltmeter will read about 2 volts.

You have just manufactured and witnessed the operation of a lead-acid cell—the very same thing that is in your boat's batteries. The only difference is that your boat's batteries consist of either three of these cells in series (6-volt battery) or six cells (12-volt battery).

Fig. 3.1 A Galley Battery, Step 1

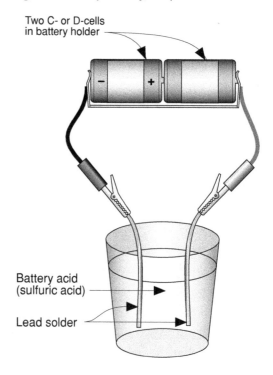

Two C- or D-cells in battery holder

Battery acid (sulfuric acid)

Lead solder

Fig. 3.2 A Galley Battery, Step 2

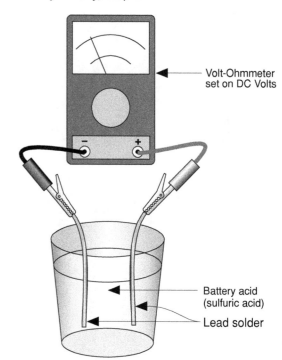

Volt-Ohmmeter set on DC Volts

Battery acid (sulfuric acid)

Lead solder

What Is Going On?

What you have just witnessed is the reversible chemical reaction found in all lead-acid batteries:

$$\begin{array}{c} \text{charging} \\ <= \\ PbO_2 + Pb + 2H_2SO_4 = 2PbSO_4 + 2H_2O \\ => \\ \text{discharging} \end{array}$$

Figure 3.3 shows the four phases of a lead-acid cell charge/discharge cycle. (See page 32 for more on specific gravity, SG.)

Fully charged. In the equation, application of an external charging voltage has driven the reaction all the way to the left. The negative electrode has become pure lead (Pb), the positive electrode is now pure lead peroxide (PbO_2), and the sulfuric acid electrolyte (H_2SO_4 + H_2O) is at its maximum concentration.

Discharging. By connecting a load (shown as a resistor in Figure 3.3), we complete the electrical circuit, allowing electrons to flow from one electrode to the other and the chemical reaction to proceed. The H_2SO_4 breaks into H and SO_4 ions (molecules with either extra or missing electrons). The H is attracted to the positive electrode where it steals the O_2 from the PbO_2 and forms water, H_2O. The now free Pb combines with the SO_4 ions to form $PbSO_4$ in place of the PbO_2. At the negative electrode, SO_4 ions also combine with the pure Pb to form more $PbSO_4$. Thus, both electrode materials are converted to lead sulfate, $PbSO_4$, while the electrolyte loses sulfuric acid, H_2SO_4, gains water, H_2O, and becomes more dilute.

Fully discharged. The cell is fully discharged when it runs out of one of the necessary ingredients. Either the PbO_2 has been totally converted to $PbSO_4$, or all of the SO_4 ions in the electrolyte have been used up, reducing it to pure water. In either case, PbO_2 and electrolyte strength have been minimized and $PbSO_4$ maximized.

Charging. By connecting a charging voltage to the cell we drive the electrons and the reaction in the reverse direction. Ideally, the negative electrode is restored to pure PbO_2, the positive terminal to pure Pb, and the acid electrolyte to its maximum strength.

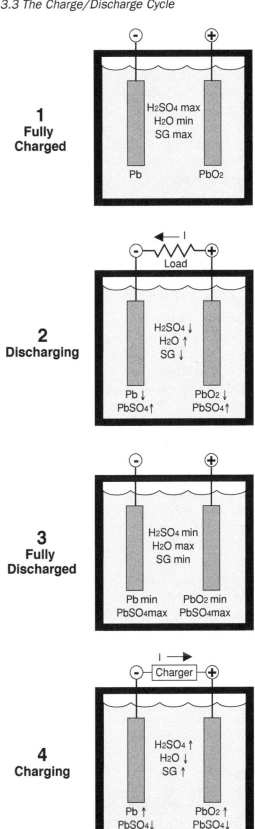

Fig. 3.3 The Charge/Discharge Cycle

A Few Messy Details

The good news is that the chemistry of the lead-acid battery is simple. The bad news is that the way in which it actually happens is a bit more complex.

Figure 3.4 shows a cross section of a cell. Both positive and negative electrodes are immersed in electrolyte. The reactive materials, lead and lead peroxide, are suspended on lead grids that serve to both support the materials and conduct electric current. So far, so simple. Now for the complications:

• Boat batteries are bounced around. In order that the plates not touch each other and short-circuit the cell, the many closely spaced plates (electrodes) are interleaved with porous fiberglass separators.

• The lead grid is chemically and electrically compatible with the active materials that it supports, but it is not very strong. To increase strength, it is alloyed with either antimony (conventional wet, deep-cycle batteries) or calcium (sealed, maintenance-free batteries).

• When the discharge reaction starts, lead sulfate first forms at the electrode surfaces. As discharge continues, the already formed sulfate forms a barrier between the electrolyte and the unreacted material beneath, slowing the reaction and limiting the current. The greater the surface area and thinner the plates, the greater the possible current flow. Engine-starting batteries have many thin plates in order to provide large currents for short periods. The electrodes are also "sponged" (made full of minute holes) in order to further increase surface area.

• Lead, lead peroxide, and lead sulfate are not of the same density. When one replaces the other, expansion and contraction tend to dislodge the materials from the grids. Each time a cell is cycled, a small amount of lead sulfate is shed and falls to the bottom of the cell. Eventually the accumulation at the bottom may short out the plates. The more complete the reaction (the deeper the discharge), the greater the loss. Batteries designed for deep-cycling have fewer but thicker plates.

• When a battery is fully charged, all of the lead sulfate of the positive plate has oxidized to lead peroxide. Further charging (overcharging) oxidizes the lead of the grid as well, turning it into lead peroxide. Lead peroxide has little mechanical strength, and the grid will ultimately fall to the bottom of the cell.

• The rest of the overcharging energy goes into hydrolysis—separation of the water of the electrolyte into H_2 and O_2—which we saw as bubbles in our kitchen battery. Various tricks are employed in sealed batteries to recombine the gases into water, but, if overcharging and gassing are too vigorous, all batteries vent gas and lose electrolyte. Water can be replaced in a conventional wet-acid battery. In a sealed or gel-cell battery, it cannot.

• As we have seen, charging regenerates the H_2SO_4 electrolyte. Pure H_2SO_4 is 1.83 times as dense as water. As the H_2SO_4 is generated, it tends to sink. Since it is the H_2SO_4 that makes the electrolyte conductive, its absence at the top of the cell limits the acceptance of charging current. In a conventional wet-acid battery, acceptance is slow until gassing begins. Rising gas bubbles then mix the electrolyte, and acceptance increases.

• Gelled-electrolyte batteries capture the electrolyte in a gel, preventing stratification and increasing initial charge acceptance. "Starved electrolyte batteries" accomplish the same goal by limiting the electrolyte to just enough to saturate the porous separators.

• Most serious is the phenomenon of sulfation. If a battery is left in a discharged state (i.e., with much of its electrodes in the form of $PbSO_4$), the initially fine, soft deposits grow into larger, harder crystals that clog the holes of the sponged electrodes. The battery becomes difficult to charge and displays reduced capacity. Vigorous overcharging and bubbling (equalization) can break up and dislodge the crystals, resulting in recovery of much of the original capacity. However, each time it is done, the plates shed more material and get closer to the end of their useful lives.

So you see that, although the basic chemistry of all lead-acid batteries is the same, there are enough variations in construction to allow battery company marketing departments a field day.

Fig. 3.4 Cross Section of a Lead-Acid Battery Cell

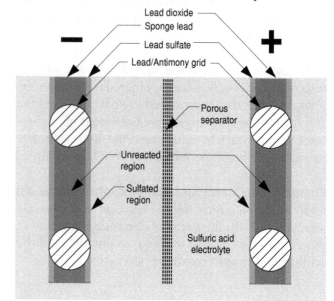

An ideal voltage source would supply unlimited current, with no drop in voltage. Considering the construction of the battery shown in Figure 3.4 and the messy complications described above, it is obvious that the lead-acid battery is not an ideal source.

For current to flow, the SO_4 and H ions have to find their way through the electrolyte. Resistance to this movement is evidenced as an internal electrical resistance, R_i.

When we disconnect a battery from an external circuit, no current should flow—at least theoretically. However, there is still voltage inside the cell ready and willing to supply current to anything that might bridge the gap between the battery's electrodes. Impurities in the electrolyte, as well as dirt and spilled electrolyte on the surface of the battery, provide such paths. They result in a parallel resistance, R_p, acting to self-discharge the battery. This is why you should never add anything but distilled or demineralized water to your battery and why it is a good idea to keep its surfaces clean.

Figure 3.5 shows the electrical model of the battery consisting of an ideal voltage source with a series internal resistance, R_i, and a parallel self-discharge resistance, R_p. Since chemical reactions always speed up with temperature, both resistances decrease with increasing temperature.

Fig. 3.5 Electrical Model of the Battery

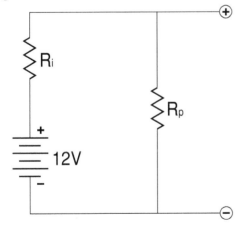

R_i in a new lead-acid battery is very small—of the order 0.01 ohm. It can be measured by drawing a known current and observing the drop in voltage at the terminals.

Example: We monitor the current drawn by a starter motor as 200 amps. As soon as we switch on the starter, we observe a drop in battery voltage from 12.5 to 9.5 volts. The battery's internal resistance, R_i, is then:

$$R_i = V/I$$
$$= (12.5 - 9.5) \text{ volts}/200 \text{ amps}$$
$$= 0.015 \text{ ohm}$$

The voltage must be measured at the battery terminals to eliminate the drop in the battery cables.

R_p is typically quite large—on the order of 1,000 to 10,000 ohms. It can be deduced by observing the drop in battery stored capacity over time.

Figure 3.6 shows the self-discharge of a typical new battery at different temperatures.

Fig. 3.6 Battery Self-Discharge vs. Time

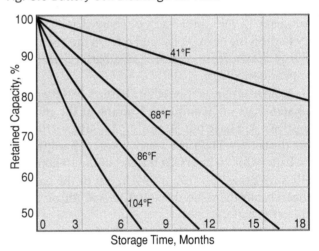

Example: At 68°F, the battery loses the first 10% of charge in three months. If this is a 100 Ah battery, it loses 10% of 100 Ah, or 10 Ah over a period of 90 days. Since there are 24 hours in a day, the discharge period is 90 × 24, or 2,160 hours. The average discharge current was thus 10 Ah/2,160 hours = 0.0046 amp. Using Ohm's Law,

$$R_p = V/I$$
$$= 12 \text{ volts}/0.0046 \text{ amp}$$
$$= 2,600 \text{ ohms}$$

The effect of temperature on R_p is evident from the discharge curves. Performing the same calculations as above, we find that R_p at 40°F is 7,900 ohms, while at 104°F it has dropped to just 930 ohms.

Monitoring Battery Health

Determining State of Charge

Short of taking a battery apart and weighing the amounts of chemicals present, how can we determine the state of charge? Later we will describe battery-charge regulators/monitors that regulate and keep track of the amperes flowing into and out of a battery. For now, we will consider the more basic methods that have been used since batteries were invented.

First, in what sorts of units do we measure the amount of energy stored in a battery? As stated in Chapter 1, electrical energy is measured in watt-hours—the watts of power dissipated by the current flowing through a load times the duration of the flow in hours. Again, watts equals current times voltage:

$$W = I \times V$$
where I = amps through the load
V = volts across the load

However, since the voltage of a battery is always nominally 12 volts until nearly discharged, it is customary to drop the term "volts" and refer to the amount of energy drawn from or stored in a battery simply as ampere-hours (Ah).

As an example, suppose we charge a battery at the constant rate of 50 amps for 2 hours. At the end of 2 hours we will have put 50 amps × 2 hours, or 100 Ah, into the battery. Then let's draw a constant 5 amps from the battery for 10 hours. At the end of the 10 hours we will have drawn 5 × 10, or 50 Ah, out of the battery. Theoretically there should be 100 Ah – 50 Ah, or 50 Ah, still in the battery.

Battery electrolyte is a mixture of water (density 1.000 gram/cubic centimeter) and sulfuric acid (density 1.830 grams/cubic centimeter). Since flow of electricity into and out of a battery results in either the generation of sulfuric acid or the loss of sulfuric acid, the amount of stored energy in a battery is, therefore, a linear function of the density of the electrolyte.

Electrolyte density is usually expressed as its specific gravity—the ratio of its density to the density of water.

Specific gravity (SG) is measured with a battery hydrometer calibrated for the range of electrolyte densities normally found in a battery, 1.000 to 1.300. Do not confuse a *battery* hydrometer with an *antifreeze coolant* hydrometer, which is designed to measure SGs of less than 1.000. When a sample of electrolyte is drawn into the hydrometer, a float indicates the SG. However, the indicated SG must be corrected to what it would be at a standard temperature, 80°F. Figure 3.7 shows the corrections to make.

Fig. 3.7 Correcting Measured Specific Gravity for Temperature

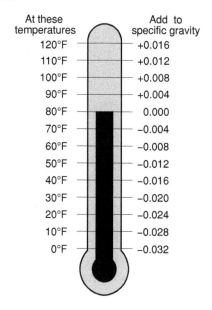

At these temperatures	Add to specific gravity
120°F	+0.016
110°F	+0.012
100°F	+0.008
90°F	+0.004
80°F	0.000
70°F	−0.004
60°F	−0.008
50°F	−0.012
40°F	−0.016
30°F	−0.020
20°F	−0.024
10°F	−0.028
0°F	−0.032

Example: A battery is located in the engine compartment. The temperature of the electrolyte is 95°F. The hydrometer reads 1.250. What is its SG, corrected to 80°F? *Answer:* 1.250 + 0.006 = 1.256.

Figure 3.8 shows the relationship between state of charge and electrolyte SG for a typical new lead-acid battery. The form of the relationship is always correct, but:

1. The high and low SG end points are particular to the individual battery, depending on age, condition, and the preferences of the manufacturer. High SG is more often between 1.265 and 1.280.
2. The SG has been measured only after the battery has rested for a time sufficient for the electrolyte to become homogeneous through diffusion, usually considered to be 24 hours.
3. The SG has been corrected to the standard temperature of 80°F.

Battery manufacturers can make the SG any value they wish. A more concentrated electrolyte (higher SG) produces higher voltage and increased capacity, but it also leads to shorter battery life. SGs are made higher in colder climates. Most new battery high SGs fall in the range 1.265 to 1.280.

Figure 3.9 shows a second electrochemical relationship—this time between SG and voltage. The open circuit (no current being withdrawn) voltage of a single lead-acid cell is determined by the homogeneous, temperature-corrected electrolyte SG as:

$$V = 0.84 + SG$$

For a 12-volt (six-cell) battery the relationship becomes that in Figure 3.9:

$$V = 6 \times (0.84 + SG)$$

Using either Figure 3.8 or Figure 3.9 requires that we actually measure the SG of the electrolyte. This operation is messy, destructive of clothing, awkward in the spaces where batteries are usually stowed, and impossible with a sealed battery.

Fortunately, Figures 3.8 and 3.9 can be combined, resulting in the more convenient relationship between state of charge and open-circuit voltage shown in Figure 3.10. The figure shows that, after 24 hours of rest, this battery would read 11.6 volts when fully discharged, 12.7 volts when fully charged, and 12.2 volts when 50% discharged.

If we can wait 24 hours, determining the remaining capacity of a battery is simple using an accurate voltmeter. The 24-hour rest period is provided by switching between two battery banks daily.

Why do we say the battery is fully discharged at 11.6 volts when the battery obviously has some amount of charge remaining? It is destructive to discharge a multicelled, lead-acid battery to 0 volts. With even small differences between cells, as 0 volts is approached, the stronger cells can drive the weaker cells into reversed polarity. Their grids will be damaged by being converted to $PbSO_4$. To avoid damage, "fully discharged" is defined as 10.5 volts at the 20-hour discharge rate. For example, for a 100 Ah battery, fully discharged is the point where the voltage reads 10.5 V, at a discharge current of 100 Ah/20 hours = 5 amps.

Self-Discharge and Winter Storage

House batteries are very heavy, so it would be nice if we could leave the really big ones on the boat over the winter. Pure water (fully discharged electrolyte) would freeze and crack the battery case. However, fully charged electrolyte (SG = 1.265) freezes at −72°F, while half-charged electrolyte (SG = 1.190) freezes at −12°F.

The question for northern boatowners thus becomes how quickly a battery that has been washed with a baking-soda solution, rinsed with fresh water, fully charged, and disconnected from its leads will self-discharge. According to Rolls Battery, at an average temperature of 50°F, such a battery would discharge at about 0.0003 SG per day. To drop from SG 1.265 to SG 1.190 (freezing point −12°F) would take 250 days.

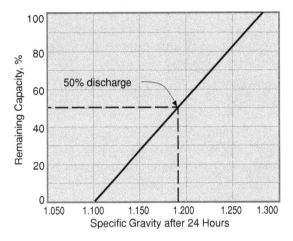

Fig. 3.8 Battery Remaining Capacity vs. Specific Gravity

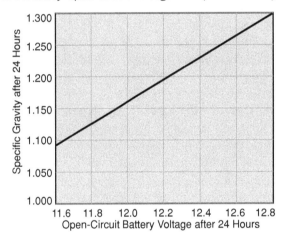

Fig. 3.9 Battery Open-Circuit Voltage vs. Specific Gravity

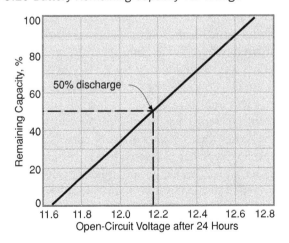

Fig. 3.10 Battery Remaining Capacity vs. Voltage

Discharge Characteristics

Earlier we noted the custom of measuring battery capacity in Ah. At small charge and discharge rates, the losses due to internal resistance are small, and the numbers of Ah we can withdraw very closely approximate the numbers of Ah we have put in.

When discharging at high currents, however, there is an apparent loss of battery capacity. As discharge current increases, the internal voltage drop through the battery's internal resistance increases, so the 10.5-volt cutoff point is reached sooner. Thus cutoff voltage for starter-motor applications is reduced to 7.2 volts.

Figure 3.11 shows discharge voltage vs. time at fractions of the 20-hour Ah capacity, C. When a battery's capacity, C, is stated as 200 Ah at the 20-hour discharge rate, it means that, when discharged at a constant rate of 0.05C (0.05 × 200 = 10 amps), the output voltage will fall to the zero-capacity cutoff of 10.5 volts in 20 hours. If the discharge rate is increased to 0.25C (50 amps), however, it will fall to 10.5 volts in about 3 hours. In the first case, 10 amps × 20 hours = 200 Ah. In the second case, 50 amps × 3 hours = 150 Ah. Discharged at 0.25C, the battery seems to have only 75% of its rated capacity.

This apparent loss of capacity vs. discharge rate is clearly shown in the more general curve of Figure 3.12. Note, that if we discharge at less than the 20-hour rate, the apparent capacity is *greater* than 100%. If this does not surprise you, it shows that you understand the effect of battery internal resistance.

Since internal resistance is strongly affected by electrolyte temperature, we would expect a family of such discharge curves for different temperatures.

Figure 3.13 shows capacity vs. both discharge rate and temperature. As in Figure 3.12, at 80°F, a battery discharged at five times the 20-hour rate (5 × 0.05C = 0.25C) gives us 75% of its rated capacity. At 0°F and 0.25C, only 45% of the rated capacity is available.

You may be wondering how this loss of Ah squares with the principle that electrons are neither created nor destroyed. Where did all those electrons go?

They are still there in the battery—they just got left behind. Due to the heavy current, the electrolyte in the plates was temporarily depleted. If we allow the battery to rest awhile, electrolyte ions will diffuse into the plates, and, when we start drawing current again, we'll find the voltage has recovered to more than 10.5 volts. This recovery is a familiar phenomenon to those who have had to start balky automobiles in subzero weather. If we are, in fact, willing to withdraw the current at a much lower rate, we will succeed in retrieving nearly 100% of our invested Ah.

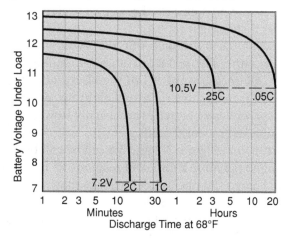

Fig. 3.11 Battery Discharge Characteristics

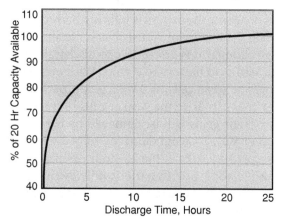

Fig. 3.12 Capacity as a Function of Discharge Time

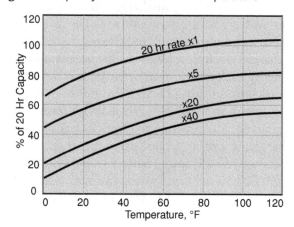

Fig. 3.13 Capacity as a Function of Temperature

Battery Discharge Ratings

Because batteries are used in widely varying applications, several standard capacity ratings have evolved:

1. *Ah at 20-hour rate*—amps a battery will supply for 20 hours at 80°F, before dropping to 10.5 volts, times 20 hours.
2. *Cold cranking amps (CCA)*—minimum number of amps a battery can supply for 30 seconds, at a temperature of 0°F, before dropping to 7.2 volts.
3. *Reserve capacity*—number of minutes a battery will supply a specified constant current (usually 25 amps) at 80°F, before dropping to 10.5 volts.

The first two ratings are of most interest to boat-owners. When running on battery power, the "house" batteries are usually required to run from the time the engine is turned off until it is turned on again. For a cruising boat, the period is likely to last from 16 to 24 hours, so the 20-hour Ah rating is an appropriate specification.

Extremely large currents are drawn by engine starting motors. You can obtain the CCA required by any engine from its manufacturer. Small diesels, in the 10 to 50 hp range, require from 200 to 500 CCAs.

Table 3.1 lists the three ratings, as well as other specifications, for the most popular marine batteries.

Table 3.1 Specifications of Popular Marine Deep-Cycle Batteries

Brand	Model	Type[1]	Capacities Ah, 20 hr	CCA	Reserve	Dimensions, in. L	W	H	Weight, lb.
				SIZE 24					
Surrette/Rolls	24HT80M	WA	80	324	163	11.0	6.8	9.5	50
Trojan	24-AGM	WA	80	440	130	10.8	6.6	8.2	52
Exide Stowaway	ST24DC140	AGM	80	400	140	10.3	6.6	9.4	–
Lifeline	24	AGM	80	550	149	10.9	6.6	9.3	53
Deka Gel-Tech	8G24	GE	74	410	140	10.9	6.8	9.9	53
				SIZE 27					
Surrette/Rolls	24HT90M	WA	90	405	183	12.5	6.8	9.5	62
Trojan	27-AGM	WA	99	560	175	12.0	6.6	8.2	66
Exide Stowaway	ST27DC180	AGM	105	500	180	12.8	6.8	9.5	–
Lifeline	27	AGM	95	575	176	12.6	6.6	9.3	63
Deka Gel-Tech	8G27	GE	86	505	170	12.8	6.8	9.9	63
				SIZE 4D					
Surrette/Rolls	12HHG185M	WA	185	800	344	20.8	8.8	10.0	122
Trojan	4D-AGM	WA	165	1110	325	20.9	8.3	8.5	115
Exide Stowaway	ST4DDC250	AGM	160	600	250	20.8	8.8	10.9	–
Lifeline	4D	AGM	210	1100	380	20.7	8.7	10.3	130
Deka Gel-Tech	8G4D	GE	183	1050	395	20.8	8.5	10.0	129
				SIZE 8D					
Surrette/Rolls	12HHG8DM	WA	275	1155	557	20.8	11.0	10.0	172
Trojan	8D-AGM	WA	230	1450	460	20.5	10.6	8.0	155
Exide Stowaway	ST8DDC400	AGM	200	800	400	20.8	11.0	10.9	–
Lifeline	8D	AGM	255	1350	461	20.6	11.0	10.2	158
Deka Gel-Tech	8G8D	GE	225	1265	500	20.8	11.0	10.0	161
				6-VOLT GOLF CART					
Trojan	T-105	WA	225	—	447	10.4	7.1	10.9	62
Exide	E3600	AGM	220	800	400	10.5	7.2	11.5	62
Lifeline	GC4	AGM	220	760	452	10.4	7.1	11.6	66
Deka Gel-Tech	8G6V200	GE	180	585	375	10.3	7.1	10.9	72

[1] WA = wet-acid, AGM = absorbed glass mat, GE = gelled electrolyte

Charging Characteristics

Charging a battery is the process of driving the lead-acid chemical reaction backward through application of an external voltage. To fully charge a battery, we must convert 100% of the $PbSO_4$ back to Pb and PbO_2.

On a boat, because charging requires running an engine, the usual goal is to recharge the battery as quickly as possible without damaging it. Damage can occur through excessive gassing, overcharging, and overheating.

Gassing. When the conversion of $PbSO_4$ to Pb and PbO_2 cannot keep pace with charging current, excess current results in hydrolysis, splitting the electrolyte's water molecules into gaseous hydrogen and oxygen. Wet-acid batteries vent the gases and thereby lose water. Through various tricks, including internal pressure, sealed batteries can recombine small amounts of gas and prevent water loss. However, even the best sealed batteries, including those with gelled electrolyte, can be overcharged to the point where they vent gas. No battery is totally immune to loss of electrolyte and subsequent loss of capacity. For this reason most gel-cell battery manufacturers specify a maximum charging voltage of 13.8 volts, as opposed to the 14.2 to 14.6 specified for wet-acid batteries.

Overcharging. A battery is fully charged when all of its $PbSO_4$ has been converted to Pb. As current continues to flow, gassing continues, as above, with the same destructive effect. Even more damaging, however, is oxidation of the positive grids into PbO_2, a relative nonconductor. The resulting increase in internal resistance decreases both the battery's charge acceptance rate and its ability to supply large discharge currents.

Overheating. A battery should never be charged when its temperature is over 120°F. Internal heat is generated by the internal resistance of the battery. At a charging current, I, of 100 amps and an internal resistance, R_i, of 0.01 ohm, the heat generated would be:

$$Watts = I^2 \times R_i$$
$$= 100 \text{ amps} \times 100 \text{ amps} \times 0.01 \text{ ohm}$$
$$= 100 \text{ watts}$$

Note that the heat generated is proportional to the square of the charging current, so a 100-amp charge rate would generate four times as much heat as a 50-amp rate. The internal temperature rise is in addition to the ambient temperature of the space where the battery is located. A good way to kill batteries is fast charging in a hot engine compartment while underway in the tropics.

Optimally Fast Charging

Optimally fast charging (charging as rapidly as possible without damage) involves four phases (Figure 3.14).

Fig. 3.14 Optimally Fast Charging

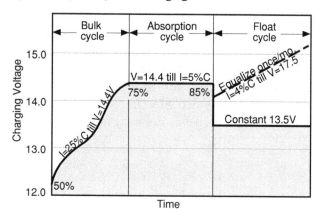

Bulk cycle. If a healthy wet-acid battery is discharged more than 25% of its capacity, C, it will readily accept charge rates of 0.25C or more, up to the point where it is about 75% charged. Gelled-electrolyte batteries, because they do not suffer from electrolyte stratification, will typically accept charge rates of up to 0.5C.

Absorption cycle. When a battery reaches its 75% charged state, the charging voltage has increased to around 14.4 volts, and gassing begins. At this point, in order to limit gassing, the charging voltage must be held constant at 14.4 volts or less, while the battery absorbs current at its own decreasing rate. At the point where the constant-voltage current has dropped to a rate of 0.05C, the battery is approximately 85% charged; at 0.02C about 90% charged; and at 0.01C nearly 100% charged. How far the absorption cycle is carried depends on whether the engine is being run only for charging (0.05C cutoff recommended), or whether the boat is under power or using shore power (0.01 to 0.02C cutoff recommended).

Float cycle. The final stage, provided the battery is still in the charge mode, is designed to just maintain the battery in its fully charged condition. If a battery is removed from all loads, as in the case of winter storage, the ideal float voltage is about 0.1 volt above the rested, open-circuit voltage, or approximately 13 volts. If the battery is in a float cycle, but still online so that current is occasionally withdrawn, either the charger should be capable of supplying the entire draw, or the float voltage should be increased to between 13.2 and 13.5 volts.

Equalization. As we saw on page 29, a fully charged battery consists of pure lead plates immersed in a sulfuric acid electrolyte; a fully discharged battery consists of lead sulfate plates in pure water. If a battery is cycled short of full charge its plates will retain the last 10% of lead sulfate. Over time this lead sulfate hardens and resists both breaking down and current flow. As a result of the electrical resistance the battery shows a falsely high voltage, appearing to be fully charged when it isn't. Over time the effective capacity of the battery shrinks.

The cure is *equalization*—a controlled overcharge, during which the cells are brought back to their fully charged states. A constant current of 0.04C is applied for 4 hours, or until battery voltage rises to the manufacturer-specified equalization voltage for the particular battery. Overcharging forces all of the $PbSO_4$ in each cell to be converted, so that, except for material previously lost by shedding, each cell is restored to its original condition. Overcharging also causes gassing and, in wet-acid batteries, loss of electrolyte. After equalization, wet-acid cells should be topped off with distilled water. Because of the gassing, equalization should be applied with care to sealed batteries and not at all to gelled-electrolyte batteries (see pages 40–41 for battery types).

Equalization should not be performed too often, however, since overcharging also oxidizes the positive plates. It should be performed whenever cell specific gravities differ by 0.030 or more, indicating a difference in capacities of 15% to 20%. Alternatively, for batteries cycled daily, a routine equalization schedule of once per month is recommended.

Each manufacturer publishes a recommended method for recharging its products. Sealed batteries are less likely than wet-acid batteries to require equalization because they ordinarily neither lose nor gain electrolyte. Furthermore, they might gas excessively and lose electrolyte if subjected to a high voltage. Constant-current charging is a possibility with wet-acid batteries because limited accidental overcharging results only in loss of replaceable water. Sealed-battery manufacturers, however, fear such an accident and so recommend constant voltage with limited-current charging.

Automotive-type regulators can be set only to a single voltage. Regulators that can be programmed for optimally fast charging will be covered in Chapter 4.

Table 3.2 compares optimally fast charging voltages and currents for most "marine" batteries.

Table 3.2 Charging Parameters for Marine Batteries (from PROsine 2.0 Inverter/Charger User's Manual)

Battery	Bulk/Absorption Vmax	Imax	Float Vmax	Equal. Vmax
Canadian Tire Nautilus 5	14.1	25	13.0	17.5
Canadian Tire Gel (Exide) 6	14.2	25	13.5	NR*
Concord AGM Valve Regulated 3	14.3	30	13.4	NR
Delco 1150, 1200, 2000, Voyager (Delphi)	16.0	20	13.5	17.5
Douglas Marine Deep Cycle 21	14.6	20	13.5	17.5
Duralast Flooded Deep Cycle/Starting	14.8	25	13.6	15.5
Duralast Flooded Starting/Deep Cycle	15.5	25	13.7	16.0
Energizer Flooded Deep Cycle/Starting	14.8	25	13.6	15.5
Energizer Flooded Starting/Deep Cycle	15.5	25	13.7	16.0
Eveready Flooded Deep Cycle/Starting	14.8	25	13.6	15.5
Eveready Flooded Starting/Deep Cycle	15.5	25	13.7	16.0
Exide Flooded 5	14.1	25	13.0	17.5
Exide Gel Master 6	14.2	25	13.5	NR
GNB Action Pac 7	14.5	25	13.5	17.5
GNB Evolyte 9	14.4	30	13.5	17.5
GNB Stowaway 8	15.3	25	14.3	17.5
GNB Sunlyte 10	14.1	30	13.5	14.2
Hawker Energy Genesis 14	15	200	13.7	NR
Interstate Flooded Deep Cycle/Starting	14.8	25	13.6	15.5
Interstate Flooded Starting/Deep Cycle	15.5	25	13.7	16.0
Interstate Optima, Normal 19	14.7	200	13.5	17.5
Johnson Contr Flooded Deep Cycle/Start	14.8	25	13.6	15.5
Johnson Contr Flooded Start/Deep Cycle	15.5	25	13.7	16.0
Keystone Solid Energy Flooded 16	14	10	13.5	16.5
Keystone Solid Energy Gel 15	14.2	12	13.7	16.5
Metra Electronic—Tsunami 19	14.7	200	13.5	17.5
Optima Blue, Red, Yellow Top 19	14.7	200	13.5	17.5
Rolls Deep Cycle (Surrette) 18	14.2	20	13.2	15.5
Sears Canada Marine (Delco)17	16.0	20	13.5	17.5
Sears Canada Marine Flooded (Exide) 5	14.1	25	13.0	17.5
Sears USA Flooded Deep Cycle/Starting	14.8	25	13.6	15.5
Sears USA Flooded Starting/Deep Cycle	15.5	25	13.7	16.0
Sears USA Gel 11	14.4	30	13.8	NR
Sonnenshein (all) 2	14.2	25	13.8	NR
Surrette Deep Cycle 18	14.2	20	13.2	15.5
Trojan (all) 1	14.4	30	13.5	17.5
West Marine Sea Volt (Trojan) 1	14.4	30	13.5	17.5
West Marine Sea Gel (Sonnenshein)	14.2	25	13.8	NR

*NR = Not Recommended

Estimating Your Daily Load

The first step in selecting storage batteries is to determine the daily consumption of electricity in Ah. Table 3.3 lists equipment commonly found on boats. Power ratings can usually be found on a nameplate, either in watts or in amps. Make your own table using the form shown in Table 3.4. To calculate the daily Ah requirement, first convert all nameplate ratings to amps by dividing watts by 12. Next multiply by the average hours used per day to get Ah. Finally, add the Ah for all the devices for the total Ah/day.

For many of the devices, two ratings have been listed: (1) the typical consumption, and (2) the consumption of the most efficient models. The table shows the total Ah/day for two cruisers: (1) with typical appliances, and (2) with the most efficient appliances.

The boat with typical appliances consumes 99 Ah/day, while the more efficient boat consumes only half as much. The more efficient boat will thus require only half as large a battery system, or, alternatively, will go twice as long before requiring recharging.

Table 3.3 Power Consumption for Cruising Boats at Anchor

Area	Appliance or Fixture		Watts	÷12 = Amps	Average Hours per Day	Typical Ah	Efficient Ah
Galley	Microwave (9 minutes/day)		550	45.8	0.15	6.9	6.9
	Toaster (5 minutes/day)		800	66.7	0.04		
	Blender (30 seconds/day)		175	14.6	0.01	0.15	0.15
	Coffee grinder (15 seconds/day)		160	13.3	0.005		
	Refrigerator	2" insulation	60	5.0	10	50.0	
		4" insulation	60	5.0	5.0		21.9
Head	Hair dryer (2 minutes/day)		1200	100	0.033		
Lighting	Reading lamp	2 incandescent 15-watt	30	2.5	2	5.0	
		2 halogen spots 5-watt	10	0.8	2		1.6
	Galley fixture	2 incandescent 25-watt	50	4.2	2	8.4	
		2 fluorescent 8-watt	16	1.4	2		2.8
	Anchor light	manual 10-watt	10	0.8	14	11.2	
		automatic 10-watt	10	0.8	11		8.8
Fans	Typical 6", 100 cfm		12	1.0	5.0	5.0	
	Most efficient, 100 cfm		4	0.3	5.0		1.5
Entertainment	Stereo	20-watt/channel	60	5.0	1.0	5.0	
		7-watt/channel	35	3.0	1.0		3.0
	Television	19-inch CRT	80	6.7	4.0		
		15-inch LCD	36	3.0	2.0	6.0	
		6-inch color	15	1.7	4.0		3.4
	VCR or DVD	typical 110-volt AC	17	1.4	1.0	1.4	
		12-volt DC play only	10	0.8	1.0		0.8
		Totals				99.1	50.9

Table 3.4 Form for Estimating Power Consumption at Anchor

Area	Appliance or Fixture		Watts	÷12 = Amps	Average Hours per Day	Estimated Ah
Galley	Microwave (9 minutes/day)		550	45.8	0.15	_____
	Toaster (5 minutes/day)		800	66.7	0.04	_____
	Blender (30 seconds/day)		175	14.6	0.01	_____
	Coffee grinder (15 seconds/day)		160	13.3	0.005	_____
	Refrigerator	2" insulation	60	5.0	10	_____
		4" insulation	60	5.0	5.0	_____
Head	Hair dryer (2 minutes/day)		1200	100	0.033	_____
Lighting	Reading lamp	2 incandescent 15-watt	30	2.5	2	_____
		2 halogen spots 5-watt	10	0.8	2	_____
	Galley fixture	2 incandescent 25-watt	50	4.2	2	_____
		2 fluorescent 8-watt	16	1.4	2	_____
	Anchor light	manual 10-watt	10	0.8	14	_____
		automatic 10-watt	10	0.8	11	_____
Fans	Typical 6", 100 cfm		12	1.0	5.0	_____
	Most efficient, 100 cfm		4	0.3	5.0	_____
Entertainment	Stereo	20-watt/channel	60	5.0	1.0	_____
		7-watt/channel	35	3.0	1.0	_____
	Television	19-inch CRT	80	6.7	4.0	_____
		15-inch LCD	36	3.0	2.0	_____
		6-inch color	15	1.7	4.0	_____
	VCR or DVD	typical 110-volt AC	17	1.4	1.0	_____
		12-volt DC play only	10	0.8	1.0	_____
Other						_____
						_____
						_____
						Total

Choosing a Battery Type

Forget the marketing terminology you have seen in battery advertisements. Batteries can be divided into four general categories:

1. Conventional, wet-acid automotive starting
2. Deep-cycle, wet-acid
3. Absorbed glass mat
4. Gelled electrolyte

Conventional, wet-acid automotive starting batteries are engineered to supply extremely high currents (200 to 1,000 amps) for periods of just a few seconds. In spite of the high current, the duration is so short that the amount of energy drawn (amps × hours, or Ah) is small. Used in this way, automotive starting batteries are typically discharged only a few percent of their capacity before returning to the float state.

The rate at which current can be drawn is proportional to plate area, so starting batteries are constructed with a large number of thin lead plates sandwiched between paper or plastic separator plates. When cycled deeply, battery plate material is shed. Since starting battery plates are so thin to start with, deep cycling will result in short life.

Don't be fooled by warranties of 60 or more months or names such as "Die-Hard." While fine for starting the engine, if used to power your cabin lights and other house loads, you will be replacing this type of battery every season or two. Used only to start the engine, provided they are recharged immediately after use, they make a good combination with a large, deep-cycle house battery.

Deep-cycle, wet-acid batteries have fewer but thicker plates designed for regular discharge to 50% or less of capacity. The largest users of such batteries are not boats but golf carts and forklifts, which require large currents and capacities, in addition to the ability to cycle thousands of times. Such batteries have the maximum cycling potential and are ideally suited to cruising boats with heavy house loads and long seasons, provided their owners are willing to spend the time monitoring and maintaining them.

In a well-equipped cruising boat, a deep-cycle house bank will also have sufficient cold-cranking capacity to start the engine. If, as recommended, the house batteries are separated into two banks, there is little need for a dedicated engine-starting battery.

Some boaters still carry a small automotive engine-starting battery as a safety backup, however.

Absorbed-glass mat batteries were developed as superior engine-starting batteries, but are being used more and more as marine house batteries. They retain all of their electrolyte in spongy fiberglass mats and are "sealed" with valve-regulated caps, which recombine charging gases under most conditions. The thin, porous plates that yield high starting-motor currents do not stand up as well as those of deep-cycle, wet-acid types. However, they can both discharge and recharge at much higher rates than wet-acid batteries. Because so many of these batteries are sold, competitive pricing makes them attractive. Provided discharge is limited to around 50%, they are suitable for the seasonal boater who expects to replace the batteries every 3 or 4 years.

Fig. 3.15 Nominal Battery Dimensions

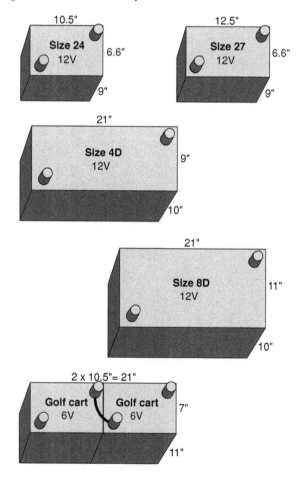

Gelled-electrolyte batteries were developed for applications where acid spills and gas venting were prohibited, such as military tanks and wheelchairs. Freedom of location and from maintenance have made them popular on boats. They cannot be deep cycled as many times as wet-acid, deep-cycle batteries, but they are less subject to damage if left in a discharged state, and accept somewhat higher recharge rates. With the caveat that their lower charging voltages must never be exceeded, gel-cells are suited to boats with large loads, long seasons, and owners who are totally unwilling to monitor and maintain their batteries. Before purchasing, however, you should seriously consider the AGM battery, which shares many of the gel's advantages, yet may be occasionally and moderately overcharged.

Figure 3.15 shows the nominal sizes of the most popular batteries. Actual sizes vary, so assume an extra ½ inch all around, or get actual specifications.

Table 3.5 compares the advantages and disadvantages of the four battery types.

Table 3.5 Comparing Battery Types

Battery Type	Advantages	Disadvantages
Wet-acid automotive	Lowest cost High cranking amps Good for engine start battery Small, lightweight	Can't stand many deep discharges Will be destroyed if left discharged Will spill electrolyte if tipped over Relatively short life Relatively fragile
Wet-acid deep-cycle	Less expensive than gels and AGMs Maximum deep-cycle life (>1,000) Individual cells accessible Can be equalized Water can be added to electrolyte	Electrolyte level must be monitored Will be destroyed if left discharged too long Will spill electrolyte if tipped over Must be installed upright Battery box should be vented overboard Extremely heavy
Gelled electrolyte (gel-cell)	Very rugged Requires least attention, provided not overcharged Can be installed in any position Doesn't require venting Won't leak even if cracked Accepts high charge rate	Most expensive May be destroyed by overcharging Moderate deep-cycle life (500 likely)
Absorbed glass mat (AGM)	Most rugged of all Can be installed in any position Doesn't require venting Won't leak unless cracked Accepts highest charge rate Tolerates moderate equalization	High initial cost Moderate deep-cycle life (250 likely)

Optimum Depth of Discharge

Figure 3.16 shows expected lifetime cycles versus depth of discharge under laboratory conditions. The shape of the curves was established with one set of data each for wet-acid, AGM, and gelled-electrolyte batteries. The golf cart curve was assumed to be of the same shape and fitted to the single published 100% discharge point.

Fig. 3.16 Expected Charge/Discharge Cycles

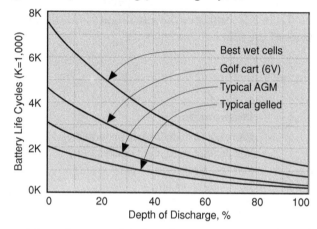

A boat is not an ideal environment, so you should count on getting about half of the cycles shown. Thus, instead of 3,000 discharges to 50% for the best wet-acid battery, you might assume 1,500 cycles. Alternating banks daily, and recharging the banks in parallel, you can project 1,500 recharges × 2 days = 3,000 days, or 8 years.

With the same 50% discharge and 2-day cycle, golf cart batteries should last about 5 years, AGMs 4 years, and gelled electrolyte batteries 2 to 3 years.

Figure 3.17 plots cost per kilowatt-hour versus depth of discharge assuming half of the life cycles shown in Figure 3.16. It was assumed the batteries were size 8D (220 Ah) and were bought for list price, less 15%. The costs (2005) assumed were: wet-acid $544, AGM $444, and gelled $308. The equivalent pair of 6-volt golf cart batteries cost $180.

Figure 3.17 leads to two conclusions:

1. Considering the cost of the batteries alone, the optimum depth of discharge is approximately 50%.
2. Due to a lower purchase cost, the golf cart battery is the most economical battery.

Charging Cutoff

Figure 3.14 showed that charging current should be reduced once a battery has been recharged to 75% of capacity. Stopping at 75%, however, results in sulfation. If the engine is run only for charging, run time becomes uneconomical beyond 85 to 90%. When charging underway or with wind or solar, run time is not an issue, and recharge to above 90% is desirable.

We will assume a boat at anchor, a discharge limit of 30 to 50%, and a recharge cutoff of 85 to 90%. Since a battery is usually considered "dead" when it has permanently lost 40% of its rated capacity, we will also derate our batteries by 20%.

Example: Our daily load is 75 Ah. We decide to discharge to 30% of capacity and charge to 85%. The required (derated to 80%) battery size is then

$$75 \text{ Ah}/0.80(0.85 - 0.30) = 170 \text{ Ah}$$

Once you have estimated your daily load and chosen your charge-discharge range, Figure 3.18 allows easy determination of the required battery size.

Fig. 3.17 Lifetime Costs per kWh of Battery Types

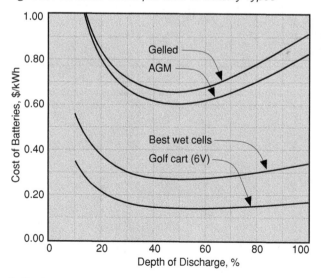

Fig. 3.18 Battery Size Selector

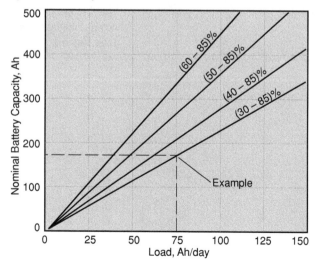

After a deep discharge, batteries will accept very high rates of charge. AGM and gelled-electrolyte batteries typically accept up to 0.5C (50% of capacity per hour), while healthy wet-acid batteries safely accept up to 0.25C. Once a battery has been recharged to 75% of its capacity, the charging rate must be reduced in order to prevent gassing in all batteries, as was shown in Figure 3.14.

The total cost per kilowatt-hour produced and stored is the sum of battery cost (Figure 3.17) and engine/fuel costs. Figure 3.19 compares battery and engine/fuel costs. Engine/fuel costs assume:
• Consumption = 0.5 gallon per hour
• Fuel price = $2.20 per gallon
• Engine life = 10,000 hours
• Engine price = $7,000
• Maintenance = $0.20 per hour

The three curves show the dramatic savings that can be realized by matching the alternator to its load. Minimum engine/fuel cost is achieved by deep discharge of AGM or gelled-electrolyte batteries and recharge at 0.5C (220 A for the example of paralleled 8D batteries). For a pair of 8D wet-acid batteries, the matched alternator would be rated at 110 A.

Solar and wind power will be discussed in Chapter 10, but costs per kilowatt-hour for solar and wind-produced power have been included in Figure 3.19 for comparison. The solar system is assumed to cost $480 per 60-watt panel, last 10 years, and be used all year in Miami. The wind machine has a 5-foot blade, costs $1,500, lasts 10 years, and is used all year in 10-knot average winds.

Solar and wind costs per kilowatt-hour are independent of discharge depth, assuming the systems are matched to the daily load. It is interesting to note that typical utility rates are $0.10 to $0.15 per kilowatt-hour.

Fig. 3.19 Total Costs per kWh of Generated Power

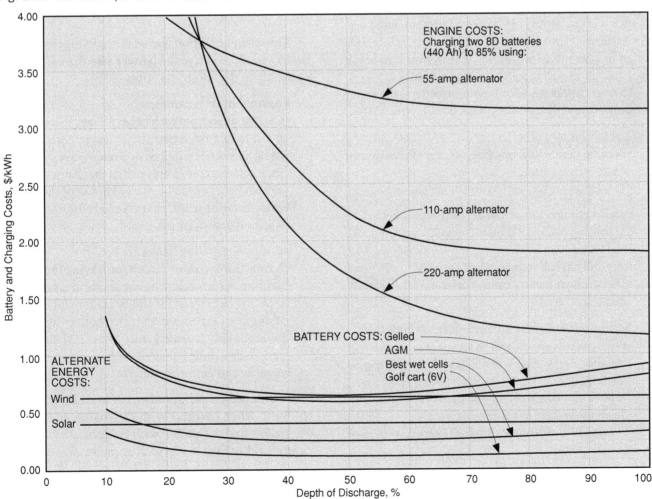

Series vs. Parallel

A battery bank consists of one or more batteries, connected to act as a single 12-volt unit. Two common questions are: (1) should a large bank consist of one very large battery, two smaller 12-volt batteries in parallel, or two 6-volt batteries in series; and (2) assuming two banks, should both be on all the time, or should they be alternated?

First, how large a bank do you need? Some say that your battery capacity can never be too large, but consider two facts:

1. Batteries should not be left in even a partially discharged condition any longer than necessary.
2. The cost of charging batteries is greater than the amortized cost of any battery, and unless a battery is discharged at least to 50%, recharging currents are restricted and charge times elongated.

These are both reasons to size each battery bank for a single day's load. If your daily load is less than about 100 Ah, you can get by with a single 4D battery (185 Ah) by cycling between 85% and 30%. The problem—unless you are young and a weight lifter—is the weight of such a large battery. As you can see from Table 3.1, 4D batteries typically weigh 125 pounds, while 8Ds weigh in at around 160 pounds. The option is to break the bank into smaller, more manageable, units.

Here are arguments for the single battery, the series connection, and the parallel connection (Figure 3.20).

A single battery is better:
• Because there is just one case, you get the maximum Ah in a given space.
• Two battery cables and terminals are eliminated.

Parallel connection of smaller batteries is better:
• Assuming isolation diodes (page 58) are used, the bad battery can be removed, and the remaining battery still has full voltage at half capacity.
• The stronger battery cannot drive a weaker battery into cell reversal.

Series connection of 6-volt batteries is better:
• Failure of a single cell will be apparent as a sudden 2-volt drop, but voltage will still be sufficient for engine starting.
• Failure of a single cell in one battery will not draw down the voltage in a paralleled battery.
• 6-volt golf cart batteries are the cheapest sources of battery power.

Fig. 3.20 Battery Size Selector

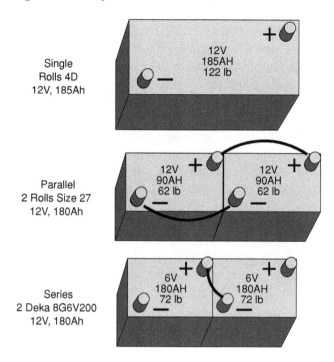

Single
Rolls 4D
12V, 185Ah

12V
185AH
122 lb

Parallel
2 Rolls Size 27
12V, 180Ah

12V
90AH
62 lb

12V
90AH
62 lb

Series
2 Deka 8G6V200
12V, 180Ah

6V
180AH
72 lb

6V
180AH
72 lb

The second question was whether, in the case of two battery banks, to leave the battery selector switch permanently in the "Both" position.

Reasons "Both" is better:
• Current drain from each battery is less, so less energy is lost to internal resistance. This is important when using an electric windlass or a microwave oven.
• Each battery receives only half of the charge currents, so both batteries can be charged in half of the time. If using solar or wind, charging near 100% capacity will less likely cause gassing.

Reasons alternating banks are better:
• A catastrophic short circuit, or leaving the anchor light on for a week, will not result in total loss of capacity. The reason for two banks is redundancy.
• Without an expensive Ah meter, battery health can be accurately assessed only after a 24-hour rest period. Switching banks allows better monitoring of capacity and performance.

Recommendation: alternate banks daily, but switch to "Both" when charging with the engine, starting the engine, hauling the anchor with an electric windlass, or running other high loads, such as microwave ovens.

There are three good reasons to house batteries in sturdy covered battery boxes: (1) to capture and vent overboard explosive hydrogen gas generated in the case of overcharging, (2) to contain electrolyte that may be spilled in rough seas, and (3) to prevent metal tools and other objects from accidently shorting the battery terminals.

Battery boxes can be purchased in a few sizes ready-made, or you can construct one to custom fit your bank. Making your own has the advantage of fitting both the space and the batteries better.

Building a Battery Box

Building a battery box is an excellent way to learn basic fiberglass techniques. No curved surfaces are required, appearance is not critical, and the plywood core forms the mold.

Figure 3.21 shows the construction of a box large enough to hold two 12-volt D4s (330 Ah total) or four 6-volt T-105 golf cart batteries (440 Ah total).

Batteries weigh about 0.75 pound and contain 2 ounces of acid per Ah. While you are making the box, consider the consequences of 330 pounds of batteries and 28 quarts of battery acid breaking loose in a storm. Also picture installing or removing batteries weighing up to 165 pounds each.

1. Mark cuts on ¾-inch AC-Exterior plywood.
2. Apply a layer of fiberglass to both sides of the uncut plywood using epoxy or polyester resin.
3. Cut the panels and apply resin to edges.
4. Glue and nail the box together.
5. Sand round all outside edges and fill inside corners with an epoxy paste.
6. Apply at least three overlapping strips of fiberglass reinforced plastic (FRP) cloth at each inside and outside corner, making sure there are no voids.
7. Apply two complete layers of fiberglass cloth over the entire outside and finish with epoxy paint.
8. Fasten the box firmly to the hull with countersunk stainless steel, flat-head (SS FH) bolts.
9. Apply two additional layers of fiberglass cloth to the inside and finish with white epoxy paint.
10. Drill a vent hole near the top of the side most convenient to venting. The hole diameter should provide a press fit for a length of garden hose.
11. Insert batteries using ¼-inch nylon line, leaving the line for later extraction.
12. Fasten the cover down and run the vent hose to a point outside the hull.

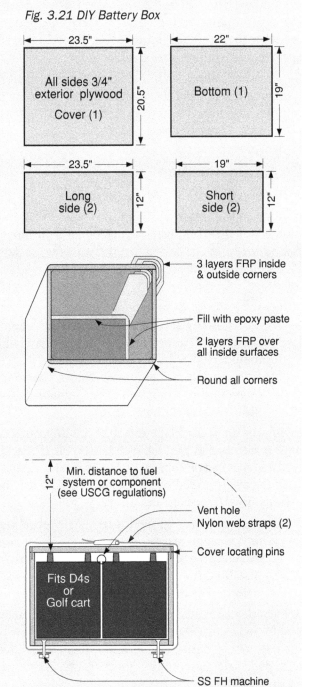

Fig. 3.21 DIY Battery Box

- 23.5" — All sides 3/4" exterior plywood, Cover (1), 20.5"
- 22" — Bottom (1), 19"
- 23.5" — Long side (2), 12"
- 19" — Short side (2), 12"

3 layers FRP inside & outside corners

Fill with epoxy paste

2 layers FRP over all inside surfaces

Round all corners

12" Min. distance to fuel system or component (see USCG regulations)

Vent hole
Nylon web straps (2)

Cover locating pins

Fits D4s or Golf cart

SS FH machine screws (FRP over) for securing

ABYC Standards for Batteries

Adapted from ABYC Standard E-10, *Standards and Recommended Practices for Small Craft*, dated December, 1996. ABYC standards conform with *Title 33, Code of Federal Regulations, Part 183—Boats and Equipment*.

E-10.6. Battery Capacity

a. Cranking batteries shall have at least the cold cranking performance rating (CCA @ 32°F) or marine cranking performance rating (MCA @ 32°F) amperage required by the engine manufacturer.

b. Accessory batteries and cranking batteries used as accessory batteries shall have a rated reserve capacity in minutes determined by the calculations in ABYC E-11, *DC Electrical Systems Under 50 Volts*.

E-10.7. Installation

a. Batteries shall be secured against shifting.

b. An installed battery shall not move more than one inch in any direction when a pulling force of ninety pounds or twice the battery weight, whichever is less, is applied through the center of gravity of the battery as follows:

(1) Vertically for a duration of one minute.
(2) Horizontally and parallel to the boat's center line for a duration of one minute fore and one minute aft.
(3) Horizontally and perpendicular to the boat's center line for a duration of one minute to starboard and one minute to port.

c. To prevent accidental contact of the ungrounded battery terminal to ground, each battery shall be protected so that metallic objects cannot come into contact with the ungrounded battery terminal. This may be accomplished by means such as:

(1) Covering the ungrounded terminal with a boot or nonconductive shield.
(2) Installing the battery in a covered battery box, or
(3) Installing the battery in a compartment specially designed only for the battery(ies).

d. Each metallic fuel line and fuel system component within twelve inches and above the horizontal plane of the battery top surface as installed shall be shielded with dielectric material to protect against accidental short-circuiting.

NOTES:

1. Terminal insulation or battery covers do not comply with this requirement since during installation or removal of a battery, these protective devices are usually removed in order to connect the cables.

2. Any nonconductive material may be used for shielding as long as it is durable enough to withstand accidental contact by a tool or the battery terminals during servicing, installation or removal.

e. Each battery shall not be installed directly above or below a fuel tank, fuel filter, or fitting in a fuel line.

NOTE: This does not prohibit a battery from being installed directly above or below an uninterrupted fuel line; however, if this fuel line is within the twelve inch envelope of the top surface of the battery it shall be shielded dielectrically as required in ABYC E-10.7.d.

f. A vent system or other means shall be provided to permit the discharge from the boat of hydrogen gas released by the battery. Battery boxes whose cover forms a pocket over the battery shall be vented.

NOTE: These provisions also apply to installations of sealed batteries.

g. If the mounting surfaces or components of the boat in the immediate vicinity of the battery location are of a material attacked by the electrolyte, a mounting means shall be provided that is made of a material that is not damaged by electrolyte.

h. Fasteners for the attachment of battery boxes or trays shall be isolated from areas intended to collect spilled electrolyte.

E-10.8. Wiring

a. Connectors to battery terminals shall be made with fitted connectors providing secure mechanical and electrical connections. Spring clips or other temporary clamps shall not be used.

b. A soldered connection that joins a battery terminal connector to a conductor may be used if the length of the soldered joint is at least 1.5 times the diameter of the stranded portion of the battery conductor.

c. Battery supply conductors must be sized to satisfy the load calculations as outlined in ABYC E-11.10. [See Chapter 6.]

CHAPTER 4

Alternators

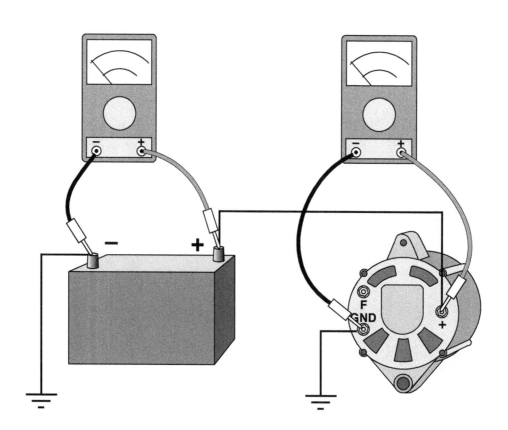

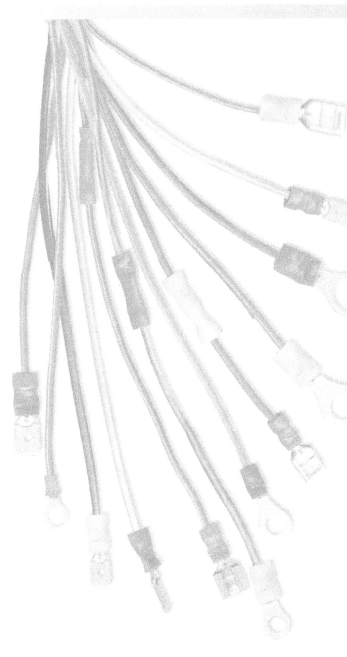

An alternator is a rotary current machine that transforms mechanical rotation into AC current. The AC current produced by the alternator coils is rectified by diodes into DC current for charging the ship's batteries.

In order not to overcharge the batteries we need a regulator for controlling the alternator. Whether the regulator field-coil wire is connected to the positive or to the negative battery terminal determines whether it is a type-P or type-N alternator. The methods of powering the voltage regulator and supplying excitation current to the field coil vary as well.

Regulator bypass controls, allowing more rapid battery charging, are popular among cruisers, the most sophisticated of all being the Link 2000-R Charge Controller.

The electrical demands of boats vary widely, so a variety of charging setups have evolved, from the simplest one alternator/one battery of the day boater to the multiple alternators/multiple batteries of the dedicated liveaboard cruiser.

Since most engines are equipped with light-duty alternators, cruisers and liveaboards having large battery banks very often upgrade to higher-output models, requiring guidance on alternator installation.

Despite the great number of alternator models and charging setups, the basic principles and components are largely the same, allowing for simple troubleshooting procedures.

A Galley Alternator

If you had fun making the galley battery in Chapter 3, try making the galley alternator in Figure 4.1. All you need are an analog voltmeter or ammeter (a multimeter with many ranges is best), a large steel nail or bolt, several feet of insulated copper wire, and a magnet.

Wrap a dozen turns of the wire around the nail and connect the bare ends to the meter. If you are using a multimeter, start with the highest amps scale. Hold the magnet as close to the head of the nail as possible without actually touching it. Now move the magnet rapidly back and forth, as shown in the illustration. The needle of the meter should jump back and forth across zero.

If the needle doesn't move, switch the meter to a lower scale. If the needle still doesn't move, increase the number of turns of wire until it does move.

What's going on? As Hans Oersted discovered in 1820, an electric current is induced in a wire whenever the magnetic field around the wire changes. Our moving magnet induces magnetism in the nail. As the permanent magnet moves back and forth, the magnetism in the nail alternates in direction, so the magnetic field through the coiled wire alternates as well. The alternating field produces pulses of current of alternating polarity as shown in the graph at the bottom of Figure 4.1.

The scale of the graph is not important to our experiment, but you should know that the current is directly proportional to the strength of the magnetic field, the rapidity of the magnet motion, and the number of turns in the coil.

Simple Two-Pole Magnet

Instead of passing the magnet back and forth across the head of the nail, we can make a rotating machine to do the same thing. Figure 4.2 shows a straight bar magnet pivoted about its center between two series-connected coils. The coils are wound in opposite directions, so that the opposite poles of the magnet produce current in the same direction. As the magnet turns, however, each coil sees alternating poles, so the current changes polarity as shown in the graph.

This type of current is called alternating current, or AC. Chapters 7 through 9 of this book deal with AC power on boats. All we need to know about AC at this point is that both voltage and current reverse, usually many times per second. One complete swing from plus to minus and back to plus again is called a *cycle*. The number of cycles per second is the *frequency*, measured in Hertz (Hz). Utility power in the United States is delivered at 60 Hertz; in Europe, at 50 Hertz.

Fig. 4.1 A Galley Alternator

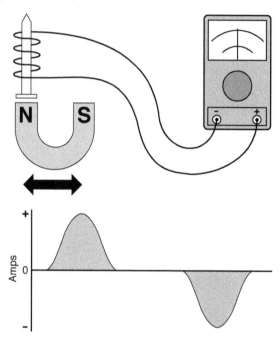

Fig. 4.2 A Rotary Current Machine

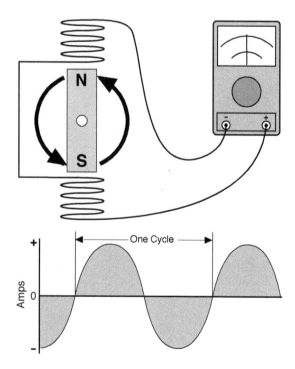

More Poles and Coils

We can make our rotary current machine more efficient by placing more magnets on the rotating shaft and by adding a corresponding number of coils of wire, as shown in Figure 4.3. With three times the number of magnets and coils, the result is three times as much generated power.

With three times as many magnet poles, each revolution of the shaft produces three times as many cycles. All of the coils still produce current in synchrony, however, so the forms of the output current and voltage remain the same as before.

Fig. 4.3 Multiple Poles and Coils

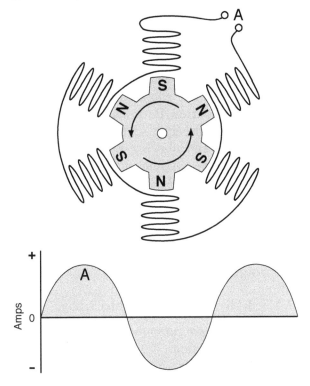

Three-Phase Current

Let's call the entire series-connected coil of Figure 4.3 coil A. Now let's add coils B and C, identical in form to coil A, but rotated one-third and two-thirds of the gap between the small coils of coil A, as shown in Figure 4.4.

The poles of the rotating magnet will pass each set of small coils in the order: A, B, C, A, B, C, etc. The currents induced in coils A, B, and C will therefore be offset by one-third and two-thirds of a cycle as shown at the bottom of Figure 4.4. We now have three identical alternating currents, offset in phase by 120° (one complete cycle equals 360°). We call this three-phase AC.

Why would we want to complicate our rotary current machine in this way?

1. We can triple power output without increasing the size of the wire in the coils.
2. It is easier to wind closely spaced coils than to increase the number of magnetic poles.
3. The three phases result in a better (smoother) output, as we'll see later.

Fig. 4.4 A Rotary Current Machine

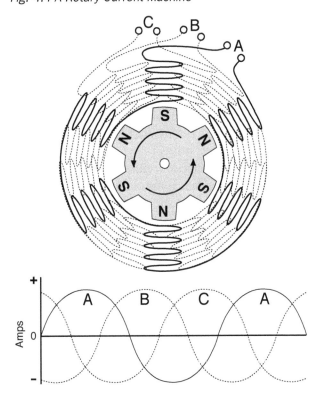

Rectification

As we saw in Chapter 3, batteries produce direct current (DC), which is always of the same polarity. To recharge batteries we need DC. The rotary current machine is of no use unless we convert its three-phase AC output to DC.

Enter the diode. As its circuit symbol (Figure 4.5, top) indicates, the diode allows current to flow only in the direction of the arrow. If you like analogies, you can think of a diode as the equivalent of a check valve in a water-supply system, allowing water to flow in one direction but not the opposite.

Fig. 4.5 Diodes and the Diode Symbol

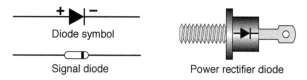

All diodes have the following three ratings:

maximum forward current—maximum current in the forward direction
peak inverse voltage—maximum voltage at which diode will block current flow in reverse direction
forward voltage drop—voltage in the direction of the arrow at which diode begins to conduct current

Diodes come in different sizes and shapes, depending on their intended uses. Tiny signal diodes are intended for low-current applications. Large rectifying diodes are used in high-current applications such as alternators. A typical alternator diode might have ratings of 50 amps, 50 volts, and 0.6 volt.

If you haven't yet put away your galley experiment, insert a diode into the circuit as shown in Figure 4.6. Now when you pass the magnet back and forth, the needle should deflect only in the positive direction. If you get a negative deflection, either the meter leads are reversed, or the diode is pointing in the wrong direction. As the current plot shows, the magnet and wire coil are still producing negative pulses, but the pulses are blocked by the diode.

Figure 4.7 shows how a diode would similarly block negative current in our rotary current machine. The process of passing current of one polarity but blocking current of the opposite polarity is called *rectification*. Passing only the positive halves of an AC wave is called half-wave rectification.

Rectification would be twice as efficient if we could pass both halves of the AC wave. This is accomplished

Fig. 4.6 The Galley Alternator with Rectifier

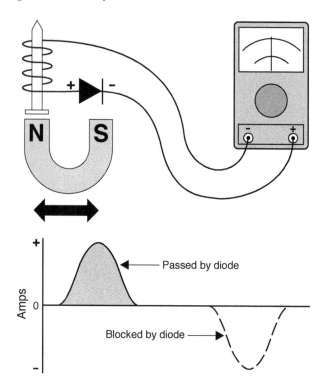

Fig. 4.7 Half-Wave Rectification

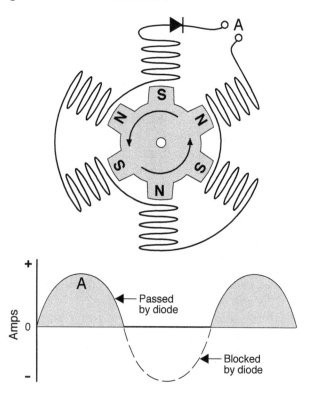

with a four-diode full-wave rectifier (Figure 4.8). No matter the polarity of current and voltage through the wire coil, there are always two of the four diodes seeing reverse voltage and acting as if they were open circuits.

Follow the currents in Figure 4.9 as they flow through the coil, the diodes of the rectifier, and the externally connected load in the alternating closed circuits labeled Path 1 and Path 2.

The first half-wave travels Path 1: from the coil,

through diode 1, into the positive terminal, through the external load, into the negative terminal, through diode 3, and back to the coil.

The second half-wave travels Path 2: from the coil, through diode 2, out the positive terminal, through the external load, into the negative terminal, through diode 4, and back to the coil.

An obvious extension would be to provide each of the coils in Figure 4.4 with their own full-wave rectifiers, as shown in Figure 4.10. This would be fine if we desired three separate outputs to recharge three separate batteries or to power three independent DC circuits, but we don't. We'd rather have a single DC system, and, although we might have three batteries, we'd rather charge them in parallel from a single source.

It would be needless torture to force you through the logic, but it turns out that connecting the ends of the three coils produces a felicitous simplification.

Fig. 4.8 Full-Wave Rectification

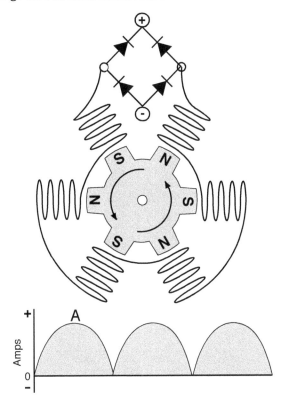

Fig. 4.10 Three Full-Wave Rectifiers

Fig. 4.9 Rectifier Current Paths

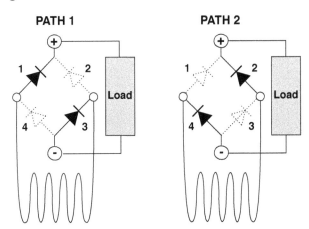

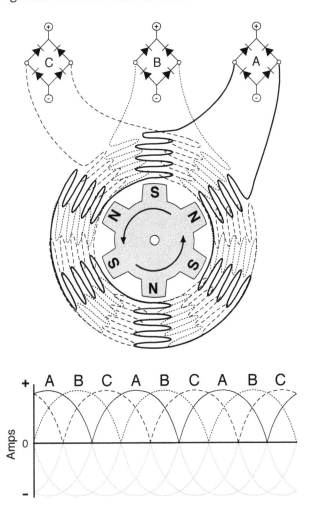

Rectification

Figure 4.11 shows the two common ways to connect the coils: the Delta and the Y. With the coils connected, half of the twelve diodes can be eliminated. With either configuration, we are left with only three coil terminals, each of which is connected to a diode pair.

Figure 4.12 shows the ends of the coils connected to a single pair of output terminals. The currents combine in such a way that total output current approximates steady DC. Our rotary current machine has finally evolved into a DC-output alternator.

Fig. 4.11 Delta and Y Coil Arrangements

Fig. 4.12 Delta and Y Connections in a Real Alternator

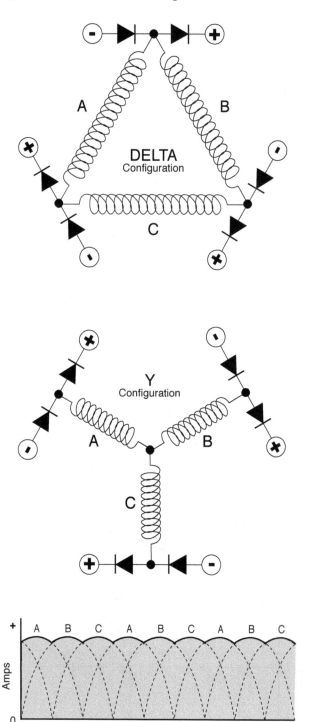

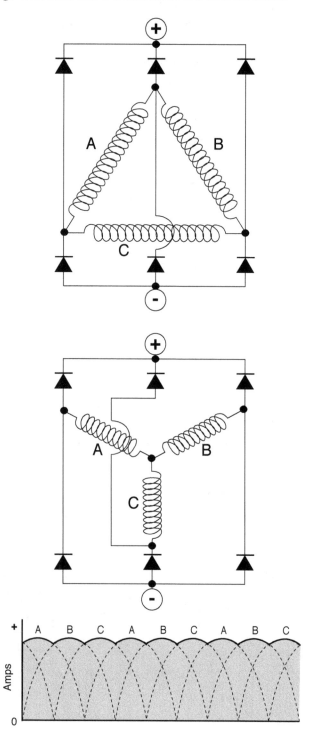

As you will recall, the output of the galley alternator in Figure 4.1 depended on three variables:

1. Strength of the magnet
2. Number of turns of wire
3. Speed of magnet movement

The alternators in Figure 4.12 are similar. We can vary their outputs only by changing engine rpm, which is inconvenient.

The problem of control in a real alternator is solved by varying the strength of the magnet. Instead of the permanent magnet in Figure 4.1, we use an electromagnet as in Figure 4.13. The iron core concentrates the magnetic field, which is generated by a current through the coil. The strength of the field generated is proportional to the current flowing in the field coil. Thus, alternator output can be controlled by varying current through the field coil.

Figure 4.13 also demonstrates a phenomenon you can verify with your galley magnet and two or more nails: A magnet will induce magnetism of opposite polarity in a second piece of iron in close proximity. For example, in Figure 4.13, two additional iron bars placed at the ends of the core also become magnets. This can be verified with either iron filings or a small compass.

Figure 4.14 shows the added iron bars replaced by iron disks with fingers that have been bent around and interleaved. In this way, current through a single field coil wrapped around the shaft results in alternating magnetic fingers around the circumference. It also shows how current can be fed to the field coil through carbon brushes riding on copper slip rings fixed to the shaft.

Figure 4.15 shows a typical alternator rotor with its interleaving magnetic poles, slip rings, and field coil wrapped around the inside shaft. This rotor assembly rotates inside the collection of stationary coils, known as the stator.

The device that controls field-coil current, and thus alternator output, is known as the voltage regulator. How it came to be known as a voltage—rather than a current—regulator, is lost in history. We will not change its name. Just remember that it controls output current, not voltage.

Fig. 4.13 Electromagnets

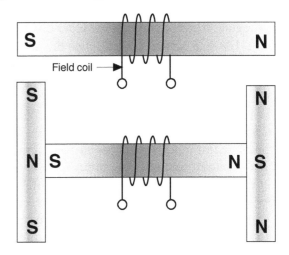

Fig. 4.14 Alternator Rotor and Brushes

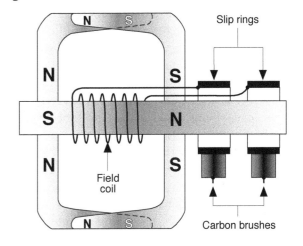

Fig. 4.15 Typical Alternator Rotor

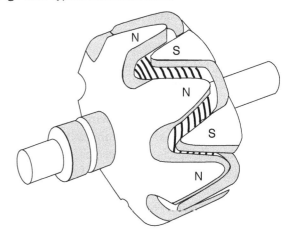

Controlling the Alternator

Voltage Regulators

We'll start with the old-fashioned electromechanical voltage regulator still found in some older boats (Figure 4.16). The field current flows through the relay arm that pivots about F and contacts the points labeled "Ignition" and "Ground." "Ignition" is connected to the battery + terminal through the engine ignition switch.

The relay arm is held up against the ignition contact by the adjusting spring. With full field current flowing, the alternator quickly produces its maximum current. If the battery voltage is low enough, the alternator continues to pump out maximum current. When battery voltage rises to a set value (between 13.8 and 14.2 volts), the increased current flowing from ignition to ground through the relay coil pulls the arm down and opens the contact. Field current drops to zero, alternator output drops to zero, battery voltage drops, and the relay arm is pulled up to the ignition contact to start the cycle again.

The greater the voltage of the battery, the greater the percentage of time the contact remains pulled down into the open position. Alternator output switches between full and zero output hundreds of times per second. The average voltage approaches a constant, while average charging current falls toward zero (plus whatever load is being drawn at the same time). Battery voltage is adjusted by turning the adjusting spring.

It is easy to check a voltage regulator. With the engine running, and after output current has dropped to a trickle, turn on a heavy load. If the regulator is working, voltage will remain the same, but alternator current will increase by the amount of the added load.

Electromechanical regulators have been replaced by solid-state regulators. Although they can be destroyed by reversing battery and ground leads and by excessive heat, they never wear out. Figure 4.17 shows a solid-state equivalent of the electromechanical regulator.

The operation of a solid-state regulator is easily understood once you understand how a transistor works. Figure 4.18 shows the most common type of transistor—the NPN. It has three leads: base (B), emitter (E), and collector (C). It can be thought of as an amplifying valve. The current flowing into the base controls the current flowing from the collector to the emitter. Because the junction between base and emitter is essentially a diode in the direction of the arrow, no current flows until the base-to-emitter voltage reaches about 0.5 volt. Above that voltage, the output current is 20 to 100 times the base current. Thus the transistor can be used as an electronic switch or current amplifier.

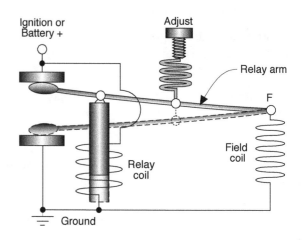

Fig. 4.16 Older Electromechanical Voltage Regulator

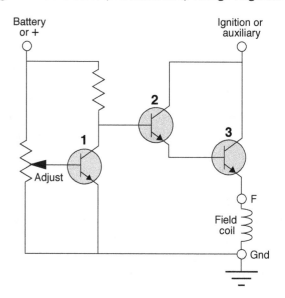

Fig. 4.17 Solid-State (Transistorized) Voltage Regulator

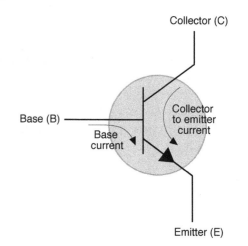

Fig. 4.18 How an NPN Transistor Works

In Figure 4.17 assume the battery voltage is low. The base of transistor 1 is therefore at a low voltage and transistor 1 is off. With transistor 1 acting as a high resistance between the base of transistor 2 and ground, the voltage of transistor 2 base is high and transistor 2 is on. Transistor 3 amplifies the collector-to-emitter current of transistor 2 by twenty times or more, causing a large current through the field coil and maximum alternator output.

Soon battery voltage increases, however, and transistor 1 switches on. The resistance from the base of transistor 2 to ground decreases, and transistors 2 and 3 switch off, cutting off the current to the field coil. With no field current, alternator output ceases.

The transistors switch on and off hundreds of times per second, with the ratio of on-to-off times controlling the average field current and alternator-output current. The analogy between electromechanical and solid-state voltage regulators is obvious.

Note that the solid-state regulator of Figure 4.17 had two positive terminals:

1. Battery, or +, is for sensing the voltage of the battery so that it can be charged at the correct voltage.
2. Ignition, or auxiliary, supplies the field current.

Not to be confused with NPN and PNP transistors, alternators and regulators can be connected in two different ways called type-P and type-N (Figure 4.19).

In type-P alternators and regulators, the regulator is connected to the positive end of the field coil. In type-N alternators, the voltage regulator is located between the negative end of the field coil and ground.

Both type-P and type-N voltage regulators draw power from the battery + terminal. If the power is not interrupted when the engine stops, the voltage regulator/alternator coil will slowly drain the battery.

Figure 4.20 shows three small diodes (the diode trio) connected to the three coil terminals in a type-N alternator. These diodes feed a terminal labeled "Aux." When the alternator is not turning, there is no current to power the regulator, so there is no drain on the battery. Reverse current flow from the battery to the auxiliary terminal is prevented by the charge diodes.

Fig. 4.20 Diode Trio

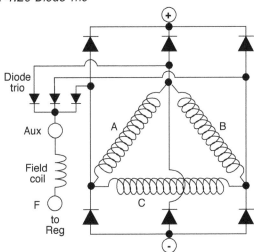

Figure 4.21 shows a second method of supplying regulator current. A large isolation diode is placed between the three charge diodes and the alternator + output terminal. This isolation diode prevents reverse current flow from the battery to the regulator.

Fig. 4.19 Type-P and Type-N Regulators

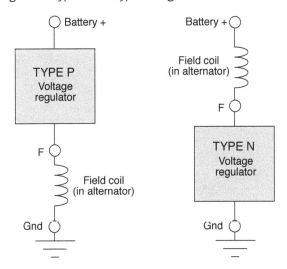

Fig. 4.21 Isolation Diode

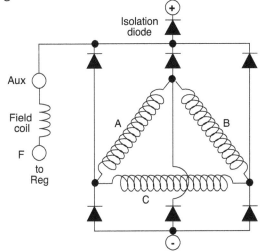

Powering the Voltage Regulator

Battery Isolation Diodes

Do not confuse the diode trio or the alternator isolation diode with *battery isolation diodes*. The first two are internal parts of the alternator and will not be seen unless the case is opened. If a boat has battery isolation diodes (Figure 4.22) they will appear as large diodes mounted on a finned heat sink. Their purpose, if present, is to prevent paralleled batteries from discharging each other. Not all marine systems have battery isolation diodes.

Exciting the Alternator

Did you spot a problem with the circuits of Figures 4.20 and 4.21? If we actually wired an alternator and regulator as shown in either of the figures, the alternator would never come on. An alternator will not generate an output current without an input field current, but there will be no field current until there is an alternator output! To solve this chicken-or-egg dilemma, alternators that derive their field currents from internal-diode trios or isolation diodes require a temporary source of field current called the excite current.

Figure 4.23 shows a typical excite circuit added to the alternator of Figure 4.21. Its operation will be familiar to anyone who owns an automobile.

When the ignition switch is turned on, current flows from the battery, through the lamp and paralleled resistor, to the alternator auxiliary terminal, and then through the field coil. As soon as the engine starts, however, the alternator begins generating current, which then makes the voltage at the auxiliary terminal 0.5 to 1.0 volt higher than the battery voltage. With only 0.5 to 1.0 volt across its terminals, the 12-volt charge-indicator lamp goes out. If it stays on or comes on again, you know that the alternator in not producing current. A resistor is placed in parallel with the lamp in order to provide excite current in case the lamp filament burns out.

An alternate and common solution is to feed the charge indicator lamp from the engine oil-pressure switch rather than the ignition switch, so that the alternator is excited as soon as oil pressure climbs. An advantage of this system is keeping the load on the engine low until it is up to speed.

Fig. 4.22 Battery Isolation Diodes

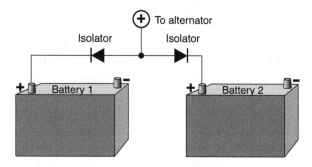

Fig. 4.23 A Common Alternator Excite Circuit

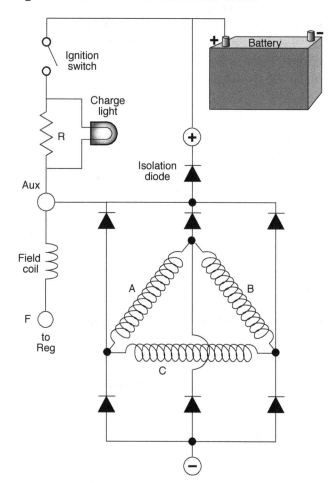

Alternators with fixed-voltage regulation are not ideal for boats. Without modification, they are simply current-limited, fixed-voltage chargers set at compromise voltages between 13.8 and 14.2 volts. As we saw in Chapter 3, 13.8 to 14.2 volts is higher than the recommended float voltage and lower than the recommended fast-charge absorption voltage. An alternator controlled by a standard regulator will never fully charge a battery in typical operation, yet will overcharge if run for days on end.

Cruising boats, particularly sailboats, impose large loads on their batteries but run their engines only a few hours per day. Worse, when a boat is at anchor the engine is usually run for the sole purpose of charging the batteries. We need a way to control the alternator output for optimally fast charging (Figure 4.24).

Figure 4.25 shows regulator bypasses installed across both type-P and type-N voltage regulators. Note that the original voltage regulators remain in place. The bypass regulators simply control field current in order to control alternator output. After the regulator bypass has accomplished its task and is switched off, the original voltage regulator resumes control.

Some regulator bypasses are manual, requiring diligent monitoring of battery-charge current and voltage. The simplest automatic bypasses come on when the engine is started, provide a constant-current bulk charge, then switch off when the battery reaches a preset voltage. More sophisticated regulator bypasses (see next page) automatically cycle through bulk, absorption, and float stages every time the engine is started. An equalization charge can also be selected when desired.

Before discussing the most sophisticated regulators (charge controllers), Figure 4.26 shows a simple manual-control regulator bypass you can build yourself. Note that the bypass circuit is the same whether used with a type-P or type-N alternator. The on/off switch allows the bypass to be switched into or out of the circuit. The 2-ohm, 25-watt fixed resistor limits the maximum field current. The 20-ohm, 100-watt rheostat (variable power resistor) allows the field current to be varied over a wide range.

Warning! Manual regulator bypasses should never be used without diligent monitoring of both battery charging current and voltage. It is easy to destroy a $300 battery with a $30 homemade regulator bypass. If you do not have the discipline to continuously monitor the charging process, you should either forgo the fast-charge option or invest in one of the sophisticated automatic models.

Fig. 4.24 Example of Optimally Fast Charging

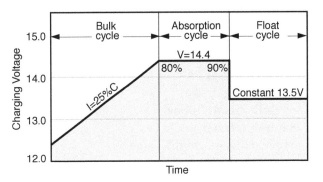

Fig. 4.25 Regulator Bypass Hookups

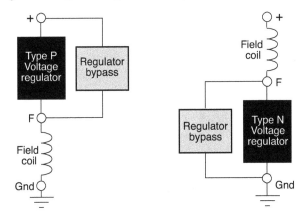

Fig. 4.26 A Manual Regulator Bypass

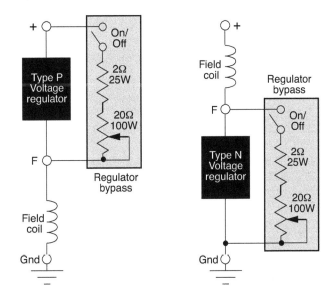

Link 2000-R Charge Controller

The Xantrex Link 2000-R Charge Controller (Figure 4.27) is a dedicated computer that monitors and controls both an inverter/charger (any of the Xantrex Freedom series) and an alternator. Parameters monitored include:

- battery voltage
- amps being drawn
- amp-hours withdrawn
- amp-hours remaining
- time remaining to discharge
- number of battery charges

When either inverter or engine is turned on, the 2000-R initiates the four-cycle optimum charge routine: charge, acceptance, float, and equalize (Figure 4.28).

Fig. 4.27 Link 2000-R Charge Controller Panel

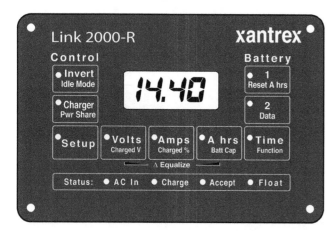

Either one or two battery banks may be monitored and controlled. Voltages for the four charge cycles are tailored both to the type of battery and to the real-time temperature of the battery (Table 4.1). Thus, the charg-

ing routine is truly ideal for any given battery type and conditions.

Fig. 4.28 Four-Cycle Charging for a Wet-Cell Battery at 70°F

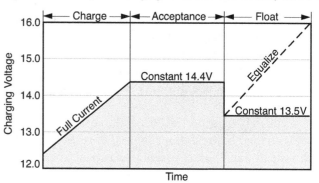

Charging Operation

The status of the four-step charging process is indicated by the horizontal row of LEDs at the bottom of the control panel (Figure 4.27 again).

Charge cycle (red LED ON). After a 2-second engine-start delay, the field current is ramped up over 20 seconds until the alternator reaches its full output. Charging at full current continues until either battery bank reaches the acceptance voltage.

Acceptance cycle (orange LED ON). Charging continues at the fixed acceptance voltage until charging current drops to 2% of the battery nominal capacity. At this point the regulator goes into an acceptance-hold status during which the acceptance voltage is maintained and the charging current is monitored. If voltage and current remain steady for 10 minutes, or if voltage holds steady but current rises during 20 minutes, the regulator goes into the float stage. If, however, battery voltage drops to below the acceptance voltage for 2 minutes, the entire charge cycle is restarted.

Float cycle (green LED ON). Battery voltage is maintained at the float voltage. The alternator supplies current up to its full output in order to supply current draw and maintain the float voltage. If battery voltage drops to below the float voltage for 2 minutes, the charge cycle is restarted.

Equalize cycle (red LED FLASHING). This is initiated manually by pressing a combination of buttons. Charge current is held at a constant 4% of capacity while voltage increases to 16.0 volts (or the acceptance voltage for gelled batteries). Equalization terminates in 3.5 hours or when charging current drops to 2% of capacity at 16.0 volts.

Table 4.1 Voltage Settings for the Link 2000-R

Temp. °F	Type 0 Wet-Cell Accept	Float	Type 1 Gel-Cell 1 Accept	Float	Type 2 Gel-Cell 2 Accept	Float	Type 3 AGM Accept	Float
120	12.5	12.5	13.0	13.0	13.0	13.0	12.9	12.9
110	13.6	12.7	13.5	13.0	14.0	13.4	13.9	12.9
100	13.8	12.9	13.7	13.2	14.1	13.5	14.0	13.0
90	14.0	13.1	13.8	13.3	14.2	13.6	14.1	13.1
80	14.2	13.3	14.0	13.5	14.3	13.7	14.2	13.2
70	14.4	13.5	14.1	13.6	14.4	13.8	14.3	13.3
60	14.6	13.7	14.3	13.8	14.5	13.9	14.4	13.4
50	14.8	13.9	14.4	13.9	14.6	14.0	14.5	13.5
40	15.0	14.1	14.6	14.1	14.7	14.1	14.6	13.6
30	15.2	14.3	14.7	14.2	14.8	14.2	14.7	13.7

Charging Setups

No battery/alternator setup is ideal for every vessel. Cost is a big issue for most boaters, but pattern of use and degree of vulnerability when dead in the water are also considerations. Here are a variety of setups, from among dozens, demonstrating the possibilities and the issues involved. Note that bilge pumps (and any other device that must never be shut off) are wired and fused directly to a battery.

Figure 4.29 shows the most common configuration in small recreational boats. All electrical loads except the bilge pump are disconnected from the battery with the simple ON/OFF switch.

Regardless of setup, an important consideration is that the alternator-to-battery + connection must never be broken while the alternator is generating current. Otherwise the energy stored in the alternator's inductive coils would produce a large voltage spike, possibly destroying both the alternator rectifier diodes and any connected electronics. Three solutions are a voltage snubber from alternator output to ground, a warning sign on the switch, and, in the case of a four-pole switch, a built-in field disconnect.

Figure 4.30 shows a common configuration in small cruising boats. Here two batteries are charged from the same alternator. Depending on the position of the four-pole switch, the charge can be directed to either battery or both batteries at the same time. Similarly, the discharge can be from either or both.

The batteries may be of unequal size—a small start battery and a large house battery—but they must be of the same type. If one were a gel and the other a wet-acid, for example, either the gel would be overcharged and destroyed, or the wet-acid would be undercharged with the same long-term result.

Figure 4.31 shows a setup where the alternator is permanently connected to the house battery, so there is no danger of damage from interrupting the alternator output. As shown the starting battery can be charged in parallel with the house battery with the switch in the "Both" position.

If, instead, the alternator were wired directly to the "Common" terminal of the switch, the setup would be the same as in Figure 4.30, with the attendant danger of interrupting the alternator output.

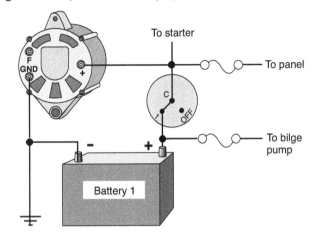
Fig. 4.29 Simplest One-Battery System

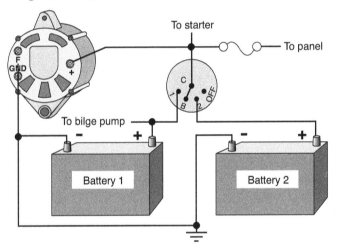
Fig. 4.30 Simplest Two-Battery System

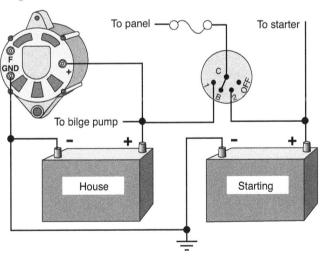
Fig. 4.31 Two Batteries with Alternator Protected

Charging Setups

Figure 4.32 shows a pair of isolation diodes. The diodes make it possible to leave both batteries connected directly to the alternator output without the danger of one battery draining the other. Because the diodes look like closed circuits in the forward direction, they also solve the open-alternator problem.

The big problem with isolation diodes is that they drop the voltage from alternator to battery by 0.6 to 1.0 volt, requiring the voltage regulator to be adjusted upward by the same amount to compensate.

Most boaters are not aware of the voltage drop, so their batteries are chronically, severely undercharged and suffer early demise.

Figure 4.33 shows a setup incorporating a series regulator. When house and starting batteries are of different size or type, one of the batteries will end up overcharged while the other is undercharged, shortening the lives of both.

A series regulator, such as Ample Power's Eliminator, is designed to solve this problem. The alternator's regulator is set up for the optimum charging of the house battery. At the same time the series regulator, set up for the characteristics of the starting battery, siphons some of the charging current to charge it.

The parallel switch can be used either to bypass the series regulator or to combine the battery outputs.

Figure 4.34 shows one way to charge two batteries from two alternators. This is useful both when the batteries are of different size and/or different type and when the batteries are larger than can be charged quickly from a single alternator. It also provides redundancy in case one of the alternators fails.

Commonly the starting battery is charged by the engine's original alternator, and a high-output alternator with multistep regulator is added to charge the much larger house bank.

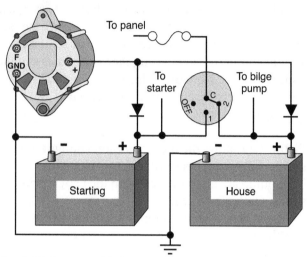

Fig. 4.32 Batteries Isolated with Diodes

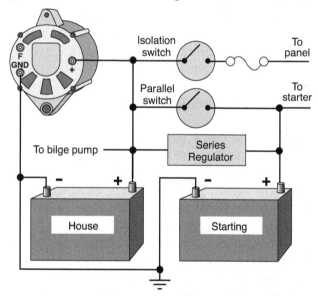

Fig. 4.33 System with Series Regulator

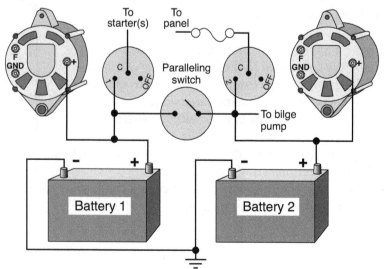

Fig. 4.34 Two Batteries and Two Alternators

When changing alternators there are four critical physical considerations: (1) mounting configuration, (2) pulley alignment, (3) belt size, and (4) belt tension.

Figure 4.35 illustrates four Balmar mounting configurations designed to be compatible with most marine engines. Most often a combination of washers, spacers, and bushings can compensate for an imperfect fit.

Figure 4.36 shows how to bring the alternator pulley into alignment with the engine drive pulley. Hold a straightedge against the faces of the two pulleys, and shim the alternator foot (or feet) with washers until the faces are in the same plane.

Alternators of up to 80 amps output can use ⅜-inch belts (width of outside belt face), up to 110 amps ½-inch belts, and over 110 amps dual belts.

Proper belt tension can be determined in two ways:

1. Turn the alternator pulley retaining nut with a wrench. If the belt slips it is too loose.
2. Press on the belt with moderate force (Figure 4.37). Deflection should be between ¼ inch and ⁵⁄₁₆ inch.

Fig. 4.36 Aligning Engine and Alternator Pulleys

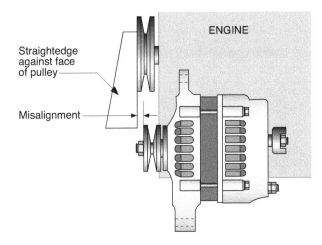

Fig. 4.37 Testing Belt Tension

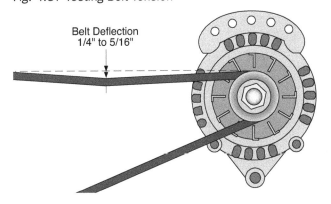

Fig. 4.35 Mounting Configurations (Balmar)

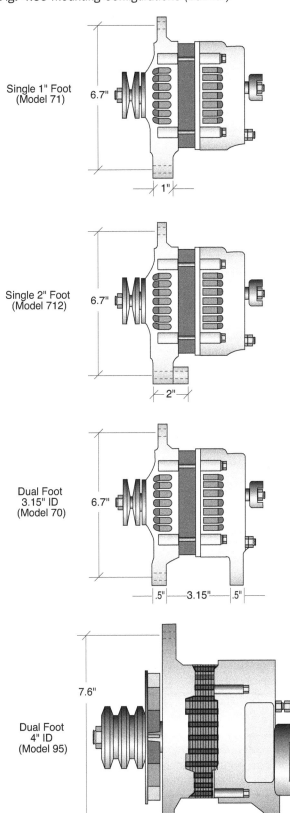

Troubleshooting

When an engine fails to turn over or batteries go flat, the fault may be in the batteries, the alternator, an external voltage regular, or the wiring. Troubleshooting the charging/starting system is made easier if you understand how each of the components work, so read Chapters 3 and 4 before using the charts and procedures that follow.

Troubleshooting 1: Engine Won't Turn Over

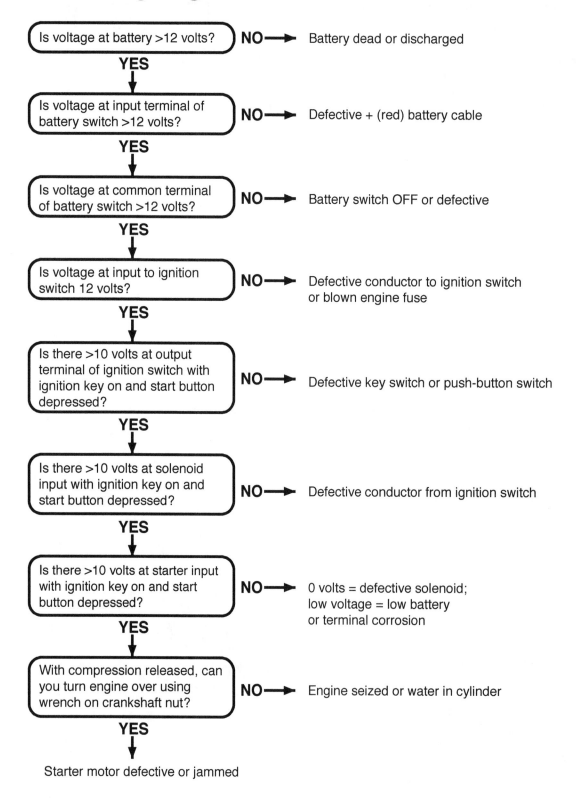

Is voltage at battery >12 volts? **NO →** Battery dead or discharged

YES

Is voltage at input terminal of battery switch >12 volts? **NO →** Defective + (red) battery cable

YES

Is voltage at common terminal of battery switch >12 volts? **NO →** Battery switch OFF or defective

YES

Is voltage at input to ignition switch 12 volts? **NO →** Defective conductor to ignition switch or blown engine fuse

YES

Is there >10 volts at output terminal of ignition switch with ignition key on and start button depressed? **NO →** Defective key switch or push-button switch

YES

Is there >10 volts at solenoid input with ignition key on and start button depressed? **NO →** Defective conductor from ignition switch

YES

Is there >10 volts at starter input with ignition key on and start button depressed? **NO →** 0 volts = defective solenoid; low voltage = low battery or terminal corrosion

YES

With compression released, can you turn engine over using wrench on crankshaft nut? **NO →** Engine seized or water in cylinder

YES

Starter motor defective or jammed

Troubleshooting 2: Batteries Not Charging Fully

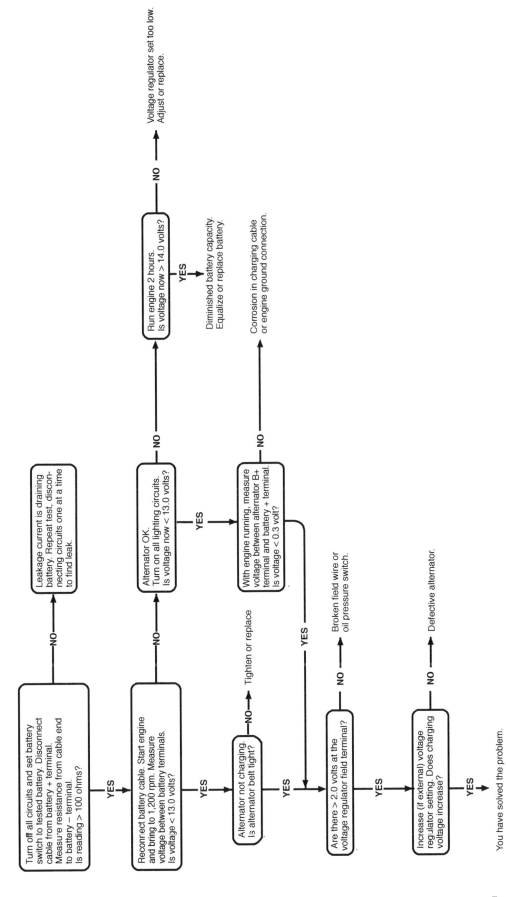

Troubleshooting 3: The Alternator

Variations in appearance, arrangement of terminals, and internal connections number in the hundreds. It is beyond the scope of this book to detail the differences, but an alternator is an alternator, and, whatever its name, it works on the principles above.

There are two basic approaches to alternator repair. The first is to carry replacements for the components most likely to fail in the field: charge diodes, diode trio, isolation diode, brushes, bearings, and voltage regulator. The second is to carry an exact replacement for the entire alternator, including the voltage regulator if external. I favor the second approach for the following reasons:

1. There will be no spare part you might have overlooked. For example, what if the problem were a broken mounting flange?
2. You don't have to carry special tools such as a bearing puller, press, or heavy-duty soldering iron.
3. Replacement takes minutes; repair takes hours.
4. The cost of the whole alternator (with trade-in) is probably no greater than the cost of a complete set of spare components.

The following troubleshooting guide should help you to discover whether the problem is with the wiring, the alternator, or the regulator.

Check the Wiring from Alternator to a Battery with Battery Isolation Diodes

STEP 1.

Turn the engine off and the battery-select switch off. The multimeter should read:
- Battery + to Ground, 12 V or more
- Alternator + to Ground, 0 V

If Alternator + to Ground reads 12 V, suspect a shorted isolation diode.

STEP 2.

Turn the engine on with the battery-select switch on. The multimeter should read:
- Alternator + to Battery +, 0.5 to 1.0 V
- Battery + to Ground, about 1 V higher than with the engine off

If not, suspect the isolation diode feeding the battery.

STEP 3.

To check a battery isolation diode definitively, disconnect it from the batteries and read resistance across the diode, reversing leads.
- An open-circuit diode reads ∞ Ω both directions
- A shorted diode reads near 0 Ω both directions
- A healthy diode reads near ∞ Ω in one direction and 0 Ω in the other direction

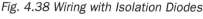

Fig. 4.38 Wiring with Isolation Diodes

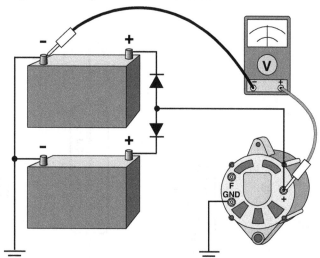

Check Wiring from an Alternator to a Battery with No Battery Isolation Diodes

STEP 1.

Turn the engine off and the battery-select switch on. The multimeter should read:
- Alternator + to Battery +, 0 V
- Alternator – to Battery –, 0 V

On the resistance scale the multimeter should read:
- Alternator + to Battery +, 0 Ω
- Alternator – to Battery –, 0 Ω

If not, suspect corrosion or a broken wire.

STEP 2.

Turn the engine on and the battery-select switch on. The multimeter should read:
- Alternator + to Battery +, < 0.5 V
- Alternator – to Battery –, < 0.5 V

If not, suspect corrosion or a broken wire.

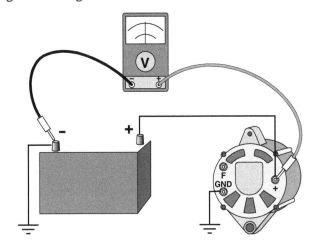

Fig. 4.39 Wiring with No Isolation Diodes

Check Alternator and Battery Voltage with No Battery Isolation Diodes

STEP 1.

Turn the engine off and turn the battery-select switch to the battery being tested (repeat tests for other batteries). On the voltage scale the multimeter should read:
- Battery + to Ground, 12 to 13 V. If not, the battery may be bad.
- Alternator + to Ground, 12 to 13 V. If not, Alternator + to Battery + cable is bad.

STEP 2.

Turn the engine on and turn the battery-select switch to the battery being tested (repeat tests for other batteries). On the voltage scale the multimeter should read:
- Battery + to Ground, about 1 V higher than with the engine off.
- Alternator + to Ground, at least 1 V higher than with the engine off. If not, the alternator is not charging.

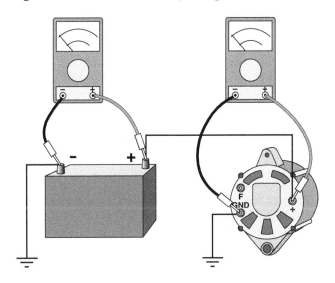

Fig. 4.40 Alternator and Battery Voltage

Check Alternator and Battery Voltage with Battery Isolation Diodes

STEP 1.

Turn the engine off and turn the battery-select switch to the battery being tested (repeat tests for other batteries). On the voltage scale the multimeter should read:

- Battery + to Ground, 12 to 13 V. If not, the battery may be bad.
- Alternator + to Ground, 0 V. If not, suspect a shorted isolation diode.

STEP 2.

Turn the engine on and turn the battery-select switch to the battery being tested (repeat tests for other batteries). On the voltage scale the multimeter should read:

- Battery + to Ground should be about 1 V higher than with the engine off. If not, the alternator is not charging.
- Alternator + to Ground should be 0.5 to 1.0 V higher than Battery + to Ground. If not, suspect a shorted isolation diode.

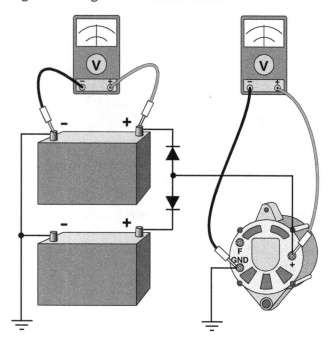

Fig. 4.41 Voltages with Isolation Diodes

Check a Type-N Alternator with No Output

STEP 1.

Turn the engine off, measure the voltage from Battery + to Ground, and note its value.

STEP 2.

Remove the wire from Alternator Terminal F.

STEP 3.

Connect a test light (minimum 12 W, such as an anchor light) from Terminal F to Ground.

STEP 4.

Start the engine and measure the voltage from Battery + to Ground again. If the voltage is about 1 V higher than it was when the engine was off, then the alternator is OK, but its regulator is bad.

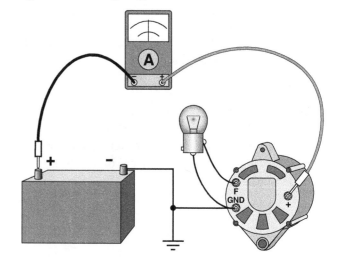

Fig. 4.42 Checking a Type-N Alternator

Check a Type-P Alternator with No Output

STEP 1.

Turn the engine off, measure the voltage from Battery + to Ground, and note its value.

STEP 2.

Remove the wire from Alternator Terminal F.

STEP 3.

Connect a test light (minimum 12 W, such as an anchor light) from Terminal F to Battery +.

STEP 4.

Start the engine and measure the voltage from Battery + to Ground again. If the voltage is about 1 V higher than with the engine off, then the alternator is OK, but its regulator is bad (see next test).

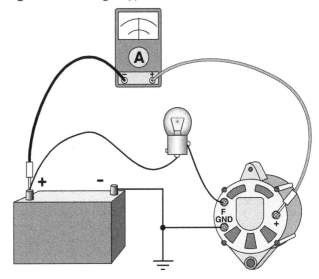

Fig. 4.43 Checking a Type-P Alternator

Check the Excite Circuit for a Type-P Alternator Regulator

If the type-P regulator tested bad above, the problem may lie not in the regulator but in its excite circuit. To test the excite circuit:

STEP 1.

Start the engine.

STEP 2.

Measure the voltage from Battery + to Ground.

STEP 3.

Momentarily connect the test light between Battery + and Alternator Terminal F. If the voltage from Battery + to Ground is now about 1 V higher than with the engine off, the alternator and regulator are OK, but the excite circuit is bad.

You can either repair the excite circuit, or you can create an excite circuit temporarily by placing a 12 W lamp between the engine oil-pressure switch and Alternator Terminal F.

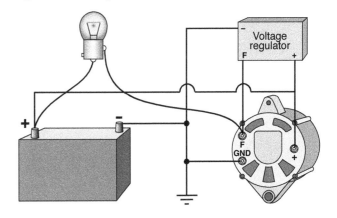

Fig. 4.44 Flashing a Type-P Alternator

CHAPTER 5

Bonding

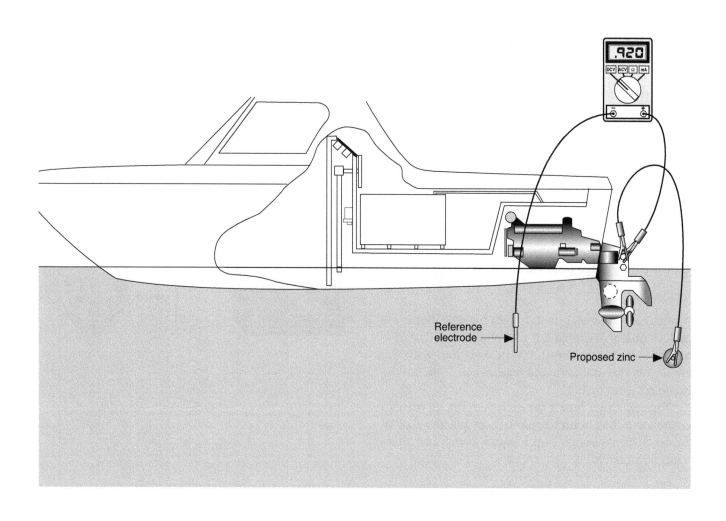

Reference
electrode

Proposed zinc

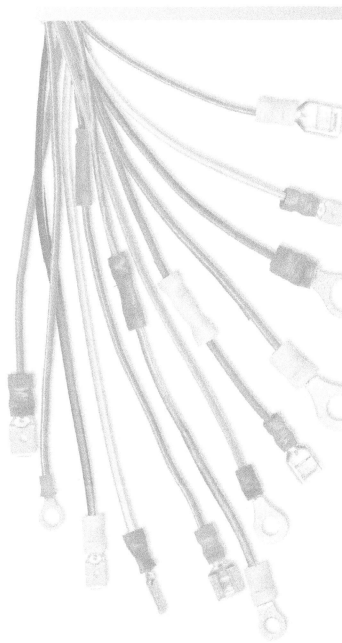

Bonding is a somewhat controversial, and often poorly understood, wiring practice. As usual, we start by answering a basic question—what is bonding?

The purposes of bonding are threefold: (1) electrical system grounding, (2) lightning protection, and (3) corrosion protection.

The bonding controversy stems from the possibility of its encouraging stray-current corrosion. So—to bond, or not to bond—that is the question we address in detail.

Fortunately, there are simple methods for testing your protection against corrosion. These, and the ABYC standards for the general application of cathodic protection, should protect your boat's underwater metals.

Though neither caused nor prevented by bonding, other types of corrosion are explained as well.

What Is Bonding?

No marine wiring topic causes more confusion than bonding. That is because there are at least three separate and compelling reasons for electrically connecting, or bonding, metal objects aboard a boat:

1. Electrical system grounding
2. Lightning protection
3. Corrosion protection

At the same time, there are reasons for *not* bonding certain items. As they occur, these exceptions will be discussed. Note that the grounding of AC systems is covered separately in Chapter 9, AC Standards and Practices. You will find there, however, that AC grounding is related to DC grounding in a simple way.

Grounded, Grounding, Bonding

Ideally, *ground* is the voltage of the water in which the boat is immersed. Unfortunately, voltage in the water may vary slightly due to stray electrical currents. As we will see, one of the purposes of the bonding system is to force the voltage of and within the hull to be as uniform as possible through the use of low-resistance conductors and connections.

As defined by the ABYC and shown in Figure 5.1:

• *Grounded conductors* are the current-carrying conductors that connect to the side of the source (almost universally the battery negative terminal), which is intentionally maintained at ground potential.

• *Grounding conductors* are normally non-current-carrying conductors, provided to connect the exposed metal enclosures of electric equipment to ground, the primary function of which is to minimize shock hazard to personnel.

• *Bonding conductors* are normally non-current-carrying conductors used to connect the non-current-carrying metal parts of a boat and the non-current-carrying parts of direct-current devices on the boat to the boat's bonding system.

All DC electrical devices receive their power through a pair of positive and negative input terminals, served by a pair of conductors. Current flows into the positive terminal from a positive conductor (wire) from the DC distribution panel and, ultimately, from the positive (+12 V) terminal of the battery. Ideally, the same amount of current returns to the battery negative terminal through the grounded conductor. All

grounded conductors are held to the same voltage (ground, or zero volts) by being connected to the DC negative bus and, ultimately, to the battery negative terminal.

So that people are not accidently exposed to live voltage from a piece of equipment shorted to a live wire, the metal enclosures of all electrical equipment are connected to ground by grounding conductors. These conductors are in addition to the grounded conductors and carry current only in the case of an electrical fault.

Bonding conductors are also separate from, and in addition to, the grounded conductors. As elaborated later in this chapter, they play important roles in both lightning and corrosion protection. They should take as short and direct routes as possible to the substantial common-bonding conductor, which usually runs near the fore-and-aft centerline of the boat. Each bonding conductor should be at least as large as the current-carrying positive and negative conductors that serve the equipment.

The engine-bonding conductor should be at least as large as the largest bonding conductor in the rest of the bonding system and large enough to carry starting current. Twin engines with crossover starting systems should be bonded to each other, as well, with a conductor large enough to carry the starting current.

The large common-bonding conductor should be bare or green. If wire, it may consist of bare, stranded, tinned copper or insulated stranded wire of minimum size 8 AWG. If solid, it may be uninsulated copper, bronze strip, or copper pipe at least 0.030 inch thick and 0.5 inch wide. The copper, bronze strip, or pipe may be drilled and tapped, provided it is thick enough to provide at least three full threads for terminal screws, or it may be unthreaded for machine screws and locknuts.

Equipment to be bonded includes: engines and transmissions, propellers and shafts, metal cases of motors, generators and pumps, metal cabinets and control boxes, electronics cabinets, metal fuel and water tanks, fuel-fill fittings, electrical fuel pumps and valves, metal battery boxes, metal conduit or armoring, and large nonelectrical metal objects as recommended in the Lightning Protection section.

Note that you may choose not to bond electrically isolated through-hull fittings, as will be discussed further in the Corrosion Protection section.

Fig. 5.1 Typical DC Negative System and DC Grounding System (Adapted from ABYC Standard E-11, Figure 18)

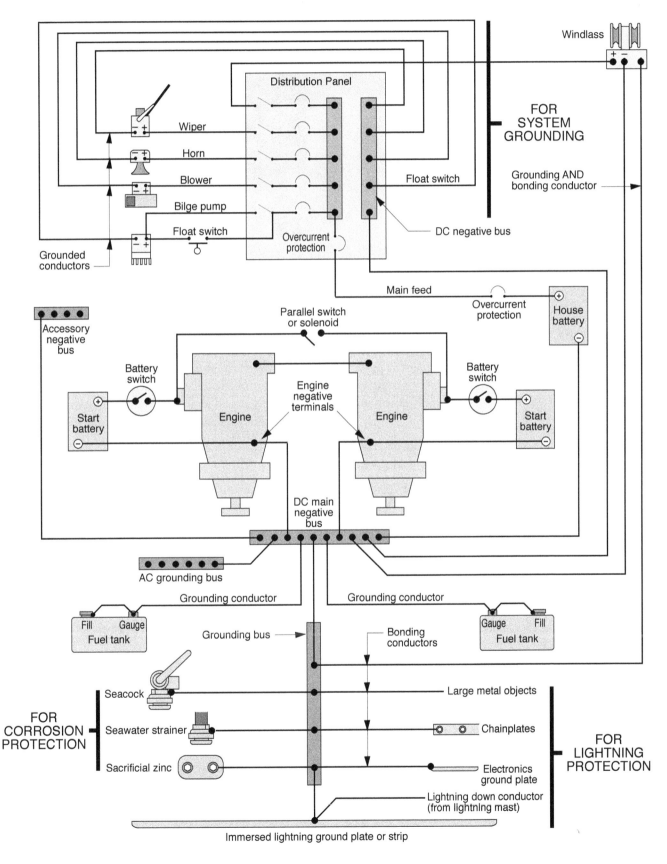

Lightning Protection

At any moment, there are approximately 2,000 lightning storms in progress around the earth, producing 100 strikes every second. In some regions lightning is a rarity. In others it is an almost daily occurrence.

To put the danger in perspective, there are approximately 24,000 lightning deaths per year in the world, 100 in the United States. From 1959 to 2003, recorded deaths in the United States included:

- Florida   425
- Texas   195
- North Carolina   181
- Ohio   136
- New York   134
- Tennessee   133

Where the deaths occurred:

- In or around the home   20%
- In vehicles (mostly open) 19%
- Taking refuge under trees 15%
- In boats   13%
- Everywhere else   33%

Considering the significant percentage of deaths occurring in boats and the low number of people in boats at any given time, it is apparent that the potential for lightning strikes on boats is a serious matter. In fact, the ABYC devotes all of Standard E-4 to the matter of lightning protection.

What Is Lightning and How Does It Act?

In all lightning theories, a combination of vertically moving water droplets and air currents results in the buildup of large quantities of oppositely charged particles within clouds and between clouds and the ground (Figure 5.2). The electrical potential differences between charges may be as high as 100,000,000 volts. By comparison, the voltage on the power lines running along a street is a mere 12,000 volts.

In particular, the base of a cloud becomes negatively charged. Since opposite charges attract, the surface of the earth directly beneath the cloud becomes positively charged. People standing in this positively charged area under a cloud sometimes report feeling their hair standing on end due to the static charge just before a lightning strike. What initially prevents the charges from combining is the extreme electrical resistance of air. Some scientists believe that lightning strikes are triggered by cosmic rays knocking electrons from air molecules. The freed electrons accelerate in the voltage field, causing the release of more electrons and ionizing the air.

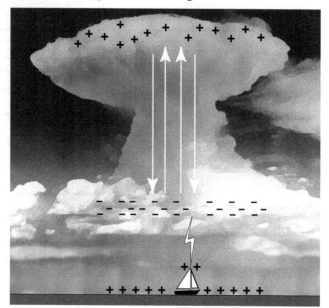

Fig. 5.2 Discharge of Cloud Charge

Ionization proceeds in steps of about 100 feet. Electrons flow downward through the ionized path and cause a faint blue-white glow, similar to the flow of electrons in the ionized gas of a neon sign. Each step requires only about 0.00005 second to ionize and fill, so that the stepped leader traverses a distance of 10,000 feet, from the base of a cloud to ground, in about 0.005 second.

The final step to ground is of most interest to a boater. Up to the last step, the presence of a boat has no influence on either the location or the direction of the discharge. When looking for that final connection to earth, however, the lightning will head for the closest accumulation of positive charge. That generally means the highest point within a radius of 100 feet. If that point is you, chances are you will be struck. If it is the tip of your mast, your mast will be struck.

After the ionization of the column has been completed by the leader, there exists a short circuit from cloud to earth. The resulting rush of accumulated charge from cloud to earth is what we see as the lightning bolt—an ionized column of air, heated to 50,000°F, conducting a typical current of 50,000 amps. The resulting rapid heating of the air produces a supersonic air-pressure wave heard as thunder. The entire 0.005-second process may be repeated several or even dozens of times during the following second, depending on the initial size of the accumulated charge.

Direct strikes are the most dangerous. Consider that the largest circuit breaker or fuse on your boat is probably rated at less than 100 amps, and that the cranking current to your starter motor is probably on the order of 200 amps. Now consider what 50,000 to 200,000 amps might do to that same wiring. Although the peak current lasts only 0.0001 second, the resistive heating is often sufficient to burn insulation, melt components, even vaporize conductors.

Much lightning damage occurs from near-hits, however. It is not uncommon for one boat to suffer a direct strike and for boats in adjacent slips to lose electronic equipment. Just as a current-carrying wire produces a magnetic field, and a varying magnetic field produces current in a conductor (the principle behind the alternator), lightning currents produce extreme magnetic fields, which then induce currents in nearby wires. These induced currents are often sufficient to destroy sensitive electronic circuits.

Just any copper conductor will not suffice to conduct currents of 50,000 amps. The conductor must be large and conductive enough to present the path of least resistance to ground (the surrounding water, in the case of a boat). Small-diameter wire, corroded connections, and too small a ground plate (area of metal in contact with the water) may cause the lightning to seek additional paths to ground, resulting in dangerous side flashes. The recommendations in ABYC Standard E-4 are intended to minimize both danger and damage from lightning.

Zones of Protection

Metal masts tend to draw the final step of a leader to themselves within a radius equal to their height. The conical zone beneath the tip is known as the zone of protection. A person or object entirely within this zone is substantially protected from a direct strike.

Figure 5.3 shows zones of protection for a powerboat with a lightning-protective mast and with the mast extended by a grounded air terminal. Powerboat hulls do not generally fall entirely within their zones of protection unless either their masts are extended by grounded antennas or outriggers, or they have more than one grounded mast.

Figure 5.4 shows the zone of protection for a sailboat mast less than 50 feet. A sailboat hull will usually lie entirely within the zone of protection. To qualify as a lightning-protective mast, the mast must either be metal or be equipped with an air terminal and metal conductor to ground (see Figure 5.6).

Figure 5.5 shows the zone of protection for a boat with a lightning-protective mast more than 50 feet. With more than one mast, zones are drawn for each mast. The combined protective zone includes all areas under one or more of the individual zones. To qualify as lightning protective, each mast must be grounded. Multihulls require grounding plates in each hull.

Fig. 5.3 Lightning-Protective Zone for Motorboat with Lightning-Protective Mast or Mast with Approved Extension

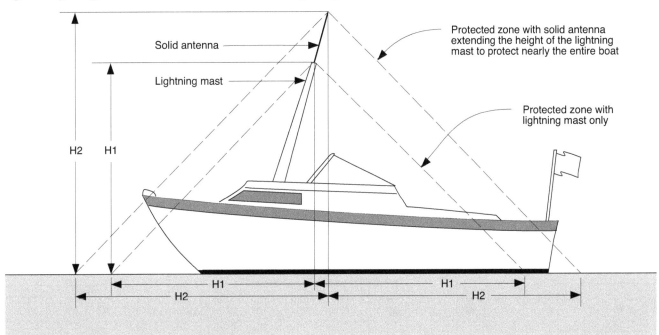

Lightning Protection

Fig. 5.4 Lightning-Protective Zone for Sailboat Mast Less Than 50 Feet

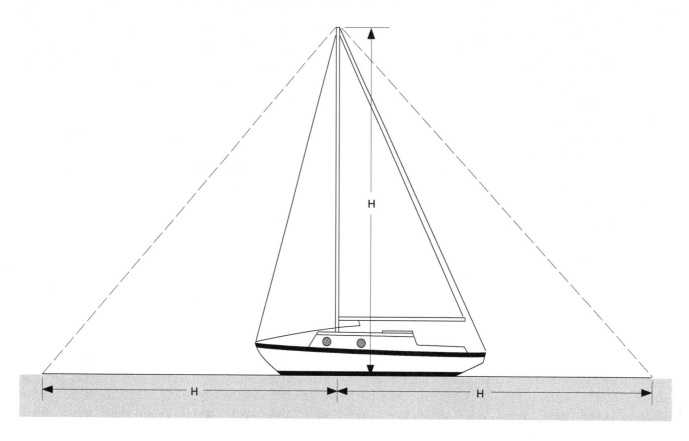

Fig. 5.5 Lightning-Protective Zone for Sailboat Mast Over 50 Feet or More Than One Mast

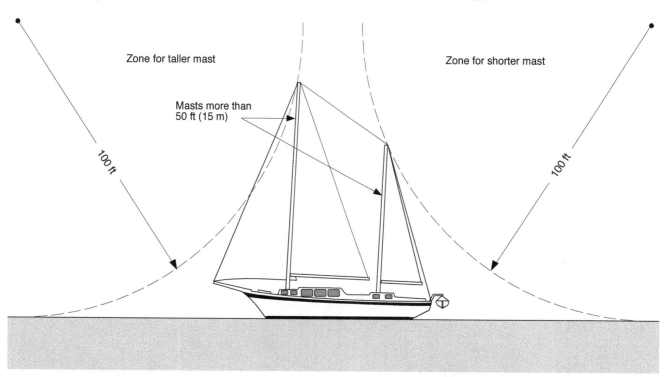

The Safe Path to Ground

Regardless of any lightning rod or charge dissipator, if your mast is the highest object in the vicinity it will be struck. The purpose of the safe path to ground is to provide a path to ground (the water) as *short, straight, and conductive as possible* to prevent side flashes to alternate routes. The path consists of two parts: the *lightning-protective mast* and the *lightning-ground connection*.

Lightning-Protective Mast

Metal masts qualify as protective masts. If nonconductive, however, a mast must be provided with a grounding conductor running from an air terminal 6 inches above the mast in as straight a line as possible to the lightning-ground connection. The conductor must be securely fastened to the mast and consist of either a stranded-copper wire of minimum size 4 AWG or a metal strip of conductivity equal to that of 4 AWG copper wire and thickness of at least 0.030 inch.

Joints, including that to the lightning-ground connection, must not be subject to immersion. In the case of 4 AWG wire, the connection must be strong enough to support a 45-pound weight for 1 minute. To avoid corrosion, all bolts, nuts, washers, and lugs must be galvanically compatible with the conductor.

A stainless steel radio antenna may serve as an air terminal provided it has either a means for direct connection to ground, or a lightning-protective gap (closely spaced electrodes, which lightning will easily jump). If not disconnected when the antenna is grounded, the antenna feed line should also have a lightning arrestor, or transient voltage surge suppressor.

Lightning-Ground Connection

A lightning-ground connection may be any underwater metal surface of at least 1-square-foot area. Metal hulls, centerboards, and external (not encased in fiberglass) keels are excellent. Although metal rudders qualify in area, the connection from mast to rudder is too long.

Where the lightning-ground connection is an immersed ground plate at the base of the mast, the backstay and other large aft metal objects, because of the distance, should be grounded to the engine instead of the ground plate.

It is commonly believed that the large surface areas of the propeller and shaft provide adequate lightning grounding. While true, relying on the conductivity of

Fig. 5.6 The Safe Path to Ground

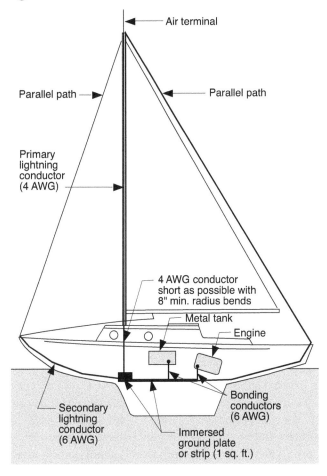

the engine, transmission, and shaft may lead to extremely large currents through main-engine- and transmission-output bearings, to their detriment. If the shaft and propeller are to be bonded, it should be through a brush riding on the shaft.

Sintered bronze plates, intended to serve as ground plates for SSB radios, are questionable as lightning grounds. Due to their porosity, these plates do have wetted areas greater than the areas of their envelopes, but evidence suggests that they are not significantly more effective than plain copper plate of the same area. In fact, it is theorized that edge length is more important than area in lightning ground plates. A 12 foot by 1 inch by ¼ inch copper strip would be six times more effective than a 1 foot by 1 foot square copper plate.

In order, the best lightning-ground connections are:

1. Metal hull
2. External metal keel (attach to keel bolts)
3. External 12 foot by 1 inch by ¼ inch copper strip
4. Large sintered bronze plate

Lightning Protection

Protecting Electronics

A well-protected boat may lose electronics. The problem is that today's solid-state electronics are very intolerant of voltage surges. It doesn't matter whether the surge comes from a direct lightning hit or from current induced in the antenna, microphone, or power leads by the magnetic field pulse of a nearby strike.

Two basic approaches to protecting electronics are: (1) shorting the surges, and (2) disconnecting all the leads.

Shorting the Surges

Figure 5.7 shows an antenna at the top of the mast. For a solid-wire antenna with base-loading coil to be an effective air terminal, there must be a lightning-bypass gap between the solid wire and the base of the antenna. If not, the inductive base coil resists the lightning current, and the lightning-protective mast originates at the base of the antenna. If the antenna is fiberglass with a less than 8 AWG conductor, its conductivity is insufficient, and the lightning protection again originates at the top of the mast.

A coaxial conductor from antenna to radio can pick up current, either as part of a direct strike, or induced by the magnetic field of a nearby strike. This surge is shorted to ground by a transient voltage surge suppressor (TVSS) several feet from the electronics enclosure.

Surges on the power supply line are shorted to ground by a metal oxide varistor (MOV), which typically acts in less than 1 microsecond. Both TVSS and MOV devices are available at ham- and marine-radio dealers.

There remain several problems with the approach:

1. Insertion of the TVSS in the antenna-feed line results in some loss of transmitted power.
2. By shorting the cable to ground, the TVSS makes it more likely that the coaxial line will be damaged by a strike.
3. By shorting the antenna feed to ground, the TVSS leads lightning current closer to the electronics than if the cable were disconnected.

Disconnecting Leads

TVSS and radio manufacturers agree the best way to protect electronics is to remove all leads, including the microphone. Switching a circuit breaker won't work because lightning will easily bridge the small breaker gap.

Fig. 5.7 Protecting Electronics from Lightning Surges

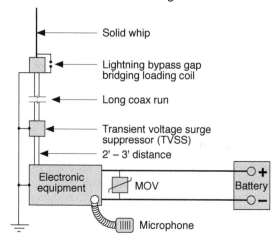

Alternative 1: Short the Surges

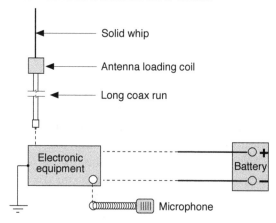

Alternative 2: Disconnect All Leads

If any of your electronics have aluminum cases, place them in a steel box, which will shield them from magnetic fields.

Protecting People

Assuming all of the protective measures above are in place, you can minimize the lightning danger to people aboard your boat by following these rules:

1. Keep everyone inside the boat.
2. Do not allow any part of anyone's body in the water.
3. Keep everyone at least 6 feet from the lightning-protective mast.
4. Don't allow anyone to touch any part of the spars, standing rigging, metal rails, or metal lifelines.
5. Don't allow anyone to touch any two grounded objects with two hands.

Every boatowner knows about corrosion. That is, they know it happens. Everywhere they look they see staining, pitting, powdering, and disintegration. Corrosion is so pervasive on a boat that it's easy to throw up your hands and accept it, like death, as inevitable. But corrosion is not inevitable. Corrosion can be prevented.

As with most problems, a solution comes only with understanding, and understanding requires an investment of mental energy. If you really, truly want to stop the corrosion on your boat, get a cup of coffee or tea, find a comfortable reading spot, and clear your mind.

What Is Corrosion?

In general terms, corrosion is the deterioration of a material by chemical or electrochemical reaction with its surroundings. As boatowners, we are most familiar with galvanic corrosion—the deterioration of the anode of a galvanic couple resulting from the flow of ions from the anode to the cathode through an electrolyte.

Relax! Those are just fancy words to describe a very common phenomenon—the chemical reaction that takes place inside a battery.

Figure 5.8 shows a carbon-zinc flashlight battery (the inexpensive type that comes with electrical toys). If we were to slice the battery in half, we would see a carbon rod in an electrically conductive paste, all inside a zinc-coated can. At A we measure the voltage between the carbon rod and the zinc can as 1.5 volts. At B,

switching the meter to amps and placing a 1.5-volt lamp in series with the meter + lead, we find that current is flowing from + terminal to – terminal as expected. Since electrons are negative, the electrons are actually flowing in the opposite direction, from – to +.

If we were to leave the lamp connected to the battery long enough, the battery voltage and current would eventually drop to zero. Upon examination, we would find that all of the zinc coating had disappeared (it had corroded). On the other hand, if we disconnected the lamp so that there was no electrical closed circuit between the carbon and the zinc, the zinc would not corrode, and the battery would retain its voltage for a very long time.

You have just witnessed galvanic corrosion in a galvanic cell. The common carbon-zinc battery is a convenient example, but it is just one example of a common phenomenon.

Another Galley Experiment

Performing the experiment in Figure 5.9 will do wonders for your understanding of corrosion on your boat.

Gather a plastic container of fresh water, a tablespoon of salt, a multimeter, two test leads with alligator clips, and an assortment of metal items. I used a stainless bolt, a small piece of aluminum pie plate, and a shaft zinc.

Fig. 5.9 Measuring Galvanic Voltage and Current

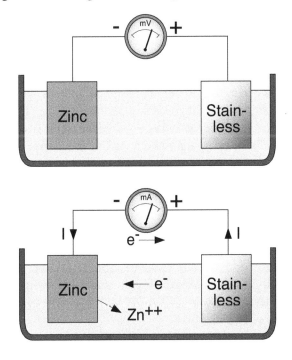

Fig. 5.8 The Battery—a Useful Form of Corrosion

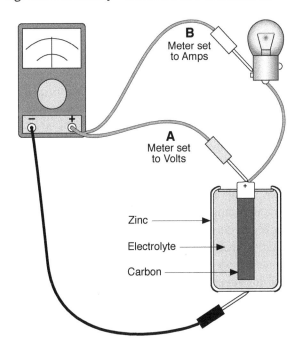

Corrosion Protection

Switch the multimeter to volts. Using the test leads, connect the negative (–) lead to the zinc and the positive (+) lead to the stainless bolt and lower both pieces into the water. Surprised? The meter will indicate a voltage.

Now switch the meter to milliamps. You may or may not read any current, but hold on. Dump the tablespoon of salt into the fresh water and stir. Depending on the sizes of the electrodes, you will now probably measure a current of about a milliamp flowing from the stainless bolt to the zinc.

What's going on? When two dissimilar metals are placed together in an electrolyte (electrically conductive medium), one of the metals will assume a higher potential than the other. In Chapter 1 we learned that current flows only in a closed circuit. Two electrodes, immersed in electrolyte, form an open circuit, and no current flows. But when we connect the two electrodes, either with a wire or by letting them touch, we complete the circuit and current flows.

In this case, the current flowing through the meter is from the stainless steel electrode into the zinc electrode. (Since electrons carry negative charge, the electron flow is actually in the opposite direction, but never mind.)

Figure 5.10 shows what is happening to the zinc on an atomic level. Zinc atoms are changing into positively charged zinc ions by giving up two electrons. These released electrons are flowing from the zinc to the stainless through the meter leads, and the newly formed zinc ions are departing the zinc electrode and migrating into the electrolyte—the zinc is corroding.

Continue the experiment if you wish by substituting other pairs of dissimilar metals. As long as the electrode metals are different in composition, they will always generate a potential difference, and current will always flow into the lower-voltage metal. The voltage difference will be the same, whether the water is salt or fresh. The currents, however, will be much greater in salt water due to its greater conductivity.

The potential difference between any two dissimilar metals can be predicted by consulting a table of galvanic potentials. The table lists the potential differences measured between the metal in question and a reference electrode, typically silver-silver chloride. Table 5.1 reproduces the values listed in Table I of ABYC Standard E-2 for metals and alloys in seawater flowing at 8 to 13 feet per second (4.7 to 7.7 knots), and at temperatures of 50°F to 80°F.

Fig. 5.10 What Happens When Zinc Corrodes

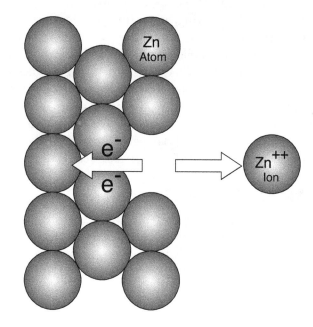

The values in the table are between a metal and a silver-silver chloride electrode. Values between any two metals are found as the differences between the table values for the two metals.

Example: What is the corrosion (galvanic) potential between silicon bronze and zinc? From Table 5.1 we find the corrosion potential of silicon bronze vs. the reference to be –0.26 to –0.29 volt (average –0.28 volt) and zinc vs. the reference to be –0.98 to –1.03 volt (average –1.00 volt). Thus the corrosion potential between silicon bronze and zinc is –0.72 volt.

By now you may be thoroughly alarmed at the thought of all the underwater metallic components on your boat—stainless bolts, stainless or bronze shaft, brass Cutless bearing shell, and aluminum outboard drive. And well you should be, with all that potential (no pun intended) for corrosion. But let's press on.

Before continuing our galley experiment, let's review what we have learned. We have found that any two dissimilar metals or alloys immersed in water will generate a potential difference. We have also found that if the two metals are isolated (neither physically touching nor electrically connected by wire), no current or corrosion will occur. Good. But what if they cannot be separated (a bronze prop on a stainless shaft), or what if we have bonded them for lightning protection (a steel rudder, several bronze through-hulls, and a copper ground strip)? Have we shot ourselves in the foot?

Table 5.1 ABYC Standard E-2, Galvanic Series of Metals in Seawater Referenced to Silver-Silver Chloride Half Cell (Seawater flowing at 8 to 13 ft./sec. [4.7 to 7.7 kn.], temperature range 50°F to 80°F—except as noted)

Metals and Alloys (Anodic or Least Noble—Active)	**Corrosion Potential, Volts**		
Magnesium and Magnesium Alloys	−1.60	to	−1.63
Zinc	−0.98	to	−1.03
Aluminum Alloys	−0.76	to	−1.00
Cadmium	−0.70	to	−0.73
Mild Steel	−0.60	to	−0.71
Wrought Iron	−0.60	to	−0.71
Cast Iron	−0.60	to	−0.71
13% Chromium Stainless Steel, Type 410 (active in still water)	−0.46	to	−0.58
18-8 Stainless Steel, Type 304 (active in still water)	−0.46	to	−0.58
Ni-Resist	−0.46	to	−0.58
18-8, 3% Mo Stainless Steel, Type 316 (active in still water)	−0.43	to	−0.54
Inconel (78% Ni–13.5% Cr–6% Fe) (active in still water)	−0.35	to	−0.46
Aluminum Bronze (92% Cu–8% Al)	−0.31	to	−0.42
Nibral (81.2% Cu–4% Fe–4.5% Ni–9% Al–1.3% Mn)	−0.31	to	−0.42
Naval Brass (60% Cu–39% Zn)	−0.30	to	−0.40
Yellow Brass (65% Cu–35% Zn)	−0.30	to	−0.40
Red Brass (85% Cu–15% Zn)	−0.30	to	−0.40
Muntz Metal (60% Cu–40% Zn)	−0.30	to	−0.40
Tin	−0.31	to	−0.33
Copper	−0.30	to	−0.57
50-50 Lead–Tin Solder	−0.28	to	−0.37
Admiralty Brass (71% Cu–28% Zn–1% Sn)	−0.28	to	−0.36
Aluminum Brass (76% Cu–22% Zn–2% Al)	−0.28	to	−0.36
Manganese Bronze (58.5% Cu–39% Zn–1% Sn–1% Fe–0.3% Mn)	−0.27	to	−0.34
Silicon Bronze (96% Cu max–0.8% Fe–1.5% Zn–2% Si–0.75% Mn–1.6% Sn)	−0.26	to	−0.29
Bronze-Composition G (88% Cu–2% Zn–10% Sn)	−0.24	to	−0.31
Bronze ASTM B62 (thru-hull) (85% Cu–5% Pb–5% Sn–5% Zn)	−0.24	to	−0.31
Bronze-Composition M (88% Cu–3% Zn–6.5% Zn–1.5% Pb)	−0.24	to	−0.31
13% Chromium Stainless Steel, Type 410 (passive)	−0.26	to	−0.35
Copper Nickel (90% Cu–10% Ni)	−0.21	to	−0.28
Copper Nickel (75% Cu–20% Ni–5% Zn)	−0.19	to	−0.25
Lead	−0.19	to	−0.25
Copper Nickel (70% Cu–30% Ni)	−0.18	to	−0.23
Inconel (78% Ni–13.5% Cr–6% Fe) (passive)	−0.14	to	−0.17
Nickel 200	−0.10	to	−0.20
18-8 Stainless Steel, Type 304 (passive)	−0.05	to	−0.10
Monel 400, K-500 (70% Ni–30% Cu)	−0.04	to	−0.14
Stainless Steel Propeller Shaft (ASTM 630:#17 and ASTM 564:#19)	−0.03	to	+0.13
18-8, 3% Mo Stainless Steel, Type 316 (passive)	0.00	to	−0.10
Titanium	−0.05	to	+0.06
Hastelloy C	−0.03	to	+0.08
Stainless Steel Shafting (Bar) (UNS 20910)	−0.25	to	+0.06
Platinum	+0.19	to	+0.25
Graphite	+0.20	to	+0.30

(Cathodic or Most Noble—Passive)

Corrosion Protection

To find out if we are in trouble, let's continue our galley corrosion experiment. First repeat the zinc vs. stainless test in Figure 5.10. Next add a piece of aluminum as a third electrode. Using alligator clip leads, connect the zinc, stainless, and aluminum electrodes, as shown in Figure 5.11. Now set the multimeter to milliamps and insert it, one at a time, in each of the leads to detect current flow.

Amazing! Electric current is flowing out of the stainless electrode and into the zinc electrode, but no current at all is flowing either into or out of the aluminum electrode. Since metal is lost only by an electrode that receives current, it seems that the zinc is protecting the aluminum by sacrificing itself.

You can repeat this experiment with any three metals you wish, and the results will always be the same: when dissimilar metals in an electrolyte are mechanically or electrically bonded, the only metal to corrode will be the one highest in the galvanic series. The metal most used in boats for this purpose is zinc.

The phenomenon just observed is called cathodic protection, and the zinc masses are called zinc anodes or just zincs.

Figure 5.12 shows two examples of cathodic protection using zincs. At top is an outboard engine mounted on the transom of a boat. A large zinc is bolted directly to the transom underwater, and a wire is run from the mounting bolts of the zinc to the outboard. The zinc protects the outboard. The zinc could also have been—and often is—bolted directly to the underwater shaft of the outboard.

At the bottom of Figure 5.12 is a sailboat with a zinc on the propeller shaft. The zinc is mechanically (and thus electrically) connected to the shaft. Protection is extended to the rudder shaft by a conductor from rudder to engine block. Rudder, rudder shaft, engine, transmission, prop shaft, and prop are all connected and thus protected by the zinc. The presence of a nonconductive plastic or rubber shaft coupling would require a jumper strap across the coupling. It should be noted that the ABYC also permits shafts and rudders to be protected separately, each by its own zinc anode.

Figure 5.13 shows a variety of zincs commonly found in chandleries. Many more shapes and forms are available from specialty suppliers. Engine zincs are mounted inside the cooling systems of engines. The guppy is used at anchor or in a marina slip and will be discussed below.

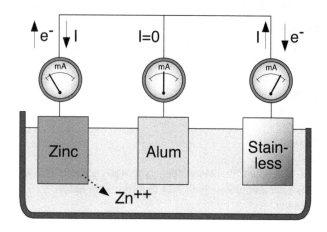

Fig. 5.11 How a Sacrificial Zinc Anode Works

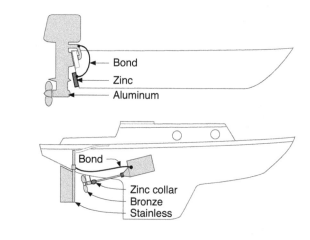

Fig. 5.12 Two Examples of Zinc-Anode Protection

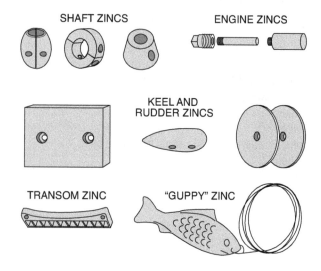

Fig. 5.13 An Assortment of Zincs

Even if you're flushed with your recent mastery of the subject of galvanic corrosion, I suggest you take a break at this point because we have to start all over again. It turns out there is more than one way to create a potential difference between underwater metals. We have another dragon to slay—stray-current corrosion.

Galley Experiment, Continued

OK, back to work. As a refresher, place two identical aluminum electrodes in the saltwater solution, as in Figure 5.14. Using the multimeter, measure the voltage between the electrodes. Then switch the multimeter to milliamps and measure the current in the wire between the electrodes. The result should be the same in both cases: zero.

Next place a 1.5-volt battery between the same two aluminum electrodes, A and B, as in Figure 5.15. Now, of course, you will measure the battery's 1.5 volts across the electrodes and, with the meter placed in series with the battery, a current flowing from the battery positive (+) terminal into electrode B. If you let the experiment go on long enough, you will observe that the electrode into which the current flows is corroding, just as it did with galvanic corrosion. It is apparent that it makes no difference whether the potential difference between the electrodes is due to their being of dissimilar metals or due to a voltage impressed on them from an outside source—the electrode receiving current always corrodes. When the impressed voltage is accidental (as from a poorly insulated electrical connection), the corrosion is termed *stray-current corrosion*. Since stray, or accidental, voltage sources can be much greater than galvanic potentials (up to 12 volts, compared to a few tenths of a volt), stray current corrosion can be much more damaging than galvanic corrosion.

Finally, we'll use four aluminum electrodes as shown in Figure 5.16. As in the previous test, Figure 5.15, we'll use electrodes A and B to force a current in the seawater. Now insert the connected pair, C and D, between A and B. Measure the current between C and D. It will be approximately the same as in the previous experiment. Likewise, electrode C will eventually show signs of corrosion.

Now you see why this insidious phenomenon is termed stray-current corrosion. Two perfectly innocent metal objects, if electrically bonded, can pick up stray current flowing through the electrolyte and participate in the corrosion process!

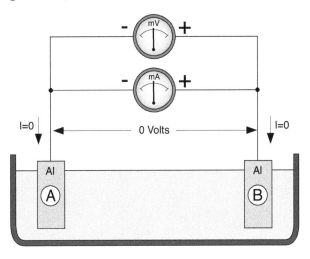

Fig. 5.14 Experiment Setup

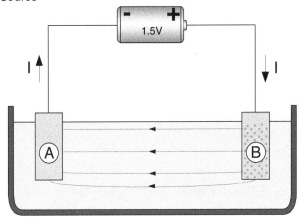

Fig. 5.15 Impressing (Forcing) Current with a Voltage Source

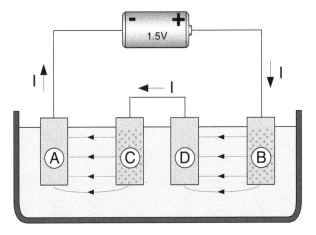

Fig. 5.16 Stray Current Impressed by Voltage Field

Stray-Current Protection

Figure 5.17 shows a boat floating in an external voltage and current field (perhaps due to an adjacent boat). The voltage difference, from left to right across the illustration, is 1.0 volt.

Since the electrical resistance of the path from ground plate to bonding wire to engine to shaft to propeller is less than that of the water path, electric current flows into the ground plate, through the bonding system and out of the propeller. And since the current is flowing into the propeller from the bonding system, the propeller will corrode.

Figure 5.18 shows that a sacrificial zinc on the shaft will divert the current flow to itself and save the prop.

Fig. 5.17 Stray-Current Corrosion Caused by an External Voltage Field

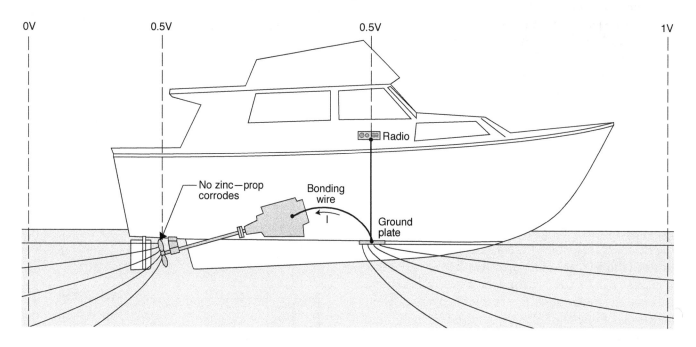

Fig. 5.18 Cathodic Protection from Stray-Current Corrosion Caused by an External Voltage Field

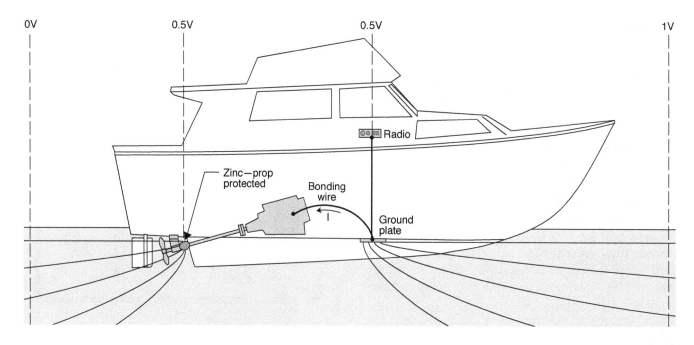

Figure 5.19 shows a stray current originating entirely inside the boat. Both a bilge pump and a bronze through-hull are sitting in bilge water. The unbonded pump develops a short from its positive power lead to its housing, establishing the pump housing at 12 volts. Current flows from the electrified housing, through the bilge water, into the through-hull, to the water outside the hull, and back through the prop, shaft, and engine path to ground. Since the through-hull is receiving current, it is also giving up ions to the sea (corroding). If the pump housing had been electrically bonded, the short would have tripped the circuit breaker, preventing corrosion and alerting the boatowner to the short.

Fig. 5.19 Stray-Current Corrosion Caused by Shorted Bilge Pump Inside Hull

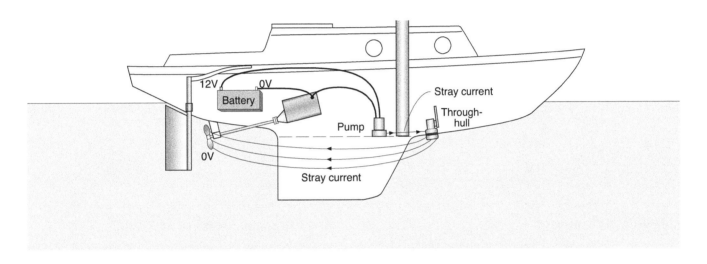

Figure 5.20 shows stray current originating from a terminal strip in the bilge. A single 12-volt/ground pair is shown here, but there are usually several pairs, serving anchor light, steaming light, and spreader lights on the mast. The terminal strip is wet, and some of the stray current finds its way back to ground by way of the through-hull–seawater connection. If the through-hull were, instead, bonded to ground, the stray current would flow back to ground by way of the bonding and not result in corrosion.

Fig. 5.20 Stray-Current Corrosion Caused by Wetted Terminal Strip in Bilge

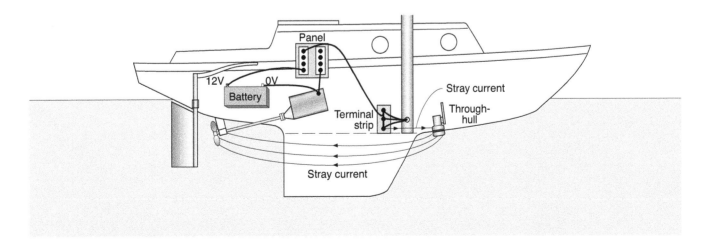

To Bond or Not to Bond

We have just seen three cases of stray-current corrosion. Two would have been *prevented* by bonding, but one was, in fact, *caused* by bonding. In general, bonding of immersed metal components *prevents* corrosion due to stray currents from *inside* the hull, but it *causes* corrosion due to stray currents from *outside* the hull.

Two opposite solutions to this dilemma are to: (1) bond everything and protect, and (2) unbond everything and isolate.

Bond and Protect

Figure 5.21 shows the bond-and-protect principle. Every underwater mass is connected to the boat's bonding system. To protect against stray currents outside of the hull, sacrificial anodes are connected to the bonding system and placed where they may best protect all underwater masses.

Fig. 5.21 The Bond-and-Protect Approach

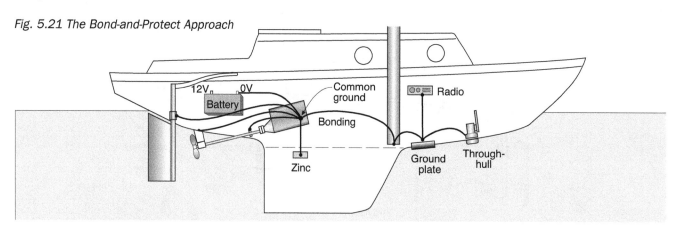

Unbond and Isolate

Figure 5.22 shows the alternative unbond-and-isolate principle. Underwater masses are isolated so neither galvanic nor outside stray current can flow between them. The only bonded underwater mass is the lightning and radio ground. Masses entirely within the hull (engine, transmission, metal tanks, and mast) are bonded to the boat's bonding system. The shaft is isolated by an insulating flexible coupling. The prop is protected by a shaft zinc if prop and shaft are of dissimilar metals.

The Pros and Cons of Bonding

Bonding and protecting offers the advantage of greater wetted surface area for the lightning and radio grounds.

On the other hand, proponents of the unbond-and-isolate approach claim that the lightning ground strip or plate provides adequate ground for both lightning and SSB radio, and that electrochemical reactions at bonded wooden hull through-hulls dangerously soften the surrounding wood. The ABYC favors the bond-and-protect approach, but specifically states that electrically isolated through-hull fittings need not be bonded.

Fig. 5.22 The Unbond-and-Isolate Approach

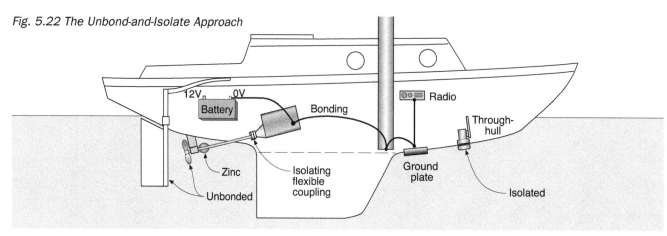

The ABYC recommends a method (in Standard E-2, Appendix 3) using a silver-silver chloride reference electrode for determining the amount of cathodic protection (size of aggregate zinc anodes) required to protect the underwater metals of a boat. The method assumes the use of zincs meeting Military Specification MIL-A-18001 (99.2% zinc minimum), excellent (metal-to-metal) electrical contact between anode and metal to be protected, and no paint on the anode.

The standard further points out that cathodic protection requirements increase with boat speed, salinity (if salt water), acidity (if fresh water), frequency of use of the boat, and deterioration over time of the anode.

ABYC Method

1. Assemble your materials:
   - silver-silver chloride reference electrode with lead (widely available on the Web or at West Marine stores for about $80)
   - digital multimeter (DMM) having at least 10 MW input impedance (even inexpensive DMMs do)
   - several high-quality zinc anodes of appropriate type (shaft collar, prop, or hull zincs)
   - two 20-foot test leads with strong clips
2. Starting with the hull free of all zinc anodes, lower the silver-silver chloride electrode into the water near the metal to be protected.
3. Set the DMM to the 2 Volts DC setting.
4. Connect the lead from the reference electrode to the DMM – input.
5. Using a test lead, connect the metal to be protected to the DMM + input. Make sure the test lead clip makes a clean electrical connection to the metal.
6. Note the DMM reading (example: –0. 720 volt).
7. Using the second test lead, connect one of the zinc anodes to the metal to be protected and lower the zinc into the water.
8. Note the new DMM reading. The zinc is adequate if it has lowered the voltage by *at least* 0.200 volt (example: from –0.720 volt to –0.920 volt or less).
9. If the second reading isn't at least 0.200 volt more negative than the first, the zinc is not sufficient. Increase either the zinc area or the number of zincs and retest.

Fig. 5.23 ABYC Method for Sizing Cathodic Protection

STEPS 1–6

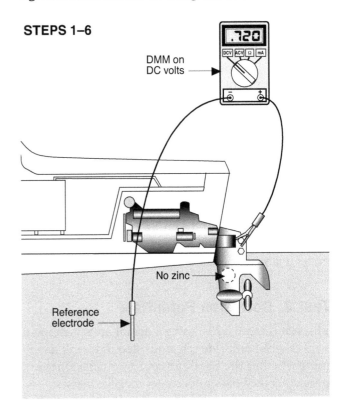

STEPS 7–9

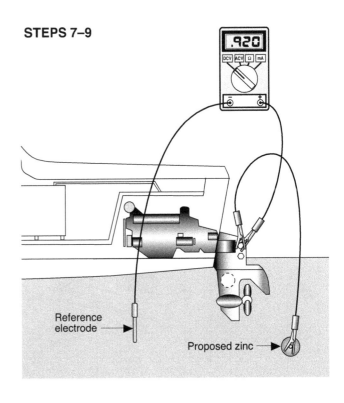

Testing Your Protection

Test 1: Stray Currents

In a bonded system, stray current will be captured by the boat's bonding conductor. Stray current in a through-hull or other accessible underwater mass can be measured with a digital multimeter on the milliamps (mA) setting as shown in Figure 5.24.

Disconnect the bonding conductor and place the meter between the end of the conductor and the metal of the through-hull. Current into or out of the through-hull will now flow through the meter. Repeat the test with each fitting, as well as the rudder shaft, prop shaft, and strut or shaft log. Remember that current flowing from the bonding conductor into the fitting, as shown, is causing corrosion of the fitting. Current of as little as 1 milliamp is reason for concern as it will, over the 8,766 hours in a year, cause serious damage to the fitting.

Test 2: Corrosion Potentials

This test (Figure 5.25), using a digital multimeter and a silver-silver chloride reference electrode, will determine whether the boat's present sacrificial zincs are protecting the boat's underwater metallic masses:

1. Set the multimeter to measure DC volts.
2. Connect the meter's + input to an underwater metallic mass or, if there is a common bonding system (as shown), to engine negative ground.
3. Connect the reference electrode to the meter's – input, and lower the electrode into the water.

Compare the reading to those of Table 5.2 to see whether the zinc anodes are adequate. If the readings indicate underprotection, replace or add zinc anodes.

Fig. 5.25 How to Evaluate Your Boat's Corrosion Potential

Fig. 5.24 Test for Stray Current

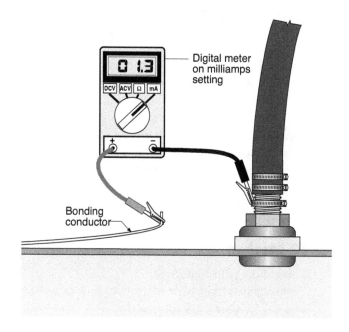

Table 5.2 Interpreting Corrosion Test Voltages

Underwater Metal	Under-protected	Protected	Over-protected
Bronze	< 0.44 V	0.44–0.70 V	> 0.70 V
Steel	< 0.75 V	0.75–0.95 V	> 0.95 V
Aluminum	< 0.90 V	0.90–1.10 V	> 1.10 V

Readings in excess of 1.10 volts usually indicate a voltage field in the water surrounding the boat. If you can't eliminate or reduce the external field, consider unbonding and isolating the underwater fittings, as shown in Figure 5.22.

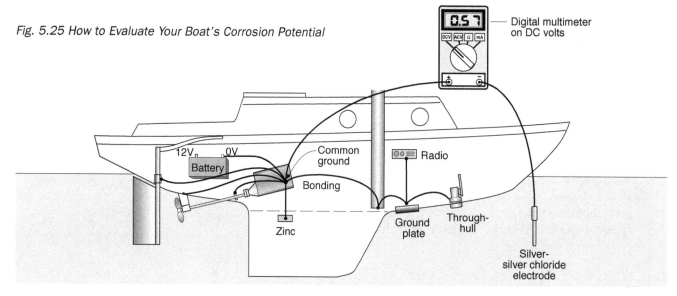

We have addressed the types of corrosion that can be eliminated by cathodic protection. There are further annoying types of corrosion on a boat that must be addressed by other means.

Dezincification

Figure 5.26 shows the dezincification of brass screws. Brass consists of a mixture of copper and zinc. Common yellow brass contains 65% copper and 35% zinc. In the presence of moisture (a very common electrolyte around boats!), the zinc and copper react galvanically, just as they would underwater, although more slowly. The result is a loss of zinc and loss of strength. When a badly dezincified screw is removed, the screw head often snaps off. The lesson: use only stainless or bronze screws around a boat.

A second instance of dezincification occurs in bronze (an alloy of copper, tin, and zinc) propellers. Loss of zinc is evidenced by a telltale change of the metal from bright yellow to a pinkish hue.

Stainless Screws in Aluminum

Figure 5.27 shows what happens when a fitting of any material, metallic or nonmetallic, is attached to an aluminum mast or boom with stainless screws. Regardless of how well machined the threads are, there are always microscopic spaces between the screw and the body. If salt water finds its way into these capillary spaces, an ideal galvanic cell is set up with resulting loss of aluminum in the area of the threads. Ultimately, the stainless screw seizes in the hole or, worse, falls out under load. Filling both sets of threads with silicone sealant or grease before fastening will fill the capillary spaces around the threads and prevent the intrusion of salt water. No seawater—no electrolyte—no corrosion.

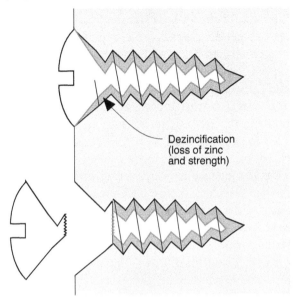

Fig. 5.26 Dezincification of Brass

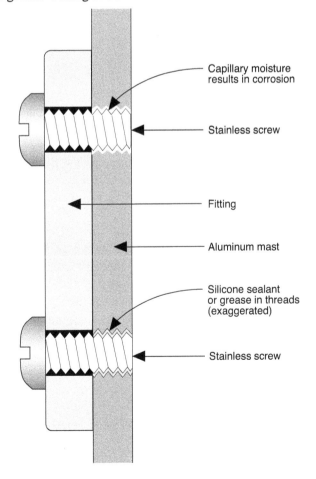

Fig. 5.27 Seizing of Stainless Screws in Aluminum

Noncathodic Corrosion

Stainless Pitting

Figure 5.28 shows how stainless (pronounce "stainless") steel develops corrosion pits. Stainless steel is principally an alloy of iron and chromium. When exposed to the oxygen in air, the chromium oxidizes and forms a shiny protective skin (the stainless is then said to be passivated). The chromium oxide skin is very noble in the galvanic series (see Table 5.1, entry 18-8, 3% Mo Stainless Steel, Type 316 [passive]), so it resists corrosion and protects the iron beneath.

If the surface is immersed in or covered with an oxygen-free liquid, however, the chromium loses its oxygen, the passive skin is lost, and the iron is free to rust. In Figure 5.27 a barnacle has attached itself to a stainless surface, depriving the chromium-oxide skin of oxygen. The unpassivated area and the surrounding passivated area then act as a galvanic couple, resulting in corrosion of the iron under the barnacle.

The same sort of corrosion occurs between stainless stanchions and their water-retaining bases, explaining the mysterious rust stains often seen in these areas.

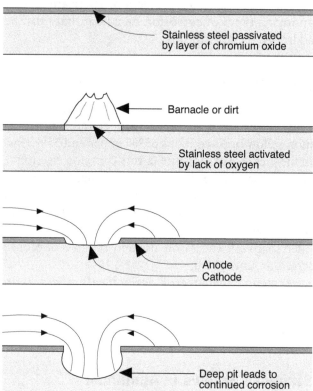

Fig. 5.28 Pitting of Stainless Steel

- Stainless steel passivated by layer of chromium oxide
- Barnacle or dirt
- Stainless steel activated by lack of oxygen
- Anode
- Cathode
- Deep pit leads to continued corrosion

Cavitation Erosion

Finally, Figure 5.29 shows cavitation erosion of the trailing edge of a propeller. Cavitation is the rapid formation and collapse of vapor bubbles just behind propeller blades. Cavitation is not galvanic corrosion. Instead, the propeller is turning so quickly that the water immediately behind the blade is left behind, forming water vapor (gaseous form of water) bubbles. As these bubbles subsequently collapse, the water hits the blade like thousands of tiny hammers. You can hear the sharp popping sound underwater when a boat passes. The result is mechanical destruction and erosion of the metal at the trailing edge of the blade. The solution is to increase the area of the blade, thereby reducing the pressure difference across the blade.

In contrast, a bronze propeller or any other bronze fitting suffering from galvanic corrosion displays a rosy-pink color instead of its normal brassy-yellow color. Galvanic corrosion selectively removes the zinc from the bronze, leaving the reddish copper behind.

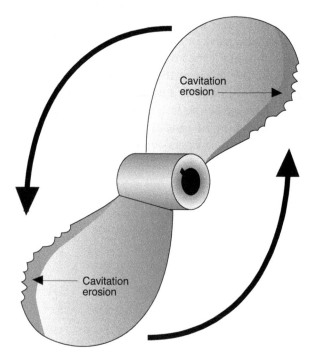

Fig. 5.29 Erosion Due to Cavitation

- Cavitation erosion
- Cavitation erosion

The following general recommendations are taken from ABYC Standard E-2, *Cathodic Protection of Boats,* Section E-2.4.

a. Although cathodic protection will, depending on the current capability of the system, help to minimize stray-current corrosion when it exists, stray-current corrosion should be controlled by:

(1) Minimizing DC and AC electrical leakage levels from electrical products, and

(2) The use of a bonding system in accordance with ABYC E-1, "Bonding of Direct Current Systems."

b. Factors that affect the type and degree of cathodic protection required:

(1) Water Velocity—Cathodic protection current requirements increase with water velocity past the hull. The current requirements can be as high as 30 times that required in still water.

(2) Boat Usage—More frequently operated vessels require more cathodic protection than vessels infrequently used.

(3) Fresh and Sea Water—Current requirements increase with salinity but higher driving potentials are required in fresh water.

(4) Deterioration of Protective Coatings—Current requirements increase as protective coatings deteriorate.

c. The need for a cathodic protection system for metal appendages on nonmetallic hulls may not be justified if the metals coupled are galvanically compatible.

d. Hull-mounted metallic trim tabs may be electrically isolated from the boat's bonding system to reduce the load on the boat's cathodic protection system, providing the trim tabs are also electrically isolated from their electrical actuating mechanism. If the trim-tab system is connected to the boat's bonding system the cathodic protection system's milliampere rating will have to be increased to provide the additional protection.

e. A cathodic protection system shall be capable of inducing and maintaining a minimum negative shift of 200 millivolts in the potential of the composite cathode being protected.

f. Since the area relationship of metals in a galvanic cell will affect current density and therefore corrosion rate, the immersed cathodic metal surfaces may be coated to obtain a more favorable anode to cathode area relationship. Coatings shall not contain pigments that will form galvanic couples with the substrate. Coatings on substrate and coatings on surfaces must be able to tolerate alkali generated by the cathodic reaction.

g. Impressed-current anodes shall have the words "DO NOT PAINT" on a visible surface when installed.

NOTE: Anodes are ineffective if painted.

h. In general, the use of several anodes instead of one large anode will tend to provide better distribution of the protective current. Sacrificial anodes may be mounted remotely; the best current distribution will be obtained with the anode(s) positioned to be as equidistant as possible from the metals to be protected.

i. Anodes should be faired and, if possible, arranged in a longitudinal row to minimize drag. After installation, peripheral crevices should be sealed.

j. Anodes shall be mounted on a sloping surface that cannot entrap gas bubbles.

k. If anodes are located near through-hull fittings they shall be positioned forward of discharge fittings and aft of intake ports. Anode locations that disturb the flow of water past the propeller should be avoided.

l. All metals which are to receive cathodic protection from the cathodic protection system must have good electrical continuity to the boat bonding system. Galvanic anodes, if used, must be affixed in a manner that electrical continuity is maintained with the metals they are to protect, either through their mounting means or through the boat's bonding system.

(1) Propeller shafts do not provide reliable electrical continuity to the boat's bonding system.

(2) Rudder posts shall be cathodically bonded by means of a flexible conductor positioned to allow full rudder movement without stressing the cathodic bonding conductor or its connection.

m. In general, sacrificial anodes may be mounted directly on the metal to be protected, but the best current distribution will be obtained by remote mounting with the anode(s) positioned to be as equidistant as possible from the metals to be protected.

n. The negative potential (–1,050 millivolts as compared to silver-silver chloride reference electrode) that can be achieved by some corrosion control systems will result in some decrease in the effectiveness of antifouling paints. Because the decrease in the effectiveness increases with higher negative voltages, the negative potential should be kept as close to the optimum value as possible. A reference potential reading in excess of –1,100 millivolts indicates excessive cathodic protection.

o. Anodes and reference electrodes shall be positioned to avoid contact with lifting slings and chocks when the boat is hauled.

p. The electrical interconnection that occurs via shore-power cables or metal mooring cables between two vessels or between a vessel and submerged metal or the dock may result in galvanic corrosion of steel or aluminum hulls and aluminum underwater appendages. An isolator or an isolation transformer can break this couple.

CHAPTER 6

DC Standards and Practices

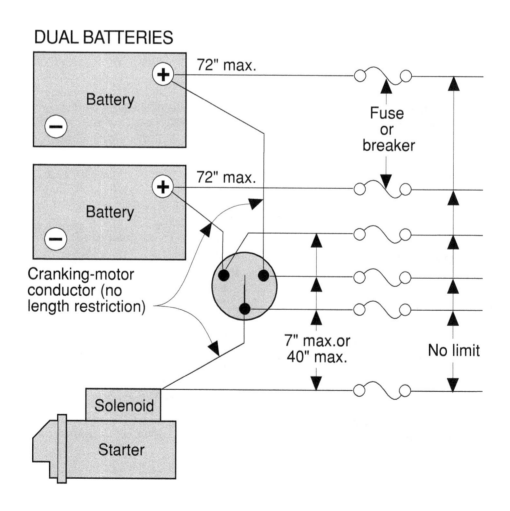

DUAL BATTERIES

Battery

Battery

72" max.

72" max.

Fuse or breaker

Cranking-motor conductor (no length restriction)

7" max. or 40" max.

No limit

Solenoid

Starter

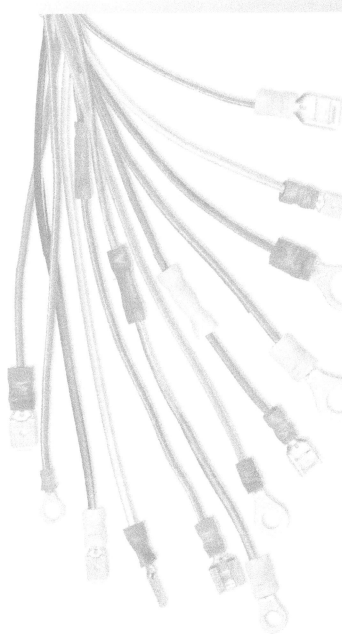

Standards and recommended practices for the wiring of boats are promoted by the American Boat and Yacht Council (ABYC). This chapter delineates and explains these standards. Preliminary to the standards, however, we first explain the wisdom of creating wiring diagrams for your boat's electrical systems.

The standards and practices start with the specification of acceptable marine wire. The ABYC DC load calculation method allows you to calculate the maximum current expected to flow in a conductor and to use the tables for allowable amperage of conductors and conductor sizes for allowable voltage drops.

Wiring and, later, troubleshooting are both facilitated by the proper identification of conductors, as well as the proper installation of wire runs.

As in a home, overcurrent protection, in the form of fuses and circuit breakers, guards against overheating and possible fire.

The marine environment, characterized by moisture, salt, and vibration, makes conductor connections critical.

The lethal mixture of gasoline vapors and open flame or electric spark dictates the ABYC-adopted Coast Guard requirements for ignition protection.

Wiring Diagrams

When you first bought your boat, you probably judged its wiring on appearances. Either it looked good or it did not. You never gave it another thought—until something went wrong. Then you discovered whether or not the boat had a wiring diagram. Chances are, if your boat was American made, it did not.

The person who wired your boat didn't need a wiring diagram. First, yours was probably one of dozens, if not hundreds, he had wired just like it. Second, he assumed he would not be there when something went wrong. Troubleshooting would be your problem.

One summer I worked in a boatyard rigging and stepping masts. One of my jobs was to check the mast wiring before the mast was stepped. Some masts had combined tricolor, anchor, and strobe light (four conductors), masthead or steaming light (two conductors), spreader lights (two conductors), windvane light (two conductors), plus a windspeed indicator (six wires in a cable) and a VHF coaxial cable—a total of ten individual conductors plus two cables.

It seemed as if every second mast had a problem. A bulb was burned out or not properly seated, connectors were corroded, or a wire was broken. The symptoms were obvious—a light at the top of the mast did not come on. Finding the cause, however, was an art. Without a wiring diagram, labeled terminals, and color-coded conductors, finding the fault sometimes required an hour of labor for two workers: one at the top end reading voltage or watching the light, the other at the bottom applying voltage to successive pairs of conductors. Did you know that the number of possible pairs of n wires is $n(n-1)/2$? For 10 wires we had to check 45 pair combinations!

Sometimes we found that a light that had worked on the ground no longer worked with the mast up. Now there were even more possibilities! Something could have happened inside the mast during stepping, or the problem could lie between the distribution panel and the base of the mast. It was here that we sometimes encountered the case of the chameleon conductor. A wire would leave the distribution panel with blue insulation, disappear into the bilge or behind a liner, and emerge at the base of the mast with yellow insulation!

One of my associates had worked for one of the best boatbuilders in the United States. Over lunch I related the case of the chameleon wire.

"Oh, sure," he said, "we used to run a wire until the spool ran out. Then we'd grab another spool of whatever color and splice it in."

A proper wiring diagram shows every electrical device: circuit breaker, fuse, switch, terminal, and conductor, as well as wire size, color, and label. It makes troubleshooting a snap. If a light doesn't come on, the diagram shows exactly where to check for voltage, all the way from the lamp back to the distribution panel. A circuit diagram also shows the best place to tie in additional electrical equipment, what spares to carry, and whether or not you are fused correctly.

Best of all, if you create your circuit diagram by visually inspecting your existing wiring, you will have looked systematically at every component and may be able to spot potential problems before they become problems underway.

Creating a Wiring Diagram

Circuit symbols are, like international road signs, intended to convey meaning at a glance. Unlike international signage, however, there is no rigorous standard for wiring symbols. Figure 6.1 shows commonly used symbols for most of the simple devices encountered in a boat. If these don't work for you, feel free to invent your own. For example, you may elect to show a fan as a fan blade and a fuse as a simple rectangle.

If you possess the repair manual for your engine (a minimal and wise investment), it probably contains a wiring diagram for the starting motor, alternator, and instrument panel. If so, you are in luck; you are already halfway there. Consider the engine diagram to be the first of your circuit diagrams and adopt its style for the rest of your diagrams.

Breaking the total system into a set of circuits has the added advantages of smaller sheets of paper, less confusion, and the ability to make changes without redrawing the entire system.

A complete set of circuit diagrams for a typical pleasure boat might include:
- Engine wiring
- Engine-starting circuit
- Cabin lights and accessories
- Navigation lights
- Instrumentation and radios
- 110 VAC system
- Main distribution panel
- Mast wiring
- Water pumps

Don't worry if several of your diagrams overlap. The intent is to locate the general area of a fault and then to isolate the exact location within that area.

Fig. 6.1 Wiring Symbols

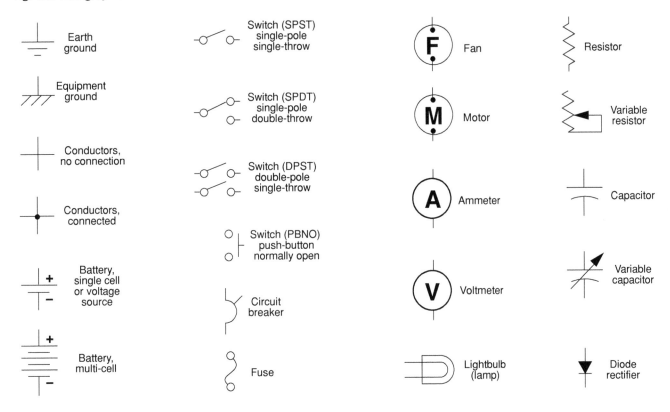

Earth ground	Switch (SPST) single-pole single-throw	Fan	Resistor
Equipment ground	Switch (SPDT) single-pole double-throw	Motor	Variable resistor
Conductors, no connection	Switch (DPST) double-pole single-throw	Ammeter	Capacitor
Conductors, connected	Switch (PBNO) push-button normally open	Voltmeter	Variable capacitor
Battery, single cell or voltage source	Circuit breaker		
Battery, multi-cell	Fuse	Lightbulb (lamp)	Diode rectifier

A Starter-Motor Circuit

Figure 6.2 shows a very simple diagram of an engine starter-motor circuit. If one day you turn on the ignition switch, push the start button, and nothing happens, this is the circuit diagram you will need. A complete engine wiring diagram would probably contain the same information, but it would also contain all of the meters, idiot lights, and alternator wiring, adding considerable visual confusion.

For the starter-motor circuit all you need to see are the:

- Battery switch
- Fuse between battery switch common terminal and engine panel
- On/Off switch
- Momentary start switch
- Wire from starting switch to solenoid
- Heavy positive cable from battery-select common terminal to solenoid
- Heavy negative cable from battery negative terminal to engine negative terminal.

If the engine won't turn over, the problem probably lies somewhere in this diagram. For guidance, see page 64.

Fig. 6.2 Typical Starter-Motor Circuit

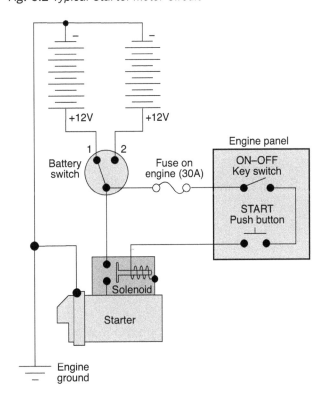

Wiring Diagrams

A Cabin Lighting Circuit

Although it shows 15 separate lights and fans, the cabin lighting diagram in Figure 6.3 is even simpler in concept than the engine starter circuit. The diagram consists of two similar, but separate, branch circuits.

On the right is the starboard cabin lighting circuit, originating at a 10-amp circuit breaker in the DC distribution panel and running forward to serve all of the lights and fans on the starboard side. The positive conductor is a red AWG (American Wire Gauge) 14 wire labeled "27." The negative conductor is a black AWG 14 wire labeled "28." Except for the two paralleled main cabin lights, each light and fan is controlled by an individual single-pole, single-throw switch. You may wish to include model numbers and specifications for each device so that you can calculate current draws and find replacement parts.

The devices are drawn on paper as laid out in the boat so that we can physically pinpoint a problem. For example, if the chart table light failed, but the main aft light still worked, the circuit diagram would allow us to immediately isolate the problem to either the chart table light or the lamp's controlling switch.

On the other hand, if the main aft, main forward, and V-berth lights failed as well, we would suspect the problem to be in either the positive or negative conductors or the connections between the night light and the chart table light.

On the left is the similar port cabin lighting circuit, originating at a 10-amp circuit breaker in the DC distribution panel and running forward to serve all of the lights and fans on the port side. The positive conductor is a red AWG 14 wire labeled "29." The negative conductor is a black AWG 14 wire labeled "30."

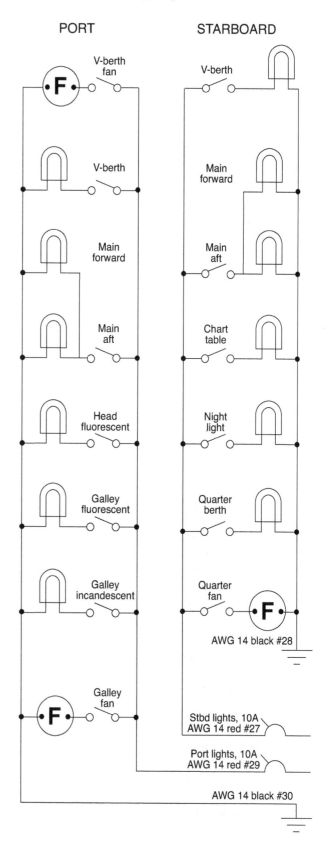

Fig. 6.3 Typical Cabin Lighting Circuits

Real circuits consist not of pencil lines on a sheet of paper, but of real metal conductors having finite electrical resistance. The conductors and their installations should satisfy a number of criteria:

1. Construction should be such that the conductor will not break under continuous vibration or an accidentally imposed force.
2. Insulation should be appropriate for the expected maximum ambient (surrounding air) temperature and degree of exposure to sunlight, moisture, and air.
3. Ampacity (current-carrying capacity) should be sufficient to avoid overheating.
4. Conductor size should be selected considering conductor length and current in order that voltage drop not impair the functioning of the load devices.

Construction

The ABYC calls for most conductors to be stranded and of size AWG 16 minimum. An exception is sheathed AWG 18 conductors that do not extend more than 30 inches beyond their sheath.

Because copper wire becomes brittle with flexing, solid wire (as used in house wiring) is not allowed at all. Type II stranding is the minimum allowed for general boat wiring, and Type III stranding should be used wherever vibration is expected, such as on an engine.

Table 6.1 shows the minimum circular-mil areas (a circular mil is the area of a 0.001-inch-diameter circle) for both AWG and SAE (Society of Automotive Engi-

neers) conductors and the minimum numbers of strands specified by the ABYC for AWG 18 through AWG 4/0 (0000) conductors.

Insulation

All single-conductor and cable insulations should be one of the types listed in Table 6.2, appropriate to its expected exposure to temperature, moisture, and oil. The letters in the designations stand for:

T	thermoplastic
M	oil resistant
W	moisture resistant
H	heat resistant to 75°C
HH	high-heat resistant to 90°C

An insulated jacket or sheathing may qualify for more than one rating and be labeled as such. The most commonly available cable suitable to all applications in the typical boat is probably UL 1426 boat cable.

Table 6.1 Minimum Circular-Mil (CM) Areas and Stranding

Conductor Gauge	Minimum CM for AWG	Minimum CM for SAE	Minimum Type II	Strands Type III
18	1,620	1,537	16	–
16	2,580	2,336	19	26
14	4,110	3,702	19	41
12	6,530	5,833	19	65
10	10,380	9,343	19	105
8	16,510	14,810	19	168
6	26,240	25,910	37	266
4	41,740	37,360	49	420
2	66,360	62,450	127	665
1	83,690	77,790	127	836
0	105,600	98,980	127	1,064
2/0	133,100	125,100	127	1,323
3/0	167,800	158,600	259	1,666
4/0	211,600	205,500	418	2,107

Table 6.2 Acceptable Insulation Types

Type	Description
	CONDUCTORS
THW	Moisture and Heat Resistant, Thermoplastic
TW	Moisture Resistant, Thermoplastic
HWN	Moisture and Heat Resistant, Thermoplastic
XHHW	Moisture and High-Heat Resistant, Cross-Linked Synthetic Polymer
MTW	Moisture, Heat, and Oil Resistant, Thermoplastic
AWM	Moisture, Heat, and Oil Resistant, Thermoplastic, Thermosetting
UL 1426	Boat Cable
	SAE CONDUCTORS
GPT	Thermoplastic Insulation, Braidless
HDT	Thermoplastic Insulation, Braidless
SGT	Thermoplastic Insulation, Braidless
STS	Thermosetting Synthetic-Rubber Insulation, Braidless
HTS	Thermosetting Synthetic-Rubber Insulation, Braidless
SXL	Thermosetting, Cross-Linked Polyethylene Insulation, Braidless
	FLEXIBLE CORDS
SO	Hard-Service Cord, Oil Resistant
ST	Hard-Service Cord, Thermoplastic
STO	Hard-Service Cord, Oil Resistant, Thermoplastic
SEO	Hard-Service Cord, Oil Resistant, Thermoplastic
SJO	Junior Hard-Service Cord, Oil Resistant
SJT	Hard-Service Cord, Thermoplastic
SJTO	Hard-Service Cord, Oil Resistant, Thermoplastic

ABYC DC Load Calculation

Ampacity

Branch circuit conductors should be sized to carry the maximum currents drawn by their loads. In the case of motors, maximum current should be for the locked-rotor, or stalled, condition.

Main feed conductors for distribution panels and switchboards should be determined using the ABYC procedure, shown in Table 6.3 (a sample calculation is shown).

Table 6.3 ABYC Load Calculation Method (for total electrical loads for minimum sizes of panelboards, switchboards, and main conductors)
NOTE: Calculations are based on the actual operating amperage for each load and not on the rating of the circuit breaker or fuse protecting that branch circuit.

Column A

List each of the loads that must be available for use on a continuous basis.

Equipment	Amperes
Navigation lights	5.5
Bilge blower(s)	2.0
Bilge pump(s)	4.2
Wiper(s)	0.0
Largest radio (transmit mode)	2.5
Depth sounder	0.9
Radar	7.5
Searchlight	12.0
Instruments	2.3
Alarm system (standby mode)	0.5
Refrigeration	5.5
Other: Autopilot	3.5
Total of Column A	46.4
Enter Total from Column B	80.0
Sum of Totals (Total Load)	126.4

Column B

List the intermittent loads. The largest load or 10% of the total, whichever is greater, will be carried to Column A.

Equipment	Amperes
Cigarette lighter	0.0
Cabin lighting	10.0
Horn	6.3
Additional electronics	10.0
Trim tabs	0.0
Power trim	0.0
Heads	0.0
Anchor windlass	80.0
Winches	0.0
Freshwater pumps	5.8
Other: Microwave	60.0
Total of Column B	172.1
10% of Column B	17.2
Largest item in Column B	80.0
Larger of above two lines—Enter in both Column A and Column B	80.0

Having the maximum load current in amps and the temperature rating of the conductor insulation, the minimum required conductor size is selected from Table 6.4.

Table 6.4 Allowable Amperage of Conductors for Under 50 Volts
(Adapted from ABYC Standard E-11, Table IV)

Conductor Size, AWG	Temperature Rating of Conductor Insulation						
	60°C (140°F)	75°C (167°F)	80°C (176°F)	90°C (194°F)	105°C (221°F)	125°C (257°F)	200°C (392°F)
	Outside Engine Spaces						
18	10	10	15	20	20	25	25
16	15	15	20	25	25	30	35
14	20	20	25	30	35	40	45
12	25	25	35	40	45	50	55
10	40	40	50	55	60	70	70
8	55	65	70	70	80	90	100
6	80	95	100	100	120	125	135
4	105	125	130	135	160	170	180
2	140	170	175	180	210	225	240
1	165	195	210	210	245	265	280
1/0	195	230	245	245	285	305	325
2/0	225	265	285	285	330	355	370
3/0	260	310	330	330	385	410	430
4/0	300	360	385	385	445	475	510
	Inside Engine Spaces						
18	5.8	7.5	11.7	16.4	17.0	22.3	25.0
16	8.7	11.3	15.6	20.5	21.3	26.7	35.0
14	11.6	15.0	19.5	24.6	29.8	35.6	45.0
12	14.5	18.8	27.3	32.8	38.3	44.5	55.0
10	23.2	30.0	39.0	45.1	51.0	62.3	70.0
8	31.9	48.8	54.6	57.4	68.0	80.1	100.0
6	46.4	71.3	78.0	82.0	102.0	111.3	135.0
4	60.9	93.8	101.4	110.7	136.0	151.3	180.0
2	81.2	127.5	136.5	147.6	178.5	200.3	240.0
1	95.7	146.3	163.8	172.2	208.3	235.9	280.0
1/0	113.1	172.5	191.1	200.9	242.3	271.5	325.0
2/0	130.5	198.8	222.3	233.7	280.5	316.0	370.0
3/0	150.8	232.5	257.4	270.6	327.3	364.9	430.0
4/0	174.0	270.0	300.3	315.7	378.3	422.8	510.0

Allowable Voltage Drop

All wire has resistance. As current flows through the wire, voltage drops according to Ohm's Law. If power is supplied to a circuit by a 12.0-volt battery and the voltage drops 0.5 volt in the positive conductor going to the load and another 0.5 volt in the negative conductor back to the battery, then the voltage across the load is not 12.0 volts, but $12.0 - 0.5 - 0.5 = 11.0$ volts. The voltage drop in the total length of conductor to and from the load is thus $1.0/12.0 = 8.3\%$.

The ABYC specifies two allowable percentage drops, depending on the effect on safety:
- 3% for panelboard feeds, bilge blowers, electronics, and navigation lights
- 10% for general lighting and other noncritical applications

Required conductor size may be determined from:

$$CM = 10.75 \times I \times L/E$$

where:
- CM = conductor circular mils (Table 6.1)
- I = current in amps
- L = round-trip length in feet
- E = voltage drop in conductor, volts

Example: What size conductor is required for an anchor light drawing 0.9 amp at the top of a 50-foot mast with a 15-foot run from panelboard to base of the mast?

The light is a navigation light, so the allowed voltage drop is 3% of 12 volts or 0.36 volt. The length of the conductor from panelboard to the light and back to the panelboard is 15 feet + 50 feet + 50 feet + 15 feet = 130 feet. The minimum circular-mil area of the conductor is thus

$$CM = 10.75 \times 0.9 \times 130/0.36 = 3{,}494$$

Table 6.1 tells us a #14 AWG conductor is required. Alternatively, we can find the answer in Table 6.5.

Table 6.5 Conductor Sizes (Minimum Circular Mils Converted to AWG by Table 6.1) for Allowable Voltage Drops in 12-Volt Systems (Adapted from ABYC Standard E-11, Tables X and XI)

Current, Amps	Round-Trip Conductor Length, ft.									Current, Amps	Round-Trip Conductor Length, ft.								
	10	20	30	40	60	80	100	120	140		10	20	30	40	60	80	100	120	140
	3% Voltage Drop										10% Voltage Drop								
1	18	18	18	18	16	14	14	14	12	1	18	18	18	18	18	18	18	18	18
2	18	18	16	14	14	12	10	10	8	2	18	18	18	18	18	18	16	16	14
5	18	14	12	10	10	8	6	6	6	5	18	18	18	16	14	14	12	12	10
10	14	10	10	8	6	6	4	4	2	10	18	16	14	14	12	10	10	8	8
15	12	10	8	6	6	4	2	2	1	15	18	14	12	12	10	8	8	6	6
20	10	8	6	6	4	2	2	1	0	20	16	14	12	10	8	8	6	6	6
25	10	6	6	4	2	2	1	0	2/0	25	16	12	10	10	8	6	6	4	4
30	10	6	4	4	2	1	0	2/0	3/0	30	14	12	10	8	6	6	4	4	2
40	8	6	4	2	1	0	2/0	3/0	4/0	40	14	10	8	8	6	4	4	2	2
50	6	4	2	2	0	2/0	3/0	4/0	–	50	12	10	8	6	4	4	2	2	1
60	6	4	2	1	2/0	3/0	4/0	–	–	60	12	8	6	6	4	2	2	1	1
70	6	2	1	0	3/0	4/0	–	–	–	70	10	8	6	6	2	2	1	1	0
80	6	2	1	0	3/0	4/0	–	–	–	80	10	8	6	4	2	2	1	0	2/0
90	4	2	0	2/0	4/0	–	–	–	–	90	10	6	6	4	2	1	0	0	2/0
100	4	2	0	2/0	4/0	–	–	–	–	100	10	6	4	4	2	1	0	2/0	2/0

Conductor Identification

The ABYC states, "Each electrical conductor that is part of the boat's electrical system shall have a means to identify its function in the system."

Two means of identification are insulation color and labels (numbers and/or letters) applied near the terminal points. The use of both is recommended.

In general, DC conductor insulation should follow the color scheme:

DC Positive	Red (R)
DC Negative	Black (B) or Yellow (Y)
DC Grounding	Green (G) or Green with Yellow (GY)

The ABYC goes on to recommend colors for specific DC positive conductors. If these colors are not used, a wiring diagram should be provided showing the conductors and their identifiers. Table 6.6 lists the recommended colors for both general and specific conductors.

Table 6.6 DC Wiring Color Code
(Adapted from ABYC Standard E-11, Tables XIV and XV)

Color	Conductor Use
Green or green with yellow stripe(s)	General DC grounding
Black or yellow	General DC negative
Red	General DC positive
Yellow with red stripe	Starter switch to solenoid
Brown with yellow stripe, or yellow	Fuse or switch to blower—If DC negative is yellow, positive must be brown with yellow stripe
Dark gray	Fuse or switch to navigation lights Tachometer sender to gauge
Brown	Generator armature to regulator Auxiliary terminal to light and regulator Fuse or switch to pumps
Orange	Ammeter to alternator or generator output and accessory fuses or switches Distribution panel to accessory switch
Purple	Ignition switch to coil and electrical instruments Distribution panel to electrical instruments
Dark blue	Fuse or switch to cabin and instrument lights
Light blue	Oil-pressure sender to gauge
Tan	Water-temperature sender to gauge
Pink	Fuel-gauge sender to gauge
Green/stripe, except G/Y	Tilt and/or trim circuits

Installation of Wire Runs

When both AC and DC conductors are run in the same area and direction, the AC conductors should be kept separate from the DC conductors by bundling, sheathing, or other means.

Continuous Support

In order to minimize flexing from vibration, conductors should be supported continuously or every 18 inches minimum by clamps or straps (Figure 6.4). Nonmetallic clamps and straps should not be used in locations where failure would result in a hazard, such as over engines, shafts, or passageways.

Metal clamps should be lined with moisture-, gasoline-, and oil-resistant material, or have smooth, rounded edges. The cable beneath unlined metal clamps should be protected by a wrapping to protect the conductors.

Fig. 6.4 Cable Support Devices

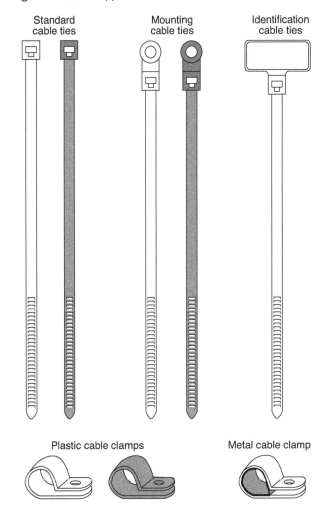

Identification and Installation

Exposure to Damage

Conductors should be protected from chafing by routing clear of engine and steering shafts and control linkages. In exposed areas conductors should be protected by conduit, raceway, or equivalent wrap. Holes in panels, bulkheads, or other structural members (Figure 6.5) should be lined.

Protecting Connections

Enclosures with electrical connections should be in dry locations or be weatherproof. If wet locations are unavoidable, nonmetallic enclosures are preferred, but metal enclosures can be mounted to prevent accumulation of moisture between the enclosure and adjacent surfaces, such as by providing a space of at least ¼ inch.

Wiring in the Bilge

The simplest routing of conductors is often through the bilge, but more than 90% of all electrical problems are due to corrosion, and nothing leads to corrosion more quickly than water—particularly of the salt variety. Current-carrying conductors should be routed as high as possible above bilge water. If routing through the bilge cannot be avoided, connections must be watertight.

Sources of Heat

Conductors should be kept away from and never run directly above engine exhaust pipes and other similar sources of heat. Minimum recommended conductor clearances are 2 inches from wet-exhaust pipes and components and 9 inches from dry-exhaust components, unless equivalent thermal insulation is provided.

Battery Cables

Unless battery cables are overcurrent protected, they should be run above bilge-water level, away from metal fuel-system components, such as fuel line and fuel filters, and away from the engine, transmission, and shaft. The grounded battery cable is excepted because contact between the grounded engine and a grounded conductor does not pose a danger.

Wiring Near Compasses

Direct current flow through a wire produces a concentric magnetic field, which may disturb a nearby compass (Figure 6.6). The direction of the magnetic field changes with current direction, so twisting positive and negative conductor pairs negates the overall magnetic field. All conductor pairs within 24 inches of a compass should be twisted, unless they are coaxial.

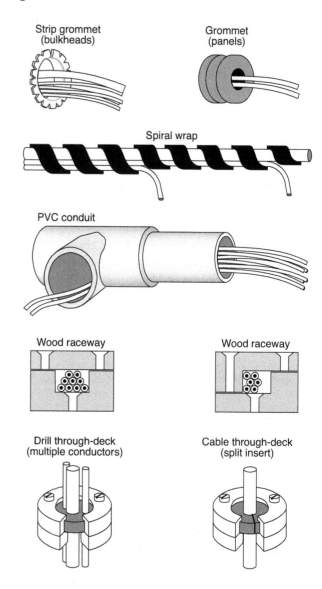

Fig. 6.5 Chafe Protection Material

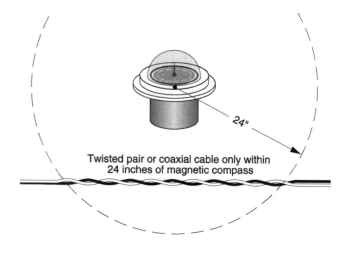

Fig. 6.6 Wiring Near Magnetic Compasses

Circuits That Require Protection

Distribution Panels and Switchboards

A distribution panel or switchboard (Figure 6.7) should be protected at its source of power (battery, battery switch, or starter solenoid) by either a fuse or a trip-free circuit breaker of capacity not exceeding the capacity of the panel or the ampacity of the feed conductors.

If there is also a sub-main fuse or breaker on the panel that does not exceed the panel or feeder ampacity, then the protection at the source of power may be rated up to 150% of the feeder capacity.

Circuits Branching from a Panel

Every ungrounded conductor originating in the panel (branch circuit) should be protected at its point of origin unless its rating is the same as that of the main or sub-main protection. The overcurrent protection rating should not exceed 150% of the conductor ampacity.

Except for engine-starter motors, all motors should be protected either internally or at the panel. The overcurrent protection rating should be low enough to prevent a fire, in the case of a stalled motor rotor, for up to 7 hours.

Fig. 6.7 Panelboard and Switchboard Overcurrent Protection

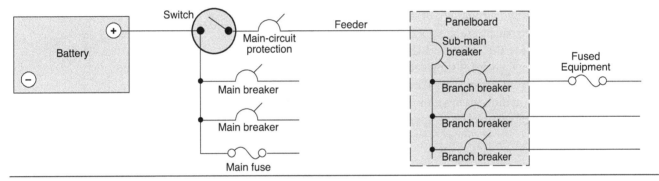

Unprotected Length Limits

Sources of power for positive-feed conductors can be a battery terminal, battery-select common terminal, or feed to the starter. The maximum allowed unprotected lengths of positive feeder conductors, as shown in Figure 6.8, are:

- Connected directly to a battery terminal—72 inches
- Connected to other than a battery terminal, but contained within a sheath or enclosure—40 inches
- All others—7 inches

Fig. 6.8 Maximum Unprotected Lengths for Positive Feeder Conductors

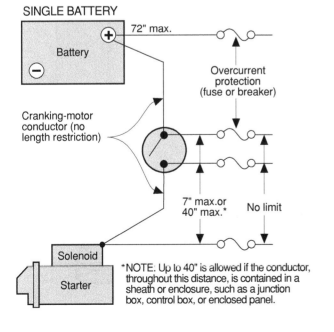

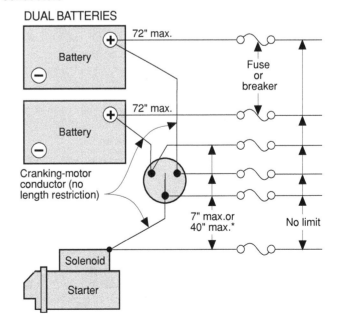

Overcurrent Protection

DC Circuit Breakers

As shown in Figure 6.7, by definition the first breaker or fuse in a circuit connected in series with the battery is considered to be the main circuit breaker or fuse. All other breakers or fuses in the circuit, including sub-main breakers and fuses, are considered to be branch circuit breakers and fuses. Note that breakers and fuses may be mixed in the same circuit. It is possible, for example, to use a main fuse ahead of a panel containing branch circuit breakers.

When installing a breaker panel, the breakers and panel should be from the same manufacturer to insure compatibility. Most manufacturers offer two sizes of breaker—small for up to 50 amps, and large for over 50 amps. Either size may be used for main or branch breakers, although many larger panels are designed to accept the larger size breaker for the main and the smaller breaker for the branches. Figure 6.9 shows the dimensions and available current ratings for Ancor brand breakers up to 50 amps and Blue Sea Systems (Bussman) surface-mount breakers rated up to 150 amps AC or DC.

Fuses

Figure 6.10 shows a wide variety of fuses for boats. The electronic types (AGC and AGU) are available from 0.25 to 30 amps, and the automotive types (ATC and ATM) are rated from 5 to 30 amps. Sea Fuses run from 100 to 300 amps, ANL ignition-protected fuses from 50 to 675 amps, and Class T fuses from 175 to 400 amps.

Fuses may be mounted in equipment, fuse blocks, distribution panels, and in-line fuse holders.

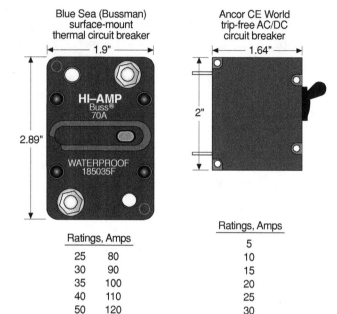

Fig. 6.9 Circuit Breakers

Ratings, Amps	
25	80
30	90
35	100
40	110
50	120
60	135
70	150

Ratings, Amps
5
10
15
20
25
30
40
50

Fig. 6.10 Common Marine Fuses and Fuse Blocks

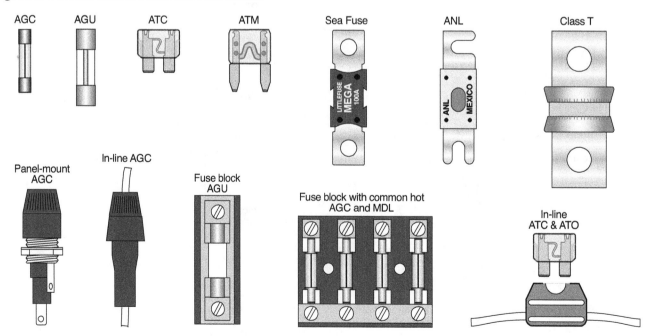

Tools

Most wiring failures occur at the connections. When copper corrodes it forms a layer of greenish copper oxide. Because it is thin, the oxide does little to the conductivity of the wire, but, because it is nonconductive, it forms a resistive barrier at surface-to-surface connections. Most remaining wiring failures are due to physical stresses on connections, such as engine vibration, or a pull on the conductor when an object or person accidentally strikes it.

Many boatowners spend as little as possible on specialized electrical tools. Instead, they attempt to make do with what they have. This is false economy. Although it is possible to make bad connections with good tools, it is virtually impossible to make good connections with bad tools.

Figure 6.11 shows a variety of specialized wiring tools. The cut, strip, and crimp tool should be your minimal investment. This tool is found in both hardware and electronics stores in a wide range of qualities. Two key considerations are:

1. The stripper holes should line up perfectly (try stripping a few wires before purchasing).
2. The tool should match the brand of terminals you will be crimping. Ideally you should be able to get both the crimp tool and connectors from the same manufacturer.

Professional electricians use ratcheting crimp tools. A single-crimp ratchet crimps just the barrel. A double-crimp ratchet crimps both the barrel and the sleeve. The advantage of the ratchet is that the tool will not release until the terminal has been crimped to the perfect degree. It is almost impossible to under- or over-crimp terminals designed for use with this tool.

Lugs are terminals for large conductors. The lug crimper in Figure 6.11 is actuated either by squeezing in a vise or by striking with a hammer.

Diagonal wire cutters ("diagonal pliers") distort the cut end, making it difficult to insert the wire into the proper size connector barrel. The wire and cable cutter shown shears the wire, resulting in cleaner cuts.

Most soldering problems are due to insufficient heat. It is better to get in and out quickly than to linger on a connector while the iron struggles to reach 400°F. The pocket-size butane soldering iron can produce all the heat you'll need, short of soldering battery lugs. It will burn for several hours on a filling and, best of all, free you from trailing cords.

Heated to 275 to 300°F, heat-shrink tubing shrinks to a third or less of its original diameter, gripping the conductor tightly. If the tubing contains adhesive, the melted adhesive seals out moisture and strengthens the connection at the same time.

Heat guns (not hair dryers) achieve temperatures in excess of 500°F and shrink the shrink tubing quickly.

Fig. 6.11 Special Tools for Wiring

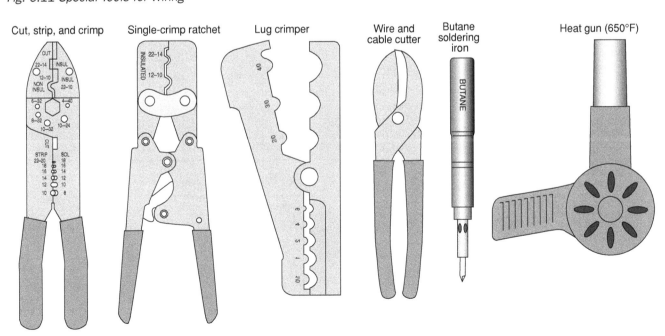

Cut, strip, and crimp   Single-crimp ratchet   Lug crimper   Wire and cable cutter   Butane soldering iron   Heat gun (650°F)

Conductor Connections

ABYC-Approved Connectors

Marine connectors differ from residential wiring connectors in being subject to vibration and other stresses. Figure 6.12 is self-explanatory and shows both approved and disapproved types of connectors. Note specifically that *the ubiquitous wire nut, so popular in household wiring, is not approved for marine use.*

Friction-type connectors (blade and bullet connectors, shown in Figure 6.12) can be used provided they resist a pull in the direction of the conductor of at least 6 pounds for 1 minute. The other connectors in Figure 6.12 must resist the tensile forces shown in Table 6.7 for at least 1 minute.

Solder

The use of solder in marine connections is controversial. Some experienced electricians feel that soldered connections are the most secure and best at eliminating terminal corrosion. Others point out that the solder in an overheated terminal may melt and allow the conductor to pull out of the terminal. A further problem is wicking of solder into the stranded conductor, resulting in a rigid portion that is liable to break like a solid conductor.

The ABYC states that solder should not be the sole means of mechanical connection in any circuit; the only exception is battery lugs with a solder-contact length of not less than 1.5 times the conductor diameter.

Solderless Heat-Shrink Connectors

Terminal systems are available that resolve all of the above problems (Figure 6.13). Although expensive (about twice the price of the usual automotive-grade materials), anything less in the hostile marine environment is false economy.

1. Pretinned, stranded conductors are available in all gauges and recommended colors. Pretinning (coating individual strands with solder) prevents oxidation of the strands, eliminates the need to cut a conductor back several inches when repairing, and facilitates soldering.
2. Heat-shrink tubing with adhesive coating, applied over both terminal and conductor, seals out moisture, makes the connection more secure, and insulates the terminal shank all at the same time. The shrink tubing may be purchased separately or already attached to terminals.

Fig. 6.12 Connectors for Marine Use

Splice	Butt	3-Way	Wire nut
Friction	Blade	Bullet or snap	
Terminals	Ring	Locking spade / Flanged spade	Plain spade
Set Screw		Indirect-bearing	Direct-bearing

Table 6.7 Tensile Test Values for Connections (Adapted from ABYC Standard E-11, Table XVI)

Conductor Size, AWG	Force, lb.	Conductor Size, AWG	Force, lb.
18	10	4	70
16	15	3	80
14	30	2	90
12	35	1	100
10	40	0	125
8	45	2/0	150
6	50	3/0	175
5	60	4/0	225

Fig. 6.13 Adhesive-Lined Heat-Shrink Tubing

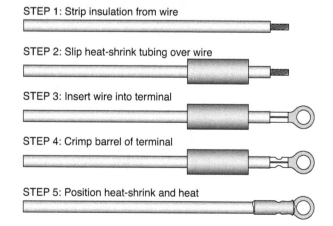

STEP 1: Strip insulation from wire

STEP 2: Slip heat-shrink tubing over wire

STEP 3: Insert wire into terminal

STEP 4: Crimp barrel of terminal

STEP 5: Position heat-shrink and heat

Other Termination Considerations

Figure 6.14 illustrates the remaining ABYC specifications for wiring connections:

1. The openings of ring and captive spade terminals should be of the same nominal size as the stud.
2. An extra length of conductor should be provided at terminations in order to relieve tension, permit fanning of multiple conductors, and allow for future repairs that might shorten the conductor.
3. Except for grounding conductors, terminal shanks should be insulated to prevent accidental shorting to adjacent terminals.
4. Connections should be in locations protected from weather or in weatherproof enclosures. If immersion is possible, connections should be watertight.
5. Terminal studs, nuts, and washers should be corrosion resistant and galvanically compatible with the conductor and terminal lug. Aluminum and unplated steel are unsuitable.
6. No more than four conductors should be attached to a single terminal stud. If necessary, two or more terminal studs may be connected by jumper straps.

Fig. 6.14 Proper Terminations

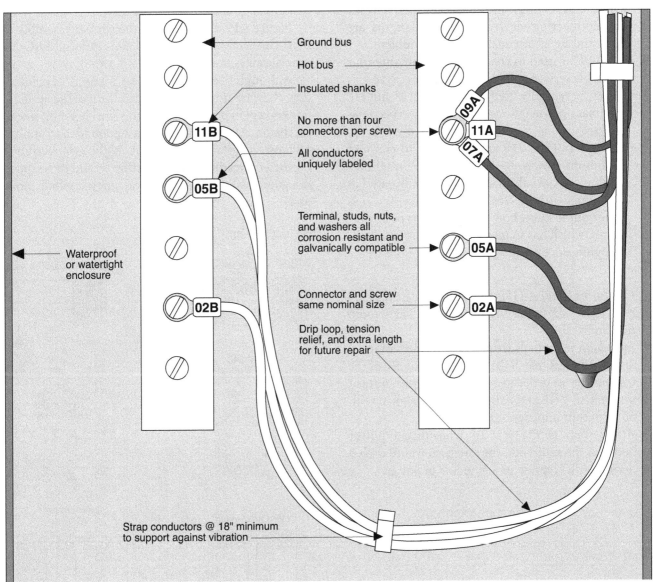

Conductor Connections

Coaxial Connectors

Coaxial cable consists of an insulated center conductor surrounded by a concentric (coaxial) grounded-shield conductor (either fine, braided strands or foil), all protected by an outer insulating jacket. Because the outer conductor (the shield) is grounded and completely surrounds the center conductor, coaxial cables neither radiate nor pick up much electrical noise. "Coax" is primarily used to connect antennas to electronic equipment, such as VHF and HF transceivers, and GPS receivers.

Like the wire used for DC wiring, coaxial cable for marine use should have pretinned, stranded center conductor and braid.

Table 6.8 lists the characteristics of five types of coaxial cable found on a boat:

- RG-58/U is very thin and is typically used only for interconnecting electronics where lengths are short and signal attenuation is not a problem.
- RG-59/U is used to connect television antennas and cable service.
- RG-8X is typically used to connect VHF and HF antennas up to lengths where attenuation becomes excessive.
- RG-8/U and RG-213 are both used to conduct maximum power to VHF and HF antennas. Marine coaxial cables are usually terminated at both ends with PL-259 8UHF connectors. It is important to know how to install this type of conductor, which has so many applications on a boat.

The significance of each of the specifications in the table is:

Conductor (size) AWG is important for heavy current flows, such as the output of SSB and ham radio transmitters.

Impedance is the high-frequency equivalent of resistance and must match the output impedance of the transmitter in order to achieve maximum output power. (All VHF and SSB radios are designed with 50 W output impedance.)

Attenuation is the loss of transmitted power between the radio and the antenna, where each 3 decibels (dB) represents a 50% loss of power.

Table 6.8 Coaxial Cables

Specification	RG-58/U	RG-59/U	RG-8X	RG-8/U	RG-213
Nominal O.D.	$\frac{3}{16}$"	$\frac{1}{4}$"	$\frac{1}{4}$"	$\frac{13}{32}$"	$\frac{13}{32}$"
Conductor AWG	#20	#23	#16	#13	#13
Impedance, ohms	50	75	50	52	50
Attenuation/100', dB					
@ 50 MHz	3.3	2.4	2.5	1.3	1.3
@ 100 MHz	4.9	3.4	3.7	1.9	1.9
@ 1,000 MHz	21.5	12.0	13.5	8.0	8.0

Figure 6.15 shows just a few of the UHF, VHF, and UHF/VHF coaxial adapters available from such sources as RadioShack.

Figure 6.16 shows the assembly of UHF connectors on both large and small coaxial cables.

Figure 6.17 demonstrates the similar assembly of BNC connectors on RG-58/U, RG-59/U, and RG-8X coaxial cables.

Although there are solderless versions of connectors, they are not recommended for marine applications except in protected locations (inside cabin) due to corrosion. After assembly, it is a good idea to apply a moisture-displacing lubricant. If the connection is exposed to weather, the connection should be wrapped in a good quality plastic electrical tape to exclude moisture.

Fig. 6.15 A Few Coaxial Adapters

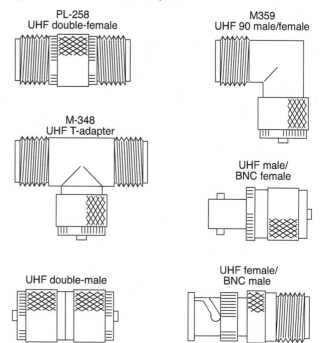

PL-258
UHF double-female

M359
UHF 90 male/female

M-348
UHF T-adapter

UHF male/
BNC female

UHF female/
BNC male

UHF double-male

Fig. 6.16 Assembly of PL-259 (UHF) Connectors

ON RG-58/U, RG-59/U, AND RG-8X CABLES

STEP 1: Slip on shell and adapter; strip outer jacket back 5/8"

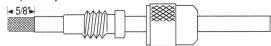

STEP 2: Bend back braided shield

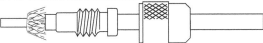

STEP 3: Slip adapter under braided shield

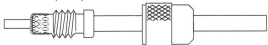

STEP 4: Strip center conductor 1/2" and tin

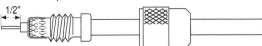

STEP 5: Screw on body and solder tip and braid through holes in body

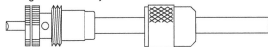

STEP 6: Screw shell onto body

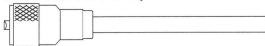

ON RG-8/U AND RG-213 CABLES

STEP 1: Slip on shell and strip to center of conductor and back 3/4"

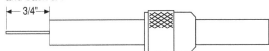

STEP 2: Strip outer jacket additional 5/16"

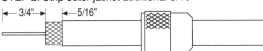

STEP 3: Slip on body, making sure shield does not contact center conductor, and solder tip and shield through holes

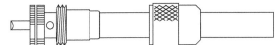

STEP 4: Screw shell onto body

Fig. 6.17 Assembly of BNC Connectors

ON RG-58/U, RG-59/U, AND RG-8X CABLES
FEMALE CONNECTOR

STEP 1: Cut cable end even and strip outer jacket back 5/16"

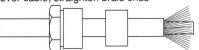

STEP 2: Slide clamp nut and pressure sleeve over cable; straighten braid ends

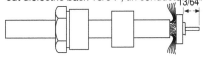

STEP 3: Fold braid back; insert ferrule inside braid; cut dielectric back 13/64"; tin conductor

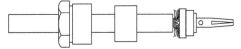

STEP 4: Trim excess braid; slide insulator over conductor into ferrule; slide female contact over conductor and solder

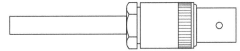

STEP 5: Slide body over ferrule and press all parts into body; screw in the nut tightly

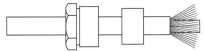

MALE CONNECTOR

STEP 1: Cut cable end even and strip outer jacket back 5/16"

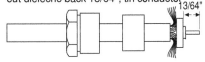

STEP 2: Slide clamp nut and pressure sleeve over cable; straighten braid ends

STEP 3: Fold braid back; insert ferrule inside braid; cut dielecric back 13/64"; tin conductor

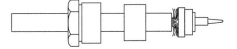

STEP 4: Trim excess braid; slide insulator over conductor into ferrule; slide male contact over conductor and solder

STEP 5: Slide body over ferrule and press all parts into body; screw in the nut tightly

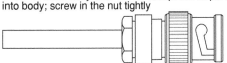

Ignition Protection

Gasoline and propane explosions are among the leading causes of marine loss of life. For this reason, the ABYC has adopted the ignition protection standards of the U.S. Coast Guard as described below.

Fuels

Boats using only diesel fuel are exempt. Boats using just a single LP (propane) or CNG appliance may exempt the gas appliance from the ignition protection standard provided:

1. Gas tank connections and regulators are outside of the hull or are located in an enclosure that is vapor-tight to the interior of the boat and vented overboard.
2. The gas supply can be shut off at the tank by a control that is part of or located near the appliance. Manual controls must provide a warning when the supply valve at the tank is open.

Boats using gasoline as a fuel for either propulsion or auxiliary generator are subject to the ignition protection standards shown here.

Isolation of Ignition Sources

Ignition sources located in the same spaces as gasoline engines, gasoline tanks, and gasoline fuel joints and fittings must be ignition-protected unless the components are *isolated* from the fuel sources. An electrical component is considered isolated from a fuel source if:

1. It is separated by a bulkhead of full width and height that leaks no more than ¼ ounce of water per hour with a water height of 12 inches or one-third the bulkhead height (whichever is less), and has no higher opening with greater than ¼-inch gap around its perimeter.
2. The electrical component is separated by a floor, deck, or other type of enclosure.
3. The distance between the electrical component and the fuel source is at least 2 feet, and the space between is open to the atmosphere, where "open" means 15 square inches of open area per cubic foot of net compartment volume.

Figures 6.18 through 6.24 illustrate these requirements for a variety of installations.

Fig. 6.18 Bulkheads (Adapted from ABYC Standard E-11, Figure 8)

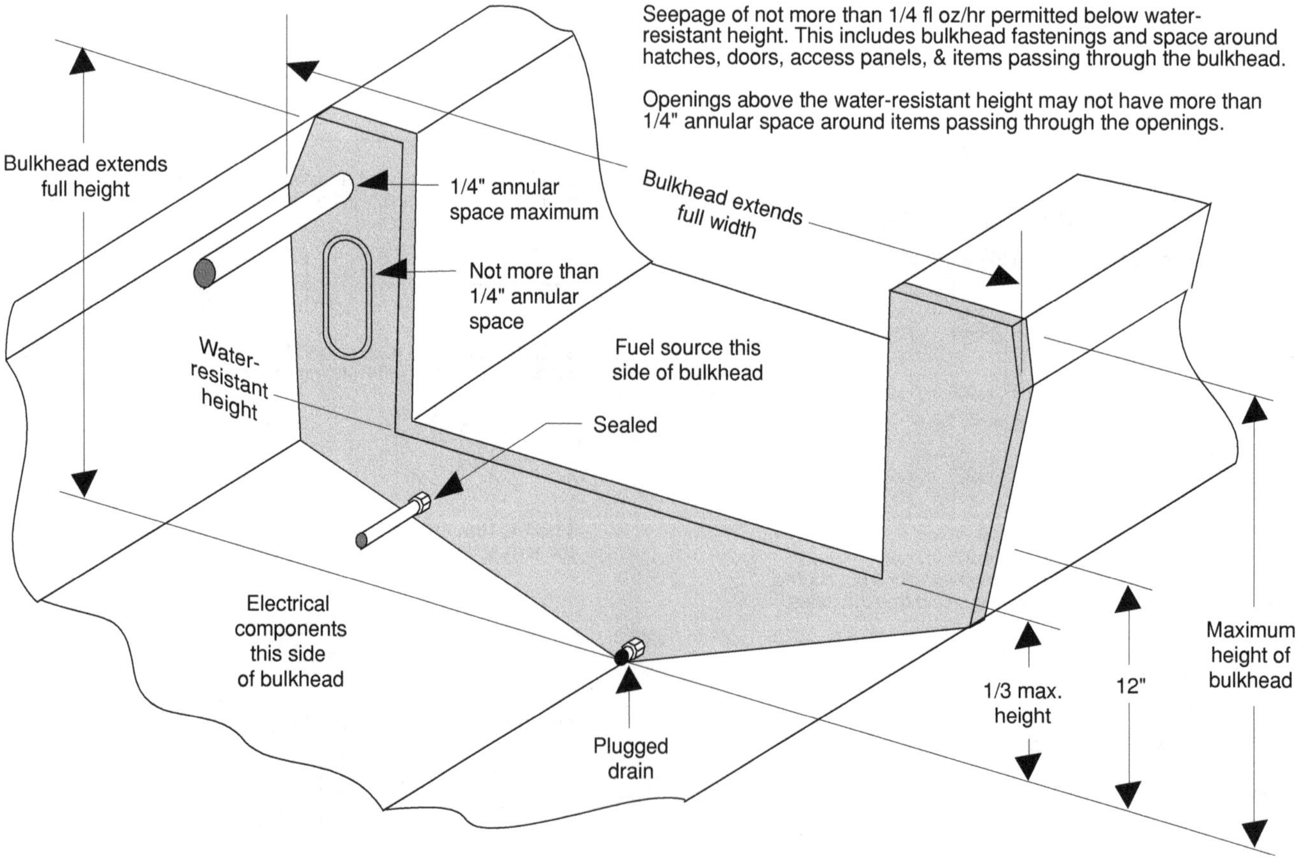

Seepage of not more than 1/4 fl oz/hr permitted below water-resistant height. This includes bulkhead fastenings and space around hatches, doors, access panels, & items passing through the bulkhead.

Openings above the water-resistant height may not have more than 1/4" annular space around items passing through the openings.

Bulkhead extends full height

1/4" annular space maximum

Bulkhead extends full width

Not more than 1/4" annular space

Water-resistant height

Fuel source this side of bulkhead

Sealed

Electrical components this side of bulkhead

Plugged drain

1/3 max. height

12"

Maximum height of bulkhead

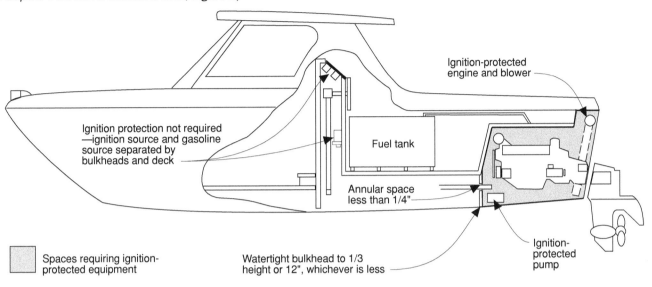

Fig. 6.19 Isolation of Ignition Sources
(Adapted from ABYC Standard E-11, Figure 1)

Ignition-protected engine and blower

Ignition protection not required —ignition source and gasoline source separated by bulkheads and deck

Fuel tank

Annular space less than 1/4"

Ignition-protected pump

Spaces requiring ignition-protected equipment

Watertight bulkhead to 1/3 height or 12", whichever is less

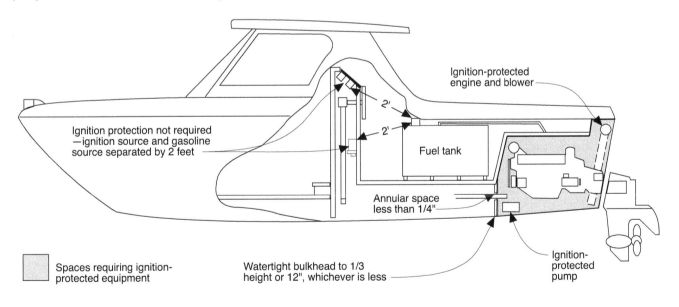

Fig. 6.20 Isolation of Ignition Sources
(Adapted from ABYC Standard E-11, Figure 2)

Ignition-protected engine and blower

Ignition protection not required —ignition source and gasoline source separated by 2 feet

2'

2'

Fuel tank

Annular space less than 1/4"

Ignition-protected pump

Spaces requiring ignition-protected equipment

Watertight bulkhead to 1/3 height or 12", whichever is less

Ignition Protection

Fig.6.21 Isolation of Ignition Sources
(Adapted from ABYC Standard E-11, Figure 5)

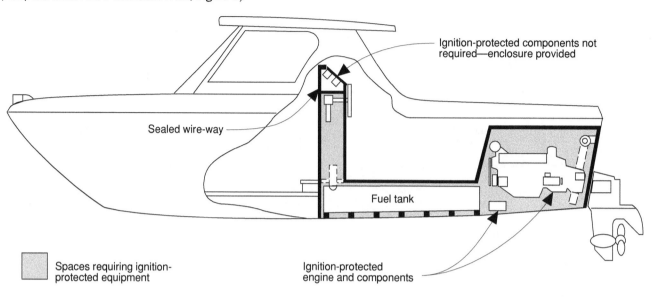

Ignition-protected components not required—enclosure provided

Sealed wire-way

Fuel tank

Spaces requiring ignition-protected equipment

Ignition-protected engine and components

Fig. 6.22 Isolation of Ignition Sources
(Adapted from ABYC Standard E-11, Figure 3)

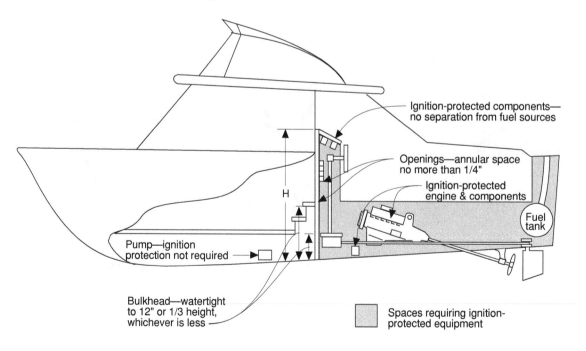

Ignition-protected components— no separation from fuel sources

Openings—annular space no more than 1/4"

Ignition-protected engine & components

Fuel tank

H

Pump—ignition protection not required

Bulkhead—watertight to 12" or 1/3 height, whichever is less

Spaces requiring ignition-protected equipment

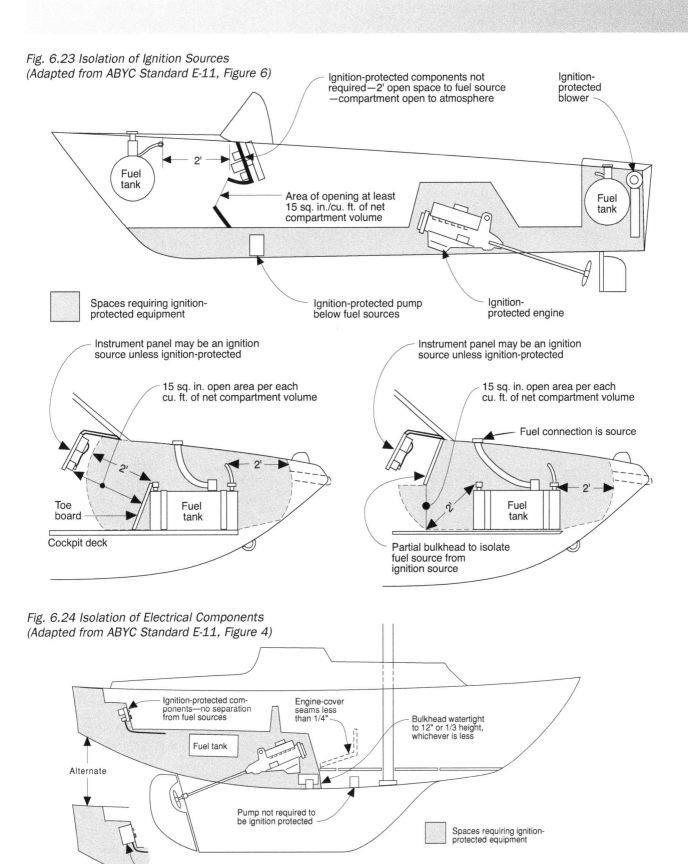

Fig. 6.23 Isolation of Ignition Sources
(Adapted from ABYC Standard E-11, Figure 6)

Ignition-protected components not required—2' open space to fuel source —compartment open to atmosphere

Ignition-protected blower

Fuel tank

Fuel tank

Area of opening at least 15 sq. in./cu. ft. of net compartment volume

Spaces requiring ignition-protected equipment

Ignition-protected pump below fuel sources

Ignition-protected engine

Instrument panel may be an ignition source unless ignition-protected

15 sq. in. open area per each cu. ft. of net compartment volume

Toe board

Fuel tank

Cockpit deck

Instrument panel may be an ignition source unless ignition-protected

15 sq. in. open area per each cu. ft. of net compartment volume

Fuel connection is source

Fuel tank

Partial bulkhead to isolate fuel source from ignition source

Fig. 6.24 Isolation of Electrical Components
(Adapted from ABYC Standard E-11, Figure 4)

Ignition-protected components—no separation from fuel sources

Engine-cover seams less than 1/4"

Bulkhead watertight to 12" or 1/3 height, whichever is less

Fuel tank

Alternate

Pump not required to be ignition protected

Spaces requiring ignition-protected equipment

Ignition protected components not required— enclosure must provide equivalent ignition protection

CHAPTER 7

AC Basics

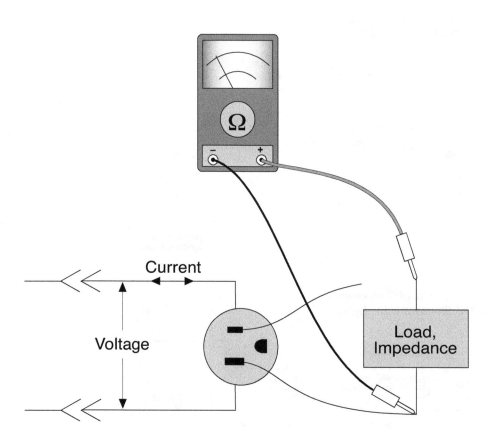

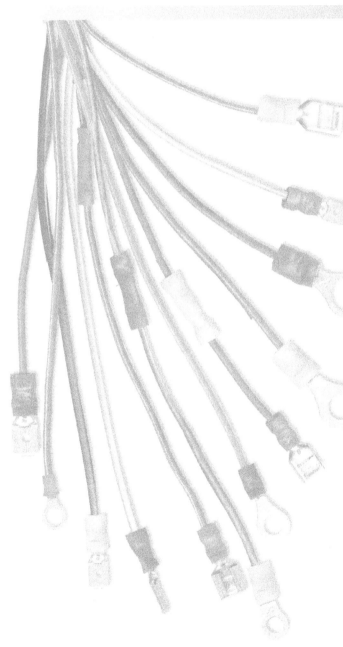

Boaters are increasingly demanding the convenience of onboard AC power. We are familiar with DC power from Chapters 1 through 6. Now we need to know how alternating current differs.

In the Will the Real Voltage Please Stand Up? section we see why 120-volt AC is variously called 110, 112, 115, 117, or even 125 volt, but in fact is none of the above!

We'll find that phase is as important as voltage and frequency. Some systems have only a single phase. Others utilize three separate phases and are called three-phase. Because voltage and current in a conductor may differ in phase, a concept termed the power factor is needed to calculate AC power.

AC safety is largely a function of grounding. Because mistaking a hot wire for a ground wire can prove fatal, conductor identification is extremely important. Even with proper conductor identification, however, we need ground fault devices to guard against breaks in the ground system.

AC is more flexible than DC because of the transformations we can achieve using (what else?) transformers.

As with DC, instruments for AC measurements permit troubleshooting AC circuits in order to uncover problems, including checking polarity of the incoming shore-power conductors.

Alternating Current

Alternating current electricity (AC) is easily understood once you have grasped the fundamentals of direct current electricity (DC). If you understand the relationships between voltage, current, and resistance in DC circuits, then you are ready for the very similar relationships in AC circuits. If you are unfamiliar with Ohm's Law, however, first review the DC concepts presented in Chapters 1 and 2.

Figure 4.2 showed us the output of a rotary current machine. Rotation of a magnet between coils of wire induces a sinusoidal current in the wire. Because the current alternates polarity, it is known as alternating current. If we used a meter to measure the voltage across, instead of current through, the coils, we would see that the voltage is of the same sinusoidal form as the current (Figure 7.1). All modern generators and alternators produce this sinusoidal current and voltage prior to rectification.

Fig. 7.1 Alternating Voltage/Current

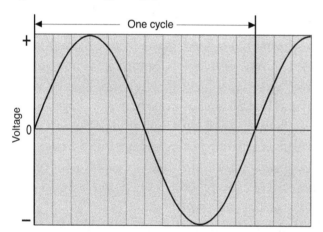

One full oscillation of voltage or current—plus, minus, and back to plus—is a cycle. The number of cycles completed in one second is the frequency. The unit of frequency (cycles per second) is Hertz, abbreviated Hz. Utility electricity in the United States is precisely regulated at 60 Hertz and in Europe at 50 Hertz. If you plugged a U.S.-built synchronous-motor electric clock into a European outlet, it would advance 50 minutes per hour instead of 60.

Many people still have not adopted the term Hertz, first introduced in the 1960s. They use the colloquial *cycles*, as in 60 cycles per second, instead of the proper 60 Hertz. Little harm is done, though, since everyone knows what is meant.

Will the Real Voltage Please Stand Up?

Read the labels on the under- or backside of your AC electric appliances, tools, and entertainment devices. Which is correct: 110, 112, 115, 117, 120, or 125 volts? There is no universal agreement as to standard AC voltage. Different utility companies aim at different nominal voltages. In addition, the voltage delivered to your home is likely to vary by a few volts, depending on the other loads in your neighborhood and the total load on the grid. In this book, we will adopt a nominal standard of 120 volts.

The first electric service supplied by utilities was in the form of 120 volts DC. The change to AC was made because AC power is easily transformed (by transformers) to higher voltage and correspondingly lower current. Since voltage drop in a wire is proportional to current and not voltage, greater voltage results in reduced loss in transmission. To take advantage of this fact, the power company distributes power over the grid at extremely high voltages (several hundred thousand), then transforms it down in progressive steps to the 120 volts AC that enters your home.

Electric lights, the first electric devices used in the home, work equally well on AC and DC, provided the power dissipated in the filament is the same. As we learned in Chapter 1, electrical power is the product of voltage and current,

$$P = V \times I$$

where: P = power consumption in watts
V = volts across the load
I = amps through the load

Using Ohm's Law, which works equally well for DC and AC with purely resistive loads, we can also express power as $P = V^2/R$. Since the resistance, R, of a lamp filament is purely resistive, equal AC and DC power dissipation reduces to:

$$(V_{DC}^2)_{ave} = (V_{AC}^2)_{ave}$$

In other words the average value of the squared AC voltage must equal the average value of the squared DC voltage.

It is easier to think in terms of equivalent DC voltage, so we say,

$$\text{Equivalent } V_{DC} = (V_{AC\ ave}^2)^{1/2}$$

The equivalent DC voltage is computed as the square root of the mean value of the squared AC voltage (the root mean square [RMS] value of the AC voltage).

In the case of a sinusoidal AC voltage, the peak AC voltage is simply $(2)^{1/2}$, or 1.414, times the equivalent DC voltage. As shown in Figure 7.2, the peak voltage of 120 volts AC is actually 1.414 × 120 volts = 170 volts.

Fig. 7.2 Peak and RMS (Effective) AC Voltages

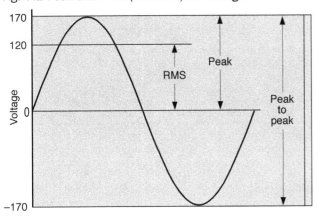

Phase

If you look at the wires coming into your home, you'll see three. Two are covered with heavy rubber insulation and are "hot." The third, forming a shield around the other two, is "neutral" and maintained at the electrical potential of the earth or ground.

If we plot the voltages between the three wires, they look as in Figure 7.3. Between wires A and C, we have 120 volts AC, just as in Figure 7.2. Between B and C, we also have 120 volts AC, but the polarity is opposite that of A and C. That is, when the voltage of wire A is at its maximum positive value, the voltage of wire B is at its maximum negative value.

If we ignore the neutral wire, C, and look at the instantaneous voltage between the two hot wires, A and B, we see it is the difference, or twice 120 volts AC.

Fig. 7.3 120/240 AC Voltages

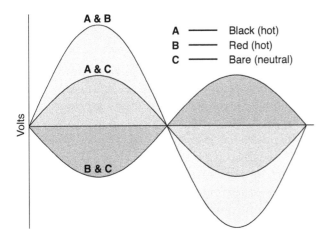

$$V_{AB} = V_A - V_B$$
$$= 120\ V_{AC} - (-120\ V_{AC})$$
$$= 240\ V_{AC}$$

Thus from the three incoming supply conductors, we actually derive three different voltage sources: 120 V_{AC}, 120 V_{AC}, and 240 V_{AC}.

The phase, Ø, of a sinusoidal wave is its horizontal position along the sinusoidal wave, as shown in Figure 7.4. Consider waveform A starting at the left. At Ø = 0°, the voltage is passing through 0 volts and rising. At Ø = 90°, the voltage is at its maximum positive value. At Ø = 180°, the voltage is zero again but decreasing. At Ø = 270°, the voltage is at its most negative value. Finally, at 360° the voltage has come full cycle.

This waveform is called single-phase (abbreviated as 1Ø) because, although changing, there is only one phase present at any time.

Figure 7.4 shows two additional waveforms, labeled B and C. Waveform B lags waveform A by 120°, while waveform C lags A by 240°. Where all three phases are present in the same voltage source (shore-power cable, generator output, distribution panel, etc.), the power is said to be three-phase or 3Ø.

Fig. 7.4 Three-Phase AC

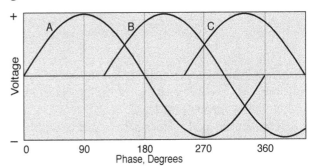

Using the same logic, the 120/240 volts AC power coming into your home (Figure 7.3) should be termed two-phase. For whatever reason, however, it is considered and termed single-phase.

Small boats with minimal AC equipment use only 120 VAC, 1Ø shore power, essentially that provided by a heavy-duty 120 VAC extension cord. Larger boats often use 120/240 VAC, 1Ø hookups to double the available power and to operate large appliances, such as electric ranges and water heaters. The largest boats may use 120/240 volts AC, 3Ø or 120/208 VAC, 3Ø hookups to increase the power even further in order to operate large appliances and take advantage of the higher efficiencies of 3Ø electric motors.

Power Factor

Figure 7.5 shows a simple AC circuit without the complications of a grounding wire. Until a load is plugged into the receptacle, the circuit from the hot (black) wire to the neutral (white) wire remains open. Although voltage exists between hot and neutral, no current flows because the circuit is not complete.

Fig. 7.5 A Simple AC Circuit

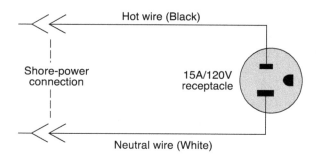

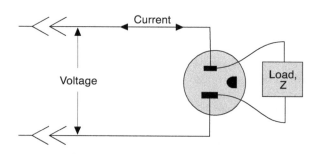

At the bottom we have plugged a load (a motor, for example) into the receptacle with a two-prong plug. Now current flows because the circuit has been closed, or completed, through the load.

Note that the load is labeled Z instead of R. Z is the symbol for *impedance*, the AC equivalent of resistance. Impedance consists of a combination of the load's DC resistance and its reactance (transient reaction to changing voltage). We won't go into the mathematics, but capacitors accept voltage changes readily, while inductors (coils) oppose voltage change. For this reason, the relationship between voltage and current in an AC circuit is not one to one, as it is in DC circuits, but is a function of frequency.

Figure 7.6 shows plots of both voltage and current in our AC motor circuit. In this example, the motor load possesses inductance, so the current lags behind the voltage by phase angle Ø. If the load were more capacitive than inductive, voltage would lag current, and Ø would be negative.

Fig. 7.6 Three-Phase AC

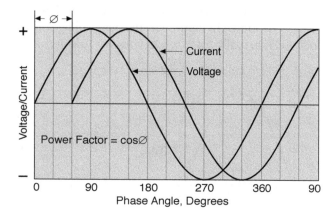

The relationship between voltage and current is usefully expressed by the load's power factor, PF.

$$PF = Watts / (Volts \times Amps)$$
where: Watts = true power consumed
Volts = measured volts
Amps = measured amps

Were the load purely resistive, voltage and current would be in phase, watts would equal volts times amps, and the power factor would be 1.0. Since the load has an inductive component, however, voltage and current are never simultaneously at their maximum values, so the true power (instantaneous product of voltage and current) is less than the maximum voltage times the maximum current, and the power factor is less than 1.0.

As shown in Figure 7.6, PF equals cos Ø, the cosine of the phase angle between voltage and current. For purely resistive loads such as incandescent lamps, Ø = 0°, so PF = 1.0. In the example shown, current lags behind voltage by 60° (Ø = 60°), so PF = cos 60° = 0.5.

The definition of PF can also be written as

$$Amps = Watts/(Volts \times PF)$$

The above equation indicates the problem with small PF. For the same wattage of useful power, halving PF doubles amps. Greater amps means larger supply conductors, greater voltage drops, greater resistive heating, and decreased efficiency.

The power factor of an electric motor can be very small when the rotor is stalled. As a result, locked-rotor and start-up currents can be three to five times normal running current, a factor which must be considered when protecting motor circuits.

Electricity is dangerous yet indispensable in our lives. Unfortunately the marine environment both worsens the hazards and degrades the materials. Understanding AC electricity and its effects on the body should convince you of the importance of AC wiring standards, such as those promoted by the ABYC.

The basic safety problem stems from the fact that the human body is an electrochemical/mechanical system. At the center of this system is an advanced computer—the brain. External stimuli are converted to electrical signals by transducers, such as the eyes (light to electricity), ears (sound to electricity) and nerves (touch and temperature to electricity). The electrical signals are conducted to the brain through nerve fibers acting much like conducting wires. The brain processes the incoming information and then sends out appropriate electrical signals in response. The most obvious effect of the outgoing signals is the stimulation and contraction of muscles. Herein lies the danger of externally applied electrical current.

Because the fluids in your body have the same approximate composition as salt water, your body has the same electrical conductivity. If you bridge an electrical circuit, you becomes a *part of that circuit*, and electric current flows through it. Muscles in your body, including your heart, cannot distinguish between electrical signals from the brain and the electric current we call a shock.

If you are fortunate, the involuntary muscle contraction propels you away from the source. A less fortunate reaction would be contraction of the muscles in the hand and a rigid grip on the source. Worst of all would be current through the chest and heart muscle, resulting in interruption of your heartbeat.

Figure 7.7 compares the dangers of various current paths through the body. The second panel shows a shock that, although painful and possibly resulting in a burn, is not usually life-threatening. Since both hot and neutral or ground conductors are in the same hand, current flow is limited to the hand muscles. Herein lies the danger of electrical shock.

The third figure explains why electricians often work with one hand in ticklish situations. If one hand were to contact a hot wire or case and the other hand a ground, the resulting current flow would be directly through the chest.

The bottom figure illustrates the second dangerous situation: contact with a hot wire or case while standing on a wet and conductive ground. The current flow is again directly through the chest and heart.

Fig. 7.7 The Dangers of Electrical Shock

Safe: Standing on nonconductive surface

Unpleasant: Hot and ground in same hand

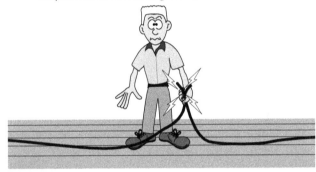

Lethal: Hot and ground in opposite hands

Lethal: Standing in/on conductive ground

Grounding

Figure 7.7 showed what happens when a person contacts a hot (live) wire or equipment case while standing on a grounded conductive surface. The body serves as a parallel return conductor to ground.

But who would ever grasp a hot wire? Figure 7.8, top, shows that it is not always necessary to touch a hot wire directly to receive a potentially lethal shock. The hot (black) and neutral (white) wires of the motor cord are intended to be isolated from each other and from the metal case. Unfortunately, through chafe or over-heating of its insulation, the hot wire has shorted to the motor case. Operation of the motor may be unaffected, but when you contact the case, the result is the same as touching the hot wire directly.

Figure 7.8, bottom, shows the solution: the green grounding wire, connected to the white neutral wire back at the power source, runs parallel to the neutral wire throughout the circuit. This green grounding wire is connected to the exterior metallic case of every electrical device. If the hot wire were to short to the case, the green grounding wire would offer the stray current a nearly zero-resistance return path to ground, thus preventing significant current through the more resistive human body.

If the short circuit from the hot conductor to the case were of low enough resistance, the short circuit current would blow the fuse or trip the circuit breaker in the black conductor. Even were the current insufficient to trip the breaker, however, the green wire would provide a low-resistance safety path. It should be obvious that this green grounding conductor should never be interrupted by a switch, fuse, or circuit breaker.

Fig. 7.8 The Green Grounding Wire

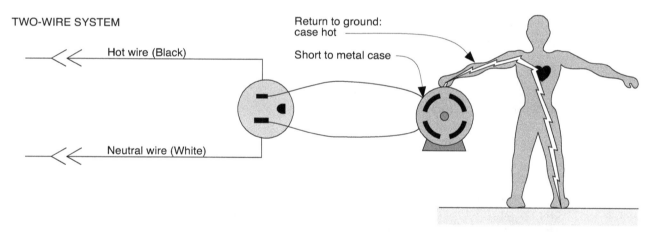

TWO-WIRE SYSTEM

Return to ground: case hot

Hot wire (Black)

Short to metal case

Neutral wire (White)

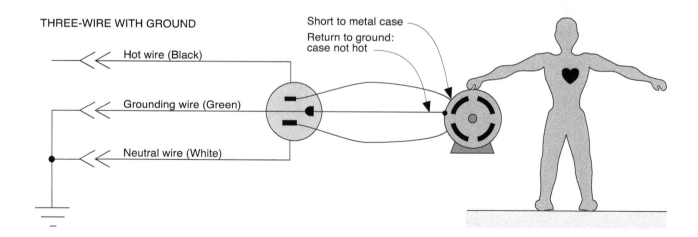

THREE-WIRE WITH GROUND

Short to metal case
Return to ground: case not hot

Hot wire (Black)

Grounding wire (Green)

Neutral wire (White)

With each conductor playing an assigned role in safety, it is critical that they not be accidentally confused and reversed. For that reason, the ABYC assigns specific colors to the insulation of each conductor in an AC circuit. Table 7.1 shows the color code for AC conductors. It is fortunate for those versed in residential wiring that the colors are the same.

Table 7.1 Color Code for AC Conductors

Source	Grounding	Neutral	Hot
120 V, 1Ø	green or bare	white	black
120/240 V, 1Ø	green or bare	white	black, red
120/240 V, 3Ø	green or bare	white	black, red, blue
120/208 V, 3Ø	green or bare	white	black, red, blue

To prevent accidental reversal of the conductors at plug and socket connections, both sockets and plugs are designed so that they can be connected in only one way, and each screw terminal is assigned a color matching its conductor.

Figure 7.9 shows the most familiar example: the 15 A/120 VAC polarized receptacle used in both residential and marine applications. Notice that the rectangular sockets and prongs are of different sizes. It is impossible to insert the mating polarized plug the wrong way and reverse the hot and neutral conductors. All screw terminals are color coded to insure proper installation. The terminal for the hot (black) conductor is darkest; the neutral (white) terminal is silver; the grounding (green) terminal is tinted green.

Fig. 7.9 Polarized 120 VAC Duplex Receptacle

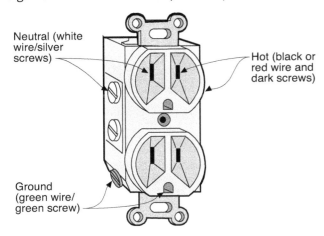

Added Safety: Ground Fault Devices

The green grounding conductor of Figure 7.8 goes a long way toward providing safety from electrocution,

but what if the green wire breaks, or the device is used on a two-wire extension cord with no grounding conductor? There are numerous ways that the purpose of the green wire can be circumvented. To protect against these accidents, an ingenious type of circuit breaker is recommended for all AC outlets located in head, galley, machinery space, or on deck.

Figure 7.10 demonstrates the operation of a ground fault circuit interrupter (GFCI). In a normally functioning AC circuit, current flow through the hot (black) and neutral (white) conductors is equal and opposite. The green grounding conductor is connected to the neutral conductor at the point of origin (the distribution panel), but not at the individual receptacles and devices. Thus, the green wire does not normally carry any current. Every electron flowing in the hot conductor is intended to be returned by the neutral conductor. Any difference in current between the hot and neutral conductors must, therefore, represent a stray (dangerous) current.

In the GFCI both hot and neutral conductors pass through a circular magnet. Current in the hot conductor induces a magnetic field in the magnet, but the equal and opposite current in the neutral conductor induces the opposite magnetic field. The net magnetic field is thus zero.

Fig. 7.10 Ground Fault Circuit Interrupter (GFCI)

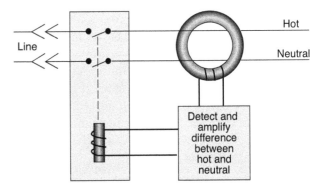

A difference in the two currents, however, produces a net magnetic field, which induces a current in the detecting coil. This current activates a solenoid that opens either the hot conductor (single-pole GFCI) or both hot and neutral conductors (double-pole GFCI). The Class A GFCI recommended for marine use opens on a current difference of only 0.005 amp—far less than a lethal current to humans. Although the sensitivity of these devices can be annoying when trying to establish a shore-power connection, it is better to be annoyed than dead.

Transformers

AC to AC

The great advantage of AC over DC power is the possibility of increasing and decreasing voltage simply.

Figure 7.11 shows a simple transformer. It consists of two insulated coils, both wound around the same iron core. AC current flowing in the input coil induces an alternating magnetic field in the core which, in turn, induces an AC current in the output coil. If the number of turns in the input and output coils are identical, output voltage is identical to input voltage. This transformer preserves the identity of the conductors and the phases of the input and output by tying the neutral conductors together. The green grounding wire is similarly uninterrupted and is bonded to the transformer case.

Figure 7.12 shows a step-down (voltage reducing) transformer. The number of turns in the output coil is less than the number of turns in the input coil. The voltage induced in the output coil is, therefore, less than the voltage in the input coil. (The ratio of voltages simply equals the ratio of turns.)

As with Figure 7.11 the identities of the input and output conductors and phases are preserved by tying the neutral conductors together. The green grounding wire is again bonded to the transformer case.

Figure 7.13 shows an isolation transformer. Here neither neutral nor grounding conductors are connected. The neutral (white) and grounding (green) conductors on the output side are connected, however, so that the transformer output acts as an independent electrical source, isolated from shore ground.

The green grounding wire from the shore-power side is connected to the shield between the input and output coils. Other common configurations include connection of the grounding wire to an inside case or to an outside case. In any case, follow the manufacturer's recommendation.

The isolation transformer is ideal for shore-power hookups because it interrupts the green grounding wire from the shore-power circuit, which might otherwise provide a path for stray corrosion currents between boats sharing the same shore-power circuit. Isolation transformers will be discussed further in Chapter 9.

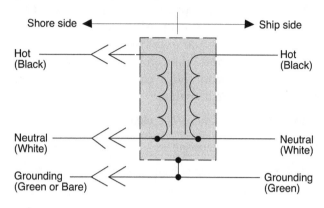

Fig. 7.11 A 1:1 Transformer

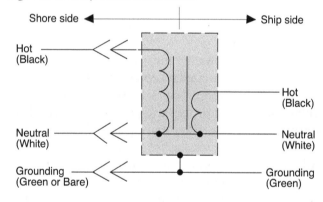

Fig. 7.12 A Step-Down Transformer

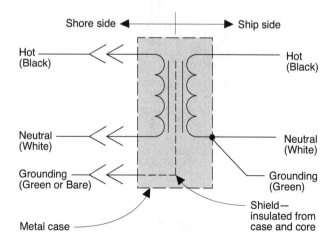

Fig. 7.13 An Isolation Transformer

Converting AC to DC

As we saw in Chapter 4, alternating current can be converted to direct current. In Figure 7.14, a diode in the output allows current to flow only in the direction of the symbolic arrow. As a result, the positive current half-waves are conducted while the negative half-waves are blocked. Although not constant, the output current never reverses polarity and is, thus, direct current.

The full-wave rectifier in Figure 7.15 employs a diode bridge of four interconnected diodes to conduct both positive and negative half-waves. During the positive current half-wave, the two diodes at the top conduct. During the negative current half-wave, the bottom two diodes conduct. Since the input and output coils are electrically isolated, both half-waves appear as positive when seen at the output.

The output voltages of both the half-wave and the full-wave rectifier still look to the eye more like alternating current than direct current, due to the extreme amount of ripple. The DC power supply in Figure 7.16 employs a large capacitor across the output to filter, or smooth, the pulses for a nearly ripple-free output.

The simple battery charger in Figure 7.17 uses the battery itself, instead of a capacitor, to smooth the ripple. As we saw in Chapter 4, the rectified output of an alternator is similarly smoothed by the large capacity of the battery it charges.

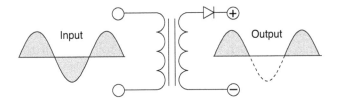

Fig. 7.14 The Half-Wave Rectifier

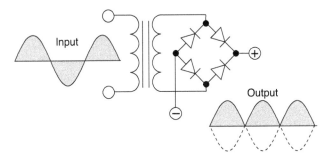

Fig. 7.15 The Full-Wave Rectifier

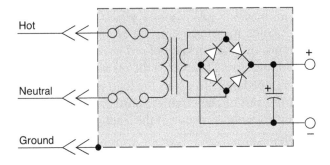

Fig. 7.16 A Filtered DC Power Supply

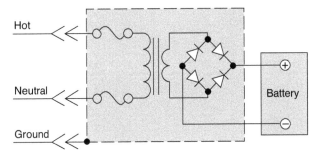

Fig. 7.17 A Battery Charger

AC Measurements

The common multimeter can be used for AC as well as DC measurements, although with fewer ranges and with reduced accuracy. Fortunately, accuracy is rarely of importance in AC measurements. While a difference of just 0.1 VDC represents about 10% of the capacity of a 12-volt battery, an acceptable range of shore-power voltage may be 110 to 125 volts AC.

AC Voltage

Figure 7.18 shows a multimeter being used to measure AC voltage. The meter employs the same internal circuitry to measure and display both AC and DC voltages, except that the AC voltage is first rectified by an internal diode bridge. In some multimeters the positive test lead must be switched to a separate AC jack that feeds the diode bridge. Attempting to measure AC volts on a DC volts setting will do no harm but will likely result in a reading of 0 volts, since the numerical average of AC voltage is zero.

AC Impedance

As we saw earlier, impedance may vary with frequency and, in the case of AC motors, with the speed of the motor. Such measurements are beyond the scope of this book and the pocketbooks of most boaters. What we can measure, however, is the resistive component of the impedance. To do so, the load must be isolated from the rest of the circuit as shown in Figure 7.19. Simply disconnecting one of the leads effects electrical isolation.

The resistance component of many AC loads is quite small, so be sure to zero the meter first by touching the test leads together and adjusting the zero-ohms knob. In digital multimeters zeroing is automatic.

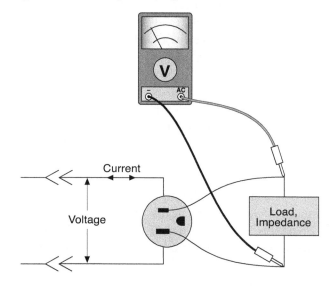

Fig. 7.18 Measuring AC Voltage

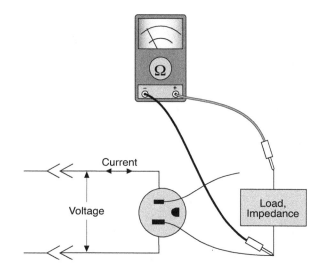

Fig. 7.19 Measuring the Resistive Component of Impedance

AC Amps

Inexpensive multimeters can measure up to 250 milliamps (0.25 amp) of AC current directly, as shown in Figure 7.20, top. To make the measurement, make sure the multimeter switches and leads are in the correct positions. Then disconnect the hot conductor from the load and insert the multimeter leads between the conductor and the load.

The trick employed in high-current ammeters can be used to measure AC currents greater than 0.25 amp. Figure 7.20, middle, shows a shunt inserted in the current-carrying conductor. A shunt is a low-ohm precision resistor that generates a voltage drop in accordance with Ohm's Law. Shunts are specified by the ratio of voltage drop across to the maximum current through the shunt. For example, a 50 mV per 100 A shunt is intended for currents of up to 100 amps and produces 50 millivolts across its terminals at full current. From Ohm's Law, we calculate the resistance of this shunt to be:

$$R = V/I$$
$$= 0.050 \text{ volt}/100 \text{ amps}$$
$$= 0.0005 \text{ ohm}$$

More expensive multimeters usually contain internal shunts allowing direct current AC measurements of up to 10 amps.

If your multimeter does not have this capability, or if you wish to measure currents greater than 10 A, you can purchase a 100 millivolts per 100 amps, 50 millivolts per 200 amps, or other shunt for less than the cost of another ammeter. You can then use your multimeter on a millivolts setting to read amps flowing through the shunt.

If you have money to spare, a more expensive, but less accurate, special-purpose AC meter employs a clamp that is placed around the hot conductor (Figure 7.20, bottom). The magnetic field around the conductor induces a current in the clamp. The current is then read as in any other type of test meter.

The advantage of the clamp-on meter is the ability to read current without disconnecting or cutting the conductor. A limitation is the requirement of physically separating the hot and neutral conductors. If both hot and neutral conductors are enclosed by the clamp, the opposing currents cancel so the meter reads zero.

A second disadvantage of the clamp-on meter is lack of sensitivity. While direct, in-line meters can measure microamps, the clamp-on meter is useful only down to milliamps.

Fig. 7.20 Measuring AC Currents

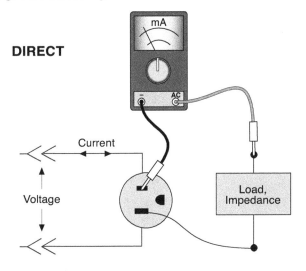

DIRECT

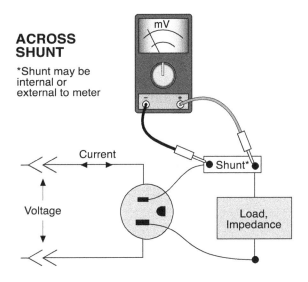

ACROSS SHUNT

Shunt may be internal or external to meter

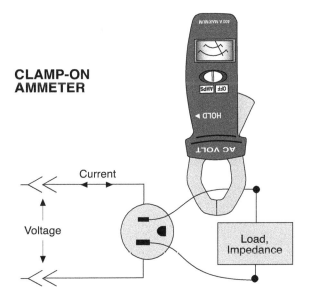

CLAMP-ON AMMETER

Troubleshooting AC Circuits

Testing an AC circuit is no more difficult than testing a DC circuit, provided you keep in mind the functions of each of the conductors in the circuit. To review the color code for AC conductors:

- Black conductors should be hot (120 VAC).
- Red (and blue if present) conductors should also be hot (120 VAC), but of different phase than the black conductors.
- White conductors should be at 0 volts relative to boat ground.
- Green or bare conductors should be at 0 volts relative to boat ground.

Figure 7.21 shows three receptacles representing the three different possible voltage sources in a 120/240 VAC system.

Set the meter to 250 VAC. At the left, insert the test probes in the two rectangular holes. Since the black conductor should be at 120 VAC and the white conductor at 0 VAC, the meter should display 120 VAC. If the meter reads zero, shift the probe from the larger rectangular socket to the U-shaped socket. If the meter now shows 120 VAC, there is a fault somewhere in the neutral conductor. If the meter still shows zero, the fault is likely in the hot conductor, including an open circuit breaker or fuse.

The test for the second circuit is identical to that for the first. Simply substitute red for black and repeat the tests.

At the right, we are testing the 240-volt leg of the 120/240-volt system. The meter is measuring the voltage difference between the two hot wires. Each hot wire should be at 120 volts, but opposite in polarity, so that the difference is 240 volts. If the meter displays zero, there is a fault in either the black or the red conductor. To discover which conductor is not working, shift one of the probes to the grounding socket. The meter should read 120 VAC. If not, the other (unshifted) probe is on the defective conductor.

Fig. 7.21 Troubleshooting AC Circuits with a Multimeter

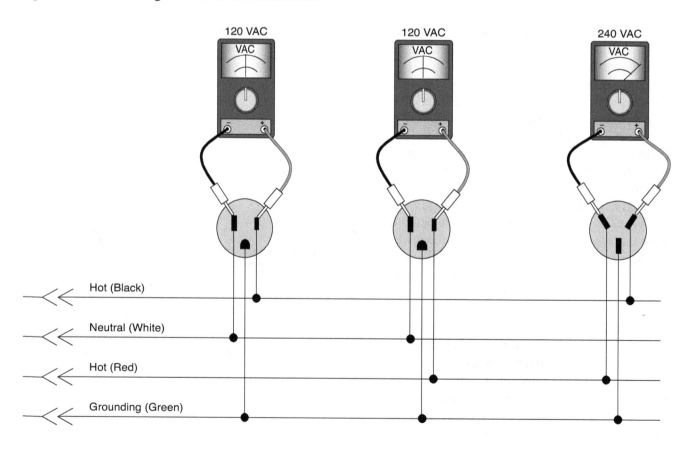

In spite of rigorous adherance to the color code, AC conductors can sometimes become switched. Most often the fault lies in a homemade shore-power cord where the mirror-image male and female plugs and receptacle patterns are easily confused.

Reverse polarity is a dangerous situation. The boat's ground is inadvertently raised to 120 VAC, *along with the seawater immediately surrounding the boat* via the bonding of underwater metal. A person swimming near the boat could be electrocuted.

Unfortunately, most AC electrical equipment will operate normally with reverse polarity. We need some way to test for proper polarity when establishing a shore-power connection.

Figure 7.22 shows how you can perform the test with a 120-volt lamp. The lamp should light whenever one of its leads is in the hot socket and the other in either the neutral or grounding socket. If the lamp lights when the leads are in the large rectangular and U-shaped sockets, then either the neutral or the grounding conductor is hot and the polarity is reversed. Fix the polarity immediately before someone is injured or electrocuted!

A proper shore-power hookup will have a reverse-polarity warning light in the AC-distribution panel (required by ABYC). If yours doesn't, you can install one as described in Chapter 14.

Alternatively, you can purchase a plug-in polarity tester at any hardware store for about $5. Plug it into an onboard AC receptacle each time you establish a shore-power connection. It may save someone's life.

Fig. 7.22 Testing the Polarity of an AC Circuit with a Lamp

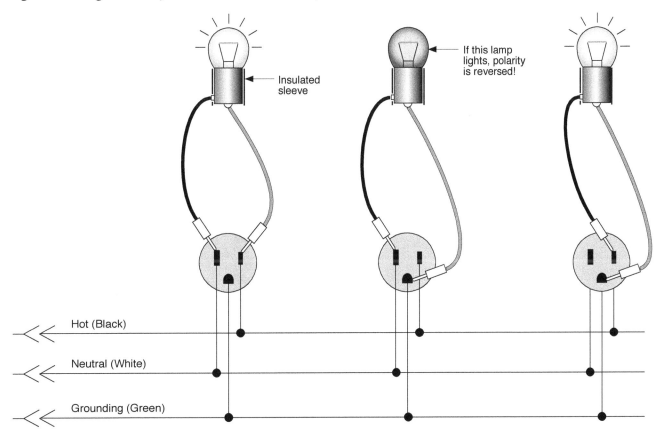

Insulated sleeve

If this lamp lights, polarity is reversed!

Hot (Black)

Neutral (White)

Grounding (Green)

CHAPTER 8

Inverters and Generators

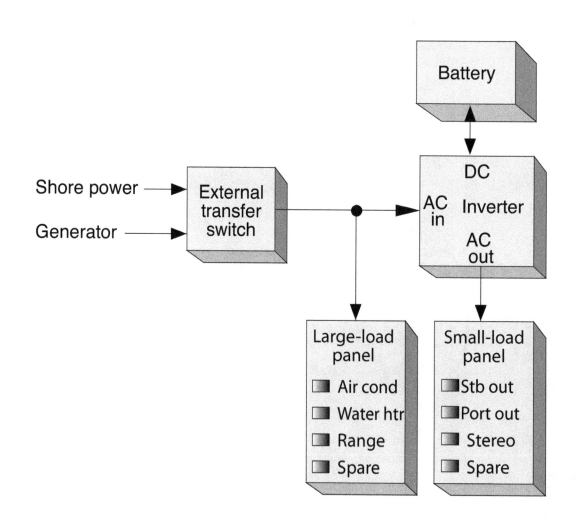

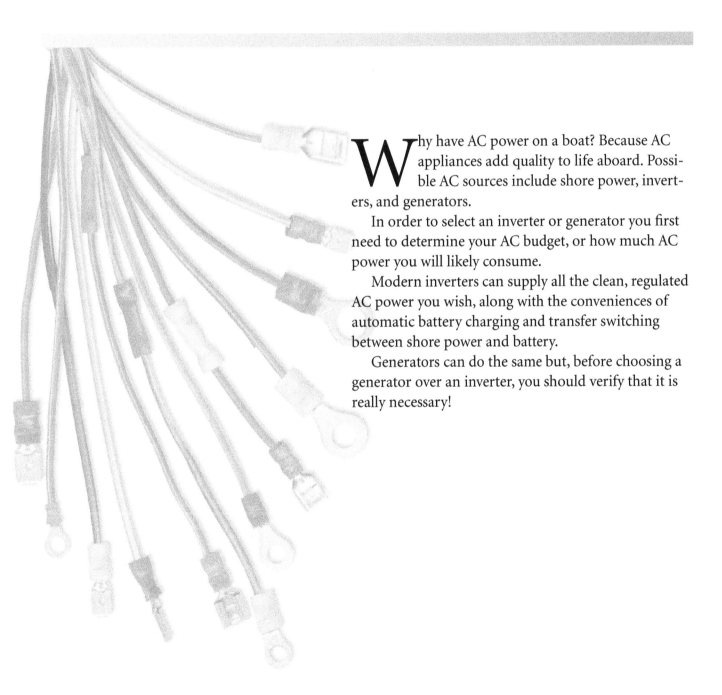

hy have AC power on a boat? Because AC appliances add quality to life aboard. Possible AC sources include shore power, inverters, and generators.

In order to select an inverter or generator you first need to determine your AC budget, or how much AC power you will likely consume.

Modern inverters can supply all the clean, regulated AC power you wish, along with the conveniences of automatic battery charging and transfer switching between shore power and battery.

Generators can do the same but, before choosing a generator over an inverter, you should verify that it is really necessary!

Why Have AC Power?

I was cruising the Bahamas a few years ago. There's not much radio or TV programming in the Bahamas so I, like most other cruisers (and Bahamians as well), was idly listening to other boaters' conversations on VHF.

Two women were chatting about the weather, their plans for the afternoon, etc. Suddenly one said, "Whoops, gotta go; the toast is up."

There was a long pause. Then, "You have a toaster?"

"Sure," said the other, "I have toast or an English muffin every morning."

Another long pause. Then, "I'm going to kill you."

My sentiments exactly. Though there is a certain pristine beauty in adherence to the old ways—reading by oil lamp, navigating by sextant, boiling coffee grounds in a pot—for most liveaboards the ascetic life wears thin after a season or two. Considering the high performance and low cost of modern inverters, the question should be, "Why *not* have AC on your boat?"

AC Versus DC

You've probably already experimented with one or more DC appliances. Your first galley appliance may have been the 12 VDC blender you saw in a marine catalog. Under the Christmas tree came the 12-volt hair dryer and coffee grinder. The first season, however, the blender screeched to a halt and the other two appliances melted in a cloud of smoke. You learned why the appliances in our homes run on 120 VAC, not 12 VDC.

You may also have noticed that the 12-volt blender, for which you paid $89.95, goes for $19.95 in its AC incarnation at Wal-Mart. Several generalizations can be made about DC versus AC appliances:

1. AC appliances cost much less because there are at least 1,000 times as many manufactured.
2. AC appliances last longer because they are designed to survive 20 years rather than a few seasons.
3. You can only get serious power (for toasters, microwaves, hair dryers) with AC.

There are also a few exceptions to the AC/DC rule. Nearly all electronic circuits run on DC. A piece of electronic equipment designed specifically for DC can eliminate the internal AC-to-DC power supply and actually be more efficient than its AC equivalent. The automobile CD player is the best example. Even with the biggest and best inverter or generator aboard, your stereo should be powered by DC, just like all of your navigation electronics.

AC Sources

You have three options for getting AC power:
- Shore power
- Diesel or gasoline generator
- DC-to-AC inverter

Shore Power

Shore power is the same power as in your home. Essentially, you connect your boat to the utility company via an extension cord. Unlike in your home, however, there are significant safeguards that should be installed to protect against dangerous shocks and stray-current corrosion of your boat's underwater metals. These installation safeguards are discussed in Chapter 9.

Generators

Generators can supply large currents—enough to power an electric range. Unless your boat is a 100-foot yacht with a soundproof engine room (not compartment), generators are too smelly and noisy to be run 24 hours per day. You may become immune to the noise, but boaters anchored near you in Paradise Lagoon will probably consider you an inconsiderate jerk.

If you really must have an electric range, water heater, and air conditioner at anchor or underway, install a generator, but concentrate the heavy loads for an hour in the morning and an hour in the evening. Smaller loads can be run off your batteries via an inverter.

Inverters

Inverters are silent sources of AC that draw battery power derived from the engine alternator, a generator, or wind, water, or solar chargers. Many modern inverters are designed specifically for marine or mobile use, are nearly 100% efficient, are better regulated in voltage than your local utility, and are capable of more sophisticated battery charging than stand-alone battery chargers.

If you spend much time dockside, you'll want a substantial shore-power hookup. Even if you spend most of the time anchored or moored, however, the cost of the most common hookup (30 A/120 VAC, 1Ø) is so small that you should install it anyway.

With an inverter, you'll be able to cast off the dock and shore-power lines and continue to use all of your small AC appliances without interruption.

If you have cloned your home with air conditioner, refrigerator, freezer, and electric range, however, you'll also need a substantial generator.

The first task is to determine how much AC power you will need. Table 8.1 lists the typical power consumptions of AC appliances and tools you may consider. The listed figures are representative and intended to be used for preliminary planning. If you already have the appliances, use their actual ratings instead.

On every tool and appliance is a nameplate listing its electrical consumption. The amps and watts shown are the maximum steady-state values at the specified voltages. Motor-driven devices often draw start-up currents several times larger than their nameplate ratings. This is usually of small concern with inverters and generators, since both are capable of surge currents far in excess of their continuous ratings. If your inverter or generator is sized to run within its steady-state capacity, it should have little trouble starting a motor.

To convert appliance ratings from amps to watts and vice versa, remember:

$$\text{Watts} = \text{Volts} \times \text{Amps}$$

Example: On the bottom of your toaster it says, "115 volt AC, 10 amps." First, ignore the fact that the voltage is listed as 115 (or 110 or 125) instead of 120. Although your toast will brown more quickly on 120 than 115 volts, the toaster will function on any voltage between 110 and 125 volts AC.

To convert from amps to watts we use the formula:

$$\begin{aligned} \text{Watts} &= \text{Volts} \times \text{Amps} \\ &= 115 \text{ volts} \times 10 \text{ amps} \\ &= 1{,}150 \text{ watts} \end{aligned}$$

The voltage of your onboard source may actually be 120 volts AC, in which case the toaster will draw slightly more than 10 amps and 1,150 watts, but we are just estimating our needs at this point.

Column 3 of Table 8.1 lists typical operating times for each appliance. You may not have a listed appliance, or you may have it but rarely use it. The figures in column 3 are suggested operating times in hours per day when applicable. These figures obviously depend on lifestyle. For example, the table lists 1.3 hours per day for a 1,500-watt water heater. A single-handed boater might halve the listed time, but a family with teenagers might quadruple the listed 1.3 hours.

After assembling your list of planned appliances, their rated wattages, and estimated hours of use, you are ready to compile your estimated daily electric load.

Table 8.2, on the next page, provides a blank form you can photocopy and complete to determine your typical daily consumption in watt-hours.

Table 8.1 Typical Appliance Power Consumption

Appliance	Typical Watts	Typical Hours Use Per Day
Air conditioner, 5,500 Btu/h	750	12
Air conditioner, 11,000 Btu/h	1,500	12
Blender	300	0.02
Broiler	1,400	0.25
Computer, desktop (w/o monitor)	60	2
Computer, laptop	60	2
Computer monitor, 17-inch CRT	65	2
Computer monitor, 15-inch LCD	30	2
Printer, inkjet	15	0.05
Printer, laser	800	0.05
Drill, ⅜-inch	350	0.02
Dryer, hair	1,200	0.05
Fan, 6-inch	25	8
Fan, 20-inch	250	8
Fry pan	1,200	0.25
Heater, space	1,200	12
Heater, water	1,500	1.3
Iron	1,100	0.15
Light	25–75	4
Microwave, 0.6 cu.ft.	800	0.15
Microwave, 1.5 cu.ft.	1,200	0.25
Mixer	240	0.05
Percolator	600	0.25
Range/element	1,200	1
Refrigerator, 6 cu. ft.	80	10
Refrigerator, 14 cu. ft.	140	10
Soldering iron	100	0.02
TV, 7-inch B&W	20	4
TV, 7-inch color	35	4
TV, 16-inch color	100	4
Toaster	1,100	0.15
VCR/DVD, play-only	20	2
VCR/DVD, play/record	80	2
Vacuum cleaner	800	0.05

Figuring Your AC Budget

Table 8.2 Daily Electrical Consumption

Appliance	Rated Watts	Typical Use, Hours/Day	Watt-Hours per Day[1]	Peak Watts	
				Inverter[2]	Generator[3]
		Totals			

[1] Watt-hours supplied by inverter.
[2] Peak watts supplied by inverter with generator off.
[3] Peak watts supplied by generator.

Tables 8.3 through 8.5 show example budgets of low, medium, and high AC-power use.

The low daily budget in Table 8.3 represents a traditional weekend cruiser with alcohol- or propane-fueled cooking, mechanical or 12-volt refrigeration, but 120-volt-AC entertainment.

This minimal budget requires an inverter with a maximum continuous rating of only about 500 watts, which draws about 35 Ah per day from the batteries.

Total battery consumption is 33 Ah (35 Ah considering inverter efficiency), plus the sum of the daily DC loads.

Table 8.3 Example of Low Daily Electrical Consumption

| Appliance | Rated Watts | Typical Use, Hours/Day | Watt-Hours per Day[1] | Peak Watts | |
				Inverter[2]	Generator[3]
Blender	300	0.02	6	300	—
Computer	100	2.00	200	100	—
Drill, ⅜-inch	350	0.02	7	—	—
Soldering iron	100	0.02	2	—	—
TV, 7-inch color	35	4.00	140	35	—
VCR/DVD	20	2.00	40	—	—
		Totals	395	435	
			(33 Ah)		

[1] Watt-hours supplied by inverter.
[2] Peak watts supplied by inverter with generator off.
[3] Peak watts supplied by generator.

The medium budget in Table 8.4 adds a small (0.6 cu. ft.) microwave, 120-volt-AC refrigerator, and hair dryer.

These significant additions require an inverter rated at about 1,300 watts continuous that draws about 125 Ah from the batteries. Since microwave use most often occurs in short bursts, and since inverters can put out much larger currents for short periods, a 1,000-watt continuous inverter would probably suffice.

Total battery drain consists of the 125 Ah inverter drain plus all DC loads.

Table 8.4 Example of Medium Daily Electrical Consumption

| Appliance | Rated Watts | Typical Use, Hours/Day | Watt-Hours per Day[1] | Peak Watts | |
				Inverter[2]	Generator[3]
Blender	300	0.02	6	300	—
Computer	100	2.00	200	100	—
Drill, ⅜-inch	350	0.02	7	—	—
Hair dryer	1,200	0.05	60	—	—
Microwave, small	800	0.15	120	800	—
Refrig., 6 cu. ft.	80	10.00	800	80	—
Soldering iron	100	0.02	2	—	—
TV, 7-inch color	35	4.00	140	35	—
VCR/DVD	20	2.00	40	—	—
		Totals	1,375	1,315	
			(115 Ah)		

[1] Watt-hours supplied by inverter.
[2] Peak watts supplied by inverter with generator off.
[3] Peak watts supplied by generator

Figuring Your AC Budget

The high budget shown in Table 8.5 includes all of the conveniences of the home. Demand in the evening is beyond the capability of standard inverters, so a generator is added to supply the largest loads, which are concentrated for an hour in the morning and an hour in the evening.

This large budget requires a 6-kilowatt generator during the hours of peak use and an inverter rated at about 3,000 watts continuous or more. Allowing for the efficiency of the inverter, the inverter alone draws about 280 Ah per day from the batteries.

Table 8.5 Example of High Daily Electrical Consumption

Appliance	Rated Watts	Typical Use, Hours/Day	Watt-Hours per Day[1]	Peak Watts Inverter[2]	Peak Watts Generator[3]
Air conditioner, 11,000 Btu/h	1,500	12.00	—	—	1,500
Blender	300	0.02	6	300	—
Computer	100	2.00	200	100	—
Drill, ⅜-inch	350	0.02	7	—	—
Hair dryer	1,200	0.05	60	1,200	1,200
Water heater	1,500	1.30	—	—	1,500
Lights	50–500	4.00	1,000	250	250
Microwave, large	1,200	0.25	—	—	1,200
Range element	1,200	1.00	—	1,200	—
Refrig., 14 cu. ft.	140	10.00	1,400	140	140
Soldering iron	100	0.02	2	—	—
TV, 19-inch color	100	4.00	400	100	100
VCR/DVD	20	2.00	40	20	20
Vacuum	800	0.05	40	—	—
		Totals	3,155 (263 Ah)	3,310	5,910

[1] Watt-hours supplied by inverter.
[2] Peak watts supplied by inverter with generator off.
[3] Peak watts supplied by generator.

How Inverters Work

Figure 8.1 shows, in simplified form, how an inverter transforms DC battery power into AC power. S_1, S_2, and S_3 are all solid-state transistors, which act as fast switches.

Fig. 8.1 Simplified Inverter Schematic

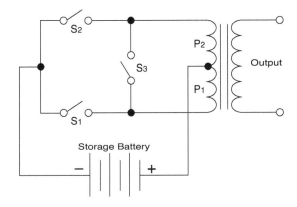

The sequence of electrical events for a single AC cycle is shown in Table 8.6. The actual circuitry is far more complex, but the switching sequence demonstrates the principle.

Table 8.6 Transistor Switching in an Inverter

S_1	S_2	S_3	Action	Result
Closed	Open	Open	12V applied to primary coil P_1	+ Output
Open	Open	Closed	primary shorted	0 Output
Open	Closed	Open	12V applied to primary coil P_2	– Output
Open	Open	Closed	primary shorted	0 Output

Figure 8.2 compares the outputs of three inverter types: square wave, pulse-width-modified sine wave, and pure sine wave. Note the differences in peak voltage for the nominal 120-volt AC waves.

The pulse-width-modified sine wave has two advantages over the square wave. First, it appears slightly more sinusoidal in shape to a load. Second, by varying the width of the output pulse, the average output voltage (area under the voltage curve) can be held constant as the input battery voltage and output peak voltage drop.

Square-wave inverters are notorious for causing 60 Hertz hum and interference. To the antenna or input transformer of a piece of sensitive electronic equip-

Fig. 8.2 Inverter Waveforms Compared

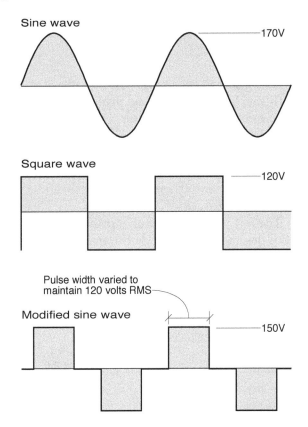

ment, the square wave appears to be a group of sinusoids at multiples of the fundamental 60 Hertz. Whether these higher-frequency components interfere depends a great deal on the quality of the equipment's grounding, shielding, and power-supply filtering.

High-quality, pulse-width-modified, sine-wave inverters emit less harmonic power but sometimes still cause difficulty in sensitive equipment. For zero interference and hum, pure-sine-wave inverters are available at significantly higher cost.

My experience in operating computers, GPS, VHF, SSB, and television receivers concurrently with a pulse-width-modified, sine-wave inverter is that the computer and GPS seemed unaffected, the television displayed minor interference patterns, and the transmissions of both VHF and SSB contained noticeable hum. I have not found the interference to be serious enough to install line filters, however.

Chapter 13 contains all of the information you require to filter the supply lines of affected equipment. If you are still concerned you can make your purchase of a pulse-width-modified, sine-wave inverter contingent on acceptable interference levels.

Inverters

Inverter Specifications

Table 8.7 lists the specifications of four popular inverters in a range of sizes.

Input Voltage

Most inverters accept a range of input voltage of about 10 to 15.5 volts DC. To avoid problems, you should make sure the voltage regulators of your engine alternator and solar and wind chargers are set to less than 15.5 volts, measured on the battery side of any isolation diodes. If you wish to bypass the regulators and equalize your batteries with a voltage greater than 15.5 volts, first turn the inverter off.

The low voltage cutoff of approximately 10 volts DC is designed to prevent destructive 100% discharge of the batteries. Some inverters sound an audible alarm before cutting off.

Output Voltage

The outputs of both Freedom inverters in Table 8.7 are pulse-width-modified sine waves, where the duration of the pulses are adjusted to produce a constant RMS (root mean square) voltage. The actual peak voltages corresponding to 120 volts AC RMS are as shown in Figure 8.2:

- Sine wave   170 volts
- Square wave   120 volts
- Modified sine wave   150 volts

Since the normal range of shore-power voltage is from 110 to 125, or 117 ±7% VAC, any regulation of 7% or better is acceptable.

The frequency regulation of most inverters is good enough to keep time by. The Freedoms' ±0.005% equates to ±4 seconds per day!

Table 8.7 Inverter Specifications

Specification	Prosine 2.0	Xantrex MS2000	Freedom Marine 10	Freedom Marine 25
Minimum input voltage, DC	10.0	10.0	10.0	10.0
Maximum input voltage, DC	16.0	15.5	15.5	15.5
Output waveform	true sine wave	true sine wave	modified sine wave	modified sine wave
Output voltage, AC	117	120	120	120
Output frequency, Hz	60	60	50 or 60	50 or 60
Frequency regulation, %	±0.05	±0.05	±0.005	±0.005
Output, continuous watts	2,000	2,000	1,000	2,500
30-minute watts	—	—	1,800	2,800
Surge watts (5 seconds)	4,500	5,000	3,000	5,200
Efficiency, peak, %	89	92	93	93
Efficiency, full load, %	81	87	85	87
Standby drain, searching, watts	2	14.4	1.5	1.5
Standby drain, inverting, watts	25	48	—	—
Battery charging current, amps	100	100	50	130
Battery charging stages	3 + manual equal.	3 + manual equal.	3 + manual equal.	3 + manual equal.
Weight, lb.	24	68	34	50
Transfer switch, AC amps	30	30	30	30
Optimal temperature range, °F	32–104	32–104	32–104	32–104

Output Power

When sizing an inverter, be careful. It was common practice in the past to define "continuous watts" as "continuous for up to 30 minutes"! For example, the maximum continuous output power of the older Heart EMS-1800 was not 1,800 watts, as you might assume, but 1,100 watts—40% less. The manufacturers no doubt reasoned that many of the larger inverter loads, such as microwaves, hair dryers, and clothes irons, lasted 30 minutes or less, so a 30-minute rating was appropriate. It may have been appropriate, but it was also misleading. Fortunately it appears that most manufacturers have now adopted a "continuous" continuous rating.

Figure 8.3 shows how the maximum output of the EMS-1800 varied with duration. The curve reflects the buildup of internal heat, not depletion of the battery, which is assumed to be a constant 13.0 volts DC. The output power versus time curves of all inverters are of similar shape.

Surge current is the momentary current drawn by electric motors at startup. As a rule of thumb, surge currents of inverters are approximately 250% of the continuous-rated currents. In fact, many manufacturers specify surge current in terms of the size of motor they will start.

Efficiency and Standby Power

The percentage of battery power converted to AC power depends on two factors:

- Efficiency is the percentage of power converted while the inverter is in operating mode
- Standby power is the drain on the battery while the inverter is in standby mode, waiting for a load to be connected

Pulse-width-modified, sine-wave inverters are typically extremely efficient at mid- to upper-output levels. Figure 8.4 shows efficiency versus output power for the Heart EMS-1800. Most inverters achieve efficiencies in excess of 90% over most of their output ranges. Efficiency drops dramatically, however, at very low power levels. For this reason, most inverters remain in standby mode (on, but not producing power) until they sense a significant load.

For Freedom inverters the minimum load required to trigger the "on" state is only 1.5 watts. Since the turn-on is instantaneous, the user is usually not aware of the standby mode unless the load is less than the trigger

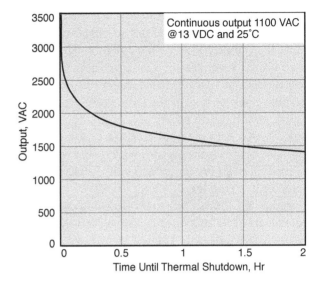

Fig. 8.3 Rated Output of Heart EMS-1800

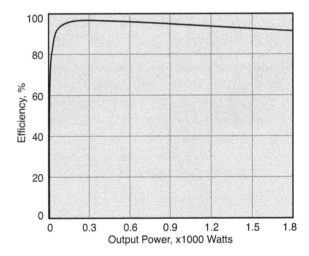

Fig. 8.4 Efficiency of Heart EMS-1800

level, as may be the case with a small nicad battery charger. To overcome the standby mode, I recharge several nicads at once.

The standby-drain specification is important because it results in a constant drain on the batteries. Freedom's 1.5 watts amounts to 3 Ah per day. With their more complex circuitry, pure-sine-wave inverters can draw an amp or more on standby, wasting at least 24 Ah per day. For example, the Xantrex MS2000 standby drain of 14.4 watts drains a hefty 28.8 Ah per day.

Inverters

Battery Charging

The most sophisticated inverters offer shore-power battery charging. In effect running backward, when external AC power is applied from either shore power or an onboard generator, a 30-amp internal transfer switch connects inverter loads directly to the external AC-power source and, at the same time, begins charging the battery. The battery-charging circuitry is as sophisticated as many multicycle stand-alone chargers costing nearly as much as the inverter. The economy is realized through the use of many of the same components for both modes.

Figure 8.5 shows the battery-charging cycles of the older Heart EMS-1800 inverter. More modern inverters are even more flexible, allowing operator choice of charging voltages, depending on the type of battery.

Bulk cycle. Assuming the battery is moderately discharged, the charging current of the EMS-1800 starts at 65 amps (100 amps for the EMS-2800). Charging current remains constant until the battery voltage reaches 13.0 volts. From 13.0 to 14.3 volts the charging current tapers from 65 amps to about half, or 30 amps.

Absorption cycle. During the absorption cycle, voltage is held constant at 14.3 volts, while the battery current acceptance drops from 30 amps to 10 amps. Referring to the recommended optimally fast charging routine for wet lead-acid batteries, shown in Figure 3.14 of Chapter 3, the 10-amp cutoff seems wise, corresponding to a 200 Ah battery (size 8D).

Float cycle. Once the current at 14.3 volts drops to 10 amps, the charger reverts to a float state, at a constant 13.3 volts. In the float state, the charger will provide up to its maximum output of 65 amps (100 amps for the EMS-2800) while maintaining 13.3 volts. Current demands over 65 amps are drawn from the battery.

Equalization cycle. As discussed earlier, the useful life of a battery can be increased by periodic equalization. Equalization consists of overcharging the battery, resulting in shedding of hardened lead sulfate from the plates. EMS inverters can be manually triggered after reaching the float state to maintain a constant 15.3 volts for 8 hours. They then revert to the float state at 13.3 volts. Note that sealed and gelled-electrolyte batteries should not be equalized because they cannot vent the generated hydrogen gas, and lost water cannot be replaced.

Fig. 8.5 Typical (Heart EMS-1800) Three-Stage Charging

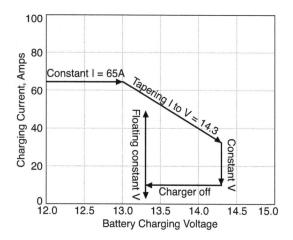

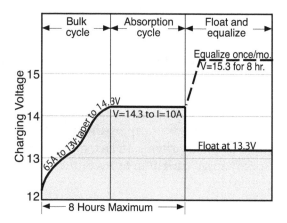

Many inverters offer a transfer switch either as standard equipment or as an option. An inverter transfer switch automatically switches boat AC loads to shore power or generator output when available, and back to the inverter output when the external source is removed. This is a great convenience on a boat that goes into and out of slips a great deal.

Boats with onboard generators require an additional transfer switch to select between shore power and generator output.

Figure 8.6 shows the internal configuration of a transfer switch. Input 1 is connected to AC source 1 (shore power, for example). Input 2 is connected to AC source 2 (internal connection to inverter output). With no AC at the terminals of input 1, power is routed from input 2 (inverter) to the output. When shore power appears at input 1, however, the solenoid pulls the switch up, and power is routed from input 1 to the output.

Operation of a shore-power/generator transfer switch can be either manual or similarly automatic.

Figure 8.7 shows the operation of an inverter with both an internal transfer switch and automatic battery charging.

With shore power on, the shore-power AC is connected to the AC output and the inverter is turned off. Simultaneously, AC power is applied to the inverter's built-in battery charger, which draws its power from the battery.

The inverter and battery combination thus operates as an "AC battery," supplying AC power when shore power is not available and recharging the batteries when it is.

Figure 8.8 shows the operation of a shore-power generator-inverter combination.

When shore power is available, the external transfer switch feeds shore power to both inverter and large-load panel. The inverter's transfer switch shunts the shore power through to the small-load panel and simultaneously charges the battery.

When shore power is not available, the external transfer switch selects the generator output, which is fed to both the inverter and the large-load panel. The inverter's internal transfer switch shunts generator power to the small-load panel and continues to charge the battery.

When neither shore power nor generator power is available, the inverter stops charging the battery and comes on to supply the small-load panel. In this mode there is no power at the large-load panel.

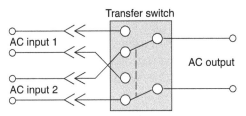

Fig. 8.6 A Transfer Switch

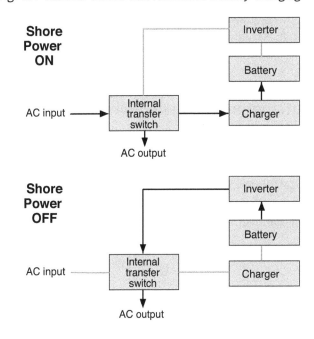

Fig. 8.7 Transfer Switch with Automatic Battery Charging

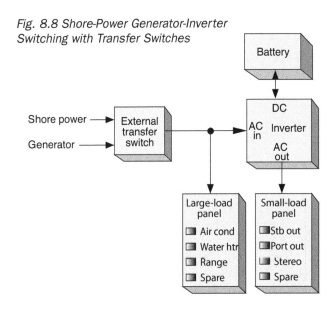

Fig. 8.8 Shore-Power Generator-Inverter Switching with Transfer Switches

Generators

Prior to the advent of efficient, low-cost, solid-state inverters, the generator was the only source of AC power away from the dock. Now, for loads up to about 2 kW, a combination of a large battery and inverter and a means for charging (such as engine alternator, solar panel, or wind machine) will produce AC power at half of the cost of power from the most economical generator. For loads greater than 2,000 watts there is still no substitute for a generator. For boats with large power budgets a generator-inverter combination is ideal. The two types of AC generator are:

1. Alternator-type, in which the output is generated by the stator.
2. Armature-type, in which the output is generated by the rotor.

Alternator-Type Generators

In an alternator-type generator the magnetic field is created by magnets and controlling field coils on the rotor. Output current is induced in fixed stator coils located around the inside of the case. In some genera-tors, the field current is generated through rectification of a portion of the AC output and fed to the rotor through brushes—just as in the automotive alternator. Most generators, however, are brushless. An exciter coil in the stator induces AC current in the rotor field coils, which is then rectified by a diode.

Figure 8.9 shows a simplified brushless alternator-type generator. There are two large windings that provide the main generator output. These may be in phase or out of phase. If in phase, there will be two 120-volt AC outputs. If out of phase, there will be two 120-volt AC outputs of opposite polarity, which can be combined for 240 volt AC. The small coil to the right provides excitation for the field coils of the rotor. The small coil to the left provides input to a bridge rectifier, which provides 12 volts DC for charging the generator's starting-motor battery.

Both main windings and the exciter winding are provided with multiple taps as shown at A, B, and C in Figure 8.9. Output voltage varies slightly with rpm and load, but the nominal voltage is changed by selecting different taps. Output frequency can be controlled only by adjusting engine rpm.

Fig. 8.9 Alternator-Type Generator

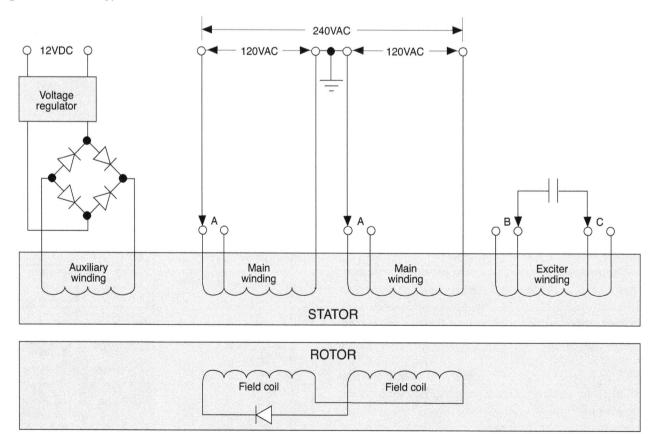

Armature-Type Generators

All generators and alternators rely on the fact that an electric current is induced in either a moving wire in a magnetic field or a stationary wire in a magnetic field that is changing in intensity.

In an armature-type generator, the magnetic field is created by a controlling field current flowing through fixed coils that are placed around the stator (stationary coil). The stator is anchored to the outside case of the generator.

Output current is induced in multiple coils wound on the rotor, which is driven at a constant 3,600 rpm (3,000 rpm in 50 Hz European models) by the speed governor of the generator's engine. Large-capacity slip rings and brushes transfer the large output currents from the moving rotor to the generator-output terminals. The output of the generator is sinusoidal in wave form.

The small DC field current is usually taken from a rectifier bridge connected across a pair of output terminals. To get around the chicken-or-egg dilemma of requiring a stator field in order to begin generating cur-

rent, the stator magnets are designed to retain a degree of permanent magnetism. A few generators solve the same problem by taking the current for the stator windings directly from the ship's batteries.

Generators with a single 120-volt AC output generally have two brushes, as shown in Figure 8.10. One brush/terminal is hot (black conductor); the other brush/terminal is neutral (white conductor) and is connected to the case of the generator and to ship's ground via the green grounding conductor. Note that single-voltage European versions produce 240 volts AC rather than 120 volts AC.

Generators having both 120-volt AC output and 240-volt AC output have either three or four brushes.

Figure 8.11 shows a four-brush generator. Brushes 2 and 3 (neutral) are tied together to the case and to ship's ground. Brushes 1 and 4 are hot. The voltages between brush 1 and neutral and between brush 4 and neutral are both 120 volts AC, but of opposite polarity. The voltage between brushes 1 and 4 is thus 240 volts AC.

Fig. 8.10 Two-Brush Armature Generator

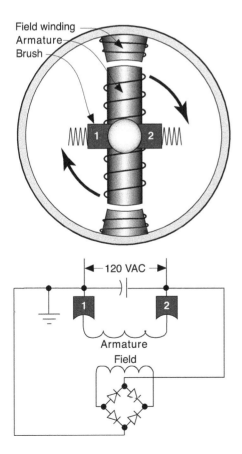

Fig. 8.11 Four-Brush Armature Generator

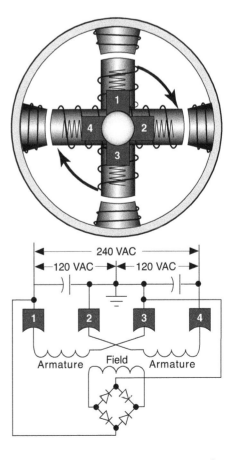

Generators

Frequency and Voltage Regulation

As you will see below, the output frequency of a generator is the key indicator of its proper operation. For this reason the importance of a frequency meter cannot be overstated. Most generators intended for permanent installation are equiped with frequency meters in their control panels, whether at the generator or in the AC distribution panel. If yours does not have such a meter, you can easily construct one from a 100-microamp panel meter and a handful of inexpensive components, as shown in Figure 8.12 and in Project 3, Chapter 14.

In a pinch you can press an old-fashioned synchronous electric clock into service. Such a clock advances in proportion to the frequency of its power supply: 60 minutes for 60 Hertz, 50 minutes for 50 Hertz, etc. Simply plug the clock into an outlet and let it run for an hour (as timed by your watch). At the end of the hour it will read the average frequency in minutes.

In both alternator- and armature-type generators, the output is taken from the output windings and thus corresponds directly with the rotation of the rotor. Frequency is therefore directly proportional to rpm. This is why fixed-drive generators cannot be driven directly by a boat's propulsion system. Hydraulic drives and variable-speed clutches are available for matching generator and propulsion engine, but they are not as popular as dedicated engines.

Engine rpm is controlled by a mechanical governor on the engine. As the engine slows under increasing load, a centrifugal weight acts to open the throttle. Mechanical governors require an rpm deviation in order to effect a throttle adjustment. The more fuel required, the larger the required deviation in rpm. Thus, generator frequency is necessarily affected by the load. Figure 8.13 shows the typical frequency versus load relationship.

Output voltage is affected by both engine rpm and output load. Since rpm is affected by load, we can think of output voltage as being affected by load. Figure 8.14 shows a typical 110- to 130-volt AC variation in output voltage from no load to full load. Voltages greater than 130 volts AC shorten the lives of resistive components, such as lamp filaments and heater elements. Low voltages cause motors to draw excessive currents and overheat, or not start at all.

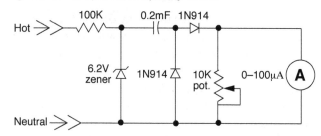

Fig. 8.12 A Simple AC-Frequency Meter

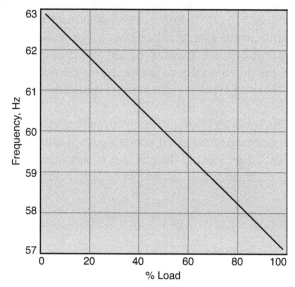

Fig. 8.13 Generator Frequency vs. Load

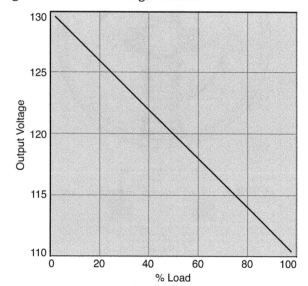

Fig. 8.14 Generator Voltage vs. Load

WARNING: The output terminals of a working generator are protected by neither a fuse, circuit breaker, nor ground fault circuit interrupter. At 120 or 240 volts AC, contact with a terminal and a grounded part of the vessel at the same time could be lethal. If you are not highly versed in dealing with generators, don't attempt measurements on the generator while it is running. As a further precaution, disable any remote-start circuitry.

The owner's manuals of high-quality generators usually contain extensive maintenance and troubleshooting guides for the specific model. If yours doesn't, purchase a copy of the shop manual, which will have the guides.

The troubleshooting guide included here is general and not intended to replace a manufacturer's guide.

Most generators have sealed bearings, which require no lubrication. This does not include the generator engine, which must be maintained to the same degree as the boat's propulsion engine. Crankcase oil should be changed every 100 hours of operation and just prior to any extended layup.

If the boat is in the north and the generator is not removed from the boat, the engine will require winterization, as well. If the engine is gasoline-fueled, the spark plugs should be replaced every year.

If the generator contains brushes, check the brushes for excessive wear (more than 50%) and the slip rings for burning and pitting. Replace worn brushes with exact replacements from the manufacturer and follow the directions for seating the new brushes.

The troubleshooting guide applies to both armature- and alternator-type generators. You will need to measure output AC volts, AC amps, and frequency. A proper generator installation should include AC volts, AC amps, and frequency panel meters in the AC distribution panel. For smaller generators use a multimeter to measure volts and amps. If you don't have a frequency meter, purchase one or build the one in Project 3, Chapter 14.

Troubleshooting Guide

Voltage Erratic

STEP 1. Check the brushes for wear. Replace if more than 50% worn.
STEP 2. Check slip rings for burning and/or pitting (requires services of a machine shop).

Voltage High (over 130 volts)

STEP 1. Check the frequency for normal range (57 to 63 Hertz).
STEP 2. Adjust the voltage regulator if possible.
STEP 3. Have the voltage regulator checked. Consult the manual for terminal changes.

Voltage Low (below 110 volts)

STEP 1. Check the voltage at the generator terminals. If OK, the problem is voltage drop in connectors or conductors.
STEP 2. If the voltage is OK initially, then drops, check the temperature of the voltage regulator. It should be cool enough to touch.
STEP 3. Adjust the voltage regulator if possible.
STEP 4. Consult manual for terminal change.

Frequency Erratic

STEP 1. Check for loads that cycle on and off.
STEP 2. If erratic with no load connected, check the engine governor.

Frequency High (over 63 Hertz)

STEP 1. Adjust the engine governor and clean and lubricate its linkage.
STEP 2. Consult the engine manual.

Frequency Low (below 57 Hertz)

STEP 1. Reduce the load. If frequency increases to normal range, the generator is overloaded.
STEP 2. Adjust engine governor and clean and lubricate linkage; consult manual.

CHAPTER 9

AC Standards
and Practices

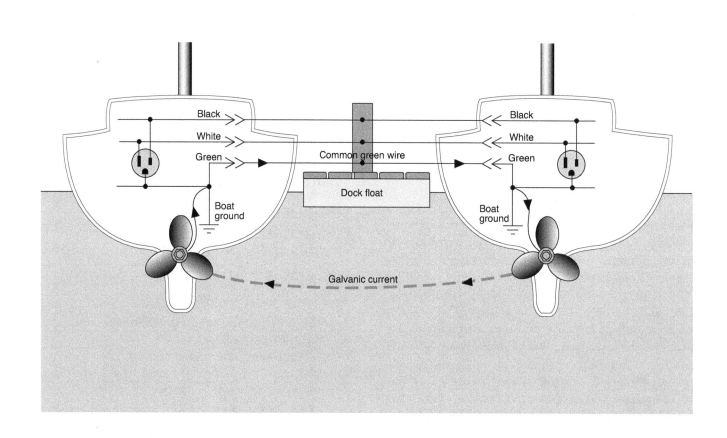

Black

White

Green

Common green wire

Dock float

Boat
ground

Galvanic current

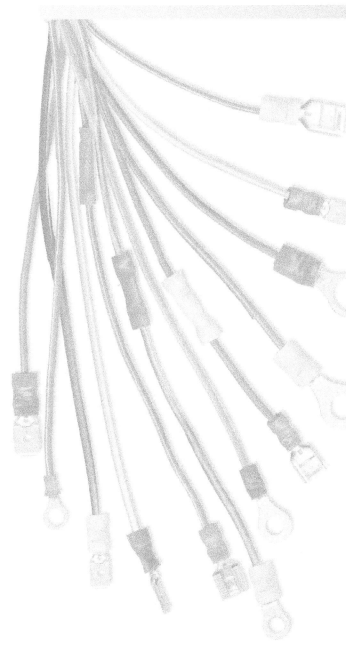

As with Chapter 6, its DC equivalent, this chapter is essentially an amplification of the ABYC standards for AC power aboard boats.

We start with sources of AC power: shore power, generators, and inverters, all of which feed the AC main panelboard.

Two primary AC safety considerations are grounding (including ground faults) and overcurrent protection.

Load calculations and ampacity tables allow us to size the overcurrent protection and to select both the approved wire and cable and receptacles for the application.

The probability of moisture, salt, and vibration, as well as the possibility of gasoline vapors, mandate standards for the installation of conductors.

As with DC wiring, the issue of galvanic protection and grounding raises the question of what to do with the green wire. The two solutions—isolating diodes and isolation transformers—are incorporated into ABYC-approved shore-power circuits.

Shore Power

The ABYC standards for AC electrical systems are designed to prevent electrical fires and shock. You should not assume that familiarity with residential wiring qualifies you to do marine wiring, however. Wiring standards for boats are more stringent than those for homes for three major reasons:

1. Boats sit in an electrically conductive medium.
2. Metal parts of boats, including electrical wiring and connections, are subject to corrosion.
3. Boats are subject to fatiguing vibration and impact.

A boat's source of AC may be shore power, an onboard generator, a DC-to-AC inverter, or a combination. The nature and operation of generators and inverters were covered in Chapter 8. The proper installation of the three sources is covered here.

Shore Power

Sooner or later someone will use the shore-power cable as a dockline, perhaps from grasping for the nearest object while headed for the water, or maybe someone forgot to unplug the power when getting underway. Plus, plugs and receptacles are subject to rain and spray from washdown hoses. For these reasons the ABYC standards for shore-power cables and inlets are rigorous.

The Boat Connection

The inlet on the boat end (Figure 9.1) must be a male connector. If in a location subject to rain, splash, or spray, it must be weatherproof, regardless of whether the cable is connected. If the location is subject to submersion, no matter how brief, the inlet must also be watertight—again, whether the cord is connected or not.

If the boat's AC system includes an isolation transformer or a galvanic isolator, the metal components of

Fig. 9.1 Shore-Power Boat Connection

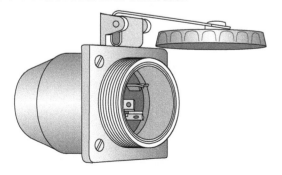

the inlet must be insulated from a metal hull or any metal parts connected to the boat's ground.

The Cable

Standards for shore-power cable are more stringent than those for cords you find in building supply outlets. The cable must be one of the types listed in Table 9.1.

Table 9.1 Shore-Power Cable

Type	Description	Temp. Rating
SOW	Hard-service cord, oil-resistant compound	60°C, 75°C
STW	Hard-service cord, thermoplastic	60°C, 75°C
STOW, SEOW	Hard-service cord, oil-resistant thermoplastic	60°C, 75°C
STOOW	Extra-hard-usage cord, oil-resistant thermoplastic	105°C

Current-carrying conductors (hot and neutral) must be sized for the capacity of the shore-power circuit, as shown in Table 9.2.

Table 9.2 Ampacity of AC Conductors

Conductor Size, AWG	Two Conductors[1] Maximum Amps	Three Conductors[2] Maximum Amps
14	18	15
12	25	20
10	30	25
8	40	35
6	55	45
4	70	60
2	95	80

[1] Not including the green grounding wire, which is considered non-conducting.
[2] For four to six conductors, reduce current rating a further 20%.

A green grounding wire is required in all shore-power cables, but since the grounding wire is considered normally non-current-carrying, it may be of smaller size than the current-carrying conductors. Commonly, it is one size smaller.

The shore end of the cable must have a locking and grounding cap with the proper male (plug) connector that matches the female shore receptacle (see Figure 9.2). The boat end of the cable must have a locking and grounding cap with the proper female (receptacle) connector to match the boat's male power inlet.

Figure 9.3 shows the boat and shore ends of a 30 A/120 VAC, 1Ø shore-power cable. The weatherproof sleeves slide over the connectors.

Fig. 9.2 Matching AC Plugs and Receptacles (U.S.)

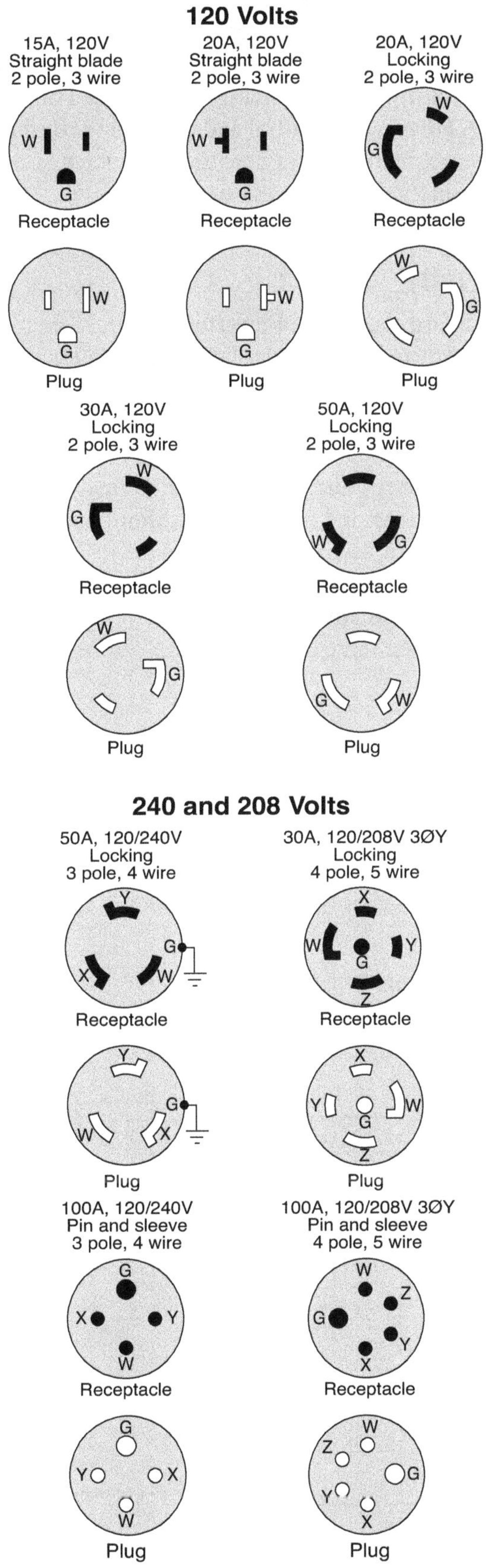

120 Volts

15A, 120V
Straight blade
2 pole, 3 wire

W [I] [I]
G
Receptacle

[I] [ ]W
G
Plug

20A, 120V
Straight blade
2 pole, 3 wire

W [⊢] [I]
G
Receptacle

[I] [⊢W]
G
Plug

20A, 120V
Locking
2 pole, 3 wire

W
G
Receptacle

W
G
Plug

30A, 120V
Locking
2 pole, 3 wire

W
G
Receptacle

W
G
Plug

50A, 120V
Locking
2 pole, 3 wire

W   G
Receptacle

G   W
Plug

240 and 208 Volts

50A, 120/240V
Locking
3 pole, 4 wire

Y
G
X   W
Receptacle

Y
G
W   X
Plug

30A, 120/208V 3ØY
Locking
4 pole, 5 wire

X
W   Y
G
Z
Receptacle

X
Y   W
G
Z
Plug

100A, 120/240V
Pin and sleeve
3 pole, 4 wire

G
X ● ● Y
W
Receptacle

G
Y ○ ○ X
W
Plug

100A, 120/208V 3ØY
Pin and sleeve
4 pole, 5 wire

W
Z
G ●
X
Y
Receptacle

W
Z ○ ○
○ G
Y ○ ○
X
Plug

Fig. 9.3 30 A/120 VAC Shore-Power Cable

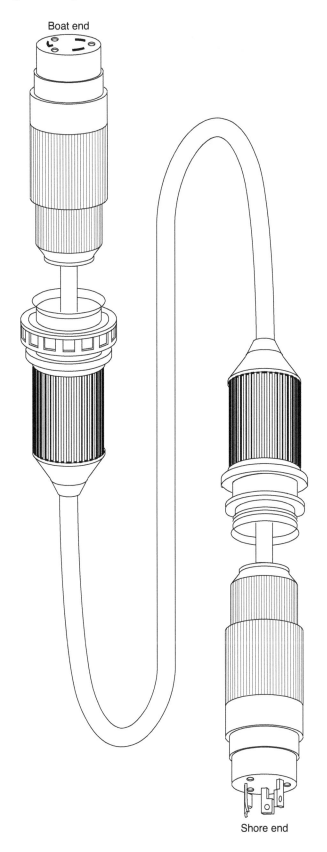

Boat end

Shore end

Generator and Inverter Sources

Transfer Switch

Connections to shore power, onboard generators, and inverters must be such that no more than one source can be connected to a circuit simultaneously. Switching between power sources must be made with a transfer switch, which prevents arc-over between the contacts of the different sources.

Grounded Neutral

Boat AC systems use a grounded neutral, as do residential systems. Where the neutral (white conductor) and grounding (green or bare conductor) are connected is critical. The neutral (white) must be grounded (connected to the green or bare conductor) *only at the power source:* an onboard generator or inverter, the secondary of an isolation or polarization transformer, or the shore-power receptacle.

Figure 9.4 shows a system consisting of shore power, onboard generator, and inverter. A two-pole transfer switch selects the power source. Note that the neutral (white) and grounding (green) wires are con-

nected at the generator, at the inverter, and (not shown) at the shore-end source.

A galvanic isolator serves to block stray current in the shore-power grounding wire. Thus, regardless of the source of power, the neutral is grounded only at its source. Further, the neutral and grounding conductors are always maintained at boat ground, which is critical for the safety of anyone on board.

Ampacity

An onboard generator or inverter must be rated to supply the entire load, as calculated later, unless the system is designed to isolate certain loads from connection.

In either case, the feed conductors from the generator or inverter must be of sufficient ampacity to carry the maximum rated output. In addition, the generator or inverter output must be protected at its output with an overcurrent device, rated at no more than 120% of the rated output, unless the generator or inverter is self-limiting to the same degree.

Fig. 9.4 Typical Use of the Transfer Switch

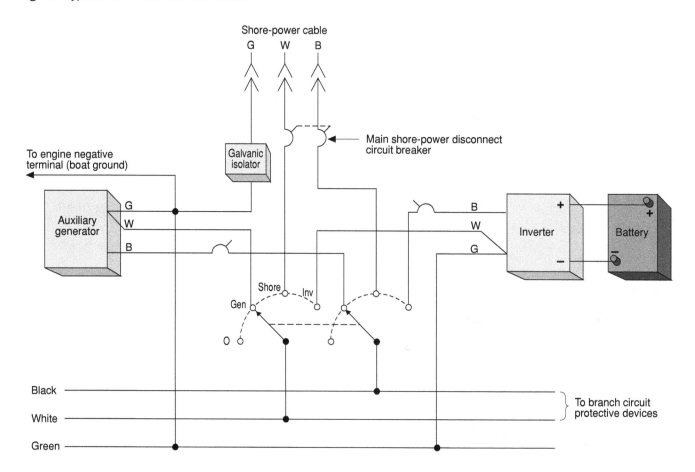

All AC systems must have a main panelboard, which may (it usually does) also serve as the AC distribution panel. The panelboard must be easily accessible and either weatherproof or in a location protected from the weather.

The panelboard must be clearly and permanently marked with the system voltage and frequency. Two common markings are "120VAC" and "120V-60Hz." If there are either AC motors or an AC generator aboard, the panelboard should also include an AC voltmeter. It is recommended that the voltmeter display upper and lower operating voltage limits.

The main panelboard should also contain a shore-power polarity indicator that warns of reversed polarity in the shore-power connection with either a continuous sound or light. A polarity indicator *must* be installed if:

1. Any of the boat's branch circuits have overcurrent protection in the ungrounded conductor only, or
2. Polarity is critical to the operation of any of the AC devices on the boat.

A polarity indicator is not needed, however, if the shore power feeds through an isolation transformer, since the transformer acts as a separate source of power on the boat, and its output conductors are permanently wired.

In order to limit current on the normally non-current-carrying green grounding wire, the impedance of polarity indication devices must be at least 25k ohms.

Figure 9.5 shows a simple polarity-indicating circuit that satisfies the 25k ohm criterion. A green light indicates correct polarity (voltage between the hot and neutral conductors). A red light indicates incorrect polarity (either neutral or grounding conductor hot).

Fig. 9.5 A Simple Polarity-Indicating Circuit (see Project 1, Chapter 14)

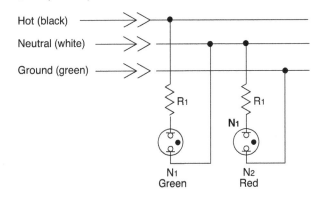

Plug-in polarity indicators, no larger than a three-prong adapter, are available at hardware stores for around $5. If your AC panel doesn't have a built-in polarity indicator, one of these devices can be used to quickly check for damaging reverse polarity when establishing a shore-power connection. Such a device does not satisfy the ABYC requirement, however.

A permanent waterproof warning placard must be displayed prominently at all shore-power inlets. Figure 9.6 shows the wording suggested by the ABYC.

Fig. 9.6 ABYC Suggested Wording for Shore-Power Connection

WARNING
To minimize shock and fire hazards:

1. Turn off the boat's shore connection switch before connecting or disconnecting shore cable.
2. **Connect** shore-power cable at the boat first.
3. If polarity warning indicator is activated, immediately disconnect cable.
4. **Disconnect** shore-power cable at shore outlet first.
5. Close shore-power inlet cover tightly.

DO NOT ALTER SHORE-POWER CABLE CONNECTORS

AC Load Calculations

Instructions

The ABYC suggests a method for determining the minimum sizes of AC panelboards, supply conductors, and AC power sources. The total load may be supplied by:

1. A single shore-power cable of required ampacity.
2. Multiple shore-power cables, provided each inlet is marked with volts, amps, phase (if 3Ø), and the load it serves.
3. One or more onboard generators of continuous rating equal to the load.
4. Shore power plus generators and inverters of combined capacity equal to the load, provided the loads connected to each are isolated.

Table 9.3 is a form that follows the ABYC-recommended procedure for calculating AC loads. As you read the instructions below, you may also find it helpful to refer to Table 9.5, the completed example.

Lighting and Small Appliances (Lines 1–7)

Lighting includes all AC-powered lights on the boat. Small appliances are those used in the galley and dining areas that have power cords and plugs, such as blenders, mixers, and toasters.

LINE 1. Add the total square feet of all of the living areas on the boat, not counting storage and engine spaces, and multiply by 2.0.

LINE 2. Multiply the number of 20-amp circuits used for small appliances in the galley and dining areas by 1,500.

LINE 3. Add Lines 1 and 2.

LINE 4. Subtract 2,000 from Line 3, and multiply by 0.35 (enter 0 if negative).

LINE 5. Add Lines 3 and 4.

LINE 6. Divide Line 5 by the system voltage (either 120 or 240).

LINE 7. If your shore-power inlet is 120 VAC, enter Line 6 in Column A. From this point on, use only the left-hand (Column A) lines. If instead you have a 240-volt AC system that splits into two onboard 120 VAC branches, enter half of Line 6 in Columns A and B. From this point on, you will have to enter values in Columns A and B separately, depending on which branch of the 240 circuit the load is on.

Motors and Heaters (Lines 8–12)

For Lines 8 through 27, you will need the amps listed on the nameplates of each piece of equipment. The nameplate is usually found on the backside of the equipment.

LINE 8. Add and enter the total amps for all fans.

LINE 9. Total the amps for all air conditioners. If there are two units, enter the larger number. If there are three or more units, multiply the total by 0.75. If the total is less than Line 10, leave Line 9 blank.

LINE 10. Total the amps for electric, gas, and oil heaters. If this total is less than the total in the previous step (before multiplying by 0.75), leave Line 10 blank.

LINE 11. Enter 25% of the nameplate amps for the largest motor in any of the appliances involved in Lines 8 through 10.

LINE 12. Enter total of Lines 8 through 11.

Fixed Appliances (Lines 13–28)

LINES 13–27. For each of the appliances shown, multiply the amps listed on the nameplates by the use factors listed after the appliance name. If the unit is a 240-volt appliance, enter the result in both Columns A and B.

LINE 28. Enter the total of Lines 13 through 27, but if there are more than three appliances listed in Lines 13 through 27, first multiply Line 28 by 0.6.

Free-Standing Range (Lines 29–31)

LINE 29. A free-standing range is one that contains both surface burners and an oven. First, read the watts listed on the range nameplate. Enter the corresponding "load watts" from Table 9.4.

LINE 30. Enter the range voltage (from the nameplate).

LINE 31. Divide Line 29 by Line 30 and enter value in both Columns A and B.

Total AC Load (Line 32)

LINE 32. Total Lines 7, 12, 28, and 31 separately for Columns A and B. The Total AC Load in Amps is the larger of A and B.

Table 9.3 ABYC AC Load Calculation Form

Line	Loads	Column A	Column B
LIGHTING AND SMALL APPLIANCES			
1.	Lighting and receptacles: Living area sq.ft. × 2	_____	_____
2.	Small appliances: number of 20-amp circuits × 1,500	_____	_____
3.	Line 1 + Line 2	_____	_____
4.	(Line 3 – 2,000) × 0.35 (Enter 0 if less than 0)	_____	_____
5.	Line 3 + Line 4	_____	_____
6.	Line 5/System voltage (either 120 or 240)	_____	_____
7.	If 120 VAC, enter Line 6 in Column A; if 240 VAC, enter 50% of Line 6 in both A and B	_____	_____
MOTORS AND HEATERS (total nameplate amps)			
8.	Exhaust and supply fans	_____	_____
9.	Air conditioners (If two, enter larger number; if three or more, enter 75% of total; omit if less than Line 10)	_____	_____
10.	Heaters (If two, enter larger number) (If figure is less than Line 9, enter 0)	_____	_____
11.	25% of largest motor in Lines 8–10	_____	_____
12.	Total of Lines 8–11	_____	_____
FIXED APPLIANCES (nameplate amps)			
13.	Disposal × 0.1	_____	_____
14.	Water heater × 1.0	_____	_____
15.	Wall oven × 0.75	_____	_____
16.	Stovetop cooking unit × 0.75	_____	_____
17.	Refrigerator × 1.0	_____	_____
18.	Freezer × 1.0	_____	_____
19.	Ice maker × 0.5	_____	_____
20.	Dishwasher × 0.25	_____	_____
21.	Clothes washer × 0.25	_____	_____
22.	Clothes dryer × 0.25	_____	_____
23.	Trash compactor × 0.1	_____	_____
24.	Air compresser × 0.1	_____	_____
25.	Battery charger × 1.0	_____	_____
26.	Vacuum system × 0.1	_____	_____
27.	Sum of other fixed appliances	_____	_____
28.	Total of Lines 13–27; if more than three fixed appliances, × 0.6	_____	_____
FREE-STANDING RANGE			
29.	Load watts from Table 9.4	_____	_____
30.	Nameplate volts (either 120 or 240)	_____	_____
31.	Line 29 divided by Line 30	_____	_____
32.	Sum of Lines 7, 12, 28, and 31; TOTAL is larger of A and B	_____	_____

AC Load Calculations

Example

Use Table 9.5 to calculate the 120 VAC load for a boat with 240 square feet of enclosed space (not including engine compartment or chain locker), one 20-amp small appliance circuit, and:

- 50-watt (0.4 amp) ventilation fan
- 1,500-watt (12 amp) water heater
- 85-watt (0.7 amp) refrigerator
- 120-watt (1 amp) air compressor
- 420-watt (3.5 amp) battery charger

Lighting and Small Appliances (Lines 1–7)

The lighting load is 2 × 240 square feet = 480 watts, which we enter on Line 1.

The small appliance load for one 20-amp circuit is 1 × 1,500 watts = 1,500 watts, which we enter on Line 2.

The sum of lines 1 and 2 is 1,980 watts, which is less than 2,000 watts, so we enter 1,980 watts on Line 3 and 0 watts on Line 4.

We divide 1,980 watts by 120 volts to get 16.5 amps. Since 120-volt shore power only has one branch, we enter the 16.5 amps on Line 7A.

Motors and Heaters (Lines 8–12)

We have only one motor—the 0.4-amp fan, which we enter on Line 8. Adding 25%, we get 0.5 amp, which we enter on Line 12A.

Fixed Appliances (Lines 13–28)

Our fixed appliances include the 12-amp water heater, 0.7-amp refrigerator, 3.5-amp battery charger, and 1-amp air compressor. The first three have a duty factor of 1.0, so we enter their amps directly. The compressor has a duty factor of only 0.10, so we enter 0.10 × 1.0 amp = 0.1 amp on Line 24A.

Adding Lines 13 through 27 we get 16.3 amps. Since there are more than three fixed appliances, we multiply the sum by the factor 0.60 and enter the result, 9.8, on Line 28.

Total AC Load (Line 32)

Adding Line 7 (16.5 amps), Line 12 (0.5 amp), Line 28 (9.8 amps), and Line 31 (0.0 amps), we get 26.8 amps. Since our system has only a single phase and, thus, a single branch, our total AC load for sizing the main AC panelboard is 26.8 amps. Rounding up, we'll call it 30 amps.

Table 9.4 Load Watts for Free-Standing Ranges (For use in Table 9.5, Line 29)

Nameplate Watts	Load Watts
0–10,000	80%
10,001–12,500	8,000
12,501–13,500	8,400
13,501–14,500	8,800
14,501–15,500	9,200
15,501–16,500	9,600

Table 9.5 ABYC AC Load Calculation Form (filled-out example)

Line	Loads	Column A	Column B
LIGHTING AND SMALL APPLIANCES			
1.	Lighting and receptacles: Living area sq.ft. × 2	480	
2.	Small appliances: number of 20-amp circuits × 1,500	1500	
3.	Line 1 + Line 2	1980	
4.	(Line 3 − 2,000) × 0.35 (Enter 0 if less than 0)	0	
5.	Line 3 + Line 4	1980	
6.	Line 5/System voltage (either 120 or 240)	16.5	
7.	If 120 VAC, enter Line 6 in Column A; if 240 VAC, enter 50% of Line 6 in both A and B	16.5	
MOTORS AND HEATERS (total nameplate amps)			
8.	Exhaust and supply fans	0.4	
9.	Air conditioners (If two, enter larger number; if three or more, enter 75% of total; omit if less than Line 10)		
10.	Heaters (If two, enter larger number) (If figure is less than Line 9, enter 0)		
11.	25% of largest motor in Lines 8–10	0.1	
12.	Total of Lines 8–11	0.5	
FIXED APPLIANCES (nameplate amps)			
13.	Disposal × 0.1		
14.	Water heater × 1.0	12.0	
15.	Wall oven × 0.75		
16.	Stovetop cooking unit × 0.75		
17.	Refrigerator × 1.0	0.7	
18.	Freezer × 1.0		
19.	Ice maker × 0.5		
20.	Dishwasher × 0.25		
21.	Clothes washer × 0.25		
22.	Clothes dryer × 0.25		
23.	Trash compactor × 0.1		
24.	Air compresser × 0.1	0.1	
25.	Battery charger × 1.0	3.5	
26.	Vacuum system × 0.1		
27.	Sum of other fixed appliances		
28.	Total of Lines 13–27; if more than three fixed appliances, × 0.6	9.8	
FREE-STANDING RANGE			
29.	Load watts from Table 9.4		
30.	Nameplate volts (either 120 or 240)		
31.	Line 29 divided by Line 30		
32.	Sum of Lines 7, 12, 28, and 31; TOTAL is larger of A and B	26.8	

Overcurrent Protection

Amp Ratings

All fuses and circuit breakers must be rated at or less than the ampacity of the conductors of the circuit being protected. *Exception:* if no breaker of correct ampacity is available, the breaker rating may exceed the ampacity of the conductors by up to 150%.

Circuit Breaker Specifications

All circuit breakers must meet the standards of either UL 489 or UL 1077, be of the manual-reset type (except if integral to a piece of equipment), and be of the trip-free type (cannot be held closed while the overcurrent condition persists).

Main Supply Protection

Specifications for overcurrent protection of the main supply conductors include:

1. The shore-power feeder conductors should be protected by multi-pole breakers. In a 120 VAC system the breakers should protect both the ungrounded (black) and the neutral (white) conductors. In any system containing either 240 VAC or 208 VAC, there should be breakers in all of the ungrounded conductors. Note that the green grounding conductor is never interrupted.
2. If there are isolation or polarization transformers in the shore-power feed, primaries should be protected by a circuit breaker that opens both primary feeders simultaneously and that is rated at no more than 125% of the primary rating. If the secondary provides 120/240 VAC, it also should be protected by a circuit breaker that opens both secondary feeders simultaneously and that is rated at no more than 125% of the rated secondary current of the transformer.
3. The maximum unprotected conductor length from boat inlet connector to circuit breaker must not exceed 10 feet. If the length is greater than 10 feet, add additional slow-blow fuses or breakers within 10 feet of the inlet. If additional fuses or circuit breakers are provided, they must be larger, but not more than 125% larger, than the main shore-power disconnect breaker.
4. The maximum unprotected conductor length from an AC generator must be less than 7 inches. However, up to 40 inches is allowed if the conductor is protected by a sheath or enclosure.

Branch-Circuit Protection

Branch circuit breakers and fuses should be rated at or less than the ampacity of the smallest current-carrying conductor in the circuit. If there is no matching breaker or fuse rating, the next larger may be used, provided it doesn't exceed 150% of conductor ampacity.

For boats wired with 120 VAC, 1Ø, both current-carrying conductors (hot and neutral) must be protected by a pair of simultaneous-trip circuit breakers. *Exception:* the ungrounded conductor alone may be protected, provided:

1. The entire system is polarized, including lighting fixtures, and there is a polarity indicator between the shore-power inlet and the main circuit breakers, or
2. The neutral and grounding conductors are connected at the secondary of an isolation or polarization transformer.

All motors must be protected by either an overcurrent or a thermal device unless they do not overheat, even when the motor is stalled (rotor locked).

Fuse or Breaker Location

The fuses or circuit breakers for a circuit must be placed at its power source, except:

1. If impractical, within 7 inches of the source.
2. If impractical within 7 inches, then within 40 inches, provided the conductor is contained in a protective sheath or enclosure.

Ground Fault Protection

GFCI Breakers

GFCI breakers must meet the same requirements as circuit breakers of the same rating. They may be used to protect individual branch circuits, or they may protect a group of associated circuits. Like other circuit breakers, they are permitted to interrupt only the ungrounded conductor, provided the system is polarized and has a polarity indicator, the system has an isolation or polarization transformer, or the system is 120/240 VAC.

GFCI Receptacles

GFCI receptacle devices must be two-pole and meet all of the requirements of standards UL 943 and UL 498. They may protect either a single receptacle or multiple receptacles in the same circuit.

No conductor may be smaller than 16 AWG, except 18 AWG inside panelboards and equipment enclosures, serving DC electronics at less than 1 amp, as less than 7-inch panelboard pigtails, and extending less than 30 inches outside a sheathed bundle. The temperature ratings of all conductors and flexible cords should be at least 140°F (60°C), except 167°F (75°C) in engine spaces. Individual conductor insulations must be rated at 600 volts minimum. Flexible cords may be rated at a minimum of 300 volts.

Conductors must be one of the types listed in Table 9.6. Flexible cords must be one of the types listed in Table 9.7. Both conductors and flexible cords must also be of the stranding as shown in Table 9.8.

The ABYC-recommended color code for AC wiring is shown in Table 9.9.

Table 9.6 Acceptable Conductor Types for AC Wiring

Type	Damp Location	Oil Resistant	Extra-Hard Usage	Hard Usage
SE, SEW	X		X	
SEO, SEOW	X	X	X	
SJ, SJW	X			X
SJE, SJEW	X			X
SJEO, SJEOW	X	X		X
SJO, SJOW	X	X		X
SJOO, SJOOW	X	X		X
SJT, SJTW	X			X
SJTO, SJTOW	X	X		X
SJTOO, SJTOOW	X	X		X
SO, SOW	X	X	X	
ST, STW	X		X	
STO, STOW	X	X	X	
STOO, STOOW	X	X	X	

Table 9.7 Acceptable Flexible Cord Types for AC Wiring

Type	Description
SO, SOW	Hard-Service Cord, Oil Resistant
ST, STW	Hard-Service Cord, Thermoplastic
STO, STOW	Hard-Service Cord, Oil Resistant, Thermoplastic
SEO, SEOW	Hard-Service Cord, Oil Resistant, Thermoplastic
SJO, SJOW, SJTW	Junior Hard-Service Cord, Oil Resistant
SJT, SJTW	Hard-Service Cord, Thermoplastic
SJTO, SJTOW	Hard-Service Cord, Oil Resistant, Thermoplastic

Table 9.8 Minimum AC Conductor Stranding

Conductor Gauge	Minimum CM for AWG	Minimum CM for SAE	Minimum Type II[1]	Strands Type III[2]
18	1,620	1,537	16	–
16	2,580	2,336	19	26
14	4,110	3,702	19	41
12	6,530	5,833	19	65
10	10,380	9,343	19	105
8	16,510	14,810	19	168
6	26,240	25,910	37	266
4	41,740	37,360	49	420
2	66,360	62,450	127	665
1	83,690	77,790	127	836
0	105,600	98,980	127	1,064
2/0	133,100	125,100	127	1,323
3/0	167,800	158,600	259	1,666
4/0	211,600	205,500	418	2,107

[1] Conductors with at least Type II stranding to be used for general-purpose boat wiring.
[2] Conductors with Type III stranding to be used where frequent flexing is expected.

Table 9.9 Color Code for AC Wiring

Conductor	Colors (Preferred First)
Ungrounded	Black or Brown
Grounded Neutral	White or Light Blue
Grounding	Green, Green with Yellow Stripe
Additional Ungrounded	Red, Blue, Orange
	Black with Red Stripe
	Black with Blue Stripe
	Black with Orange Stripe

Ampacity

The minimum ampacities of AC current-carrying conductors are shown in Tables 9.10 through 9.15 on the following pages.

Ampacity Tables

Table 9.10 Allowable Amperage of No More Than Two Bundled Conductors
(Adapted from ABYC Standard E-11, Table VII-A)

Temperature Rating of Conductor Insulation

Size AWG	60°C 140°F	75°C 167°F	80°C 176°F	90°C 194°F	105°C 221°F	125°C 257°F	200°C 392°F
Outside Engine Spaces							
18	10	10	15	20	20	25	25
16	15	15	20	25	25	30	35
14	20	20	25	30	35	40	45
12	25	25	35	40	45	50	55
10	40	40	50	55	60	70	70
8	55	65	70	70	80	90	100
6	80	95	100	100	120	125	135
4	105	125	130	135	160	170	180
2	140	170	175	180	210	225	240
1	165	195	210	210	245	265	280
1/0	195	230	245	245	285	305	325
2/0	225	265	285	285	330	355	370
3/0	260	310	330	330	385	410	430
4/0	300	360	385	385	445	475	510
Inside Engine Spaces							
18	5	7	11	16	17	22	25
16	8	11	15	20	21	26	35
14	11	15	19	24	29	35	45
12	14	18	27	32	38	44	55
10	23	30	39	45	51	62	70
8	31	48	54	57	68	80	100
6	46	71	78	82	102	111	135
4	60	93	101	110	136	151	180
2	81	127	136	147	178	200	240
1	95	146	163	172	208	235	280
1/0	113	172	191	200	242	271	325
2/0	130	198	222	233	280	316	370
3/0	150	232	257	270	327	364	430
4/0	174	270	300	315	378	422	510

Table 9.11 Allowable Amperage of Three Bundled Conductors
(Adapted from ABYC Standard E-11, Table VII-B)

Temperature Rating of Conductor Insulation

Size AWG	60°C 140°F	75°C 167°F	80°C 176°F	90°C 194°F	105°C 221°F	125°C 257°F	200°C 392°F
Outside Engine Spaces							
18	7	7	10	14	14	17	17
16	10	10	14	17	17	21	24
14	14	14	17	21	24	28	31
12	17	17	24	28	31	35	38
10	28	28	35	38	42	49	49
8	38	45	49	49	56	63	70
6	56	66	70	70	84	87	94
4	73	87	91	94	112	119	126
2	98	119	122	126	147	157	168
1	115	136	147	147	171	185	196
1/0	136	161	171	171	199	213	227
2/0	157	185	199	199	231	248	259
3/0	182	217	231	231	269	287	301
4/0	210	252	269	269	311	332	357
Inside Engine Spaces							
18	4	5	8	11	11	15	17
16	6	7	10	14	14	18	24
14	8	10	13	17	20	24	31
12	10	13	19	23	26	31	38
10	16	21	27	31	35	43	49
8	22	34	38	40	47	56	70
6	32	49	54	57	71	77	94
4	42	65	71	77	95	105	126
2	56	89	95	103	125	140	168
1	67	102	114	120	145	165	196
1/0	79	120	133	140	169	190	227
2/0	91	139	155	163	196	221	259
3/0	105	162	180	189	229	255	301
4/0	121	189	210	221	264	295	357

Ampacity Tables

Table 9.12 Allowable Amperage of Four to Six Bundled Conductors
(Adapted from ABYC Standard E-11, Table VII-C)

Temperature Rating of Conductor Insulation

Size AWG	60°C 140°F	75°C 167°F	80°C 176°F	90°C 194°F	105°C 221°F	125°C 257°F	200°C 392°F
			Outside Engine Spaces				
18	6	6	9	12	12	15	15
16	9	9	12	15	15	18	21
14	12	12	15	18	21	24	27
12	15	15	21	24	27	30	33
10	24	24	30	33	36	42	42
8	33	39	42	42	48	54	60
6	48	57	60	60	72	75	81
4	63	75	78	81	96	102	108
2	84	102	105	108	126	135	144
1	99	117	126	126	147	159	168
1/0	117	138	147	147	171	183	195
2/0	135	159	171	171	198	213	222
3/0	156	186	198	198	231	246	258
4/0	180	216	231	231	267	285	306
			Inside Engine Spaces				
18	3	4	7	9	10	13	15
16	5	6	9	12	12	16	21
14	7	9	11	14	17	21	27
12	8	11	16	19	23	26	33
10	13	18	23	27	30	37	42
8	19	29	32	34	40	48	60
6	27	42	46	49	61	66	81
4	36	56	60	66	81	90	108
2	48	76	81	88	107	120	144
1	57	87	98	103	125	141	168
1/0	67	103	114	120	145	162	195
2/0	78	119	133	140	168	189	222
3/0	90	139	154	162	196	218	258
4/0	104	162	180	189	227	253	306

Table 9.13 Allowable Amperage of Seven to 24 Bundled Conductors
(Adapted from ABYC Standard E-11, Table VII-D)

Temperature Rating of Conductor Insulation

Size AWG	60°C 140°F	75°C 167°F	80°C 176°F	90°C 194°F	105°C 221°F	125°C 257°F	200°C 392°F
			Outside Engine Spaces				
18	5	5	7	10	10	12	12
16	7	7	10	12	12	15	17
14	10	10	12	15	17	20	22
12	12	12	17	20	22	25	27
10	20	20	25	27	30	35	35
8	27	32	35	35	40	45	50
6	40	47	50	50	60	62	67
4	52	62	65	67	80	85	90
2	70	85	87	90	105	112	120
1	82	97	105	105	122	132	140
1/0	97	115	122	122	142	152	162
2/0	112	132	142	142	165	177	185
3/0	130	155	165	165	192	205	215
4/0	150	180	192	192	222	237	255
			Inside Engine Spaces				
18	2	3	5	8	8	11	12
16	4	5	7	10	10	13	17
14	5	7	9	12	14	17	22
12	7	9	13	16	19	22	27
10	11	15	19	22	25	31	35
8	16	24	27	28	34	40	50
6	23	35	39	41	51	55	67
4	30	46	50	55	68	75	90
2	40	63	68	73	89	100	120
1	47	73	81	86	104	117	140
1/0	56	86	95	100	121	135	162
2/0	65	99	111	116	140	158	185
3/0	75	116	128	135	163	182	215
4/0	87	135	150	157	189	211	255

Ampacity Tables

Table 9.14 Allowable Amperage of 25 or More Bundled Conductors
(Adapted from ABYC Standard E-11, Table VII-E)

Temperature Rating of Conductor Insulation

Size AWG	60°C 140°F	75°C 167°F	80°C 176°F	90°C 194°F	105°C 221°F	125°C 257°F	200°C 392°F
Outside Engine Spaces							
18	4	4	6	8	8	10	10
16	6	6	8	10	10	12	14
14	8	8	10	12	14	16	18
12	10	10	14	16	18	20	22
10	16	16	20	22	24	28	28
8	22	26	28	28	32	36	40
6	32	38	40	40	48	50	54
4	42	50	52	54	64	68	72
2	56	68	70	72	84	90	96
1	66	78	84	84	98	106	112
1/0	78	92	98	98	114	122	130
2/0	90	106	114	114	132	142	148
3/0	104	124	132	132	154	164	172
4/0	120	144	154	151	178	190	204
Inside Engine Spaces							
18	2	3	4	6	6	8	10
16	3	4	6	8	8	10	14
14	4	6	7	9	11	14	18
12	5	7	10	13	15	17	22
10	9	12	15	18	20	24	28
8	12	19	21	23	27	32	40
6	18	28	31	32	40	44	54
4	24	37	40	44	54	60	72
2	32	51	54	59	71	80	96
1	38	58	65	68	83	94	112
1/0	45	69	76	80	96	108	130
2/0	52	79	88	93	112	126	148
3/0	60	93	103	108	130	146	172
4/0	69	108	120	126	151	169	204

Table 9.15 Allowable Amperage of Flexible Cords[1,2]
(Adapted from ABYC Standard E-11, Table XIII)

Size, AWG	Nominal CM Area	Outside Engine Space 30°C Ambient		Inside Engine Space 50°C Ambient	
		Three Conductors	Two Conductors	Three Conductors	Two Conductors
16	2,580	10	13	6	8
14	4,110	15	18	9	11
12	6,530	20	25	12	15
10	10,380	25	30	15	20
8	16,510	35	40	20	25
6	26,240	45	55	30	35
4	41,740	60	70	35	40
2	66,360	80	95	50	55

[1] Current ratings are for flexible cords containing no more than three conductors. For four to six conductors, reduce ampacity to 80%.
[2] Shore-power cables rated at 86°F (30°C).

Conductor Installation

Note that the conductor specifications and wiring techniques for DC and AC systems are nearly identical. Some of the illustrations used in Chapter 6 are repeated here to save the reader from having to flip back and forth.

Connections

Fabrication and installation of wiring connections should not damage the conductors. Special tools (see Figure 6.10 and discussion in Chapter 6) are available for making approved crimp-on connections.

All connection components (conductors, terminals, studs, washers, and nuts) should be galvanically compatible and corrosion resistant. Specifically, aluminum and unplated steel are not appropriate for studs, nuts, and washers.

Marine connectors also differ from the more common electronic-type connectors in that they must withstand vibration and tensile stresses. Figure 9.7 shows the types of connectors approved for marine use, along with several types specifically disapproved.

Friction connectors (the blade and bullet variety in Figure 9.7) are allowed, provided they resist a 6-pound pull. The other approved connectors must resist the pulls shown in Table 9.16 for at least 1 minute.

Although not specified in the ABYC standard, pre-tinned conductors are preferred in marine use. The reason will be apparent when you attempt to repair a conductor that has been on a boat for a few years. Chances are, if it is untinned, it will be corroded far up into the insulating sleeve, due to capillary wicking of moisture into the stranded conductor. Soldering corroded copper wire is ineffective and definitely not recommended.

Although solder can make a strong connection, the ABYC states that solder must not be the sole means of mechanical connection in any circuit. One reason is that the solder may melt if the terminal overheats, due to either an overcurrent condition or high resistance in the connection. Without any other means of attachment, a melted solder connection may separate. If you wish to use solder (and many professionals do), first crimp the connector to the conductor, then flow solder into the crimped joint.

As an alternative to solder, adhesive-lined, heat-shrink tubing is available. It seals out moisture, mechanically strengthens the connection, and electrically insulates the terminal shank at the same time. Figure 9.8 shows how to make a terminal connection using adhesive-lined, heat-shrink tubing.

Fig. 9.7 ABYC Approved and Disapproved Marine Connectors

Splice	Butt	3-Way	Wire nut
Friction	Blade	Bullet or snap	
Terminals	Ring	Locking spade / Flanged spade	Plain spade
Set Screw		Indirect-bearing	Direct-bearing

Table 9.16 Tensile Test Values for Connections (Adapted from ABYC Standard E-11, Table XVI)

Conductor Size, AWG	Force, lb.	Conductor Size, AWG	Force, lb.
18	10	4	70
16	15	3	80
14	30	2	90
12	35	1	100
10	40	0	125
8	45	2/0	150
6	50	3/0	175
5	60	4/0	225

Fig. 9.8 Adhesive-Lined, Heat-Shrink Tubing

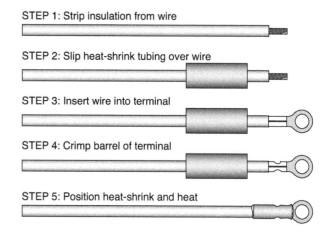

STEP 1: Strip insulation from wire

STEP 2: Slip heat-shrink tubing over wire

STEP 3: Insert wire into terminal

STEP 4: Crimp barrel of terminal

STEP 5: Position heat-shrink and heat

Conductor Protection

Exposed conductors must be protected by conduit, self-draining loom, tape, raceway, or equivalent means. Loom materials must be self-extinguishing.

Except for battery cables up to 36 inches in length and outboard engine cables, conductors must be either supported continuously or secured every 18 inches maximum with clamps or straps.

Nonmetallic clamps are allowed except over an engine, shaft, machinery, or passageway, where clamp failure could result in danger. Clamp materials must also be resistant to oil, gasoline, and water.

Metal clamps must have smooth, rounded edges, and the cable must be protected from the metal by tape or other wrapping to protect the conductors.

Conductors should be clamped close to their connections to remove strain from the connections.

Receptacles

Maintaining Polarity

AC receptacles (Figure 9.9) must be of the grounding type with one terminal connected to the green grounding wire. To prevent polarity reversal all plugs and receptacles must match and must not be interchangeable with plugs and receptacles of the DC system. Terminals must be identified either by letter or by using the color scheme shown in Table 9.17:

Table 9.17 AC Wiring Color Code

Conductor	Wire Color	Terminal Color
Ungrounded	Black, Red	Dark (Copper/Brass)
Grounded	White	Light (Silver)
Grounding	Green	Tinted Green

Location

Galley receptacles should be placed so that appliance cords do not cross a stove, sink, or traffic area, as shown in Figure 9.10.

Receptacles that are located in the head, galley, machine spaces, or above deck should be protected by a Type-A (trip-on fault current of 5 milliamps [0.005 amp]) GFCI.

Receptacles normally should be installed in locations that are protected from weather, spray, and flooding. If not, they should be protected when not in use by a spring-loaded cover. Receptacles subject to submersion must be watertight.

Conductor Routing

Route conductors well above the bilge or any other area where water might accumulate. If routing through such an area cannot be avoided, both the conductors and the connections should be watertight.

Conductors should also be kept clear of exhaust pipes and other heat sources. Minimum clearances, except for engine wiring and exhaust-temperature sensor wiring, should be 2 inches for wet exhausts and 4 inches for dry exhausts, unless equivalent heat barriers are provided.

Conductors should also be kept clear of sources of chafing such as engine shafts, steering cable and linkages, steering gears, and engine controls.

If AC and DC conductors are run together, the AC conductors must be sheathed or bundled separately from the DC conductors.

Fig. 9.9 Polarity Provisions in AC Receptacles

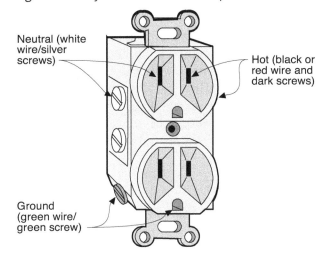

Neutral (white wire/silver screws)

Hot (black or red wire and dark screws)

Ground (green wire/ green screw)

Fig. 9.10 Receptacle Placement in Galleys

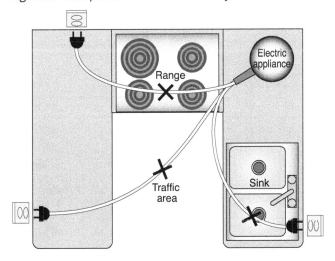

Electric appliance

Range

Sink

Traffic area

The Green Wire

The green wire in AC circuits provides a life-saving return path for stray electric currents. Figure 9.11 illustrates the danger the green wire is designed to protect against. The engine, through the transmission, shaft, and water surrounding the boat, is at earth potential. In the illustration one of the hot conductors of a piece of electrical equipment (a water heater) has short-circuited to its metal case. With one hand on the metal engine and the other on the water heater jacket, the person in the illustration serves as a return-to-ground path for the AC current. Were there a green grounding wire connected to the heater jacket and to the engine, it would provide a very-low-resistance return path for the return current and hold the case and engine at the same potential. With no driving potential difference, there would be no reason for electrical current to flow through the person.

Boaters familiar with residential wiring often assume that a boat is just like a house. On that assumption, they connect the neutral (white) and grounding (green) shore-power conductors at the boat's AC panel.

Figure 9.12 shows what can happen in such a case. As always, all of the current in the hot (black) conductor somehow finds its way back to the shore-power ground. In a properly wired system, the sole return path would be the neutral (white) conductor. In the system shown, however, the return current flows through three paths: the neutral conductor, the green

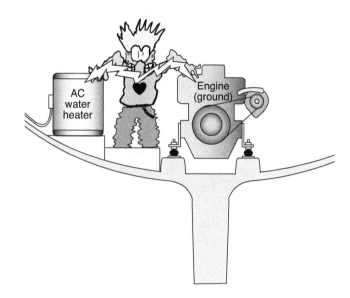

Fig. 9.11 What the Green Wire Protects Against

grounding conductor, and—via the boat's grounded underwater metal—the seawater.

If resistance or a break develops in the white and green conductors, much of the return current could be through the water, exposing a person in the water near the boat to great danger.

Principle: Connect the green and the white conductors at the source, be it shore power, generator, or inverter.

Fig. 9.12 Mistake #1: Connecting White (Neutral) and Green (Grounding) Conductors on a Boat

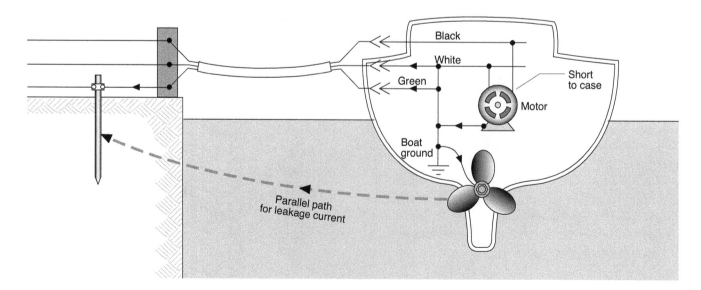

Figure 9.13 shows a second mistake. This time the white and green wires are properly separated on the boat, but, intending to prevent stray-current corrosion of the boat's underwater hardware, the misguided owner has cut the green wire to the boat's ground (engine and metallic underwater hardware). If a short develops in a piece of electrical equipment, the green wire will carry current. If there is, however, resistance in the green wire and its connections, the equipment case may still be above ground potential. A person contacting both the equipment case and a piece of metal underwater hardware may be shocked (literally) to find that he is a parallel return path through the water.

Principle: Connect the green wire to the boat's ground.

Fig. 9.13 Mistake #2: Not Connecting the Green Grounding Conductor to Boat Ground

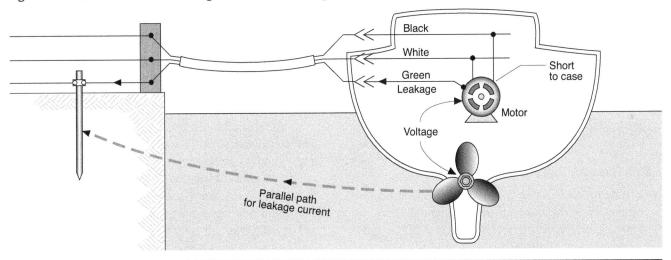

We have found that the green and white wires must not be connected on a boat, but that the green wire must be connected to the boat's ground. Unfortunately, we still may experience a problem. We may have unwittingly created a galvanic cell, which, as we saw in Chapter 5, leads to corrosion of underwater metals.

Figure 9.14 shows two boats in a marina on shore power. The green wires are properly connected to their respective boat grounds, but they are also connected to each other through the common shore-power connection.

We have now created a galvanic cell: one boat is the anode and the other boat is the cathode. Even were the underwater metals of the two boats of identical composition, they could suffer from impressed-current corrosion were there a voltage field in the water.

Woe is us; is there ANY safe solution which doesn't cause corrosion? Actually, there are two.

Fig. 9.14 Galvanic Cell Created by Marina Common Ground

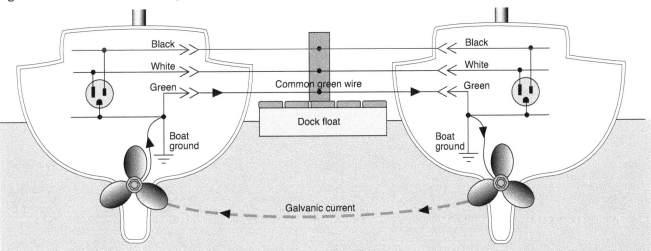

Solution 1: The Galvanic Isolator

A galvanic isolator, placed on the ship's green grounding wire immediately after the shore-power connector, blocks DC current. Figure 9.15 shows how it works. At top is a simple pair of parallel and reversed diodes. Diodes pass current in the direction of the arrow but block current in the opposite direction. In the forward direction a small voltage drop (0.6 volt for a silicon diode) occurs. Thus the pair of diodes will block current until the voltage reaches 0.6 volt in both directions.

Adding diodes in series doubles the voltage rating. Parallel and reversed diode pairs will thus block current until the voltage reaches 1.2 volts in either direction.

Finally, a nonpolarized capacitor allows AC current to pass, while still blocking DC currents up to ±1.2 volts.

ABYC Galvanic Isolator Recommendations

According to the ABYC, a galvanic isolator should:
- be tested by an independent testing laboratory
- have a current rating not less than that of the main shore-power disconnect circuit breaker
- not introduce a voltage drop greater than 2.5 volts at 100% of the shore-power cable ampacity rating
- not pass less than 0.030 ampere at DC voltages of 1.2 volts in either direction
- not pass less than 0.030 ampere at DC voltages of 0.5 volt in either direction with 3.0 amperes RMS AC current superimposed

In addition the galvanic isolator should provide audible or visible status monitoring indicating:
- shorted or open diode
- failure to block galvanic current at 1.1 volts DC
- continuity of the shore grounding circuit
- operational status of the monitoring device

Fig. 9.15 Galvanic Isolators

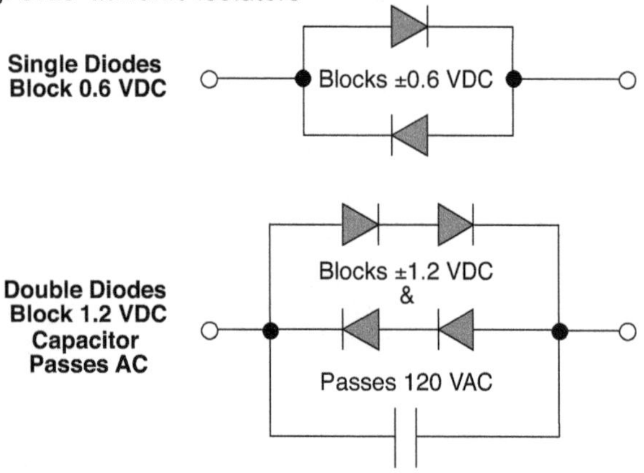

Single Diodes Block 0.6 VDC   Blocks ±0.6 VDC

Double Diodes Block 1.2 VDC Capacitor Passes AC   Blocks ±1.2 VDC & Passes 120 VAC

Solution 2: The Isolation Transformer

If we had a source of electricity that acted like an onboard generator, there would be no need for a green wire to run back to the shore-power ground, and we could break the galvanic connection to other marina-bound boats. An isolation transformer is the answer, regenerating onboard power without direct electrical connection to shore power.

Figure 9.16 shows an isolation transformer. To meet ABYC requirements, isolation transformers must be tested and labeled by an independent laboratory.

The primary coil is connected to the hot and neutral shore-power conductors. The secondary coil is connected to the hot and neutral ship's-power conductors.

A metal shield, electrically isolated from all other parts of the transformer, is placed between the primary and secondary coils, and a lead is brought out from the shield. The shield must withstand a voltage of 4,000 volts AC, 60 Hz, for 1 minute, applied between the shield and other components such as windings, core, and outside enclosure.

The transformer case must be metal and have a grounding terminal.

The ship's neutral (white) and grounding (green) conductors are connected at the transformer output, since the transformer secondary is a new source of electricity. As you will see on the following pages, connections between shield, conductor, transformer case, shore-power ground, and ship's ground vary with the transformer. Follow the manufacturer's directions.

Fig. 9.16 Isolation Transformer

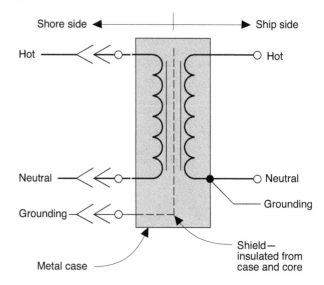

The following pages contain a variety of shore-power circuits, adapted from ABYC Standard E-11. They range from the simplest and most common small-boat, 120-volt AC, 30-amp circuit to the heavy-duty 120/240 VAC systems found on large power yachts. Each circuit incorporates galvanic protection in the form of either a galvanic isolator or an isolating transformer. For ease in finding the appropriate circuit for your application, here is a guide:

Figure	Volts	Phases	Galvanic Protection	ABYC Reference
9.17	120	1	Galvanic isolator	E-11.7.2.2.1
9.18	120	1	Galvanic isolator and generator	E-11.7.2.2.1
9.19	120	1	Galvanic isolator and polarity indicator	E-11.7.2.2.1
9.20	120/240	1	Galvanic isolator and generator	E-11.7.2.2.2
9.21	240	1	Polarization transformer and generator	E-11.7.2.3
9.22	120	1	Isolation transformer	E-11.7.2.4
9.23	120	1	Isolation transformer	E-11.7.2.5
9.24	120	1	Isolation transformer and GFCI	E-11.7.2.6
9.25	240	1	Isolation transformer	E-11.7.2.7
9.26	240	1	Isolation transformer	E-11.7.2.8
9.27	240	1	Isolation transformer and GFCI	E-11.7.2.9
9.28	120	1	Polarization transformer and galvanic isolator	E-11.7.2.10
9.29	240	1	Isolation transformer	E-11.7.2.11

Approved Shore-Power Circuits

Fig. 9.17 Single-Phase, 120-Volt System with Shore-Grounded Neutral and Grounding Conductors

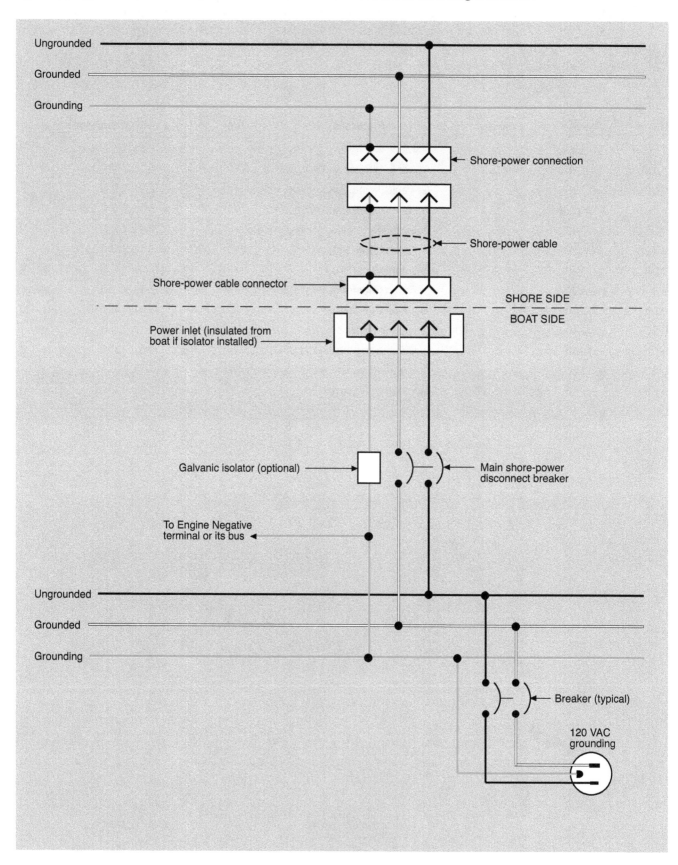

Fig. 9.18 Single-Phase, 120-Volt System with Shore-Grounded Neutral and Grounding Conductors

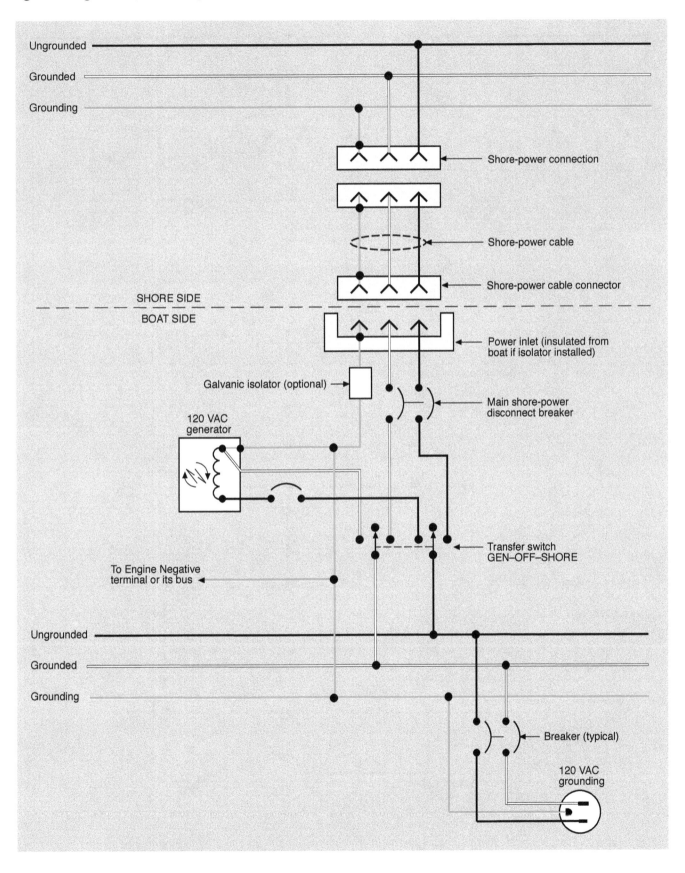

Approved Shore-Power Circuits

Fig. 9.19 Single-Phase, 120-Volt System with Shore-Grounded Neutral and Grounding Conductors

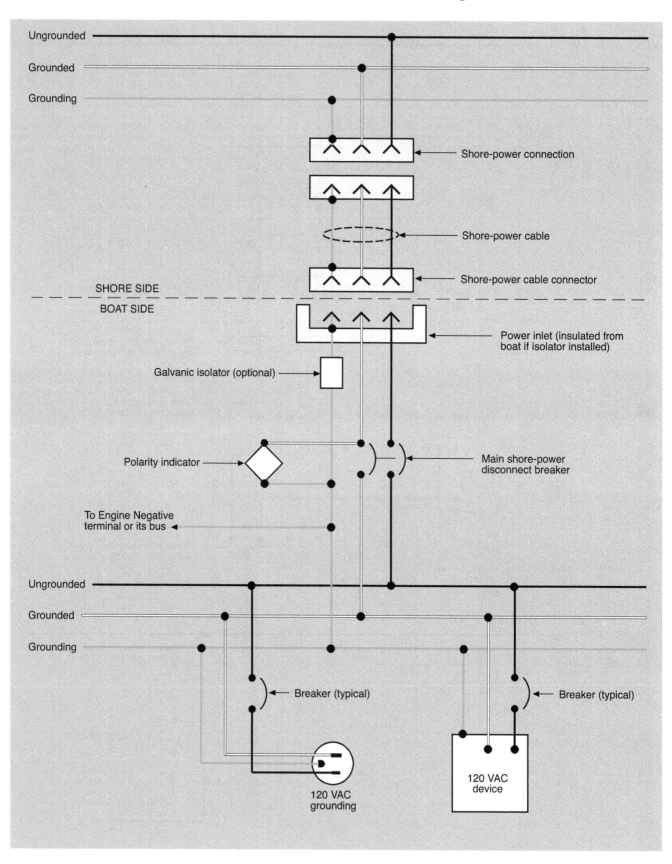

Fig. 9.20 Single-Phase, 120/240-Volt System with Shore-Grounded Neutral and Grounding Conductors

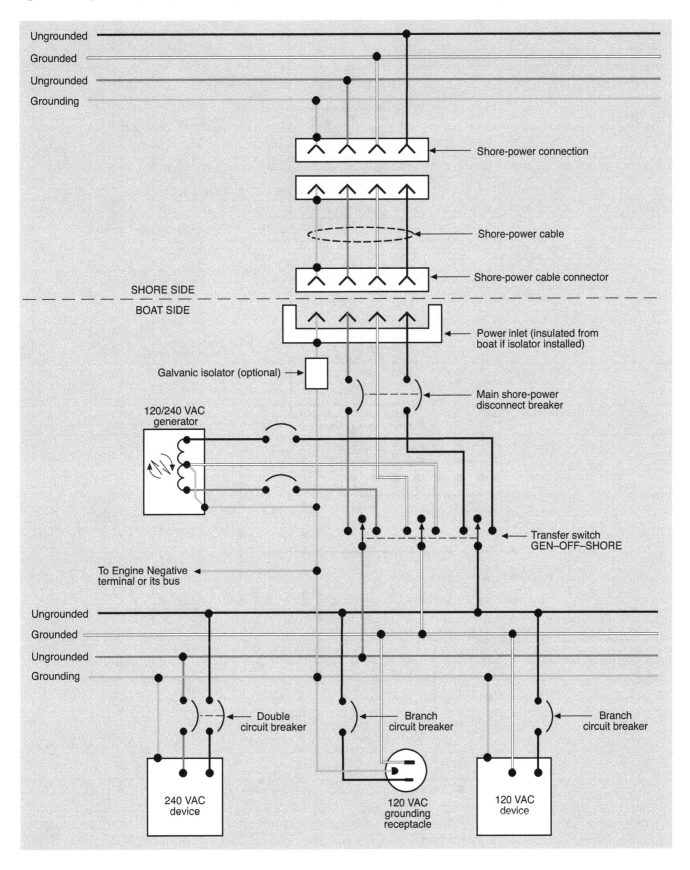

Ungrounded
Grounded
Ungrounded
Grounding

Shore-power connection

Shore-power cable

Shore-power cable connector

SHORE SIDE
BOAT SIDE

Power inlet (insulated from boat if isolator installed)

Galvanic isolator (optional)

Main shore-power disconnect breaker

120/240 VAC generator

Transfer switch GEN–OFF–SHORE

To Engine Negative terminal or its bus

Ungrounded
Grounded
Ungrounded
Grounding

Double circuit breaker

Branch circuit breaker

Branch circuit breaker

240 VAC device

120 VAC grounding receptacle

120 VAC device

Approved Shore-Power Circuits

Fig. 9.21 Polarization Transformer System with Single-Phase, 240-Volt Input, 120/240-Volt Output, and Generator

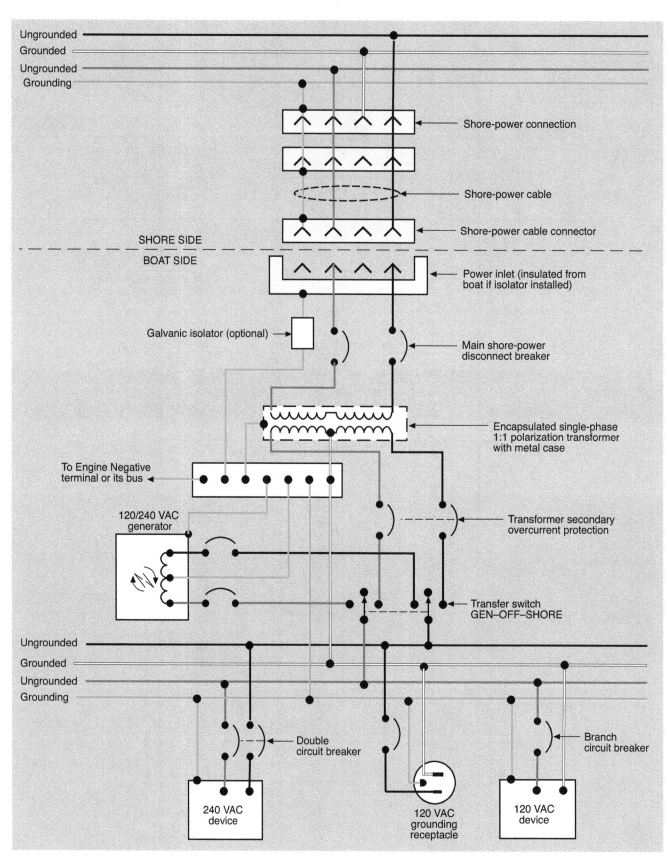

Fig. 9.22 Isolation Transformer System with Single-Phase, 120-Volt Input and 120-Volt Output

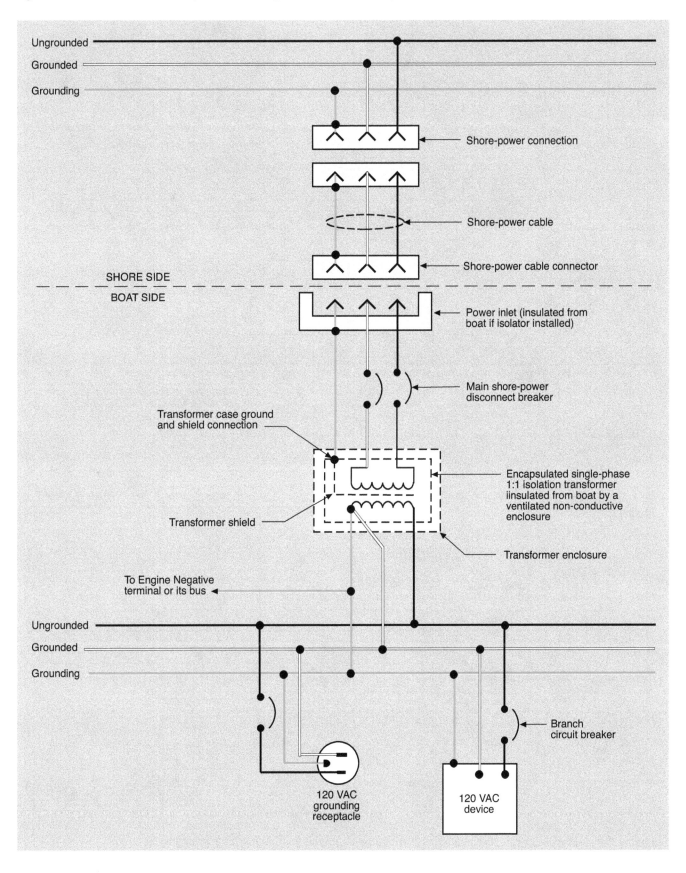

Approved Shore-Power Circuits

Fig. 9.23 Isolation Transformer System with Single-Phase, 120-Volt Input and 120-Volt Output

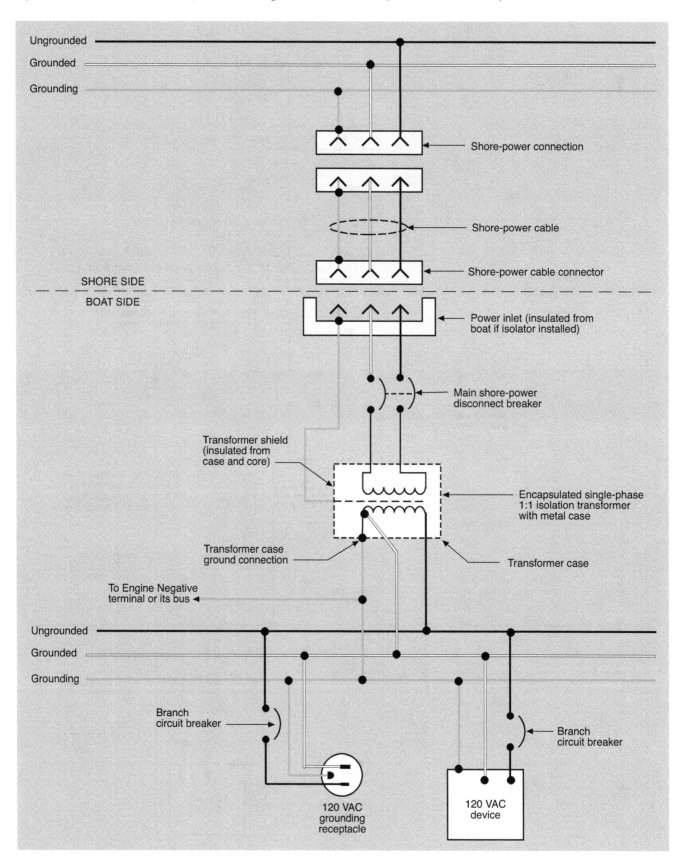

Ungrounded

Grounded

Grounding

Shore-power connection

Shore-power cable

SHORE SIDE

BOAT SIDE

Shore-power cable connector

Power inlet (insulated from boat if isolator installed)

Main shore-power disconnect breaker

Transformer shield (insulated from case and core)

Encapsulated single-phase 1:1 isolation transformer with metal case

Transformer case ground connection

To Engine Negative terminal or its bus

Transformer case

Ungrounded

Grounded

Grounding

Branch circuit breaker

Branch circuit breaker

120 VAC grounding receptacle

120 VAC device

Fig. 9.24 Isolation Transformer System with Single-Phase, 120-Volt Input and 120-Volt Output with Ground Fault Protection

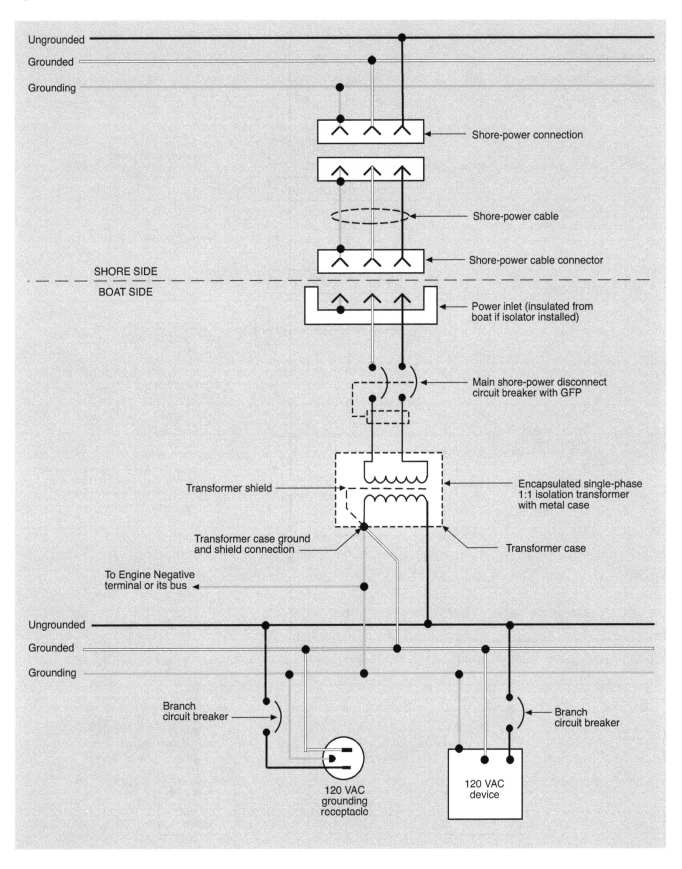

Ungrounded
Grounded
Grounding

Shore-power connection

Shore-power cable

Shore-power cable connector

SHORE SIDE
BOAT SIDE

Power inlet (insulated from boat if isolator installed)

Main shore-power disconnect circuit breaker with GFP

Transformer shield

Encapsulated single-phase 1:1 isolation transformer with metal case

Transformer case ground and shield connection

Transformer case

To Engine Negative terminal or its bus

Ungrounded
Grounded
Grounding

Branch circuit breaker

Branch circuit breaker

120 VAC grounding receptacle

120 VAC device

Approved Shore-Power Circuits

Fig. 9.25 Isolation Transformer System with Single-Phase, 240-Volt Input and 120/240-Volt Output

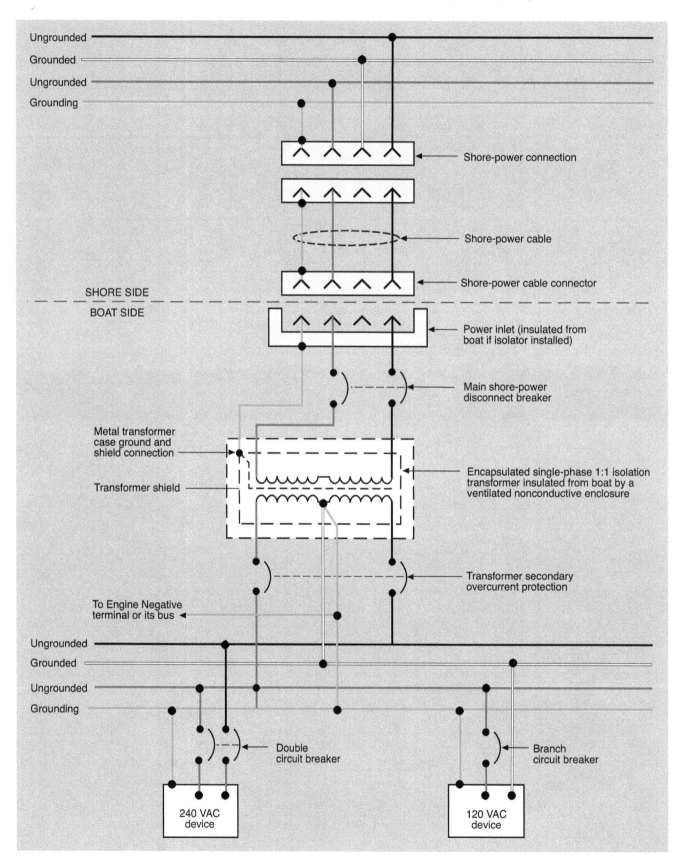

Ungrounded

Grounded

Ungrounded

Grounding

Shore-power connection

Shore-power cable

SHORE SIDE

Shore-power cable connector

BOAT SIDE

Power inlet (insulated from boat if isolator installed)

Main shore-power disconnect breaker

Metal transformer case ground and shield connection

Encapsulated single-phase 1:1 isolation transformer insulated from boat by a ventilated nonconductive enclosure

Transformer shield

Transformer secondary overcurrent protection

To Engine Negative terminal or its bus

Ungrounded

Grounded

Ungrounded

Grounding

Double circuit breaker

Branch circuit breaker

240 VAC device

120 VAC device

Fig. 9.26 Isolation Transformer System with Single-Phase, 240-Volt Input and 120/240-Volt Output

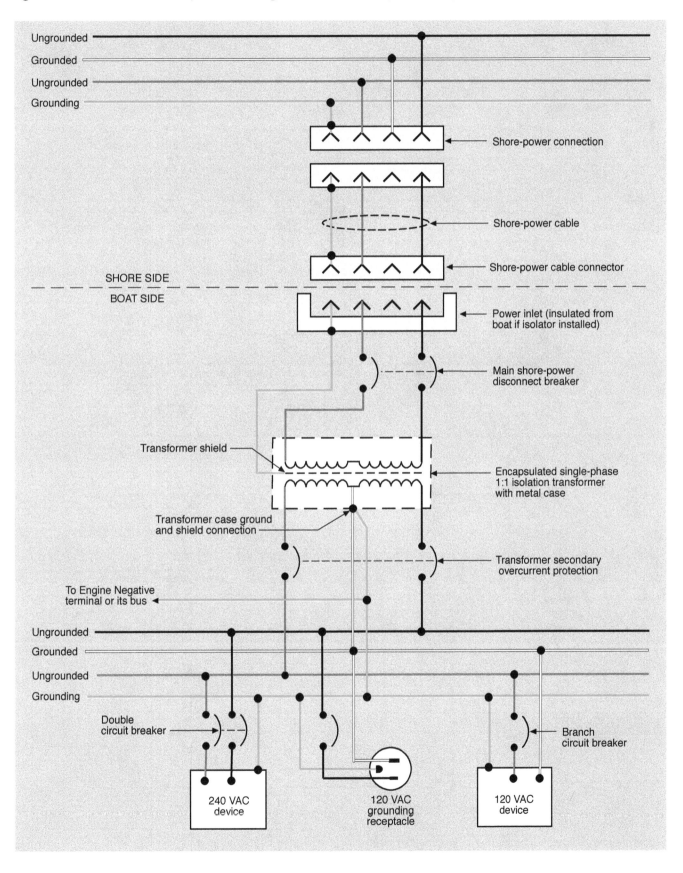

Approved Shore-Power Circuits

Fig. 9.27 Isolation Transformer System with Single-Phase, 240-Volt Input and 120/240-Volt Output with Ground Fault Protection

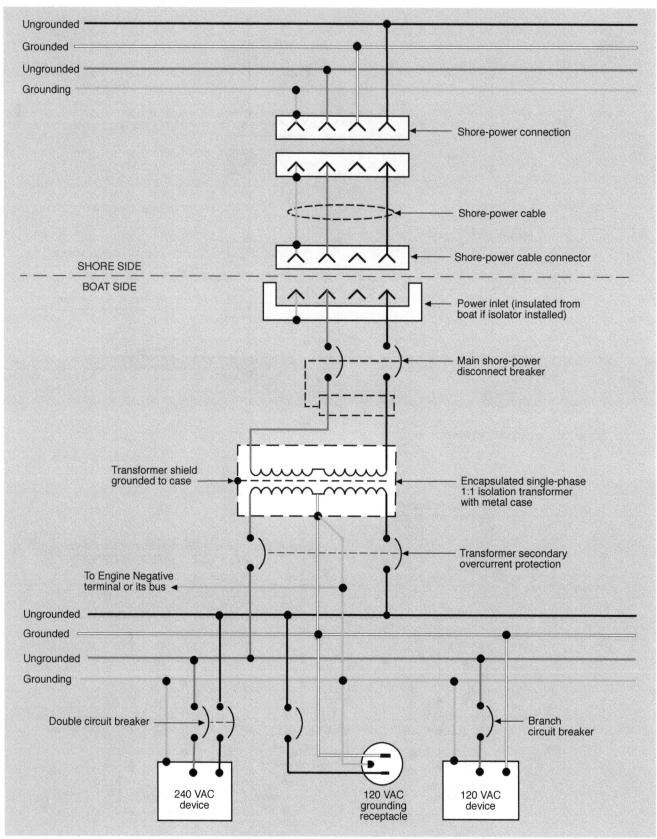

Fig. 9.28 Polarization Transformer System with Single-Phase, 120-Volt Input and 120-Volt Output

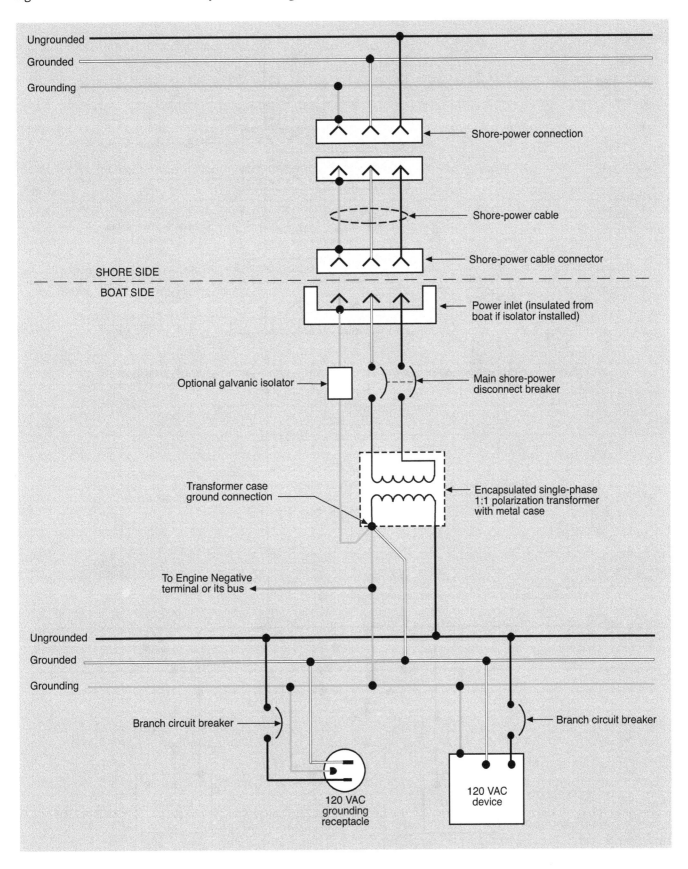

Ungrounded

Grounded

Grounding

Shore-power connection

Shore-power cable

Shore-power cable connector

SHORE SIDE

BOAT SIDE

Power inlet (insulated from boat if isolator installed)

Optional galvanic isolator

Main shore-power disconnect breaker

Transformer case ground connection

Encapsulated single-phase 1:1 polarization transformer with metal case

To Engine Negative terminal or its bus

Ungrounded

Grounded

Grounding

Branch circuit breaker

Branch circuit breaker

120 VAC grounding receptacle

120 VAC device

Approved Shore-Power Circuits

Fig. 9.29 Polarization Transformer System with Single-Phase, 240-Volt Input and 120/240-Volt Output

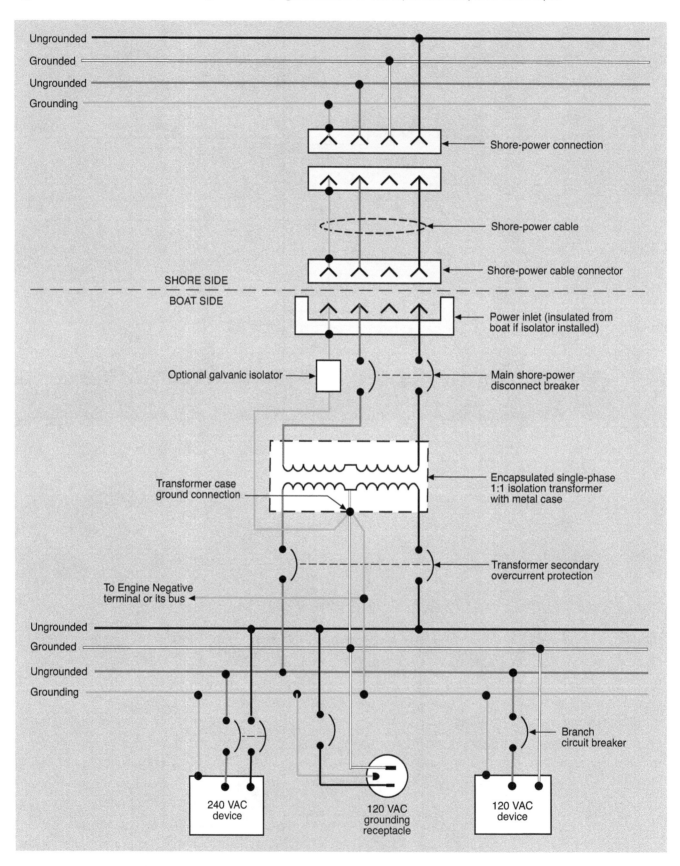

Ungrounded

Grounded

Ungrounded

Grounding

Shore-power connection

Shore-power cable

Shore-power cable connector

SHORE SIDE

BOAT SIDE

Power inlet (insulated from boat if isolator installed)

Optional galvanic isolator

Main shore-power disconnect breaker

Transformer case ground connection

Encapsulated single-phase 1:1 isolation transformer with metal case

Transformer secondary overcurrent protection

To Engine Negative terminal or its bus

Ungrounded

Grounded

Ungrounded

Grounding

Branch circuit breaker

240 VAC device

120 VAC grounding receptacle

120 VAC device

CHAPTER 10

Conservation for Liveaboards

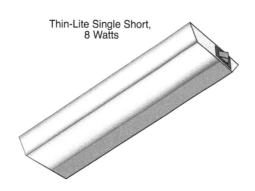

Thin-Lite Single Short,
8 Watts

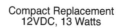

Compact Replacement
12VDC, 13 Watts

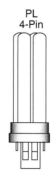

PL
4-Pin

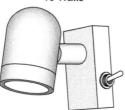

Mini Reading Light
10 Watts

Halogen Mini-Spot
5 Watts

LED All-Round Light
3 Watts

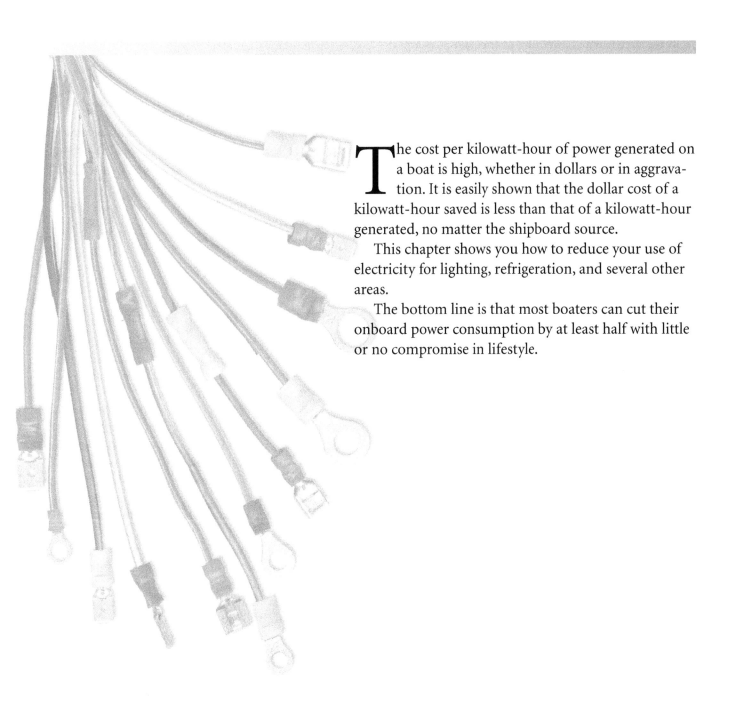

The cost per kilowatt-hour of power generated on a boat is high, whether in dollars or in aggravation. It is easily shown that the dollar cost of a kilowatt-hour saved is less than that of a kilowatt-hour generated, no matter the shipboard source.

This chapter shows you how to reduce your use of electricity for lighting, refrigeration, and several other areas.

The bottom line is that most boaters can cut their onboard power consumption by at least half with little or no compromise in lifestyle.

Costs per Kilowatt-Hour

Before considering solar and wind power, the live-aboard boater should consider the less expensive alternative form of energy—conservation.

Put yourself to the following test. Your already leaky boat becomes more leaky. Which solution first comes to your mind? If it is to install a second or larger bilge pump, then forget conservation, solar, and wind, and get yourself to a slip where you can tap into shore power. If fixing the leak seems more logical to you, however, then read on.

If we have learned anything in the past 20 years, it is that, with modest investment and attention to detail, we can save a lot of expensive energy in our homes and offices. The same is true of boats.

If your boat is typical, this chapter can show you how to reduce the drain on your batteries by half with virtually no effect on your lifestyle. By cutting consumption in half, you will also reduce the required sizes and costs of the solar and wind systems you may be considering adding to your boat. In fact, you may reduce your consumption to the point where you never need run your engine again just to charge your batteries!

The old saying "A penny saved is a penny earned" has its analog in energy conservation: "A kilowatt saved is a kilowatt made." If we can save energy without dimishing lifestyle, then it is fair to compare the cost of saving a kilowatt-hour to the cost of producing a kilowatt-hour in order to see which is the better deal.

Costs of Producing Electricity

Figure 10.1 shows the costs per kilowatt-hour of electricity produced by:
- 220-amp alternator on a 20 hp diesel
- 110-amp alternator on a 20 hp diesel
- 55-amp alternator on a 20 hp diesel
- Solar panel at $8 per peak watt
- 5-foot wind machine at $1,500

The assumptions used include:

Diesel Power
- Used at anchor
- Fuel consumption, 0.5 gallon/hour
- Fuel price, $2.20/gallon
- Price including controls, $7,000
- Life, 10,000 hours
- Maintenance, $0.20/hour

Solar Power:
- Used all year
- Size, 50 watts peak output
- Price including controls, $400
- Life, 10 years
- Average daily sunshine, 5.2 hours
- Annual maintenance, $0

Wind Power:
- Used all year
- Size (blade diameter), 5 feet
- Price including controls, $1,500
- Life, 10 years
- Average wind speed, 10 knots
- Annual maintenance, $100

Assuming the alternators cycle the battery between the charge states of 50% and 90%, the relative production costs per kilowatt-hour shown in Figure 10.1 of electricity are:
- 220-amp alternator, $1.25
- 110-amp alternator, $2.30
- 55-amp alternator, $4.10
- Solar panel, $0.42
- 5-foot wind machine, $0.59

The Costs of Conserving Electricity

Now let's compare the costs per kilowatt-hour of electricity *saved* by two simple changes: switching from incandescent to fluorescent lighting, and halving the losses of a DC-powered refrigerator.

Lighting Conversion

An 8-watt fluorescent fixture puts out nearly as much light as a 40-watt incandescent lamp. Assume each replacement fluorescent fixture costs $30. Fluorescent bulbs cost four times as much as incandescent bulbs, but they last proportionally longer, so the cost of bulb replacement is the same.

Assuming a 10-year fixture life, and that the lamp is operated an average of 2 hours per day throughout the year, the lifetime savings of the fluorescent replacement fixture is 124 kilowatt-hours. The cost per kilowatt-hour saved is $30/124 = $0.24—half the cost of electricity produced by the cheapest alternative means, and one-tenth the cost of the 110-amp alternator power.

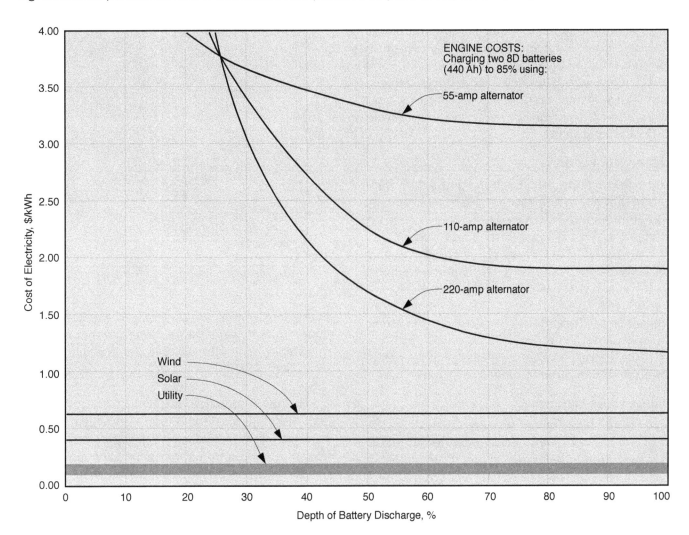

Fig. 10.1 Costs per Kilowatt-Hour of Generated Power (based on 10 years of daily consumption)

ENGINE COSTS:
Charging two 8D batteries
(440 Ah) to 85% using:

55-amp alternator

110-amp alternator

220-amp alternator

Wind
Solar
Utility

Cost of Electricity, $/kWh

Depth of Battery Discharge, %

Refrigerator Losses

Assume that our 8-cubic-foot refrigerator with 2-inch foam insulation draws 5.5 amps at 12 volts DC and has a 40% duty cycle. Its daily consumption would be: 5.5 amps × 24 hours × 0.40 = 52.8 Ah, or 0.63 kilowatt-hour.

If we were to double the insulation of the refrigerator walls to 4 inches, install a better door gasket and install a trap in the drain, we would probably reduce the refrigerator's total heat loss by half, or 0.315 kilowatt-hour/day. Over 10 years of continuous use, the savings would amount to 1,186 kilowatt-hours.

The most effective way to double the refrigerator insulation would be to line the inside of the box with 2-inch polyurethane foam board and then glass over the foam. If accessible, cavities between the box and the hull and cabinetry can be filled with expanding foam.

The first method has the advantage of simplicity, but reduces the volume of the box. The second method retains the box dimensions, but its effectiveness is uncertain without disassembly of the cabinetry.

Method one could be accomplished for about $50 in materials and $200 in labor by a reasonably competent fiberglass technician. Cost per kilowatt-hour saved is thus $250/1,186 kilowatt-hours = $0.21/kilowatt-hour.

Both of our retrofits are at least twice as cost effective as adding solar and wind power, and ten times cheaper than generation by shipboard diesel.

Caveat: The above calculations assume year-round use of the boat for 10 years. If you use your boat only 10% of the year, then solar and wind costs per kilowatt-hour should be multiplied by a factor of 10. That is why this chapter is titled Conservation for Liveaboards.

Lighting Savings

Most boats come from the factory equipped with incandescent lighting. Both the bulbs and the fixtures are inexpensive, but it is a false economy for the owner. You can reduce your lighting load by a full two-thirds through three simple retrofits (see Figures 10.3 and 10.4): fluorescent galley and head fixtures, halogen reading-light fixtures, and, for those who anchor out a lot, a light-actuated anchor light switch or a 3-watt LED all-around light.

Fluorescent Fixtures

The galley requires bright lighting, but 8-watt fluorescent slim-line fixtures cast as much light as common 40-watt incandescent fixtures. For serious chefs, larger fluorescents rated at 13 watts (65 W), 16 watts (80 W) and 26 watts (130 W) are available. The head is another good location for the same types of fluorescent lighting.

If you have 120 VAC light fixtures aboard, you can convert them with compact fluorescent screw-in replacement bulbs and then run these fixtures from a DC-to-AC inverter for similar savings.

If the fluorescent fixtures affect any of your electronics, install the filters described in Chapter 13.

Halogen Spot Fixtures

Many of the lights below deck are for reading. The most common small incandescent fixtures spread the light from 15-watt bulbs over an area ten times that of a page. These lamps can be directly replaced with 5- or 10-watt halogen spot-task lamps, which achieve the same light intensity by concentrating the beam from a high-efficiency halogen bulb onto a page or task.

You can save further lighting energy by installing the solid-state dimmer circuit described in Chapter 14. You can then dim the lights for a warmer ambience, save electricity, and double the lifetime of the lamps, all at the same time.

LEDs

The future of marine lighting is all about LEDs. While Figure 10.2 shows the present efficacy range of LEDs as 22 to 42 lumens per watt (about twice that of incandescents and half that of fluorescents), there is little doubt that 60 to 100 lumens per watt will ultimately be achieved.

The same efficiency as fluorescents, 10 to 100 times the life of halogens and incandescents, indestructible packaging, and easily and efficiently dimmed: sounds like a no-brainer.

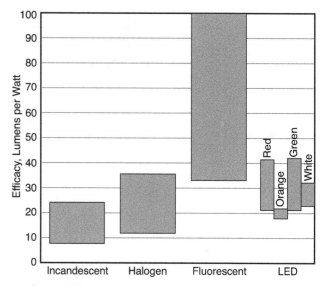

Fig. 10.2 Efficacy of Light Sources

Anchor Lights

International navigation law requires boats less than 20 meters long to display an anchor light that is visible for at least 2 nautical miles. The required luminance is equivalent to that produced by a 10-watt incandescent lamp.

The battery-powered "marker lights" many boaters employ do not meet the 2-mile requirement. Simply reducing incandescent lamp wattage puts your boat in jeopardy—at least from the standpoint of liability.

Two legal, energy-saving alternatives are:

1. Using an automatic anchor light switch
2. Switching to an LED all-round light

Anchor light switch. To run the light from sunrise to when you wake up (or when you first remember the light is on, which may be considerably longer) is wasteful, however. The automatic anchor light switch in Chapter 14 turns the anchor light on and off precisely at sunset and sunrise, saving about 2 Ah per day. If you leave your boat unattended it will save an average of about 10 Ah per day. If building the circuit yourself isn't your idea of a fun way to spend a weekend, several commercial versions are also available.

LED all-around light. Perko (no doubt others will follow suit) has developed an LED all-round light that satisfies the 2 nm visibility requirement for vessels under 20 meters. The design takes advantage of both the LED's inherent efficiency (two times that of incandescents) and its narrow beam (±5°) to focus the light at the horizon. The result is a 75% power reduction, from 10 to 12 watts to only 3 watts.

Fig. 10.3 Bulbs for Boats

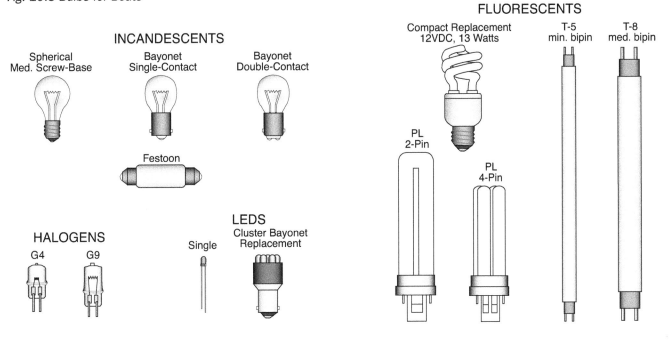

INCANDESCENTS

Spherical
Med. Screw-Base

Bayonet
Single-Contact

Bayonet
Double-Contact

Festoon

HALOGENS
G4   G9

LEDS

Single

Cluster Bayonet
Replacement

FLUORESCENTS

Compact Replacement
12VDC, 13 Watts

T-5
min. bipin

T-8
med. bipin

PL
2-Pin

PL
4-Pin

Fig. 10.4 A Collection of Efficient Fixtures

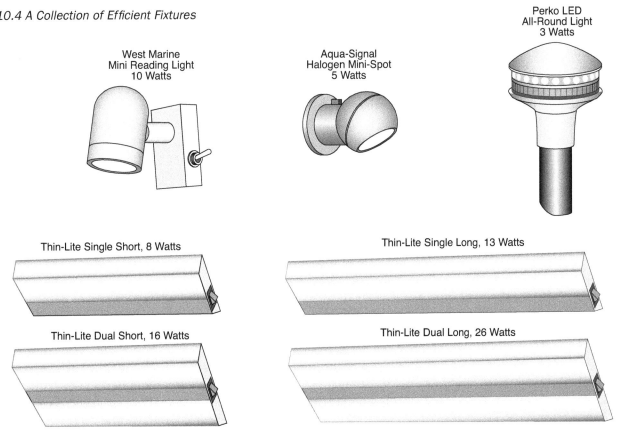

West Marine
Mini Reading Light
10 Watts

Aqua-Signal
Halogen Mini-Spot
5 Watts

Perko LED
All-Round Light
3 Watts

Thin-Lite Single Short, 8 Watts

Thin-Lite Single Long, 13 Watts

Thin-Lite Dual Short, 16 Watts

Thin-Lite Dual Long, 26 Watts

Refrigeration Savings

How Refrigeration Works

If you know that water boils (turns from a liquid to a gas) at 212°F at normal atmospheric pressure, but that its boiling temperature rises at higher pressure (such as in a pressure cooker), and that evaporating water absorbs a lot of heat (think of getting out of the water on a windy day), then you are well on your way to understanding how refrigerators, air conditioners, and heat pumps work.

Unfortunately, the boiling point of water is too high to use it as a refrigerant, but other fluids exist that boil at below the freezing point of water! One such refrigerant is ES-12a (see Figure 10.5), one of many refrigerants developed to replace R-12 (Freon), now banned due to its adverse effect on the earth's ozone layer.

As shown in Figure 10.5, at atmospheric pressure (15 psi), ES-12a boils at about –26°F. If we compress it to a pressure of 150 psi, its boiling temperature rises to about 110°F. Since this rise approximates the range from freezer temperature to maximum atmospheric temperature, ES-12a may prove useful.

In the refrigeration system in Figure 10.6, the refrigerant is sucked into a compressor. The compressor works like the piston of an internal combustion engine, except power is applied to the piston by the crankshaft instead of the other way around. The piston compresses the gas to about 150 psi, in the process raising its temperature to about 120°F.

The hot, compressed gas then flows through the discharge line to a condenser—a heat exchanger—where it is cooled to below its condensation point and changes back to a liquid. In order to condense the 120°F gas, the condenser must be located in a cool space or be cooled by seawater.

From the condenser the hot liquid first passes through a drier, which assures no water contaminates the refrigerant, then on to an expansion valve.

The function of the expansion valve is to control the release of the hot liquid into the low pressure of the evaporator coil. When the fluid emerges from the expansion valve, the dramatic drop back to near atmospheric pressure causes it to boil (evaporate) at about –25°F, absorbing heat from the evaporator coil. The evaporator coil is the frost-covered tubing you see in an older refrigerator or freezer.

From the evaporator the now-cool gas is again sucked into the compressor, and the cycle is repeated.

Now for some details:

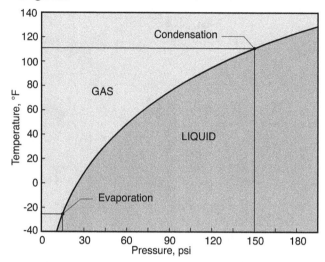

Fig. 10.5 Pressure-Temperature Curve for ES-12a Refrigerant

Condenser

Efficient condenser operation requires efficient heat removal from the tubing. Air-cooled condensers utilize metal fins on the tubing and air flow over the fins to remove the heat. The efficiency of such an arrangement depends on both the temperature of the air and the rate of airflow. A stuffy engine compartment is obviously not a good location for the condenser.

Evaporator

The evaporator shown has little heat-storage capacity. As a result the compressor will cycle on and off every few minutes. A lot of energy is lost starting the compressor, so the efficiency is relatively low. A better system encloses the evaporator coil in a holding plate filled with a liquid having a low freezing point. The compressor runs until all of the holding-plate liquid freezes. The holding plate then functions like a block of ice. Properly sized for the refrigerator box, a holding-plate system requires running the compressor just once a day for an hour or so. By running such a system only when the engine is running, all of the considerable load is removed from the boat's batteries.

Controls

A small temperature-sensing bulb on a capillary tube is attached to the suction end of the evaporator coil. The temperature-dependent pressure in the tube controls the rate of fluid flow through the valve, and thus the temperature of the evaporator coil. When the temperature of the refrigerator box rises, a thermostat switches the compressor on to move and compress refrigerant, cooling the box.

Fig. 10.6 How Refrigerators Work

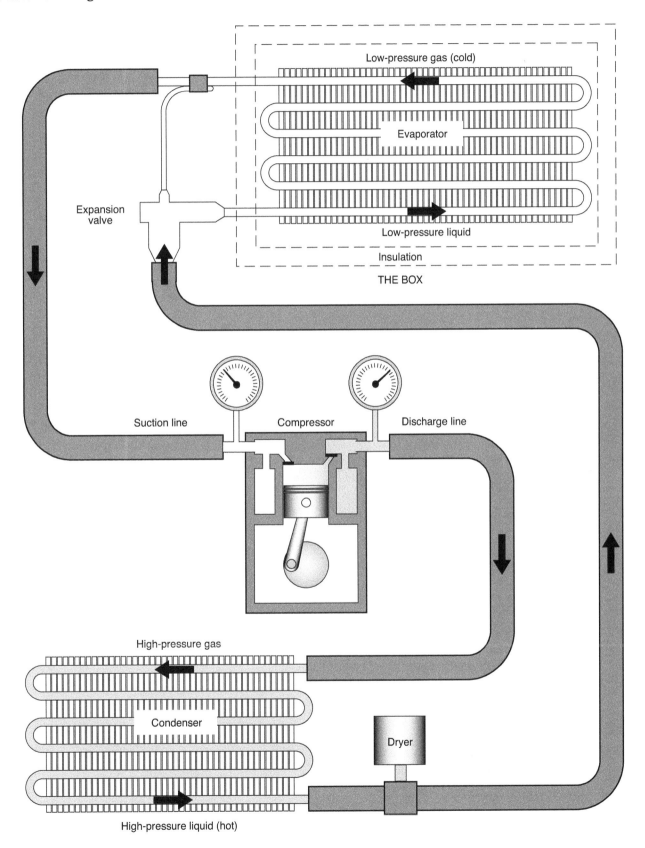

Calculating the Cooling Load

First, two definitions:
- Btu = heat that changes the temperature of 1 pound of water by 1F°.
- Heat of fusion of water (heat absorbed by 1 pound of ice when it melts) = 144 Btu.

Next, Figure 10.7 shows the basic equation of conductive heat loss:

$$H = A \times \Delta T / R$$

where:

H = heat loss through A, in Btu/hour
A = area of surface in square feet
ΔT = temperature difference, $T_{outside} - T_{inside}$F°
R = thermal resistance

To this conductive heat loss through the refrigerator walls we have to add the losses of infiltration (air leakage through the lid and drain) and cooldown (heat that must be removed from warm objects added to the box).

The Refrigerator Box

Figure 10.8 shows the dimensions of a typical 8-cubic-foot refrigerator. The walls are constructed of 2-inch urethane foam, lined with fiberglass. Plugging the numbers into the heat-loss equation above:

A = 28 square feet (insulation mid-plane)
ΔT = 75°F outside − 40°F inside
    = 35F°
R = 2 inches × R-6/inch
    = 12
H = 28 × 35/12
    = 82 Btu/hour

If this box had a perfect lid and we never opened it, it would melt 82 Btu/hour/144 Btu/pound = 0.57 pound of ice per hour or 13.7 pounds of ice per day. If we add another third (27 Btu/hour) to the heat loss for infiltration and cooldown, our totals become 109 Btu/hour and 18 pounds of ice per day.

How much electricity will it take to replace the ice? The answer is—it all depends. It depends primarily on the efficiency of the refrigeration system, the refrigerator's coefficient of performance (COP), defined as:

COP = watts removed/watts used

We'll also need a conversion factor:

Ah/day = 0.586 × Btu/hour

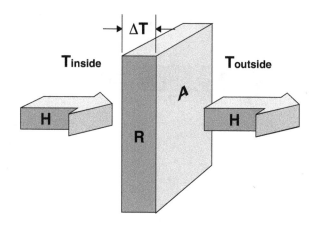

Fig. 10.7 Conductive Heat Loss

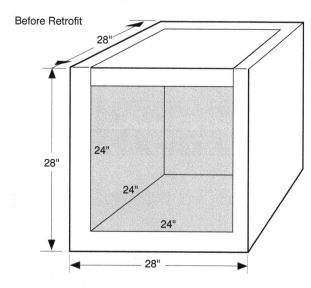

Fig. 10.8 Typical Refrigerator Box

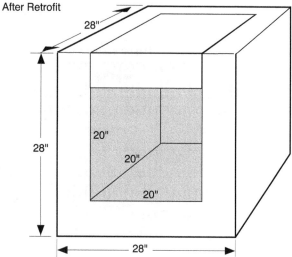

COP depends on how hard the compressor has to work pumping heat from the evaporator (cold) side to the condenser (hot) side. When the temperatures of evaporator and condenser are the same, the compressor can remove about 3 Btu of heat energy, using the equivalent of 1 Btu of electrical energy, yielding a COP of 3.0.

At the opposite extreme, the typical refrigerator is capable of moving heat across a maximum difference of about 150F°, at which point its COP becomes zero.

Figure 10.9 shows the relationship between COP and condenser temperature for a typical small refrigerator, assuming the evaporator is at 20°F.

The temperature of the condenser depends on its type and location. Table 10.1 shows typical condenser operating temperatures and resulting COPs for different condenser types and locations in the boat.

Assume the condenser is located in free air at 75°F but has no fan. According to Table 10.1, its COP will be about 1.3. Our example refrigerator will then draw 190 Btu/hr × 0.586/1.3 = 49 Ah/day.

A Typical Refrigerator Retrofit

To reduce the refrigeration load we can take three steps:

1. Increase wall insulation.
2. Decrease infiltration with a better lid gasket and a drain trap.
3. Increase condenser COP with a fan.

Wall Insulation

At the cost of 3.4 cubic feet of interior space, we can double the insulation of all surfaces and increase their R-values to R-24. Because we also have decreased the heat loss area (measured at the midpoint of the insulation) to 24 square feet, conductive heat loss is decreased by 47 Btu/hour to 35 Btu/hour.

Infiltration

By installing a better gasket on the lid and a better melt-water drain trap, we might decrease the losses due to air leaks by half, or 13 Btu/hour, and the total heat loss by 60 Btu/hour to 49 Btu/hour.

Condensor COP

By installing a thermostatically controlled 12-volt DC fan to move air through the condenser coils, we can increase the condenser COP from about 1.3 to 1.7 at the cost of about 2 Ah per day to power the fan. Most

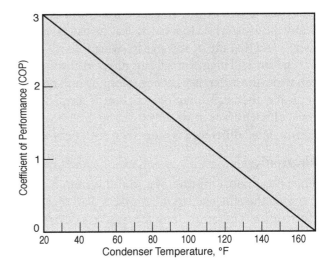

Fig. 10.9 Refrigerator COP vs. Temperature

Table 10.1 Refrigerator COP vs. Location

Condenser/Location	Condenser Temp., °F	COP
Air-cooled in 110°F engine compartment, no fan	140	0.6
Air-cooled in 110°F engine compartment with fan	120	1.0
Air-cooled in 75°F free air with no fan	105	1.3
Air-cooled in 75°F free air with fan	85	1.7
Water-cooled, intake water 75°F	85	1.7
Water-cooled, intake water 60°F	70	2.0

marine and RV refrigeration manufacturers offer such fans as an option. If not, small fans that run on 12 VDC are readily available at electronics stores, such as RadioShack. DIY Project 13 (Chapter 14) is a circuit to control such a fan.

Manufacturers also sometimes offer water cooling, where the condenser is cooled by water circulated to a heat exchanger mounted on the bottom of the hull. While more efficient in cooler waters, such systems are susceptible to becoming fouled with growth.

Net Refrigerator Savings

With the above improvements, our new refrigeration load becomes 60 Btu/hour × 0.586/1.7 = 20.7 Ah/day—a decrease of more than 50%.

Other Savings

Cabin Fans

The most efficient way to cool a hot cabin is with a wind chute attached to a hatch, but its use assumes a breeze and that the boat is free to swing into it.

On hot, still nights, small fans directed at your body can make the difference between sleeping and not. The typical 6-inch cabin fan draws about 1 amp, but the most efficient fans draw only 0.3 amp. In 8 hours the accumulated difference is more than 5 Ah per fan.

Electronics

The power consumption of a sound system depends more on the efficiency of the speakers than that of the electronics. Therefore, look for speakers designed to be driven by computers, as they are the most efficient.

No one is willing to watch black and white television any longer, so the choice is between the older standard cathode-ray (CRT) color television and the newer, solid-state LCD versions. Wattage is roughly propor-

tional to the area of the screen (diameter squared). From a 19-inch CRT to a 6-inch LCD there is a 65-watt, or 5-amp, difference. If you are an average 4-hour-per-day boob-tube watcher, the daily difference is greater than the drain of the anchor light. An excellent way to save energy is, therefore, to install a 6-inch LCD television and sit closer!

VCRs and DVD players are becoming very popular on boats. In fact, trading videotapes and DVDs is nearly as common as trading paperback books. The typical 120-volt AC record/play VCR/DVD machine draws about 17 watts. Portable 12-volt DC play-only models draw 10 watts.

The Bottom Line

Table 10.2 shows, as promised, how the daily power consumption of a typical cruising boat can be reduced by half with no significant degradation of lifestyle.

Table 10.2 Power Consumption of a Typical versus an Energy-Efficient Liveaboard Boat

Area	Device		Watts	Amps	Hours/ Day	Typical Ah	Efficient Ah
Galley	Microwave		550	45.8	0.15	6.9	6.9
	Toaster		800	66.7	0.04		
	Blender		175	14.6	0.01	0.1	0.1
	Coffee grinder		160	13.3	0.01		
	Refrigerator	2" insul.	60	5.0	10.00	49.0	
		4" insul	60	5.0	5.00		20.7
Head	Hair dryer		1,200	100.0	0.03		
Lights	Reading	2 incand., 15 W	30	2.5	2.00	5.0	
		2 halogen, 5 W	10	0.8	2.00		1.6
	Galley	2 incand., 25 W	50	4.2	2.00	8.4	
		2 fluor., 8 W	16	1.4	2.00		2.8
	Anchor	manual, 10 W	10	0.8	14.00	11.2	
		auto., 10 W	10	0.8	11.00		8.8
Fans	Typical 6-inch, 100 cfm		12	1.0	5.00	5.0	
	Most efficient, 100 cfm		4	0.3	5.00		1.5
Electronics	Stereo	20 W/channel	60	5.0	1.00	5.0	
		7 W/channel	35	3.0	1.00		3.0
	Television, color, 19" CRT		80	6.7	2.00	13.4	
		15" LCD	36	3.0	2.00		
		6" LCD	15	1.25	2.00		2.5
VCR or DVD	Typical 120-volt AC		17	1.4	1.0	1.4	
	12-volt DC play-only		10	0.8	1.0		0.8
					Totals	105.4	48.7

CHAPTER 11

Solar Power

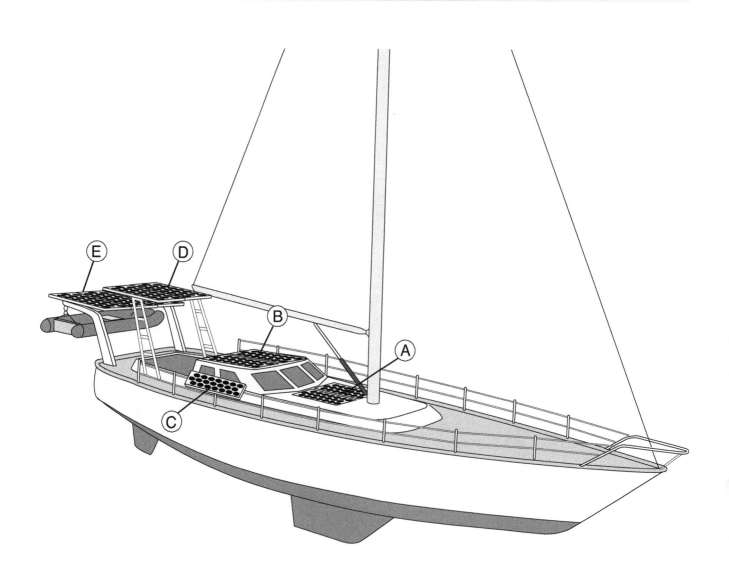

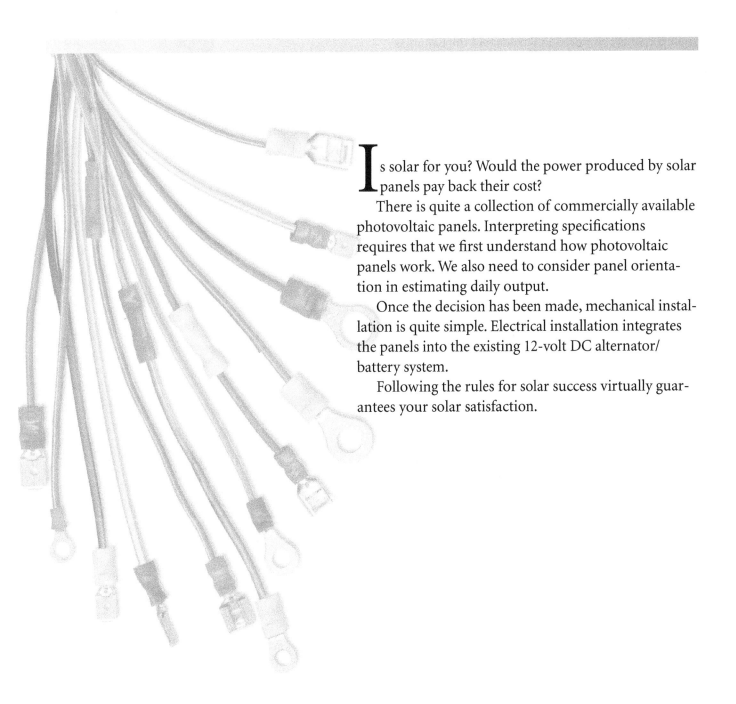

I s solar for you? Would the power produced by solar panels pay back their cost?

There is quite a collection of commercially available photovoltaic panels. Interpreting specifications requires that we first understand how photovoltaic panels work. We also need to consider panel orientation in estimating daily output.

Once the decision has been made, mechanical installation is quite simple. Electrical installation integrates the panels into the existing 12-volt DC alternator/battery system.

Following the rules for solar success virtually guarantees your solar satisfaction.

Is Solar for You?

A solar, or photovoltaic, installation is a one-time investment with a fuel- and maintenance-free lifetime of 10 years or longer. Whether a photovoltaic system would prove cost effective on your boat, however, depends very much on how you use the boat. If you live aboard and are away from the dock at least half of the time, the answer is a definite "yes." If you cruise 1 month each summer, the answer is probably "no."

Figure 11.1 shows the percentage of daily electrical load supplied by photovoltaic panels among 71 live-aboard cruisers surveyed in Florida and the Bahamas. The average installation was far smaller than optimal, yet the average percentage of power supplied was a significant 40%. Had the array sizes been optimal, I am sure the power supplied would have been in the 80 to 100% range.

Also note from Figure 11.1 that cruisers who had both solar and wind systems garnered more than 90% of their power from the combination. Those having wind power, but no solar, generated 60% from the wind.

Figure 10.1 compared the costs per kilowatt-hour of electricity produced by photovoltaic panels, wind machines, and engine-driven alternators. The photovoltaic cost of $0.42/kilowatt-hour assumed:
- System used year-round
- Panel size—50 watts peak output
- Price including controls—$400
- Life—10 years
- Average daily sunshine—5.2 hours
- Maintenance—$0

Such a panel would produce on average 5.2 hours × 50 watts = 0.26 kWh per day, or 95 kWh per year. An alternative source of power would be a high-output, 110-amp alternator, charging batteries on a 50 to 85 percent-of-charge cycle. This, according to Figure 10.1, would produce power at a cost of $2.30 per kilowatt-hour.

Compared to the cost of alternator power, solar savings would be $2.30 − $0.42 = $1.88 per kilowatt-hour. At 95 kilowatt-hours per year, annual savings would be $179, and the photovoltaic system would pay for itself in $400/$177 = 2.2 years. That amounts to receiving a tax-free return on investment of 45%. Try to match that at your local bank!

On the other hand, if the boat were used but 1 month out of the year, the payback would be 27 years—longer than the projected life of the system.

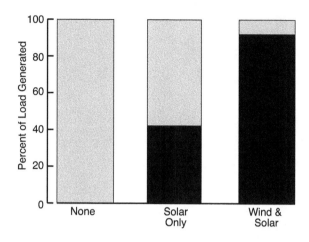

Fig. 11.1 Solar Energy Production among 71 Cruisers

Figure 11.2 shows how a photovoltaic panel works. Solar energy in the form of photons penetrates the photovoltaic material. Each photon transfers enough energy to the photovoltaic atoms to release an electron. If we connect the grid on the sunlit side to the conducting base on the backside, the free electrons will flow through the external conductor and load to rejoin atoms having missing electrons.

Each free electron has a potential of about 0.6 volt. A panel typically consists of from 30 to 36 cells, connected in series to produce an open-circuit voltage of from 18 to 22 VDC. The theoretical maximum efficiency of this conversion of light energy to electrical energy is about 28%. As we will see, however, the efficiencies achieved in manufacture are improving but still fall far short of theory.

Photovoltaic collector materials take three common forms: monocrystalline silicon, polycrystalline silicon, and amorphous silicon. Crystalline silicon is grown in the form of large crystals, which are sawn into thin wafers to form the cells.

Monocrystalline cells consist of single, large crystals grown and drawn from melted silicon in the form of large rods. Due to their crystalline perfection, they have the highest efficiencies, ranging from 14 to 17%.

Polycrystalline silicon is formed by pouring melted silicon into blocks, the molten silicon forming many small crystals on cooling. These polycrystalline blocks are then sawn into cells. Because of defects between the crystals, the conversion efficiency of polycrystalline silicon ranges between 13 and 15%.

Amorphous silicon is produced by the less expensive process of depositing vaporized silicon onto a metal substrate. In addition to being less expensive to produce, amorphous silicon can be fabricated into semirigid and flexible panels. Semi-rigid panels attached to a thin steel backing can be adhered to a deck and stepped on without damage. Flexible panels with a heavy fabric backing can be attached to boat canvas. Unfortunately, the efficiency of amorphous silicon is only 5 to 7%, so twice as much collector area is required as for crystalline panels.

Most crystalline photovoltaic panels are warranted for 20 years, but there is no reason, barring physical damage, that they would not last 30 years or longer.

Amorphous silicon panels, because they are not enclosed in a rigid, protective frame, are generally warranted for only 5 years.

Fig. 11.2 How Photovoltaics Work

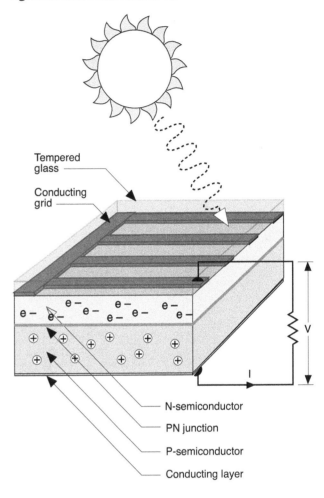

Tempered glass

Conducting grid

N-semiconductor

PN junction

P-semiconductor

Conducting layer

Photovoltaic Panels

Table 11.1 lists the specifications of the most popular photovoltaic panels. All panel output ratings are for 25°C (86°F). Rigid panels are in aluminum frames, and can be mounted to davits, bimini frames, and stanchions. Semirigid panels may be adhered directly to the deck. Flexible panels may be draped anywhere. On average you can expect (in 2005) to pay about $6 per rated watt for rigid panels, $8 for semirigid, and $12 for flexible. Add about $2 per rated watt for controls and mounting hardware.

Table 11.1 Photovoltaic Panel Specifications[1]

Model	Rigid (R) Semirigid (S) Flexible (F)[2]	Dimensions, inches	Rated Watts	Rated Amps	Open-Circuit Volts	Short-Circuit Amps	Warranty Years
ICP Solar Pro[3]							
Plug'n'Play 30	R	41 x 12.4	30	2.00	—	—	Life
Plug'n'Play 50	R	41.3 x 20	50	3.30	—	—	Life
Plug'n'Play 75	R	50 x 23.3	75	5.00	—	—	Life
Plug'n'Play 100	R	60.3 x 28	100	6.70	—	—	Life
Solara							
SM40M	S	16.6 x 10.7	10	0.50	21.0	—	20
SM60M	S	24.4 x 9.8	15	0.90	21.0	—	20
SM80M	S	16.9 x 17.7	20	1.10	21.0	—	20
SM120M	S	23.2 x 17.7	30	1.70	21.0	—	20
SM160M	S	29.0 x 17.7	40	2.20	21.0	—	20
SM225M	S	29.5 x 24.0	56	3.00	21.0	—	20
United Solar (Unisolar)							
USF-5	F	21.3 x 9.7	5	0.30	16.5	0.33	5
USF-11	F	21.3 x 16.7	11	0.62	16.5	0.69	5
USF-32	F	55.8 x 16.7	32	1.94	16.5	2.10	5
Kyocera							
KC35	R	18.5 x 25.7	35	2.33	18.8	2.50	25
KC40	R	20.7 x 25.7	40	2.34	21.5	2.48	25
KC50	R	25.2 x 25.7	50	3.00	21.5	3.10	25
KC60	R	29.6 x 25.7	60	3.55	21.5	3.73	25
KC70	R	34.1 x 25.7	70	4.14	21.5	4.35	25
KC80	R	38.4 x 25.7	80	4.73	21.5	4.97	25
KC120-1	R	56.1 x 25.7	120	7.10	21.5	7.45	25
Shell Solar (Siemens)							
SM20	R	22.3 x 12.9	20	1.38	18.0	1.60	10
SM46	R	42.7 x 13	46	3.15	18.0	3.35	25
SM55	R	50.9 x 13	55	3.15	21.7	3.45	25
SM75	R	47.3 x 20.8	75	4.40	21.7	4.80	25
SM110	R	51.8 x 26	110	6.30	21.7	6.90	25
BP Solar (Solarex)							
BP MSX5L	S	10.8 x 10.5	4.5	0.27	20.5	0.30	5
BP MSX10L	S	17.5 x 10.5	10	0.58	21.0	0.65	5
BP MSX20L	S	17.5 x 19.5	20	1.17	21.0	1.29	5
BP MSX30L	S	24.3 x 19.5	30	1.75	21.0	1.94	5
BP MSX40	R	29.9 x 19.7	40	2.37	21.0	2.58	20
BP MSX60	R	43.5 x 19.7	60	3.56	21.0	3.80	25

[1] All ratings at 25°C (86°F).
[2] Flexible panels for mounting directly to deck.
[3] Plug'n'Play panels include a charge controller.

Figure 11.3 shows the voltage-current curve for a typical 30-cell photovoltaic panel in full sunlight. With output terminals shorted, the panel put out its short-circuit current (here 3.3 amps). With output terminals not connected, current is zero, but output voltage is the open-circuit voltage (here 18.0 volts). Maximum power output is achieved at the knee of the curve where the rated current (3.0 amps) times the rated voltage (14.7 volts) equals the panel's rated power (44 watts).

Fig. 11.3 Typical Photovoltaic Panel Output Curve

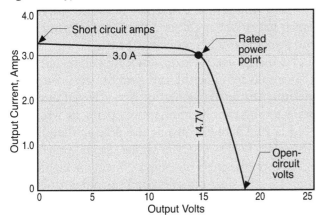

Figure 11.4 shows how the voltage-current curves vary both with number of cells and with panel temperature. Panel specifications are given for a panel (not air) temperature of 25°C (86°F). Both voltage and current decrease at higher temperatures. For this reason, panels should be mounted with free airflow beneath to minimize operating temperature. Panels in the tropics should have higher voltage ratings as well.

The effect of shading is not shown in manufacturers' voltage-current curves. Shading the panel from direct sun does not affect open-circuit voltage, but reduces power output under load roughly in proportion to the percentage of shaded area.

Finally, unless built in, you should install a Schottky blocking diode to prevent reverse-current flow from the batteries at night. Better yet, install a regulator that opens the circuit whenever the panel voltage is less than that of the battery.

A common mistake in selecting solar panels is failing to account for all of the voltage drops. Select a panel whose rated voltage at your expected operating temperature is at least 14.8 volts, since 14.8 volts − 0.4 volt (blocking diode drop) = 14.4 volts, the voltage required for fully charging lead-acid batteries. In order to equalize the batteries, the blocking diode can be temporarily shorted with clip leads, raising the voltage to 14.8.

Fig. 11.4 Typical Photovoltaic Output vs. Number of Cells and Panel Temperature

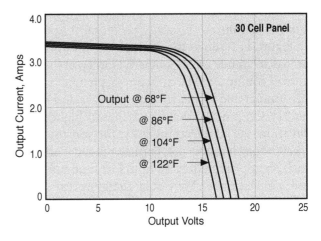

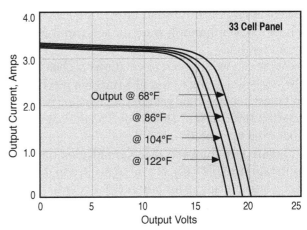

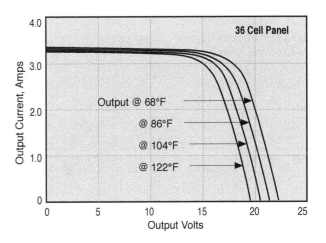

Panel Orientation

To understand how panel orientation affects the output of a photovoltaic system, we must consider how the sun moves through the sky, both throughout the day and with the seasons.

Figure 11.5 shows the track of the sun over a boat located at latitude 24°N (southern Florida) at the spring and fall equinoxes (March 21 and September 21), and the summer and winter solstices (June 21 and December 21). On June 21, the sun reaches its highest noon elevation, 90°. On December 21, the sun reaches its lowest noon elevation, 43°. Further, the sun is above the horizon approximately 16 hours in June but only 8 hours in December. We would, therefore, expect a lot less solar input in December than in June.

Panel output ratings assume full sunlight with the sun's rays normal (perpendicular) to the panel surface. Panels in large utility "solar farms" are mounted on frames that continuously track the sun's orbit for maximum output.

What can we do about orientation on a boat? You're obviously not going to install a tracking mechanism, and most people would get tired of adjusting panel orientation three or four times a day. So the question is: what fixed tilt is best?

Figure 11.6 compares the solar radiation on a horizontal surface (tilt = 0°) and surfaces tilted to the south at the latitude angle, for latitudes 24°N (Miami) and 40°N (New York), on both the longest (June 21) and shortest (December 21) days. On June 21, if we are both smart and mobile, we will be at, or around, latitude 40°N. Figure 11.6 shows that a horizontal panel will collect 119% of the radiation collected by a fixed panel tilted south at 40°.

On December 21 we hope to be in the neighborhood of Miami, where our horizontal panel will collect 72% as much radiation as a fixed panel tilted south at 24°.

Thus we see, averaged over the year, a horizontal panel will perform as well as a fixed, south-tilted panel.

"But," you say, "if I were at a dock, I could tilt my panels toward the noon sun." But if you were at a dock, you wouldn't need photovoltaic panels.

Further, if you were on a mooring or anchor, your boat would swing without regard for the position of the sun. Any fixed orientation you selected might be perfectly right at one moment but perfectly wrong an hour later. There is only one orientation that doesn't change as a boat swings: horizontal (facing straight up).

To show the effect of compass direction, Figure 11.7 compares the solar radiation on horizontal panels and vertical panels facing north, east, south, and west. Although vertical east and west panels collect significant amounts of radiation in morning and afternoon respectively, both collect for only half a day, so their total collection is small. Conclusion: the only practical solar panel orientation on a cruising boat is horizontal.

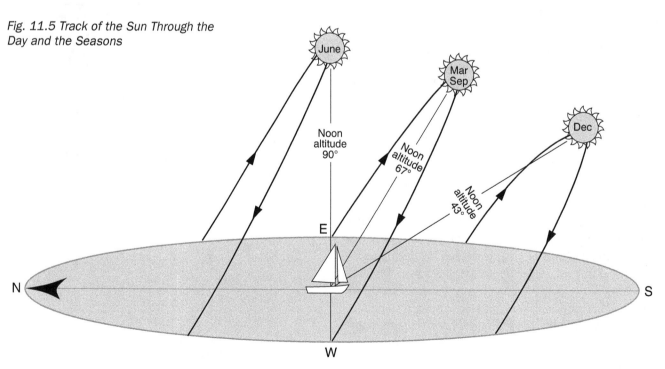

Fig. 11.5 Track of the Sun Through the Day and the Seasons

Fig. 11.6 Hourly Radiation on Horizontal and Tilted Surfaces

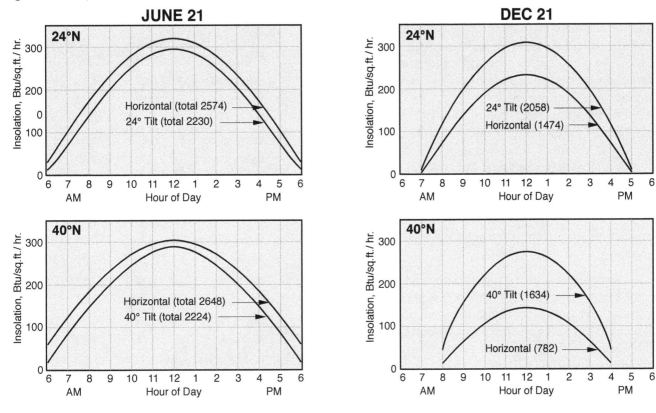

Fig. 11.7 Hourly Radiation on Horizontal and Vertical Surfaces

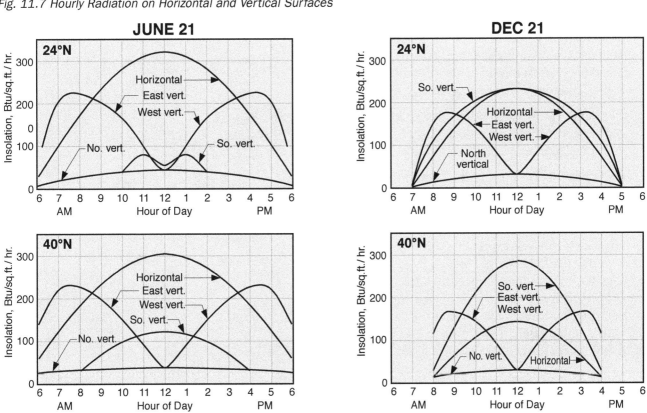

Estimating Output

Because the fixed horizontal orientation is the most practical on a non-stationary platform, solar-availability tables and maps often show total radiation on a horizontal surface. Figure 11.8 contains such seasonal maps. Table 11.2 lists, for selected locations, more precise values of average daily solar radiation falling on horizontal surfaces during:

- the sunniest month (Highest Month)
- the least sunny month (Lowest Month)
- the entire year (Annual Average)

The values are in equivalent hours of full sunlight, where full sunlight is defined as 1,000 watts/meter^2.

These values allow easy estimation of solar panel performance: the average daily output is simply the panel rating in watts times the equivalent hours of full sunlight.

Example 1—always in a sunny location: How many kilowatt-hours of output can you expect over an entire year from a horizontally mounted, 60-watt panel in Miami, FL? In Table 11.2 we find for Miami an annual average figure of 5.62. Thus we can expect a 60-watt panel to produce an average of 60 watts × 5.62 hours = 337 watt-hours per day. Over the entire year, we would expect 365 × 337 watt-hours = 123 kilowatt-hours.

Example 2—Florida in winter and Maine in summer: With the limited figures in Table 11.2, the simplest approximation would be to use the Lowest Month figure for Miami for the 6 months centered on winter and the Highest Month figure for Portland, ME, for the 6 months centered on summer.

Miami, FL: 60 × 5.05 × 365/2 = 55.3 kWh
Portland, ME: 60 × 5.23 × 365/2 = 57.3 kWh
Annual total = 112.6 kWh

In Chapter 10, we retrofitted a boat to reduce its electrical load to 48.7 Ah per day. As we saw in the examples above, in a sunny climate, or for a liveaboard boat following the sun, a solar array consisting of two 60-watt panels could be expected to provide an average of 2 × 112.6 = 225 kWh/yr. Dividing by 12 volts and 365 days, the array output averages 51.4 Ah/day or less than 100% of the boat's load. Provided the battery bank was sized at roughly four times the daily draw, this cruiser would rarely, if ever, have to use his engine for the sole purpose of charging the batteries.

Table 11.2 Average Daily Radiation on a Horizontal Surface, in Equivalent Hours of Full Direct Sunlight

State	City	Highest Month	Lowest Month	Annual Average
AK	Fairbanks	5.87	2.12	3.99
AK	Matanuska	5.24	1.74	3.55
CA	La Jolla	5.24	4.29	4.77
CA	Los Angeles	6.14	5.03	5.62
CA	Santa Maria	6.52	5.42	5.94
DC	Washington	4.69	3.37	4.23
FL	Apalachicola	5.98	4.92	5.49
FL	Belle Is.	5.31	4.58	4.99
FL	Miami	6.26	5.05	5.62
FL	Tampa	6.16	5.26	5.67
HI	Honolulu	6.71	5.59	6.02
IL	Chicago	4.08	1.47	3.14
LA	Lake Charles	5.73	4.29	4.93
LA	New Orleans	5.71	3.63	4.92
MA	Boston	4.27	2.99	3.84
MA	E. Wareham	4.48	3.06	3.99
MD	Silver Hill	4.71	3.84	4.47
ME	Portland	5.23	3.56	4.51
NC	Cape Hatteras	5.81	4.69	5.31
NJ	Sea Brook	4.76	3.20	4.21
NY	New York City	4.97	3.03	4.08
NY	Rochester	4.22	1.58	3.31
OR	Astoria	4.76	1.99	3.72
OR	Corvallis	5.71	1.90	4.03
OR	Medford	5.84	2.02	4.51
RI	Newport	4.69	3.58	4.23
SC	Charleston	5.72	4.23	5.06
TX	Brownsville	5.49	4.42	4.92
TX	San Antonio	5.88	4.65	5.30
VA	Richmond	4.50	3.37	4.13
WA	Prosser	6.21	3.06	5.03
WA	Seattle	4.83	1.60	3.57

*Fig. 11.8 Maps of Average Daily Radiation on a Horizontal Surface,
in Equivalent Hours of Full Direct Sunlight*

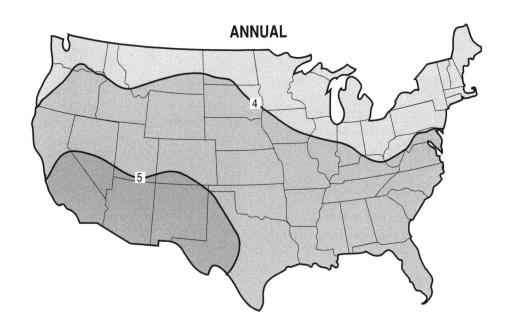

ANNUAL

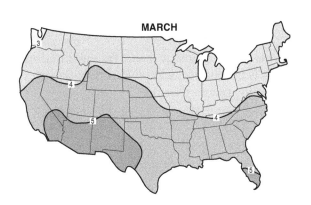

MARCH

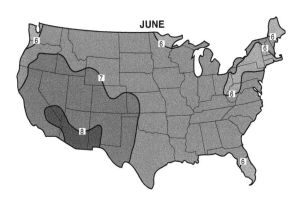

JUNE

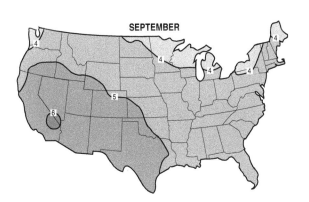

SEPTEMBER

DECEMBER

Mechanical Installation

Fastening

Solar panels are extremely lightweight and strong. Their extruded aluminum frames make mechanical fastening a snap. Multiple panels can be fastened together loosely using stainless machine screws, locknuts, and rubber grommets as shown in Figure 11.9. The assembly of panels can then be fastened to the stainless or aluminum tubing of a dodger, bimini, radar arch, or davits. Alternately, each panel can be fastened individually, or multiple panels can be fastened within a frame, and the frame fastened to the boat.

Panel Location

The critical part of panel installation is choosing the location. Figure 11.10 shows five locations for a system of four panels.

> *Location A*, on the deck just aft of the main mast, is shaded by both mast and boom, is in the way during mainsail operations, and is a target for objects dropped from the mast.
>
> *Location B*, on top of a pilot house, is a better location than A because it is out of the way and farther from the drop zone. And, to avoid shading, the boom could be swung to the side with a preventer.
>
> *Location C* is often seen because solar suppliers offer the mounting hardware and because it allows tilting of the panels. As we saw above, however, tilting the

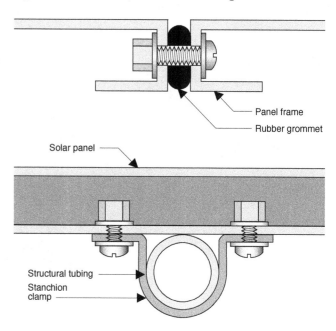

Fig. 11.9 Panel Clamp for Bimini or Dodger Frame

Panel frame

Rubber grommet

Solar panel

Structural tubing

Stanchion clamp

panels offers no advantage. Worse is the fact that the panels extend beyond the rail, where they are subject to damage while docking.

> *Location D*, in a horizontal frame on top of a radar arch, is both out of the way and free from shade.
>
> *Location E*, in a similar frame fastened to dinghy davits, is as good as Location D. It is shade-free, out of the way, and very secure.

Fig. 11.10 Candidate Panel Locations

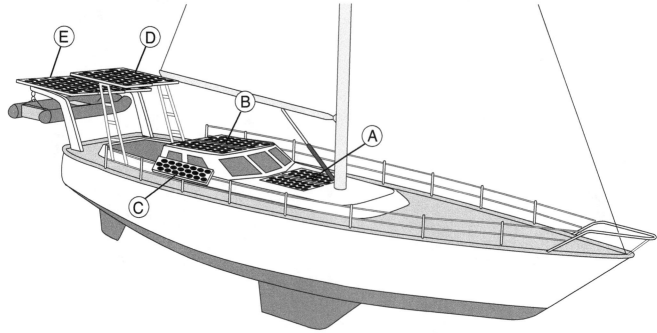

Figure 11.11 shows a typical proper photovoltaic installation. The important elements are:

1. *Fuse or circuit breaker.* The positive leads from all charging sources except the alternator should be overcurrent protected by fuses or circuit breakers, as close to the battery as possible. The reason is that unprotected leads might short, melting the conductor insulation, damaging the batteries, and possibly starting a fire. Furthermore, if the output current of a short-circuited solar panel could exceed the conductor capacity, the charge controller should be fused, as well.

2. *Blocking diode.* There should be blocking diodes between the battery and panel positive terminals to prevent reverse flow at night (unless the charge controller opens the circuit when panel voltage is too low). The diodes should connect to the battery side of any isolation diodes from the alternator to avoid the double voltage drop of isolation diode and blocking diode.

3. *Charge controller.* Unless the total panel-rated

current is less than 0.5% of total battery capacity (2 amps for a 400 Ah battery bank), a charge controller is required to prevent overcharging the batteries. A switch should be provided to bypass the controller, however, so that a battery equalization charge might be applied occasionally. If panel voltage is marginal, you might install a switch to temporarily bypass the blocking diodes as well.

The simplest way to satisfy all three requirements is to purchase a charge controller that contains all three features. The best controllers allow full current up to about 14.4 volts, then taper to a float charge. Some controllers automatically switch excess panel output to a resistance load, such as a 12-volt DC water heater element, thereby extracting maximum use from the panel output.

Naturally, all DC wiring standards, such as conductor ampacity, stranding, insulation, and fastening, apply as well to solar installations.

Fig. 11.11 Electrical Hookup of Solar Panels (Wind Generator Optional)

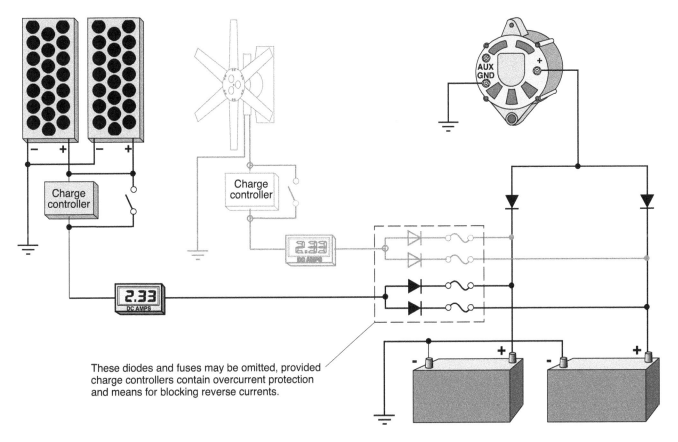

These diodes and fuses may be omitted, provided charge controllers contain overcurrent protection and means for blocking reverse currents.

Rules for Solar Success

If you want a photovoltaic system to supply all or nearly all of your electrical energy needs, you must:

1. Reduce your average daily electrical consumption to 60 Ah or less. See Chapter 10 for suggestions.

2. Install sufficient panel area. Use Figures 11.8 through 11.10 to calculate the required panel wattage for the areas you plan to cruise.

3. Install the panels in a permanent, horizontal, shade-free location.

4. Do not depend on tilting of the panels, removing shading objects, or controlling boat orientation to increase panel output.

5. Select panels with sufficient rated voltage to overcome the voltage drops due to blocking diodes (if present), operating temperature, and anticipated shading.

6. Install a charge controller that does not require blocking diodes.

7. Make solid, corrosion-free electrical connections and protect with corrosion inhibitor.

8. Clean the panel surfaces of dust and salt spray regularly.

CHAPTER 12

Wind Power

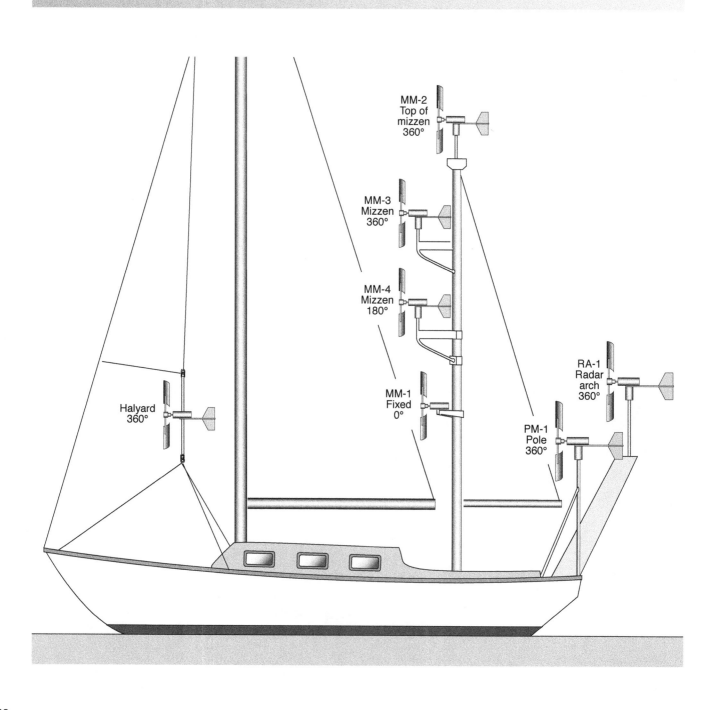

MM-2
Top of
mizzen
360°

MM-3
Mizzen
360°

MM-4
Mizzen
180°

RA-1
Radar
arch
360°

MM-1
Fixed
0°

Halyard
360°

PM-1
Pole
360°

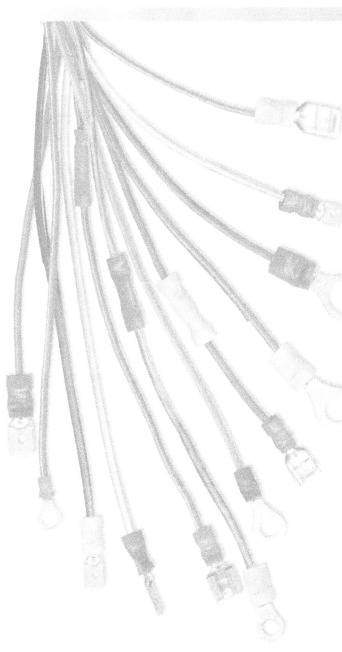

If not solar power, then is wind power for you? Again, calculating the economics will tell.

Getting power from the wind explains how the kinetic energy of moving air can be converted to electrical energy.

In order to estimate the daily output of a wind machine, we need to know how much wind there is where we will be cruising and the specifications of our wind machine.

The most difficult part of mechanical installation is simply selecting the best location on the boat. As in the case of solar panels, the electrical installation of a wind machine requires integration with the existing alternator battery system.

At least one popular wind machine can be converted into a water generator—a feature long-distance cruisers may wish to consider.

Is Wind Power for You?

The variables determining the viability of wind power on a boat are much more complicated than those for photovoltaics, but the general criteria remain the same—if you live aboard, are away from the dock at least 6 months of the year, and actively seek out windy areas, the answer is probably yes; if you use your boat only 1 month per year, the answer is no.

Before delving into the economics of wind power production, you should note several non-economic factors that are unique to wind:

1. *Maintenance.* Wind machines are of two types: the familiar alternator, and DC electric motors running backward. Both produce AC electricity, but rectify it (change AC to DC) in different ways. As we saw in Chapter 4, alternators employ solid-state diode bridges. The DC-motor types, however, rely on brushes and commutators, both of which are subject to wear and maintenance. Also, both types contain bearings which will require replacement.

2. *Noise.* All wind machines make noise, ranging from the barely perceptible whisper of a small, six-bladed Ampair, to the "woof, woof, woof" of a large, two-bladed, mizzen-mounted machine. Generally, the more power being generated, the louder the noise. Some find the noise of a large machine satisfying, an audible reminder that their batteries are being recharged for free. Others—particularly sailors on nearby boats—find the sound annoying. You would be wise to spend time on a boat with a particular model before purchasing.

3. *Safety.* The higher the wind speed, the greater the output of a wind machine. But wind speeds over about 30 knots pose several potential problems, particularly with the larger-diameter machines: (1) the high centrifugal forces and vibration on the blades may cause fatigue and failure (throwing a blade), (2) the electrical output may become too much for the batteries or charge regulator to handle, and (3) it may prove impossible to shut the machine down, either manually (picture trying to stop an airplane propeller) or automatically. All of the manufacturers have addressed this issue, but in various ways. Make sure you understand the shutdown mechanism of the machine you are thinking of purchasing, and talk to several owners about their experiences.

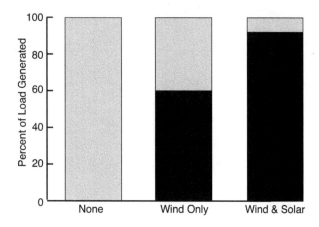

Fig. 12.1 Wind Power Production on Cruising Boats

Economics

Figure 12.1 shows the percentage of daily electrical load supplied by wind among 71 liveaboard boats surveyed in Florida and the Bahamas. Most of the wind machines were of the large (60-inch blade diameter) variety. The fact that 40% of the average daily load still had to be supplied by running the engine shows that wind is not constant. Decreasing the daily load through conservation (see Chapter 10) and increasing battery capacity could increase the wind contribution to 80% or more.

An interesting alternative is the combination of wind and solar, which, as shown in Figure 12.1, supplied an average of 96% of the daily load.

Figure 10.1 compared the costs of power generated by wind, solar, and alternators of various sizes. The $0.59 kilowatt-hour cost of wind power assumed:
- Wind machine lifetime—10 years
- Installed cost—$1,500
- Annual maintenance—$100
- Blade diameter—60 inches
- Conversion efficiency—30 percent
- Average wind speed—10 knots

Such a wind machine would produce 420 kilowatt-hours per year in a steady 10-knot wind. One of the conventional alternatives, also shown in Figure 10.1, is a 110-amp engine alternator charging the batteries on a 50 to 90% cycle at a cost of $2.25 per kilowatt-hour.

The example wind machine savings would thus be $2.25 – $0.59 = $1.66 per kilowatt-hour, or $697 per year. The machine would pay for itself in a little over 2 years. Unfortunately for the majority of boaters, if the wind machine were used only 1 month per year, the savings would fall to $58 per year, and the payback period would increase to over 25 years.

The electrical power that a wind machine can extract from the wind is:

$$P = K \times E \times D^2 \times V^3$$

Where:
P = power in watts
K = 0.0653
E = mechanical efficiency in %
D = blade diameter in meters
V = wind speed in knots

Example: Calculate the power output of a wind machine having a blade diameter of 5 feet (1.52 meters) and efficiency of 30% in a steady 10-knot wind.

$$P = 0.0653 \times 0.30 \times 1.52^2 \times 10^3 = 45 \text{ watts}$$

The equation highlights the important factors in selecting and sizing a wind machine to satisfy a boat's electrical demand:

Efficiency, E, can never be 100%. If it were, the blades would extract 100% of the kinetic energy of the wind, bringing the wind to a complete halt. The maximum theoretical, aeronautical efficiency of a wind machine is 59.3% but, due to losses in the generating coils, rotor bearings, and transmission gearing, the actual efficiencies are around 30%.

Diameter, D, enters the equation squared. Doubling blade diameter quadruples power output. Most marine wind machines have blade diameters of either 1 m (39 inches) or 5 feet (1.52 m). Squaring the ratio of diameters shows that the theoretical maximum output of the 5-foot machines is 230% that of the 1 m machines.

Wind speed, V, is the most important factor of all because it enters the equation cubed. The difference between 8 knots and 10 knots may be barely noticeable when sailing, but doubles the output of a wind machine. Don't guess; use the wind-power maps on the following pages when making the purchase decision.

Figure 12.2 plots wind machine output versus wind speed. The two theoretical curves (dashed) assume efficiencies of 30% and output at 14 volts. The curves for actual machines were drawn to fit manufacturers' data.

You would be wise to question the output figures claimed by wind machine manufacturers. The important specification is continuous rated output at 14 VDC, not maximum output.

Since average wind speeds are rarely above 15 knots, output at wind speeds in excess of 15 knots is not important in your choice of a wind machine.

Fig. 12.2 Manufacturer-Claimed Output of Marine Wind Generators

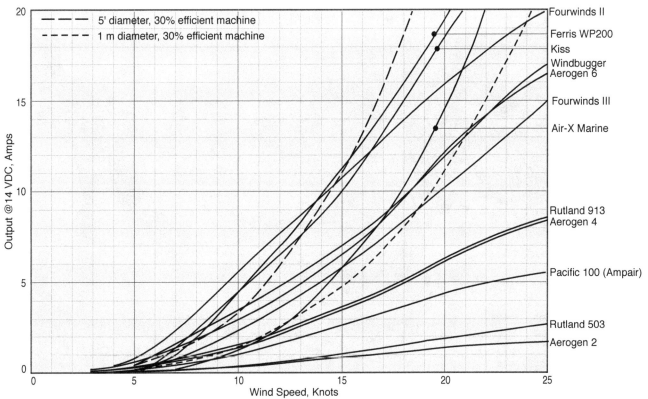

How Much Wind Is There?

Figures 12.3 through 12.7 show average wind power, in watts per square meter, from the *Wind Energy Resource Atlas of the U.S.* The figures are the power contained in the wind and must be multiplied by wind machine efficiency and area swept by the blades to predict electrical output.

What is most striking about the maps is the predominance of low average wind speed. While we all know of places where the wind blows much harder, you would be well advised to ignore such places. In reality, it is human nature to seek refuge from the wind. Since most boaters seek shelter when on the hook, the wind speeds shown may, in reality, be a little too high.

The wind speeds shown in the figures were observed in exposed locations, such as airports, and at an average height above ground of 10 meters. Figure 12.8 shows how wind speed and power vary with actual height in both open-water and harbor locations.

Over open water a wind machine at a height of 10 feet will be exposed to 90% of the 10-meter wind speed and produce about 72% as much power. In a protected harbor, the same 10-foot height will result in about 80% of the 10-meter wind speed and only 50% of the power.

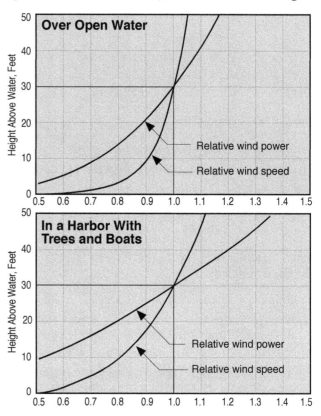

Fig. 12.8 Variation of Wind Speed and Power with Height

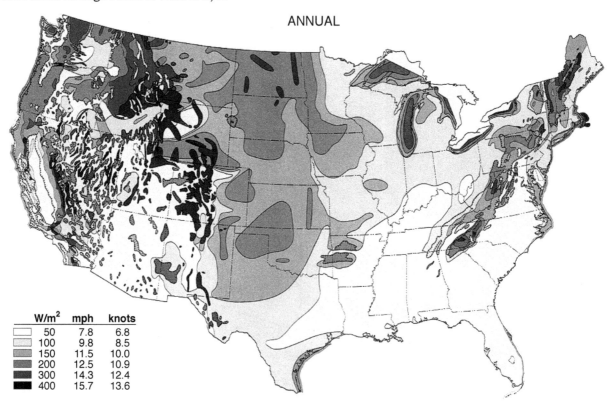

Fig. 12.3 Annual Average Power in Wind in W/m²

W/m²	mph	knots
50	7.8	6.8
100	9.8	8.5
150	11.5	10.0
200	12.5	10.9
300	14.3	12.4
400	15.7	13.6

Fig. 12.4 Spring Average Power in Wind in W/m²

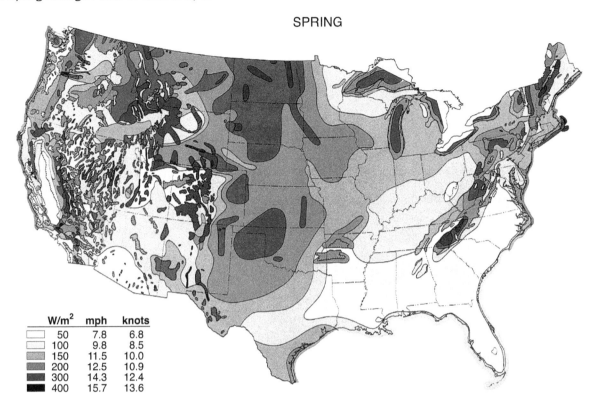

SPRING

W/m²	mph	knots
50	7.8	6.8
100	9.8	8.5
150	11.5	10.0
200	12.5	10.9
300	14.3	12.4
400	15.7	13.6

Fig. 12.5 Summer Average Power in Wind in W/m²

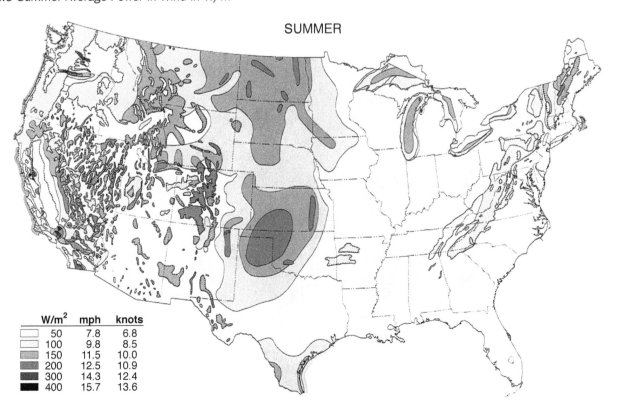

SUMMER

W/m²	mph	knots
50	7.8	6.8
100	9.8	8.5
150	11.5	10.0
200	12.5	10.9
300	14.3	12.4
400	15.7	13.6

How Much Wind Is There?

Fig. 12.6 Fall Average Power in Wind in W/m²

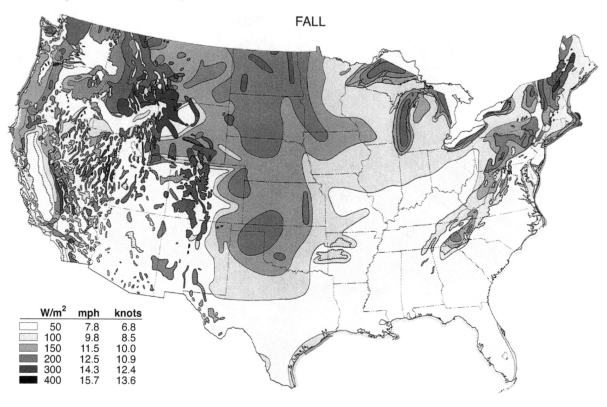

FALL

W/m²	mph	knots
50	7.8	6.8
100	9.8	8.5
150	11.5	10.0
200	12.5	10.9
300	14.3	12.4
400	15.7	13.6

Fig. 12.7 Winter Average Power in Wind in W/m²

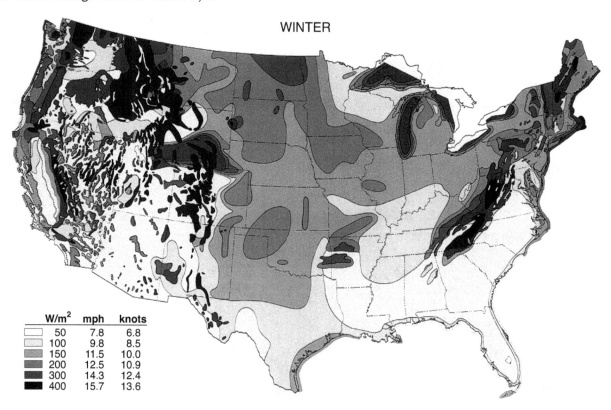

WINTER

W/m²	mph	knots
50	7.8	6.8
100	9.8	8.5
150	11.5	10.0
200	12.5	10.9
300	14.3	12.4
400	15.7	13.6

Selecting the right size wind machine for your boat is not quite the same as designing a solar system. While you have a variety of solar panel sizes to select from, there are really only two sizes of wind machine: 1 meter, and 5 feet. So selecting a wind machine comes down to deciding whether one of the two available sizes is worth the investment.

Start by determining your average daily load in Ah, just as in Chapter 11. Next, determine the available power in the wind for the areas you plan to cruise, using either the annual map (Figure 12.3) or the seasonal maps (Figures 12.4 through 12.7).

Calculating the expected average electrical power from a wind machine is then a simple matter of multiplying the area swept by the blades by the machine efficiency and the power shown in the map for the area(s) you intend to cruise.

The area of a circle is $\pi \times D^2/4$ (Figure 12.9), so

$$\text{Watts} = \pi \times D^2 \times E \times P/4$$

where:

$\pi = 3.14$
$D = $ blade diameter in meters
$E = $ wind machine efficiency, 0.00 to 1.00
$P = $ annual wind power in W/m^2

Assuming $E = 0.30$ (30%):
$$\text{Watts} = 0.24\,D^2 \times P$$
$$\text{kWh/yr} = 2.10\,D^2 \times P$$
$$\text{Ah/day} = 0.44\,D^2 \times P$$

Example 1: How much power can you expect from a wind machine of 5-foot (1.52 m) blade diameter, 30% efficiency, and 12-foot height in protected harbors in New England in summer and the Florida Keys in winter?

Answer 1: Both locations have average wind power of about 100 W/m^2 at 33-foot height. Assuming harbor locations, at 12-foot height (Figure 12.8) the available power is 60% of the power at 33 feet. Therefore,

$$
\begin{aligned}
\text{Watts} &= 0.24\,D^2 \times P \\
&= 0.24 \times 1.52^2 \times 0.6 \times 100 \\
&= 33 \text{ watts} \\
\text{kWh/yr} &= 2.10\,D^2 \times P \\
&= 2.10 \times 1.52^2 \times 0.6 \times 100 \\
&= 292 \text{ kilowatt-hours} \\
\text{Ah/day} &= 0.44\,D^2 \times P \\
&= 0.44 \times 1.52^2 \times 0.6 \times 100 \\
&= 61 \text{ Ah}
\end{aligned}
$$

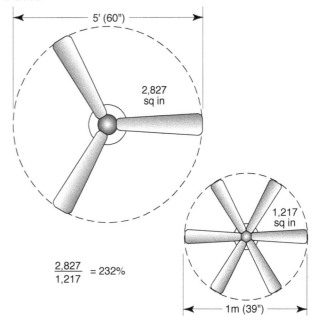

Fig. 12.9 Areas Swept by 5-Foot and 1 m Wind Generator Blades

$$\frac{2{,}827}{1{,}217} = 232\%$$

This wind machine would be well matched to the load of the energy-efficient boat discussed in Chapter 10.

Note that the output of this wind machine could be increased by either of two steps:

1. Changing to a 33-foot mizzen mount would theoretically increase output by a factor of 100%/60% = 1.67.
2. With the 12-foot mount, anchoring in unprotected locations would theoretically increase output by a factor of 75%/60% = 1.25.

Example 2: For the same conditions as in Example 1, how much power would a 1 m wind machine produce?

Answer 2: The ratio of blade diameter 1 to blade diameter 2 is:

$$
\begin{aligned}
D2/D1 &= 1.00 \text{ m}/1.52 \text{ m} \\
&= 0.66
\end{aligned}
$$

The ratio of outputs is the ratio of diameters, squared:

$$
\begin{aligned}
(D2/D1)^2 &= 0.662 \\
&= 0.43
\end{aligned}
$$

The output of a 1 m machine would therefore be: 14 watts, 126 kilowatt-hours per year, and 26 Ah per day.

Specifications

Table 12.1 Wind Machine Specifications

	Number of Blades	Blade Diameter	Weight, pounds	Warranty, years	Amps @10 kn	Amps @15 kn
Aerogen 2 (LVM)	5	23"	11	3	0.3	0.9
Aerogen 4 (LVM)	6	34"	24	3	1.4	3.5
Aerogen 6 (LVM)	6	48"	28	3	3.0	6.6
Air-X Marine	3	45"	13	3	1.3	5.8
Ferris WP200	2	60"	19	1	4.0	11.2
Fourwinds II	3	60"	22	3	5.6	10.7
Fourwinds III	3	40"	20	3	3.0	6.0
Kiss	3	30"	23	3	4.5	10.0
Pacific 100 (Ampair)	6	36"	20	3	1.0	2.7
Rutland 503	6	20"	8	2	0.3	1.0
Rutland 913	6	36"	28	2	1.6	3.8
Windbugger	3	54"	38	1	4.0	10.0

Table 12.1 lists the specifications for the wind machines included in Figure 12.2. As the manufacturers say, "specifications subject to change without notice," so get the latest information before making your purchase.

Number of Blades

Theoretically, the efficiency of a wind machine is unrelated to the number of blades. A two-bladed machine can be as efficient as a six-bladed machine. However, noise level decreases with increased number of blades, and blade diameter. All six-bladed machines are quieter than the two- or three-bladed machines.

Blade Diameter

As already discussed, power output varies with diameter squared, so a large diameter is necessary for large output. On the other hand, weight, noise, and potential danger all increase with diameter as well.

Weight

Weight is a two-edged sword. Light weight makes the machine easier to handle—particularly in the case of a halyard mount—but light weight may equate to a flimsier construction and smaller continuous rated output.

Amps at X Knots

Watch out! This may be the output when the machine is cold, before self-regulation kicks in. Make sure the rating for maximum continuous output is at least as large as the claimed 15-knot output.

Other Specifications

Voltage

Some machines are regulated to produce constant voltage. If so, select a regulator that can be adjusted for your battery type. As pointed out in Chapter 3, gelled-electrolyte batteries can be ruined by long-term charging at over 14.1 volts DC. When a manufacturer claims its machine is "battery regulated," watch out! Such machines cannot be left unattended for long periods.

Brushes

If a machine is used continuously, it may require new brushes every year. If this sort of maintenance doesn't appeal to you, check with the manufacturer, or go with a brushless machine.

Slip Rings

Slip rings pass current from a swiveling wind machine to the power cables leading to the battery. Without slip rings a wind machine cannot make more than a few revolutions before fouling its cable. A ±180° swivel-mount has no slip rings but tracks the wind 99% of the time.

Shutdown

This is the most important safety factor. A machine that must be manually secured in high winds is at best inconvenient and at worst dangerous. Even if the machine has an automatic governor or brake, make sure the braking device is guaranteed to at least 50-knot winds. Otherwise, you are likely to have a broken or burned-out machine within a year.

Figure 12.10 shows a wind machine electrical installation. Voltage and current meters are not shown but are often supplied with wind machines. If they are, simply follow the manufacturer's directions for installation.

A solar system is also shown in the figure because wind and solar are often combined. The installation is designed so that the wind and solar systems are completely independent, though complementary. Deleting the solar system has no effect on the wind system hookup.

Elements of the installation include:

1. *Fuses or circuit breakers.* Because a short circuit in one of the battery positive leads could lead to fire or explosion of the battery, all positive battery leads except those from the alternator are required to be overcurrent-protected, as close to the positive battery terminals as possible.
2. *Blocking diodes.* Most wind machines are little more than DC motors. Blocking diodes prevent current from the batteries from spinning the wind machine backward in the absence of wind. They also act as isolation diodes, preventing the battery with greater charge from discharging into the battery with lesser charge when there is

no wind. Note that the blocking diodes are installed downstream (down-current) of the alternator isolation diodes so that the voltage drops are not additive.

3. *Charge controller.* Unless the wind machine contains a voltage regulator, a charge controller should be inserted in the output to prevent overcharging of the batteries. The manual bypass switch shown is provided to allow periodic equalization of the batteries.

Some charge controllers dump excess current into heat-sinked transistors. Others divert current to an external load, such as a 12-volt water heater element. In any case make sure the controller can handle the maximum output current.

All of the DC wiring standards and practices discussed in Chapter 6 apply to wind machine installations as well. Make sure the ampacity of the output conductors exceeds the wind machine's maximum output. Sizing the conductors for a 3% maximum voltage drop is not as important with wind machines as with solar panels, however, since the open-circuit voltage in winds over 10 knots is at least 20 volts and the voltage regulator is clamped at less than 15 volts. I'd use a 10% drop.

Fig. 12.10 Electrical Hookup of Wind Generator (Solar Optional)

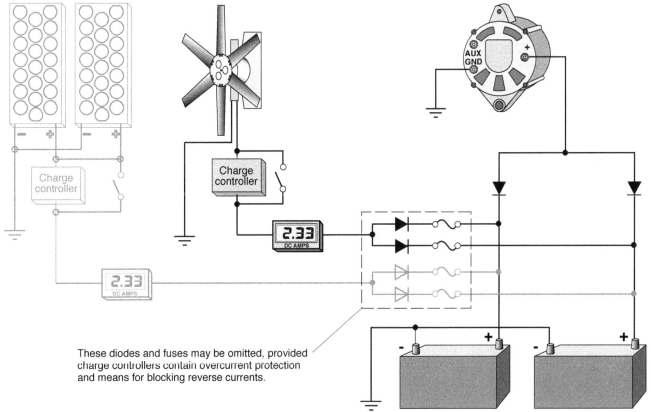

These diodes and fuses may be omitted, provided charge controllers contain overcurrent protection and means for blocking reverse currents.

Mechanical Installation

Figure 12.11 shows a common large wind machine (the 5-foot Fourwinds) mounted in all possible configurations on a 35-foot ketch. Most wind machines can be mounted in several configurations with mounting accessories available from the manufacturer. Check with dealers for the possibilities.

Pole Mount

Of the three mounting options, the stern pole is the most common. The pole is usually of 2-inch schedule-40 or 80 pipe. Bracing is provided either by two lengths of rigid stainless tubing to the deck or by one rigid standoff to the backstay plus two guywires to the deck. Pole height should be such that the blade clears the head of the tallest crew, but can be secured without standing on a pulpit rail.

The advantages of the pole mount are that it is accessible from the deck and that it allows use while under sail. Disadvantages include smaller output due to low height, relatively high noise level, and potential danger to unwary crew.

Mizzen Mounts

Mizzen mounts, for boats with a second mast, raise the wind machine for greater output and decreased danger. In spite of the height, if an unbalanced machine is mounted near the midpoint of the mast, noise levels may be even greater than those for the pole mount. Blade distance from the mast is also important in reducing noise levels. Note that Fourwinds offers four different mizzen mounts.

The four types of mizzen mounts differ chiefly in the ability to swivel into the wind: 0° (fixed in forward direction), 180°, and 360° (unlimited). The fixed mount is extremely limiting, being useful only when the boat is anchored or on a mooring. The 180° mount allows operation in all conditions except running downwind. This is a small disadvantage, however, since the apparent wind speed is reduced by the speed of the boat. If a lot of downwind sailing is contemplated, some wind machines (Fourwinds, Ferris, and Ampair) can be adapted to towing behind the boat.

Halyard Mount

While the ability to raise a wind machine to great height would seem to promise the highest output, least noise, and greatest safety, a halyard-mounted machine should not be raised beyond the reach of a person standing on deck. Shutdown or recovery of a halyard-mounted machine in a high wind can be exceedingly dangerous. In addition, the hassle of deployment, recovery, and storage at every anchoring makes them less popular.

In spite of these negatives, some owners swear by the halyard mount, claiming deployment and recovery in less than 3 minutes, as well as lowest initial cost.

Large halyard-mount machines are usually two-bladed because they are most conveniently stored in the V-berth and handled through a forward hatch.

Radar Arch Mount

In line with the modern trend of mounting *everything* on an aft radar arch or on davits, the Fourwinds offers a radar arch mount with 360° freedom. The mount makes logical sense, but many feel it compromises the aesthetics of a sailing vessel.

Noise

After safety, the most common concern about wind machines is the level of noise generated at moderate to high wind speeds. Manufacturers have made some progress in recent years in abating noise.

First, as pointed out earlier, the fewer the blades, the greater the noise. Because of this, only one two-blade machine (the Ferris) remains on the market. The majority now offer either three or six blades.

Second, the more aerodynamic (more like an airfoil) the shape of the blade, the less the noise. The blades of the newest machines closely resemble airplane propellers.

Third, mounting a machine rigidly on a pole or mast directly connected to the deck results in vibration being transmitted to the deck. The deck then acts like a drumhead, amplifying the sound. Some manufacturers now offer rubber shock mounts to decouple the vibrations before reaching deck level.

Fig. 12.11 Wind Generator Mounting Options

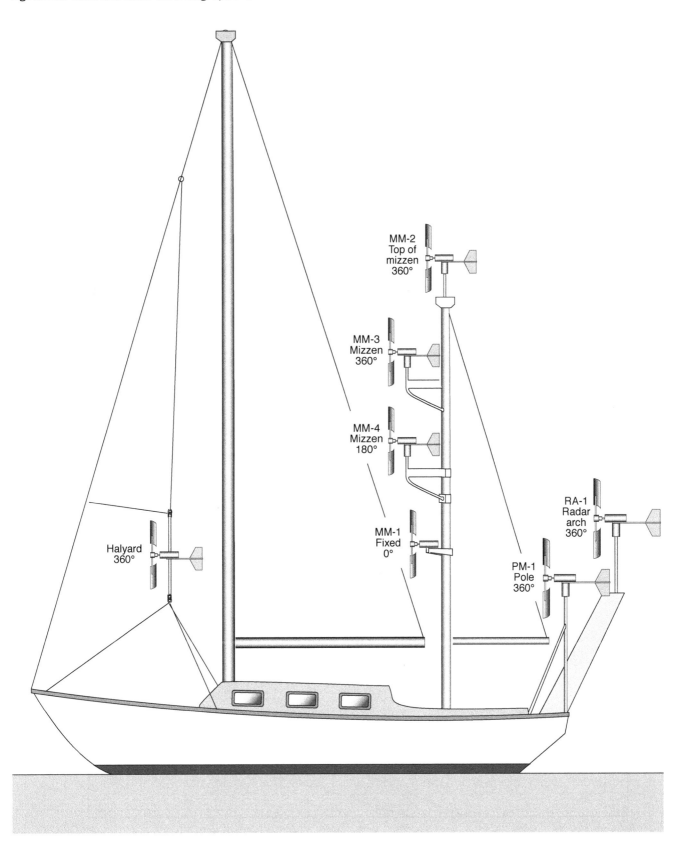

Water Generators

Many wind machines can be converted to water generators. Figure 12.12 shows the outputs of four water generators versus water speed. All are sized to carry the electrical load of a typical cruising boat at less than hull speed. The drag typically slows a boat by a small fraction of a knot, and they are usually deployed only as needed to recharge the batteries.

They are popular with downwind passagemakers who are already equipped with wind machines, since relative airspeed downwind is low, but water speed is high. Most mount the generator on the stem rail and trail the propeller unit with a line sufficiently stiff to transmit the torque to the generating unit (Figure 12.13). Manufacturers generally recommend carrying several spare propeller units on long passages. The reason is obvious: the spinning prop looks suspiciouly like live bait to a large fish!

The electrical installation for dual units is the same for both wind and water operation, and is described in Figure 12.10.

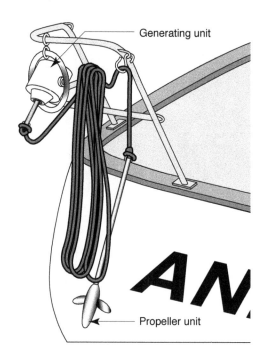

Fig. 12.13 Aquair 100 Mounted on a Stern Rail

Fig. 12.12 Water Generator Output Curves

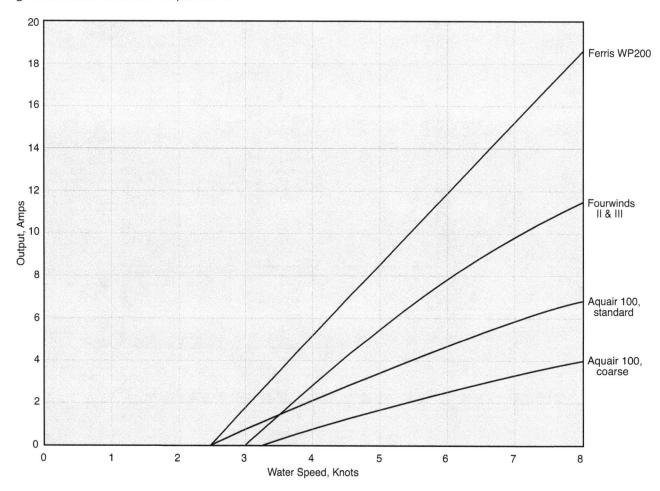

CHAPTER 13

Installing Electronics

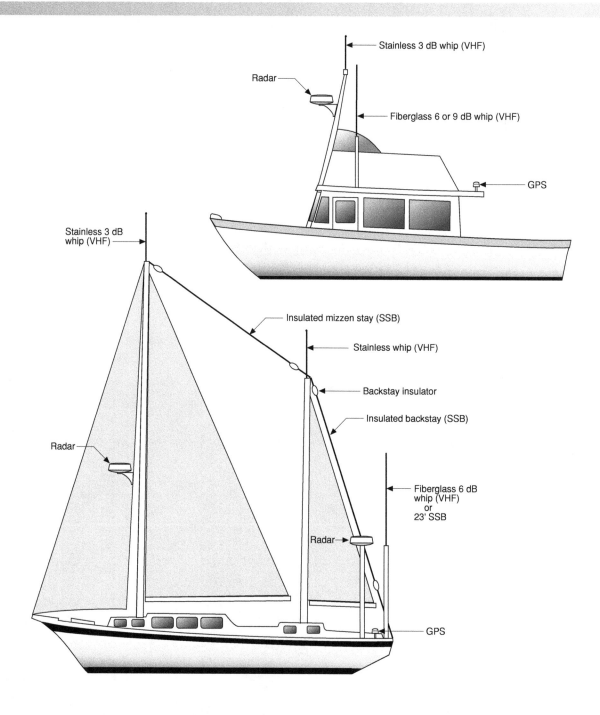

Stainless 3 dB whip (VHF)

Radar

Fiberglass 6 or 9 dB whip (VHF)

GPS

Stainless 3 dB whip (VHF)

Insulated mizzen stay (SSB)

Stainless whip (VHF)

Backstay insulator

Insulated backstay (SSB)

Radar

Fiberglass 6 dB whip (VHF) or 23' SSB

Radar

GPS

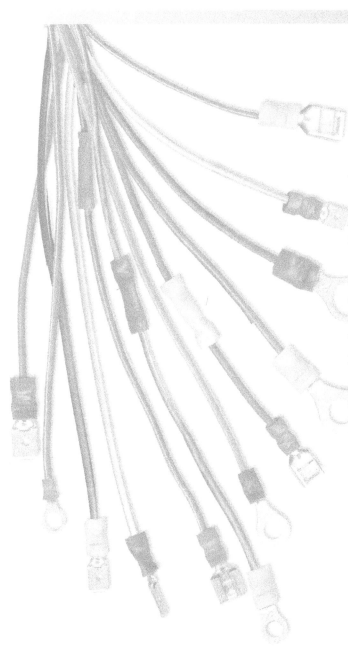

If you can install a towel rack, you can install an electronic cabinet or case. But there is often more to a successful electronic installation than meets the eye.

This chapter focuses on communication and navigation electronics—that is, electronics that use antennas.

Antennas are intended to receive signals. It is important that the incoming signals not be attenuated, so much attention must be paid to antenna cable and connectors in addition to proper receiver and transmitter installation. Receivers and transmitters include VHF radio, GPS, SSB, and radar.

The problem is they also receive electrical noise, so we give step-by-step procedures for identifying the sources and reducing the level with electrical filters.

Antennas

Few things are as satisfying as installing your own electronics. Repairing digital electronic circuitry is beyond the abilities of most, but installation is not.

Installation requires only an understanding of the DC wiring standards and practices in Chapter 6, wire and connectors available through chandleries and mail-order catalogs, and the principles outlined in this chapter.

With these in hand, you should be able to install any piece of marine electronic equipment over a weekend, and as well as any professional. The obvious benefits are a significant costs saving and satisfaction at accomplishing a professional job. The less obvious benefit occurs when something goes wrong, and you find that you are now able to retrace your steps and often locate the problem.

The equipment covered in this chapter includes VHF and SSB radios, GPS, and radar. From an installation standpoint, all marine electronics are similar. You'll find that the principles and techniques apply to stereos, televisions, depth sounders, and wind indicators, as well.

Antenna Types

You can find books on antenna design and specific antenna designs in electronics and ham radio magazines. My advice, however, is to start with the antenna recommended or supplied by the manufacturer of the equipment. Many antennas are designed to work only with a specific brand and model of equipment. After you have the equipment up and running, you may decide to experiment with a different antenna. The original antenna will then serve as a reference.

Antenna Location

Figures 13.1 and 13.2 show a variety of antennas and locations that will be referenced in the discussions of particular equipment types.

VHF and radar signals travel in straight lines, so their antennas should be mounted high.

GPS signals travel line-of-sight from outer space and, except for the requirement for a relatively clear view of the sky, are independent of height.

SSB and ham signals arrive from space, having bounced one or more times off the ionosphere. While antenna performance is independent of height, their great lengths (23 to 60 feet) require height at one end.

Radar and GPS have wavelengths of the same order,

or smaller than, objects on the boat. Objects with a diameter less than 1 inch (such as a mast) can reflect or block the signal, creating blind zones.

Finally, signals are at least partially absorbed by grounded rigging. Antennas placed too close to metal standing rigging thus suffer loss of signal strength. The exception that proves the rule is the use of an insulated (ungrounded) backstay as a long SSB or ham antenna. To avoid interference, antennas that are used to transmit as well as receive should be spaced from other antennas.

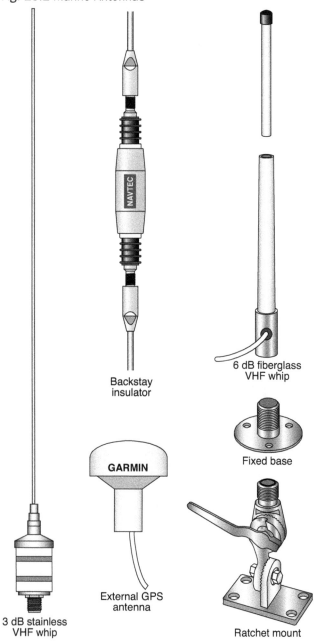

Fig. 13.1 Marine Antennas

Backstay insulator

6 dB fiberglass VHF whip

Fixed base

GARMIN

External GPS antenna

Ratchet mount

3 dB stainless VHF whip

Fig. 13.2 Locating Antennas

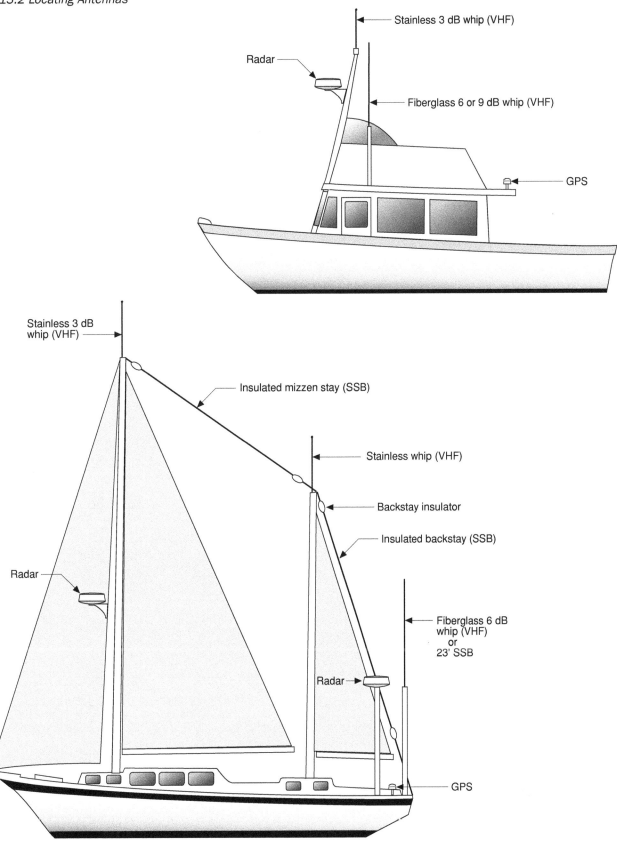

Stainless 3 dB whip (VHF)

Radar

Fiberglass 6 or 9 dB whip (VHF)

GPS

Stainless 3 dB whip (VHF)

Insulated mizzen stay (SSB)

Stainless whip (VHF)

Backstay insulator

Insulated backstay (SSB)

Radar

Fiberglass 6 dB whip (VHF)
or
23' SSB

Radar

GPS

Antenna Cable and Connectors

To minimize interference from shipboard electrical noise, all antennas aboard a boat are, or should be, connected to their respective receivers with coaxial cable. Table 13.1 lists the most common coaxial cable types and their specifications.

Table 13.1 Coaxial Cables

Specification	RG-58/U	RG-8X	RG-8/U	RG-213
Nominal O.D.	³⁄₁₆"	¼"	¹³⁄₃₂"	¹³⁄₃₂"
Conductor AWG	#20	#16	#13	#13
Impedance, ohms	50	50	52	50
Attenuation per 100 Feet				
@ 50 MHz	3.3 dB	2.5 dB	1.3 dB	1.3 dB
@ 100 MHz	4.9 dB	3.7 dB	1.9 dB	1.9 dB
@ 1,000 MHz	21.5 dB	13.5 dB	8.0 dB	8.0 dB

Conductor size (AWG) is important in transmitters where large currents may result in resistive loss of power in the cable.

Impedance of the antenna cable should match the output impedance of the transmitter in order to maximize signal strengths.

Attenuation is the loss of transmitted power in the cable between transmitter and antenna. Each 3 decibels (dB) of loss is equivalent to a reduction in power at the antenna of 50%.

Coax cables may have identical specifications, yet vary greatly in quality. Cables aboard boats are exposed to salt spray, sunlight, oil, and sometimes battery-acid mist. Use only the highest-quality cable, consisting of tinned center conductor and braid, solid polyethylene dielectric, and UV-resistant, non-contaminating outer jacket.

Figure 13.3 shows the cable adapters and feed-throughs available at most chandleries and radio stores.

Figure 13.4 shows the assembly of UHF connectors on both large and small coaxial cables. Figure 13.5 demonstrates the similar assembly of BNC connectors on RG-58/U, RG-59/U, and RG-8X coaxial cables.

Solderless versions are not recommended in marine applications due to the moist environment and the likelihood of corrosion, which solder excludes. After assembly the connector and cable should be sealed with adhesive-lined, heat-shrink tubing, as shown in Figure 13.6, to exclude moisture.

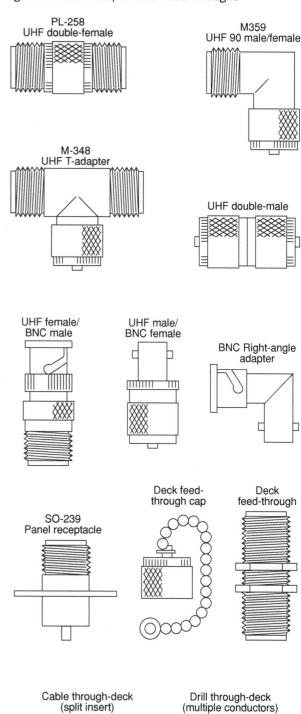

Fig. 13.3 Cable Adapter and Feed-Throughs

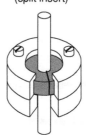

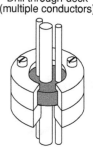

Fig. 13.4 Assembly of PL-259 Connectors

ON RG-58/U, RG-59/U, AND RG-8X CABLES

STEP 1: Slip on shell and adapter;
strip outer jacket back 5/8"

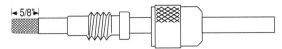

STEP 2: Bend back braided shield

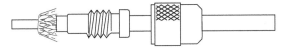

STEP 3: Slip adapter under braided shield

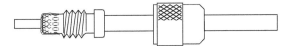

STEP 4: Strip center conductor 1/2" and tin

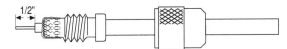

STEP 5: Screw on body and solder tip and braid
through holes in body

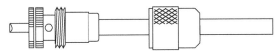

STEP 6: Screw shell onto body

ON RG-8/U AND RG-213 CABLES

STEP 1: Slip on shell and strip to center of conductor
and back 3/4"

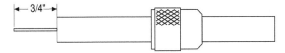

STEP 2: Strip outer jacket additional 5/16"

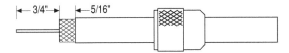

STEP 3: Slip on body, making sure shield does not contact
center conductor, and solder tip and shield through holes

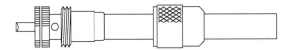

STEP 4: Screw shell onto body

Antenna Cable and Connectors

Fig. 13.5 Assembly of BNC Connectors

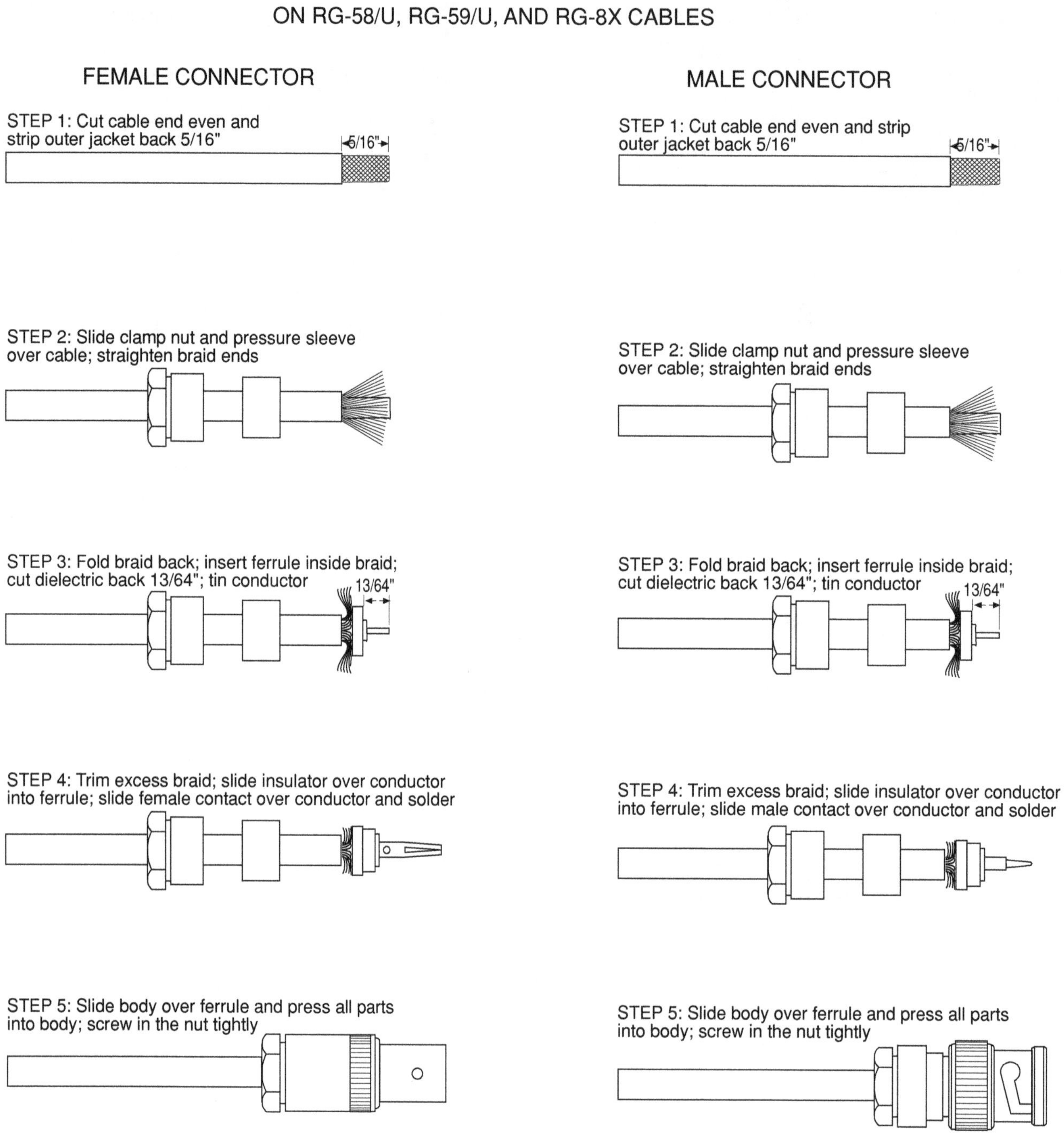

ON RG-58/U, RG-59/U, AND RG-8X CABLES

FEMALE CONNECTOR

STEP 1: Cut cable end even and strip outer jacket back 5/16"

|←5/16"→|

STEP 2: Slide clamp nut and pressure sleeve over cable; straighten braid ends

STEP 3: Fold braid back; insert ferrule inside braid; cut dielectric back 13/64"; tin conductor

13/64"

STEP 4: Trim excess braid; slide insulator over conductor into ferrule; slide female contact over conductor and solder

STEP 5: Slide body over ferrule and press all parts into body; screw in the nut tightly

MALE CONNECTOR

STEP 1: Cut cable end even and strip outer jacket back 5/16"

|←5/16"→|

STEP 2: Slide clamp nut and pressure sleeve over cable; straighten braid ends

STEP 3: Fold braid back; insert ferrule inside braid; cut dielectric back 13/64"; tin conductor

13/64"

STEP 4: Trim excess braid; slide insulator over conductor into ferrule; slide male contact over conductor and solder

STEP 5: Slide body over ferrule and press all parts into body; screw in the nut tightly

Moisture is the enemy of marine connectors. At least 90% of all marine electronics problems are due to corrosion in connectors and conductors. Water that penetrates the connector wicks into the stranded center conductor and shield and travels far into the cable. Corrosion turns copper into powdery copper oxide, thinning the conductors. In addition, the copper oxide is an insulator, so resistance goes up and signal strength goes down.

Figure 13.6 shows three defenses against moisture:

1. Making a nonwaterproof connection inside a waterproof box with the conductors entering the box from beneath.

2. Drip loops near the connector force water running along the conductor to drop off before reaching the conductor. The loops cannot prevent incursion of water falling directly on the connector, but they minimize guttering. A single drip loop at the base of a vertical run diverts water running down the mast.

3. Adhesive-lined, heat-shrink tubing seals the connector to the cable, preventing water leaks. The heated tubing shrinks (up to 85%), and the adhesive flows, sealing the connection.

Fig. 13.6 Protecting Coax Connections Against Moisture

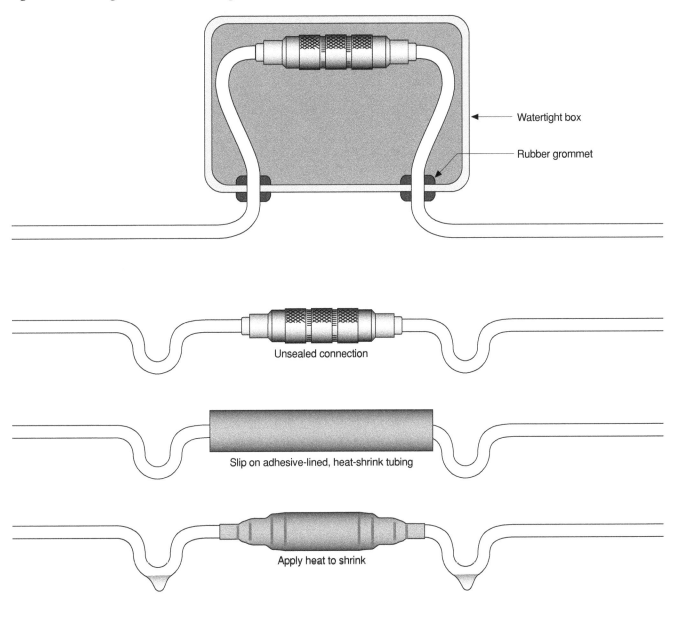

Watertight box

Rubber grommet

Unsealed connection

Slip on adhesive-lined, heat-shrink tubing

Apply heat to shrink

VHF Radio

Three factors affect how far a properly working VHF radio can be heard:

1. *Cable transmission loss.* As indicated in Table 13.1, power loss increases with frequency and decreases with cable diameter. At the VHF frequency of 157 MHz, the lengths of coaxial cable for a 3 dB (50%) power loss are RG-58—49 feet; RG-8/X—66 feet; and RG-8/U—111 feet. A sailboat with a 50-foot mast and a 16-foot run will lose half its VHF transmitting power if it uses RG-8X (most boats do). The loss would be reduced by 50% by switching to the larger-diameter RG-8/U or RG-213.

Fig. 13.7 VHF Antenna Gain

2. *Antenna gain.* As shown in Figure 13.7, antennas can be designed to concentrate the radiation toward the horizon to a greater or lesser degree. The concentration is expressed as gain in dB. Generally, the longer the antenna, the greater the gain. Popular models and their lengths are 3 dB—38 inches; 6 dB—8 feet; and 9 dB—19 feet. A masthead, 3 dB, 38-inch whip antenna is the most appropriate for a sailboat because mast height compensates for low gain, and the less flattened pattern allows for heeling under sail. Bridge-mounted 6 dB and 9 dB antennas are best for powerboats because they do not heel.

3. *Antenna height.* VHF transmission is line of sight. Transmit/receive distance is the same as the distance two observers at the same heights can see each other. Figure 13.8 demonstrates the principle. Table 13.2 lists the distances, versus the heights, of the two antennas.

Table 13.2 Line-of-Sight Distance, D₁ + D₂, for VHF Radios

Receiver Height, ft	Transmitter Height, feet								
	5	10	20	40	60	80	100	200	400
5	5	6	8	10	12	13	14	19	26
10	6	7	9	11	13	14	15	20	27
20	8	9	10	13	14	16	17	22	29
40	10	11	13	15	17	18	19	24	31
60	12	13	14	17	18	20	21	26	33
80	13	14	16	18	20	21	22	27	34
100	14	15	17	19	21	22	23	28	35

The distances in Table 13.2 are based on the formulas:

$$D = 1.17\sqrt{H}$$
$$D_1 + D_2 = 1.17(\sqrt{H_1} + \sqrt{H_2})$$

where D is in nautical miles (nm) and H is in feet.

Actual transmission distances are observed to be about $1.22\sqrt{H}$, about 4% greater than the theoretical values under average conditions. Thus, two sailboats with 60-foot masts can be expected to communicate about 19 nm.

Powerboaters sometimes make the mistake of raking a high-gain VHF antenna back to make the boat look more streamlined. This leads to a radiation pattern that will be into space in the forward direction and into water aft.

Fig. 13.8 Line-of-Sight Transmit/Receive Distance for VHF Radio

GPS

GPS receivers are supplied with matched antennas. With signal frequencies of about 1.5 gigahertz, the wavelengths are about 8 inches, and the antennas tiny. Location requirements are that the antennas have clear views of the sky and be located outside the radar beam and a few meters away from VHF and SSB antennas. Antenna power is low, so RG-58 cable is acceptable.

SSB or Ham

Both marine single-sideband and ham HF transceivers operate in the same approximate frequency bands. SSB transmissions are restricted to designated SSB frequencies, and ham radio transmissions are restricted to FCC-designated ham bands. The two transceiver types, however, are otherwise functionally identical. Although it is illegal to operate a ham transmitter as an SSB transmitter (except in an emergency), removal of a single diode allows the ham radio to transmit on all frequencies, from 300 kilohertz to 30 megahertz.

There are two types of SSB antennas. A 23-foot whip antenna works well down to 4 megahertz on both power- and sailboats. The antenna should be mounted vertically and located out of easy reach, since touching it may result in radiation burns.

A second option, available on sailboats, is an insulated backstay. The backstay, insulated with special fittings at upper and lower ends, acts as a simple "longwire" antenna. To protect crew from radiation burns, either the bottom insulator and electrical connection should be placed at least 7 feet above the deck, or a length of rubber hose should be slid over the exposed lower portion.

Both antennas require tuners to achieve maximum output. The tuners may be built into the radio chassis or a separate unit installed near the antenna. Most ham operators feel the separate units work better in the relatively low-frequency SSB bands.

Both antenna types work well. The advantages of the 23-foot whip include smaller size, lower cost, and a vertical orientation for omnidirectional transmission. The insulated backstay results in a cleaner deck and captures more incoming signals.

Use either RG-8 or RG-213 coax to connect transceiver and tuner. Attenuation is less in the 2- to 12-megahertz SSB bands than in the 157-megahertz VHF band, but output currents are much greater for the 150-watt SSB than the 25-watt VHF, so we need a larger center conductor.

Fig. 13.9 Single-Sideband (SSB) Antenna and Ground Connections

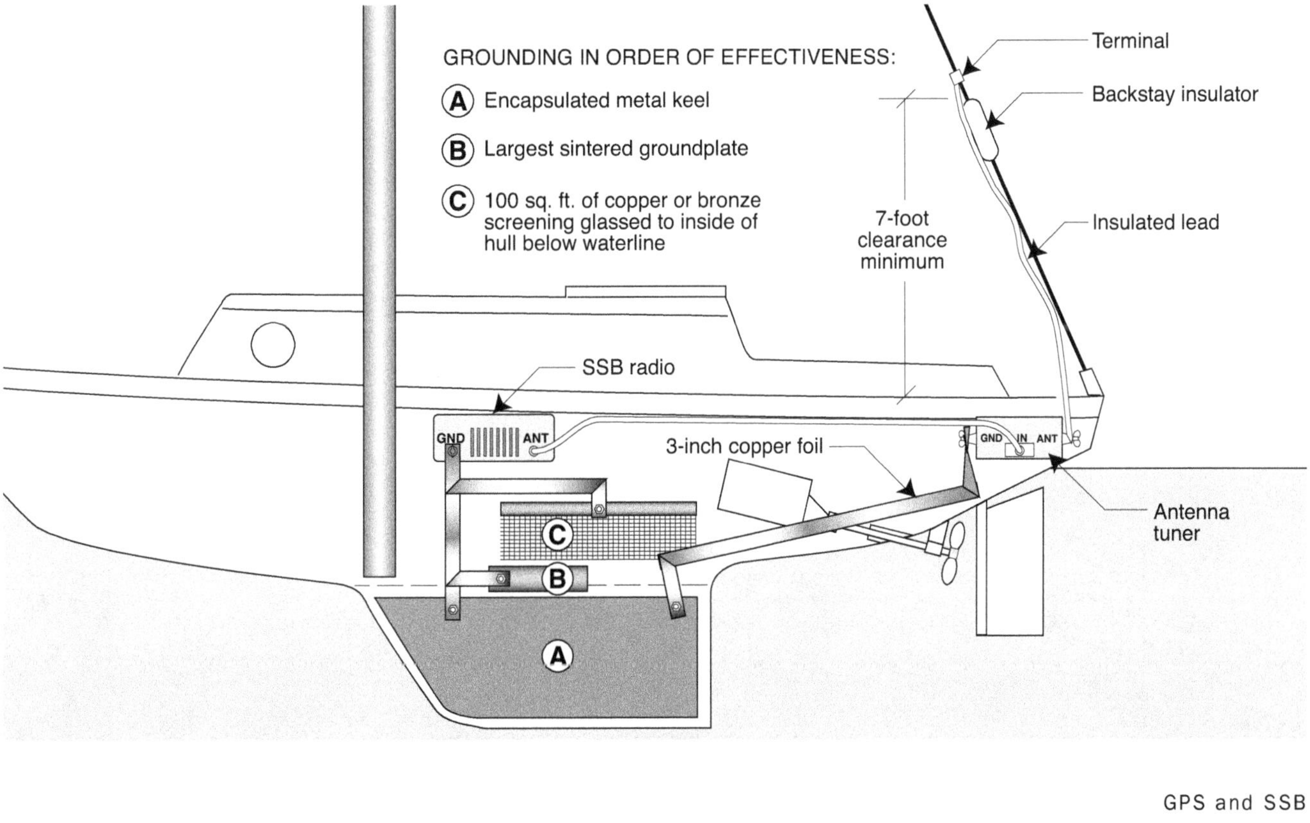

Radar

As with GPS, radar units include matching antennas. The transmission frequency of around 9,500 megahertz (9.5 gigahertz) corresponds to a wavelength of about 1 inch. The radar waves are therefore easily blocked by metallic objects, such as masts, greater than 1 inch in diameter.

A second location requirement is that the antenna—essentially a microwave generator—be located a minimum of 2 feet from humans. (The first microwave ovens were aptly named *Radar Ranges!*) Just forward of the steering station on a flying bridge is not a good location!

The third location criterion is height. Since radar transmission is line of sight and limited in distance by the curvature of the earth, the higher the antenna, the farther you can see. On the other hand, the radiation has a vertical beam width of about 40°, so objects more than 20° below the horizontal will not be seen either. In choosing an antenna height, you thus need to balance the need to see large, distant targets and small, close objects.

Figure 13.10 shows both far ($D_1 + D_2$) and near (N_1) distances. Table 13.3 lists the far distances (range) for combinations of radar and target heights. Table 13.4 similarly shows the near distances (blind zone) for combinations of radar and target heights.

The near distance can be calculated from:

$$N_1 = H_1/\text{tangent } 20°$$
$$= 2.75 \times (H_1 - H_0)$$

For example, a 40-foot-high antenna cannot see surface objects closer than 110 feet. Reducing the antenna height to 20 feet reduces the blind zone radius to 55 feet.

Note that it is the difference in height between the antenna and the target that determines the blind zone. A 40-foot-high antenna can see a 20-foot-high target, such as another boat, at a distance of 55 feet.

The cable between the radar antenna assembly and the display unit typically contains a dozen conductors. Use only the type of cable supplied with the unit.

Assuming you are skilled at soldering multi-pin connectors, you can shorten the supplied cable by any degree. A longer cable can generally be ordered as well. A third option is to purchase an extension cable with matching connectors.

The extension cable is very useful in the case of mast-mounted antennas in sailboats. Provided the original cable and the extension cables join at the mast step, stepping and unstepping the mast requires only connecting and disconnecting the cable. In any case, never locate cable connectors in the bilge, where they may be subject to corrosion.

Table 13.3 Radar Line-of-Sight Range in Nautical Miles

Radar Ht (H_1), ft	Target Height (H_2), feet								
	5	10	20	40	60	80	100	200	400
5	5	6	8	10	12	13	14	19	26
10	6	7	9	11	13	14	15	20	27
15	7	8	10	12	14	15	16	21	28
20	8	9	11	13	14	16	17	22	29
25	9	10	11	13	15	16	18	22	29
30	9	10	12	14	16	17	18	23	30
40	10	11	13	15	17	18	19	24	31
50	11	12	14	16	17	19	20	25	32

Table 13.4 Radar Near Range (Blind Zone), N_1, in Feet

Radar Ht (H_1), ft	Target Height (H_0), feet								
	0	1	2	3	5	10	15	20	30
5	14	11	8	5	–	–	–	–	–
10	27	25	22	19	14	–	–	–	–
15	41	38	36	33	27	14	–	–	–
20	55	52	49	47	41	27	14	–	–
25	69	66	63	60	55	41	27	14	–
30	82	80	77	74	69	55	41	27	–
40	110	107	104	102	96	82	69	55	27
50	137	135	132	129	124	110	96	82	55

Fig. 13.10 Radar Range and Blind Zone vs. Heights of Antenna and Target

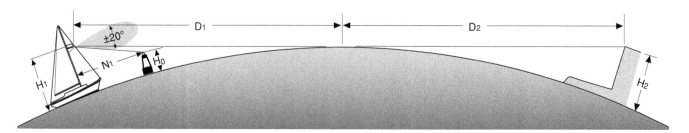

Location

1. *Install in a dry location.* As we saw in Chapter 3, moisture serves as an electrolyte and promotes corrosion. Salt spray has a way of infiltrating anything located on deck or in the cockpit. A thin film of salt on a circuit board may have much lower resistance than many of the circuit components, effectively shorting them out and altering, if not disrupting, performance. In my experience a standard enclosure in a dry location causes fewer problems than a "waterproof" enclosure in a wet location.

2. *Prevent overheating.* Electronics are designed to operate in any temperature a person can tolerate. They are designed to dissipate internally generated heat either by conduction through the case, by natural convection through vents, or by fan-forced convection. The most common mistakes are to restrict ventilation and to pile heat-producing electronics on top of each other with insufficient space between.

3. *Do not strain cables.* Install the equipment so that both antenna and power cables are secure but not taut. Excessive tension on the conductors can pull the connectors apart.

4. *Keep away from magnetic compasses.* Direct current produces a magnetic field around a conductor. The fields can be reduced but not eliminated if the power leads are either coaxial or twisted. Even stronger magnetic fields are caused by radio-speaker magnets and ferrite-rod radio antennas.

5. *Secure firmly at a good viewing/listening angle.* Equipment cases are usually supplied with convenient mounting brackets that allow either vertical or horizontal mounting. Secure the mounting bracket to a bulkhead or overhead with panhead self-tapping stainless screws.

12-Volt DC Power Hookup

1. Do not install more than one radio on a single circuit. If you do, VHF and SSB radios may interfere with each other through their power leads.

2. GPS receivers contain memories that retain coordinates and reduce settling time considerably. Turning off the equipment's power switch does not disconnect the power to the memory, but a drop in voltage may erase the memory. Powering navigation electronics from the house battery rather than the engine-starting battery will help prevent memory loss.

Grounding

If there is a separate chassis, or case, ground (usually a wing nut labeled "Gnd"), then:

1. Run a #10 AWG minimum green or bare copper grounding wire to ground.

2. Run a separate ground from each chassis.

3. On a steel or aluminum boat, ground to the hull as close as possible to the equipment. On a wood or fiberglass boat, make the common ground point either the engine negative terminal or an external ground plate.

4. SSB/ham transmitters require special attention to ground (see Figure 13.9). Grounding conductors should be of 3-inch-wide copper foil and connected to a large area of bronze screening epoxied to the inside of the hull, a large sintered copper external ground plate, or an internal metal keel. Provided that all underwater metals are bonded, the boat's ground may prove sufficient. Remember, however, that bonding all underwater metals may increase corrosion.

Harnessing Electrical Noise

Conducting a Noise Audit

If you still have a loran set, don't deep-six it until you have first conducted a noise audit of your boat's electrical system. Most loran sets will display the signal-to-noise ratio (SNR) of their received 100-kilohertz loran signals. In this mode, they are marvelous tools for detecting radio frequency noise aboard your boat. Here's how:

1. Disconnect shore power.
2. Turn off all electrical equipment, including lights, refrigeration, receivers and transmitters, inverter, generator, and engine.
3. Turn on the loran and let it settle.
4. Call up the SNR display (see your owner's manual). If any of the SNRs (at least one master and three slave stations per master should be available anywhere in the United States for display) is greater than 50, proceed to the next step. If all of the SNRs are less than 50, select another loran chain having greater SNRs.
5. Note on a pad of paper the SNR values of one of the stations for a few minutes, then average the values to obtain the "clean-boat" reference SNR.
6. Start the engine and bring it up to its normal cruising rpm. Compare the SNR now displayed with the engine running to the previous averaged clean-boat reference SNR. If the SNR has dropped by more than 20% (from 50 down to 40, for example), your engine alternator or generator is a source of noise.
7. Repeat Step 6 for each additional piece of equipment, one at a time; i.e., turn off the previous piece of equipment before testing the next item. Any item that causes a greater than 20% drop in SNR is a source of noise that needs to be corrected. Between each of the tests recheck the reference SNR, with all equipment off, to make sure it hasn't changed.

Curing Noise

The first step in curing a noise problem is to recognize how electrical noise is generated and how it penetrates electronic equipment. Figure 13.11 shows that electrical equipment can be divided into *noise generators* (alternators, generators, ignitions, regulators, DC motors, fluorescent fixtures, and some types of digital electronics) and *noise receivers* (radios and electronic navigation devices).

Sometimes a single piece of equipment falls into both categories. I am reminded of my autopilot, whose DC motor caused noise in my radios, but whose electronic control went crazy when I transmitted on a nearby handheld VHF.

Fig. 13.11 Radio Frequency Interference (RFI) Generators and Receivers

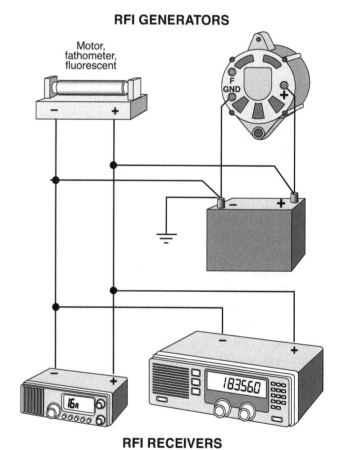

RFI GENERATORS

Motor, fathometer, fluorescent

RFI RECEIVERS

Cures fall into two categories: shielding and filtering.

Shielding consists of enclosing sensitive electronics in a metal case and connecting the case to ground, thereby shunting radiated noise to ground. By enclosing power and signal leads in shielded cable and connecting the cable shield to the metal case, we shunt noise induced in the leads to ground, as well.

Filtering utilizes capacitors and inductors. Capacitors conduct AC but block DC, while inductors conduct DC but block AC. The ideal 12-volt source is pure DC. Noise, on the other hand, is AC, either generated by the alternator or generator, or picked up by power leads acting like antennas. To reduce the amount of AC in a DC supply, we place capacitors across the + and – leads and inductors in series with the leads.

Capacitors for 12-volt DC applications should be rated at 50 working volts (50 WVDC) minimum. Large capacitors are generally polarized electrolytics, so make sure you observe proper polarity.

Inductors are rated by the maximum continuous DC current they can carry, as well as the value of inductance. For electronic navigation equipment, a 5-amp rating is generally sufficient. For DC motors (pumps and autopilots), a 10-amp rating is common. Alternators and generators require ratings that match or exceed their peak output ratings. Inductors with 50-, 70-, and 100-amp ratings are common.

In the case of noise on power leads, the unprotected length of lead serves as an antenna, picking up the noise. Thus, it is important to install the filter as closely as possible to the noise generator or the receiver.

Sometimes a single capacitor or inductor will reduce the noise to an acceptable level. More powerful solutions are provided by a variety of special commercially available filters, combining capacitors and inductors, as shown in Figure 13.12.

Fig. 13.12 A Typical RFI Filter

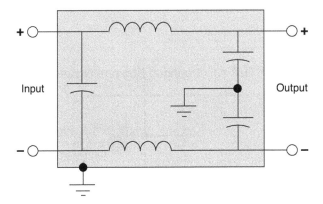

Figure 13.13 lays out a step-by-step attack on electronic noise. The first six steps attack the noise sources, since killing but a single source may reduce the noise to an acceptable level on all receivers. The last four steps treat the receivers individually.

The plan also proceeds roughly in order of increasing cost. It is assumed that, as each step is implemented, all previous cures are left in place.

1. Run separate grounding conductors from the alternator (or generator) case and from the cases of the affected equipment to boat ground.
2. Install a 10,000 µF, 50 VDC electrolytic capacitor across the alternator + output and ground terminals.
3. Install a 1 µF, 50 VDC capacitor from the voltage regulator battery terminal to ground.
4. Install 1 µF, 50 VDC capacitors across the + and – power input leads of all motors, fluorescent fixtures, and the depth sounder.
5. Install an alternator filter across the alternator + output and ground terminals. The filter rating must exceed the output ampere rating of the alternator.
6. Install commercial 10-amp filters across the + and – power input leads of all motors and 10-amp filters across the + and – power input leads of fluorescent fixtures and the depth sounder.
7. Install 1 µF, 50 VDC capacitors across the + and – power input leads of all affected electronics.
8. Install 1 µF, 50 VDC nonpolarized capacitors from the + power lead to chassis ground and the – power lead to chassis ground.
9. Install commercial 5-amp line filters across the + and – power input leads of each piece of affected electronics.
10. Enclose affected electronic equipment in screened-metal enclosures, or wrap in foil tape and connect the enclosure, or tape, to boat ground.

In case all of the above grounding, shielding, and filtering prove insufficient, the only remaining option is relocation of the antenna, cables, or the equipment itself. Remove both antenna and equipment chassis from their mounts and connect temporary power and antenna leads. Experiment with the location of the antenna and chassis and the routing of supply and antenna cables until the best results are obtained.

Electrical Filters

Fig. 13.13 Incremental Attack on Electronic Noise (see text)

STEP 1. Ground All Cases

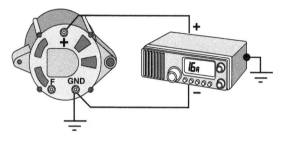

STEP 2. Capacitor across Alternator Output

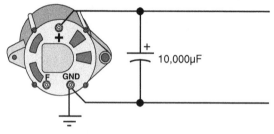

STEP 3. Capacitor on Regulator Input

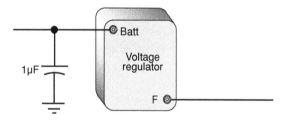

STEP 4. Capacitor on Accessory Supply

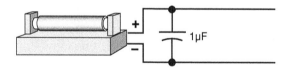

STEP 5. Alternator Filter

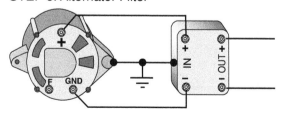

STEP 6. Filter on Accessory Supply

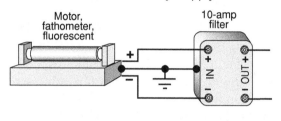

STEP 7. Capacitor on Equipment Supply

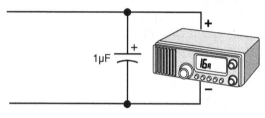

STEP 8. Capacitors from Supply to Gnd

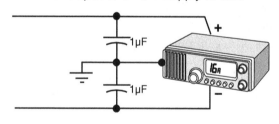

STEP 9. Filter on Equipment Supply

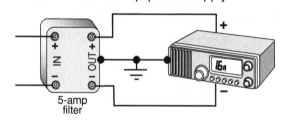

STEP 10. Grounded Equipment Screen

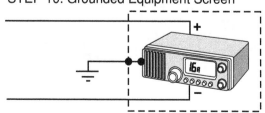

CHAPTER 14

Do-It-Yourself Projects

PROJECT 6: Expanded-Scale Analog Battery Monitor

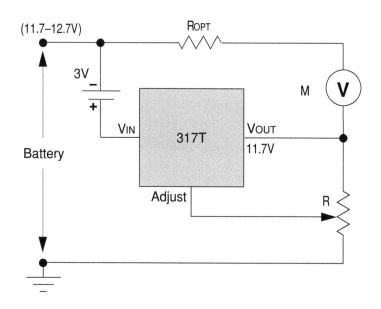

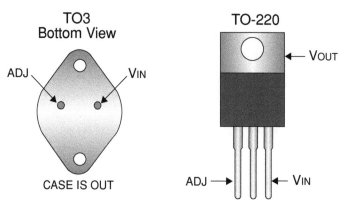

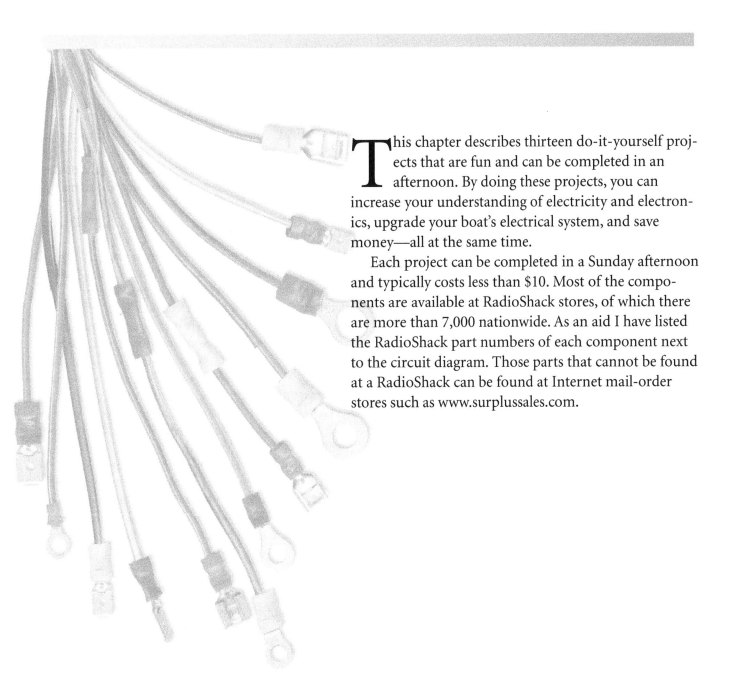

This chapter describes thirteen do-it-yourself projects that are fun and can be completed in an afternoon. By doing these projects, you can increase your understanding of electricity and electronics, upgrade your boat's electrical system, and save money—all at the same time.

Each project can be completed in a Sunday afternoon and typically costs less than $10. Most of the components are available at RadioShack stores, of which there are more than 7,000 nationwide. As an aid I have listed the RadioShack part numbers of each component next to the circuit diagram. Those parts that cannot be found at a RadioShack can be found at Internet mail-order stores such as www.surplussales.com.

Passive Circuit Components

Projects are always more fun and generally more successful when you understand how they work. To understand the behavior of a circuit, you first have to understand how each of its components works. A few of the integrated circuits listed are actually complex circuits containing, in a single small package, hundreds of components. For these we will have to settle for an action/reaction, or input/output understanding. Each of the discrete components is described in a thumbnail sketch below.

Conductors

No connection. A conductor is shown as a solid line. Where conductors simply cross in a circuit diagram, there is no connection.

Connected conductors. When two or more conductors are electrically connected, the connection is indicated by a dot at the intersection. Think of the dot as a small blob of solder on the connection.

Connectors. Connectors are used to mate conductors when assembling or installing equipment. Connectors may mate single conductors, as in AC and DC distribution circuits; a shielded pair, as in coaxial antenna connections; or dozens of conductors, as in computer applications.

Resistors

Fixed resistor. A zigzag symbol indicates a fixed-value resistor. The resistance in ohms is constant regardless of current, temperature, or any other variable. The ability of a resistor to dissipate heat (calculated as $W = I^2 \times R$, where W = watts, I = amps, and R = ohms) is determined mostly by the size of the resistor. The value (ohms and precision) of a resistor is shown by a series of colored bands, as shown on page 267.

Variable resistor. A zigzag with an arrow through it indicates a resistor whose resistance value can be changed. Externally there are three terminals: one at each end of the full resistance, and a third ("wiper") connected to a contact, which slides along the resistance wire or film. The contact is generally moved by turning a screw or knob.

The value of the variable resistor is its maximum value, which can be read with an ohmmeter across the

two end terminals. By connecting to the wiper terminal and the appropriate end terminal, we can have a resistance that increases or decreases with clockwise rotation of the screw. Using all three terminals, you have, in effect, two resistors, which form a voltage divider.

Low-power variable resistors are known as trimmers or trimpots; medium-power variable resistors are potentiometers; and high-power variable resistors are rheostats.

Thermistor. In reality a semiconductor, the thermistor (T) is a component whose resistance changes with temperature. Thermistors are specified by their resistance at 25°C, for example 10 kW (10,000 ohms) at 25°C.

If the variation of resistance with temperature were linear, measuring temperature with an ohmmeter would be a simple matter. Thermistors are more often used to control temperature, however, using the deviation in resistance from a set point as an error signal.

Capacitors

Nonpolarized capacitor. If electricity is like water, then capacitors are like pressurized water tanks: the higher the voltage you place across them, the more electric charge they store. Electric charge is measured in coulombs, which equal 6.24×10^{18} electrons. A 1-farad capacitor stores 1 coulomb of charge at a potential of 1 volt, 10 coulombs at 10 volts, etc.

Electronic circuits require much smaller charge storage, however, so the more common units of capacitance are the microfarad, or μF (10^{-6} farad), and the picofarad, or pF (10^{-12} farad).

Most capacitors are made of extremely thin, interleaved or wound, films of insulation (the dielectric) and aluminum. At high potentials the insulation can break down, so capacitors are also rated by their maximum working voltage.

Polarized capacitor. A device that is halfway between a capacitor and a battery is the electrolytic capacitor, which stores charge in a chemical electrolyte. The advantage is large capacitance in a small size. The disadvantage is that, as with a battery, reversing the voltage will damage the capacitor. Such polarized capacitors can be used only where the applied voltage is always of the same sign.

You can identify polarized capacitors by the + and − markings next to their leads.

Batteries

Single cell. A single electrochemical cell is generally used to supply power at low voltage. Nominal voltages for common cells are:

• Alkaline	1.50
• Carbon zinc	1.50
• Lead acid	2.10
• Lithium ion	3.60
• Lithium metal hydride	1.20
• Mercury oxide	1.35
• Nickel cadmium	1.25
• Zinc air	1.45
• Zinc chloride	1.50

Battery. The word *battery* means a group of cells. By packaging cells in series, manufacturers create batteries of nearly any voltage, the most common being 6, 9, and 12 volts. You can create a battery of nearly any voltage yourself by connecting cells in battery holders, which are designed to hold multiples of AAA-, AA-, C-, and D-size cells.

Switches

SPDT switch. The single-pole, double-throw is the simplest form of switch, allowing a single conductor (pole) to be routed to either of two routes (throws).

Think of the SPDT switch as a switch in a railroad track, shunting the track to either of two destinations. Of course, one of the destinations can lead nowhere, in which case the switch acts like a simple On-Off light switch. An SPDT switch used in the simple On-Off mode can be wired to be normally open (NO) or normally closed (NC).

DPDT switch. Going back to the railroad analogy, if you consider the two rails to be two conductors, then the railroad switch is analogous to the double-pole, double-throw switch. Two poles are switched simultaneously to one of two destinations. You can also think of the DPDT switch as being two SPDT switches ganged, or locked together.

Given enough layers and contacts, rotary switches can switch any number of poles to any number of destinations. They are specified as X-pole, Y-position.

Examples include: 1-pole, 12-position; 3-pole, 4-position; 2-pole, 8-position.

PB switch. Push-button switches are of two types: push-on, push-off; and momentary contact. The first is often used to control power On-Off and to activate options. The second is to activate a circuit or function briefly, such as a battery indicator or a microphone transmit switch.

Relay. The relay is an electrically activated switch. Current through its coil pulls on a magnetic slug, which activates a switch. The automotive solenoid is a high-current relay where a few amps from the keyed ignition switch activate the high-current (several hundred amps) switch on the starter motor. Electronic relays are rated by:

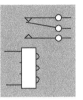

1. Input coil characteristics
2. Output switch maximum voltage and current

Sometimes the input coil voltage and resistance are specified, allowing you to calculate the current using Ohm's Law.

Example:
Coil: 12 VDC, 43 milliamps
Contacts: 2 amps, 120 VDC

Relays can have more than two poles, but they are always either single- or double-throw.

Overcurrent Devices

Fuse. A fuse (fusible link) protects a circuit from excessive current and damage by melting and breaking the circuit. The fuse is obviously a one-shot deal! In spite of the hassle of having to carry replacements, the fuse is still popular, due to low cost and high reliability.

Circuit breaker. You can think of the circuit breaker as a relay whose input current is routed through its output switch. The rated current of the circuit breaker is also the current required to activate the relay. Upon reaching its rated current, the circuit breaker disconnects itself, interrupting current flow to everything downstream of its output. Most circuit breakers operate on the same magnetic principle as coil relays. Some, however, contain a thermally activated bimetallic switch that opens at high temperature and won't close again until the temperature drops. Such thermal breakers are common in motors.

Passive Circuit Components

Lamps

Incandescent. The incandescent lamp is simply a miniature version of the ubiquitous household lightbulb. Its tungsten filament acts like a high-temperature resistor, glowing white-hot at normal operating voltage. Incandescent bulbs are rated by volts, either amps or watts, and type of base. By filling lamps with a halogen gas, which does not react with the filament, lamp manufacturers have been able to increase filament operating temperatures, which results in both greater light output and higher efficiency. The halogen lamps recommended in Chapter 10 are examples.

Neon. Neon bulbs contains no filaments to burn out. Instead, light is emitted by neon gas, which is stimulated by electric current. Neon bulbs require at least 60 volts to operate, and give off little light, but they consume little power and last indefinitely. They are often used as indicator lights in 120 and 240 VAC circuits.

Meters

Ammeter. The principles of both ammeters and voltmeters were discussed in Chapter 2. The ideal ammeter passes current with no voltage drop. In other words, it appears to a circuit as a resistor of near-zero resistance. Real ammeters come very close to the ideal with resistances on the order of 0.001 ohm.

There are two fundamentally different ammeter styles: analog and digital. The difference between analog and digital presentation is best exemplified by analog (sweep hands) and digital (LCD digits) watches. Analog is best for quick recognition; for accuracy you need digital.

Beware of cheap analog meters. They do not stand up well to the marine environment. On the other hand, the differences between high- and low-cost digital meters are often more in styling and name than in performance. The integrated circuitry inside the cases may be identical.

Voltmeter. Voltmeters are just ammeters with a high resistance in series with the input. The ideal voltmeter would appear to a circuit as an infinite resistance. The input resistance of real voltmeters ranges from 5,000 to 50,000 ohms per volt for analog meters and 1 to 10 megohms for digital meters.

Neither ammeters nor voltmeters must always be dedicated. A single panel meter can monitor an unlimited number of voltages or amperages by routing its input through a rotary switch. I use a $10 pocket digital volt-ohm meter Velcroed to my electrical panel, with its leads plugged into test jacks. When I need it for troubleshooting, I simply unstick it and substitute whatever test leads are appropriate to the job.

Motors

Motor. The most common motor on a boat is that driving the bilge pump. All small-boat bilge pump motors run on 12 VDC and consume from 2 to 20 amps. Start-up and locked-rotor currents can be three to four times as great, however, so contact ratings of switches and relays are important.

Fan. Most of the fans in a boat run on 12 VDC. A useful fan for the do-it-yourselfer is a zero-maintenance, brushless, and nearly noiseless fan originally developed for cooling computers. Sizes range from about 2 to 6 inches square. Drawing little current, they are ideal for circulating air through the condenser coils of small marine refrigerators under thermostatic control.

Acoustic Devices

Speaker. Speakers reproduce a range of frequencies, i.e., voice or music. They may also be used to emit very loud fixed-frequency sounds, as in burglar alarms and ship's horns. Speakers are rated by maximum power consumption in watts, frequency range, and input impedance, which is nearly always 8 ohms.

Piezo electric buzzer. A buzzer is an acoustic transducer that produces a single-frequency sound. Its primary use is as an alarm, indicating such things as:

- Too high voltage
- Too low voltage
- Too high temperature
- Too high water in the bilge

They are available in fixed frequencies from about 1 to 5 kHz. Current consumption depends on sound level and ranges from about 10 milliamps, which can be driven directly by integrated circuits, to 100 milliamps, which requires a driver transistor or relay.

Diodes

Rectifier diode. The most common diode passes current in the direction of the arrow but blocks current in the reverse direction. Actually, a minimum voltage of about 0.6 volt must be exceeded in the silicon diode (0.25 volt in a germanium diode) before current begins to flow in the forward direction. In the forward direction the diode looks, to a circuit, like nearly zero resistance and a voltage drop of 0.6 volt. In the reverse direction, it looks like infinite resistance.

With too high a forward current, diodes can overheat and be destroyed; at excessive reverse voltage, they will break down.

Diode specifications, therefore, include maximum forward current and peak reverse voltage. For example, a 1N4001 diode is rated at 1-amp continuous forward current and 50 volts peak reverse voltage.

Rectifier diodes are used in high-current applications, such as power supplies and battery chargers. Signal diodes handle a few milliamps and are used in signal processing. An example is the 1N914, rated at 10-milliamps continuous forward current and 75 volts peak inverse voltage.

Zener diode. All diodes break down and pass current in the reverse direction when the voltage exceeds their rating. Zener diodes are carefully manufactured to break down at precise voltages, ranging from 2 to 200 volts. The characteristic of switching from nonconducting to conducting at a precise voltage is used to regulate voltage in a circuit.

Light-emitting diode (LED). When free electrons flow across a diode junction, some electrons fall back into their normal, lower-energy states, releasing the extra energy in the form of radiation. In the rectifier and zener diodes, the frequency of the radiated energy is outside the range of visible light. In the LED gallium, arsenic, and phosphorus replace silicon, and the released radiation falls within the visible range. LEDs are available in red, green, yellow, and white.

Threshold voltages (voltage at which the LED begins to emit light) are typically 1.5 volts, rather than 0.6 volt. LEDs are rated, in addition to color, by maximum forward current and maximum reverse voltage. In practice, a resistor is placed in series with the LED to limit the forward current to the nominal value. Light

output, however, is nearly linear with forward current, so the LED can run usefully at lower current and light levels simply by increasing the series resistance.

Since LEDs can be destroyed by reversing the leads, it is important to distinguish the anode (+ voltage lead) from the cathode (– voltage lead). If a specification sheet with a drawing is not available, polarity can be checked by connecting to a battery of 1.5 volts, which is sufficient to cause light output but generally less than the peak inverse voltage.

Active Circuit Components

NPN transistor. Transistors are usually explained in terms of electrons and holes. I prefer a water analogy, which will serve our purposes well enough.

Figure 14.1 shows the three terminals of the NPN transistor: base, collector, and emitter. The small arrows show the direction of current flow in the leads: I_B, I_C and I_E. Note that the arrow in the emitter lead serves the same purposes and distinguishes the NPN from the PNP transistor.

The transistor is constructed like a pair of diodes connected back-to-back. Current I_B will flow from the base to the emitter, in the direction shown, whenever the base is at a higher voltage than the emitter.

Now the analogy—the base acts like a valve in the collector-to-emitter waterpipe. A small change in I_B results in a large change in I_C and I_E. The ratio of current changes is called the forward current gain:

$$h_{FE} = \Delta I_C / \Delta I_B$$

Typical values of h_{FE} range from 20 to 100.

The most common use of the transistor is to multiply current and, thus, increase the power of a signal.

PNP transistor. The PNP transistor functions in exactly the same way as the NPN transistor, except that its diodes are reversed. Figure 14.2 shows the lead definitions and current directions in the PNP transistor. Due to the reversal of diodes, current I_B will now flow whenever the base is negative relative to the emitter. Current gain is again defined as:

$$h_{FE} = \Delta I_C / \Delta I_B$$

The choice between PNP and NPN transistors depends on the supply voltage configuration of the circuit.

MOSFET. Both the field effect transistor (FET) and the metal-oxide semiconductor field effect transistor (MOSFET) act like transistors, except that the controlling input signal is a voltage rather than a current. Since almost no current flows into the input lead (the gate), the input resistance of the MOSFET is virtually infinite. FETs and MOSFETs are therefore primarily used where high input resistance is required. Applications where this characteristic is especially useful are operational amplifier inputs and digital voltmeters. Figure 14.3 shows the circuit symbol and the pin designations of the IRF510 power MOSFET.

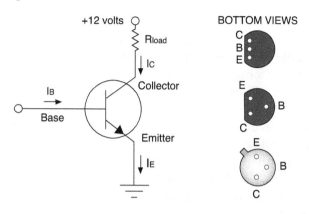
Fig. 14.1 NPN Transistor

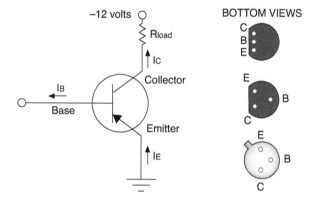
Fig. 14.2 PNP Transistor

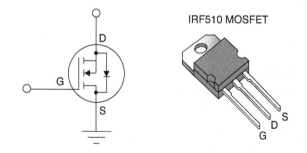
Fig. 14.3 MOSFET (IRF510)

Operational amplifier. If we were to describe a perfect amplifier, its specifications would read:

- Voltage gain = ∞
- Input resistance = ∞ Ω
- Input offset voltage = 0 volts

A real opamp, the LM353, costs less than $1.00 in single quantity and has the following specifications:

- Voltage gain $>10^6$
- Input resistance = $10^{12}\Omega$
- Input offset voltage < 0.002 volt

The usefulness of the opamp derives from its essentially infinite voltage gain and input resistance. Figure 14.4A shows the basic opamp. Since the output voltage is limited by the supply voltage (usually ±15 VDC, although single-voltage operation is possible too), infinite voltage gain implies zero volts between the positive (V_{in+}) and negative (V_{in-}) inputs. Further, since the input resistance is infinite, no current flows into either input.

Figure 14.4B shows the opamp as a voltage follower.

Zero difference voltage means that $Vin_+ = V_{in-}$, and since $V_{out} = V_{in-}$, then $V_{out} = V_{in}$. The voltage follower is used to simply boost current while maintaining voltage.

Figure 14.4C shows an inverting amplifier with voltage gain. Since no current flows into the – input, and since the – input is at the same potential as the + input (ground), then the input current flowing through R_1 must cancel the feedback current through R_2: $I_1 = -I_2$.

Then, using Ohm's Law,

$$I = V/R,$$
$$V_1/R_1 = -V_2/R_2$$
$$V_2 = -V_1(R_2/R_1)$$

Figure 14.4 shows a variety of other useful opamp configurations (D, E, F). To understand how they work, you need remember only that $V_{in+} = V_{in-}$.

The equation relating V_{out} to V_{in} can then be derived from equating the input and (negative) feedback currents flowing into each input.

Fig. 14.4 A Few Useful Operational Amplifier Circuits

A. Basic Operational Amplifier

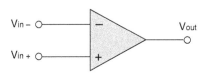

B. Unity-Gain Voltage Follower:
Vout = Vin

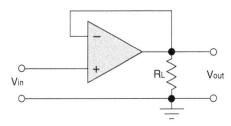

C. Inverting Amplifier
Vout = – Vin

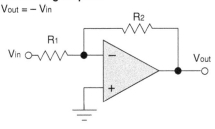

D. Non-Inverting Amplifier
Vout = Vin(R2/R1)

E. Summing Amplifier
Vout = – (Rf/R1 x V1 + Rf/R2 x V2 + ...)

F. Difference Amplifier
Vout = – (V1 – V2)R2/R1

1. AC Polarity Indicator

The ABYC recommends reverse-polarity indicators on all AC main panels. It also suggests that the resistance of such indicators be at least 25,000 ohms in order that they not bypass any isolation transformer or galvanic isolation diodes installed in the shore-power circuit. This two-lamp circuit consists of a green neon lamp across the hot and neutral conductors and a red neon lamp across neutral and ground. Proper polarity is indicated by a green light alone. If the red light comes on, either alone or with the green, something is wrong. To install the lamps, drill $\frac{5}{16}$-inch holes in the distribution panel and press in.

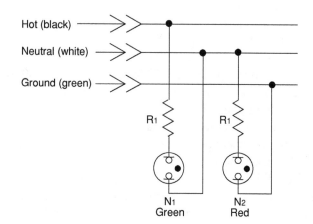

Components

Part	Description	RadioShack #
N1	Green 120-volt neon lamp	272-708
N2	Red 120-volt neon lamp	272-712
R1	33 kΩ, ¼-watt resistor	271-1341

2. LED Panel Indicator

Many DC distribution panels come only with circuit breakers or fuses, so it is difficult to tell at a glance whether a circuit is on or off. Others come with battery-draining incandescent indicator lamps. One of these low-current LED indicators can be installed on the output side of each circuit breaker and fuse to indicate, with a soft glow, when the circuit is on. The LED specified consumes only 0.012 amp. Ten LEDs will consume 3 Ah of battery power per 24 hours. To install, drill press-fit holes in the panel adjacent to each fuse switch or circuit breaker. Press in the LED and solder the 1 kΩ resistor between the LED anode (see specification sheet for lead identification) and the hot terminal. Connect the LED cathode to the panel ground bus.

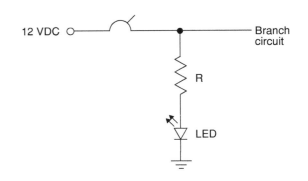

Components

Part	Description	RadioShack #
R	1 kΩ, ¼-watt resistor	271-1321
LED	Red, T1 (3 mm), LED	276-026

3. AC Frequency Meter

The ABYC recommends an AC frequency meter on the AC distribution panel fed by any onboard generator. The zener diode in this circuit clips incoming 120-volt AC sine waves to 6.2-volt DC square waves. Capacitor C_1 differentiates the square waves into positive and negative pulses. Diode D_1 shorts the negative pulses to ground, but diode D_2 passes the positive pulses, which are then averaged by the inertia of the ammeter, M.

To calibrate, connect the circuit to shore power (60 Hz), and adjust R_2 until M reads exactly 60 mA.

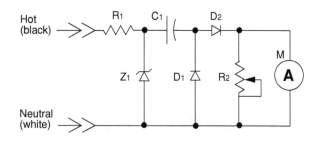

Components

Part	Description	RadioShack #
R1	100 kΩ, ½-watt resistor	271-1131
R2	10 kΩ, 1-turn potentiometer	271-1715
C1	0.22 µF capacitor	272-1070
D1, D2	1N914 signal diode	276-1122
Z1	6.2 V zener diode	276-561
M	0–100 µA panel meter	none

4. Small Battery Eliminator

If you are tired of replacing expensive batteries in your electronics, you can make a "battery" that will supply up to 1.5 amps at any voltage from 1.5 to 10 volts DC, drawing from your ship's battery. The 317T is an adjustable, three-terminal, integrated-circuit voltage regulator in a package smaller than a dime.

To install, solder the circuit as shown, connect V_{in} to 12 VDC and adjust trimpot R until V_{out} reads the desired voltage. Then connect V_{out} and Ground to the battery terminals of the electronic equipment.

You may wish to pack the circuit into a cardboard or plastic cylinder of the same dimensions as the battery you are replacing. An alternative is to wrap the circuit in foam and then stuff it into the battery slot. If the 317T gets too hot to touch, mount it on the optional heat sink.

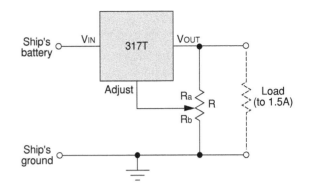

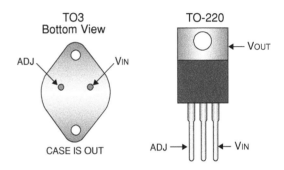

Components

Part	Description	RadioShack #
317T	Adjustable voltage regulator	276-1778
R	1kΩ trimpot	271-280
*	Optional heat sink (not shown)	276-1368

Projects

5. Low-Battery Voltage Alarm

In this circuit a 741 operational amplifier compares the voltage of zener diode, Z, to a voltage determined by the ship's battery and the voltage divider, R_3 and R_2.

When the battery voltage falls below the preset lower-voltage limit, the voltage at the opamp's V_{in-} terminal drops below the zener's 6.2 volts, and the output of the opamp rises to the battery voltage, lighting the LED. A 10-milliamp Piezo buzzer could replace the noiseless LED for an audible alarm.

To set the battery's low-voltage alarm point, monitor the battery voltage with a digital voltmeter. When the voltage reaches 12.00 volts, for example, adjust R_3 until the LED or buzzer just comes on.

A two-stage alarm can easily be constructed, which will give a visual LED warning at 50% discharge, for example, and a more dire audible warning at 75% discharge.

To construct, replace the 741 with a 1458 dual operational amplifier, feed the – input of the second amplifier with a second R_2/R_3 voltage divider, and drive the Piezo buzzer with the output of the second amplifier. Calibrate the two setpoints as before, using a digital voltmeter to monitor battery voltage.

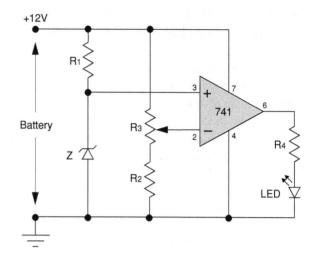

Components

Part	Description	RadioShack #
R_1	10 kΩ, ¼-watt resistor	271-1335
R_2	1 kΩ, ¼-watt resistor	271-1321
R_3	10 kΩ, 15-turn trimpot	271-343
R_4	1 kΩ, ¼-watt resistor	271-1321
Z	1N4735, 6.2 V zener diode	276-561
LED	Red, T1 (3 mm), LED	276-026
741	741 operational amplifier	276-007

6. Expanded-Scale Analog Battery Monitor

The problem with monitoring battery voltage with an analog panel meter is that the normal 5% accuracy of the meter is equivalent to about 50% of the battery's capacity. What is needed is an electronic magnifying glass to focus on the battery's 11.7- to 12.7-volt range.

In this circuit, a 317T adjustable voltage regulator is used to provide a constant 11.70 VDC. The 0- to 1-volt DC voltmeter then reads the difference between the ship's battery voltage and the reference 11.70 volts. Assuming 12.70 and 11.70 volts represent 100% and 0% charge, 0 to 1 volt on the voltmeter represents 0% to 100% charge.

The 3 VDC alkaline battery (can be two AA alkaline cells in a battery holder) boosts the regulator source so that the output can still deliver 11.7 volts, even when the ship's battery drops to 11.7 volts.

The 0- to 1-volt voltmeter can be replaced by R_{opt} and an ammeter, as shown in the component list.

Of course a digital voltmeter may be used, in lieu of the analog meter.

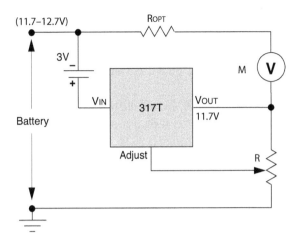

Components

Part	Description	RadioShack #
317T	Adjustable voltage regulator	276-1778
R	1 kΩ, 15-turn trimpot	271-342
M	0–1-volt DC meter	none
R_{opt}	10 kΩ resistor for 100 µA meter	271-1335
R_{opt}	1 kΩ resistor for 1 µA meter	271-1321

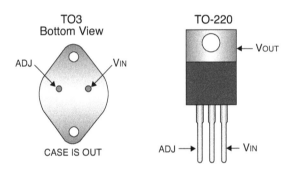

Projects

7. Expanded Digital Battery Monitor

This circuit utilizes the incredibly useful, yet inexpensive, LM3914 Dot/Bar Display Driver to display the charge status of a boat's batteries in 0.1-volt increments.

The LEDs can be of different colors, further enhancing the status indication. For instance, if your normal discharge range is 90 to 50%, the top five LEDs could be green (indicating OK) and the bottom five LEDs red (indicating need to charge).

To calibrate the circuit, connect a digital voltmeter to the battery terminals. First charge the battery fully and let it come to its fully charged rest voltage (approximately 12.65 volts). Adjust potentiometer R_3 until LED #10 lights, indicating full charge. To establish the fully discharged state, let the battery discharge until the voltmeter reads 11.65 volts, and adjust potentiometer R_2 until LED #1 lights.

From this point on, the battery voltage will be indicated by which LED is lit, in increments of 0.1 volt.

As an option, and at the cost of slightly higher power consumption, the display can be converted to a bar graph simply by connecting pin 9 to Battery +.

Components

Part	Description	RadioShack #
LM3914	Dot/bar display driver	900-6840
R_1	47 kΩ, ¼-watt resistor	271-1342
R_2	200 kΩ, 15-turn trimpot	none
R_3	100 kΩ, 15-turn trimpot	none
C_1	47 µF electrolytic capacitor	272-1027
C_2	0.1 µF capacitor	272-1069
LEDs	10-segment LED bar graph	276-081
	or individual red	276-026
	or individual green	276-022

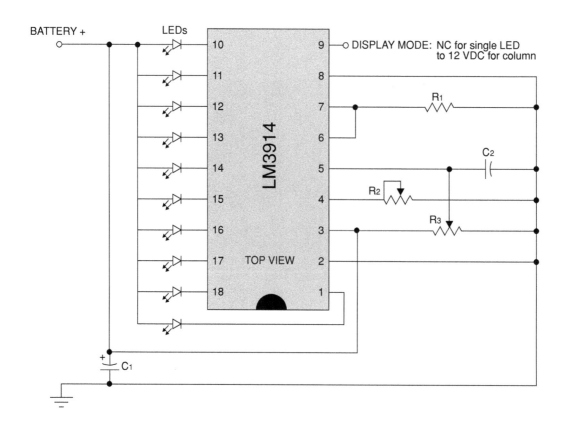

8. Automatic Anchor Light

The typical mast-top anchor light consumes 12 watts. Over a 12-hour period, it will drain 12 Ah from the battery. If you leave the boat unattended and leave the anchor light on (as you must legally), it will draw down the battery at 24 Ah per day!

This circuit saves battery power by automatically switching on at sunset and off at sunrise. At sunset, the resistance of the cadmium sulfide photoresistor increases, increasing the voltage to the NPN transistor, Q. The transistor provides the current to close the coil of the relay and feed 12 VDC to the anchor light.

The red LED indicates when the anchor light is on. A single-pole, three-position rotary switch allows selection between automatic, manual, and off modes.

Note that the cadmium sulfide photoresistor must be placed so that it is not illuminated by the anchor light. Otherwise it will interpret the anchor light as sunlight and cause the light to turn on and off rapidly.

Components

Part	Description	RadioShack #
R_1	1 kΩ, ¼-watt resistor	271-1321
R_2	10 kΩ, 1-turn potentiometer	271-282
R_3	1 kΩ, ¼-watt resistor	271-1321
P	Photoresistor	276-1657
Q	2N2222 NPN transistor	276-2009
Relay	12 V, 400 Ω, 10 A SPDT	275-248
SW	SPDT switch, center Off	275-654
LED	Red, T1 (3 mm), LED	276-026
741	741 operational amplifier	276-007

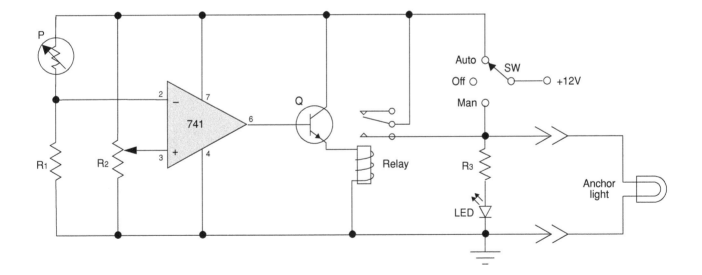

9. Cabin Light Dimmer

Halogen cabin lamps are great for reading, but not very romantic for dining. Furthermore, dimming your cabin lights will save on battery power.

The heart of this circuit is the integrated circuit 555 timer. The 555 runs as a multivibrator (digital oscillator) with its frequency determined by R_1, R_2, R_3, and C_1. Pin 3 of the 555 controls the gate of the MOSFET, Q, which supplies current to the cabin lamps in the form of square waves of modulated width.

The percentage of normal voltage supplying the lamps is equivalent to the percentage-on time of the pulses, which is controlled by adjusting trimpot R_2. This effective voltage across the lamps can be varied from about 4.5 to 11.0 VDC.

The dimmer circuit is switched in and out of the circuit by switch SW. Individual cabin lights can still be switched on and off with their own switches.

Since the life of the very expensive halogen lamps is extended markedly by reduction in supply voltage, you might consider leaving the dimmer circuit on all the time, set at the minimum power level required for the task at hand.

If the circuit load is more than 5 watts, check the operating temperature of the 555. If too hot to touch, attach a heat sink to the integrated circuit.

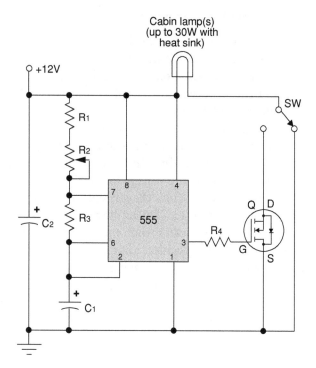

Cabin lamp(s)
(up to 30W with
heat sink)

Components

Part	Description	RadioShack #
R_1	100 Ω, ¼-watt resistor	271-1311
R_2	5 kΩ potentiometer	271-1714
R_3	1 kΩ, ¼-watt resistor	271-1321
R_4	10 kΩ, ¼-watt resistor	271-1335
C_1	0.047 µF capacitor	272-1068
C_2	22 µF capacitor	272-1026
Q	IRF-510 power MOSFET	276-2072
555	555 timer integrated circuit	276-1723
SW	SPDT switch, center Off	275-654
*	Heat sink for Q (not shown)	276-1368

10. Bilge High-Water Alarm

Automatic bilge pump switches are notorious for failing. Although not usually dangerous, having bilge water rise above the cabin sole is not very good for the rugs or the joinery. This circuit gives an audible warning when the bilge water rises to the level of the normally dry probe.

The 741 opamp acts as a voltage comparator. The – input voltage is set at +6 VDC by the voltage divider formed by R_2 and R_3. With a dry probe, the + input voltage is near 0 VDC, so the output of the 741 is near 0 VDC.

With the probe immersed in water, however, the voltage at the + input rises to over 6 VDC, and the 741 output goes to 12 VDC. Transistor Q boosts the output of the 741 to drive the Piezo transducer. R_4 prevents the + side of the probe from shorting to ground through the bilge water.

An inexpensive and convenient probe can be made from a section of television twin lead with each conductor stripped back about 1 inch and tinned (soldered) to prevent corrosion. The probes should be mounted well above the normal bilge high-water level, so that they remain dry except when the regular bilge switch fails.

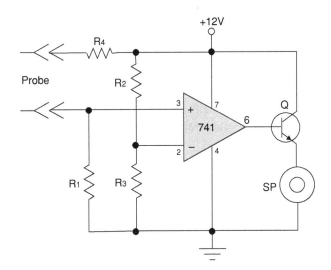

Components

Part	Description	RadioShack #
R_1	100 kΩ, ¼-watt resistor	271-1347
R_2	100 kΩ ¼-watt resistor	271-1347
R_3	100 kΩ, ¼-watt resistor	271-1347
R_4	10 kΩ, ¼-watt resistor	271-1335
Q	2N2222 NPN transistor	276-2009
741	741 operational amplifier	276-007
SP	Piezo transducer	273-075
Probe	TV twin-lead antenna wire	15-0004

Projects

11. Water Tank Monitor

Few things are more annoying than unexpectedly running out of water or having to lift deck hatches and unscrew access plates to check the level of water in your tanks. This circuit gives a visual warning when your water tank reaches a predetermined level.

The 741 operational amplifier acts as a voltage comparator. The + input voltage is set by the voltage divider formed by trimpot R_2.

Run a length of television twin-lead antenna cable into your water tank from above. Strip about 1 inch of insulation from each of the two conductors and solder the exposed wire to prevent corrosion.

With the probe immersed in water, the voltage at the − input is near +12 VDC. As soon as the water level drops below the probe leads, the resistance between the leads increases to near infinity and the − input voltage drops to zero. The amplifier output rises to the supply voltage and lights the LED warning light.

Add a switch to the +12 VDC power lead if you don't wish to monitor the tank continuously.

Components

Part	Description	RadioShack #
R_1	220 kΩ, ¼-watt resistor	271-1350
R_2	100 kΩ trimpot	271-284
R_3	1 kΩ, ¼-watt resistor	271-1321
LED	Red, T1 (3 mm), LED	276-026
741	741 operational amplifier	276-007

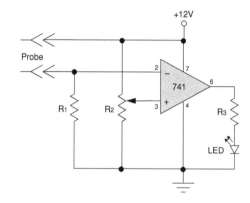

12. Electronic Ship's Horn

The circuit is a multivibrator (Q_1 and Q_2) with a frequency of $2\pi/R_1C_1 = 280$ Hz. Transistor Q_3 boosts the output current to drive the 8 Ω, 25-watt speaker. Pushing the momentary contact switch, SW_1, sounds the horn.

Play with resistors R_1 to achieve the pitch that is most pleasing to you, although 280 Hz is close to the frequency of most commercial horns. A speaker with higher impedance can be used with an impedance-matching transformer.

Using switch SW_2, the speaker can be connected to the hailer output found in the rear of many VHF radios, allowing the speaker to be used as a bullhorn as well.

Components

Part	Description	RadioShack #
R_1(2)	100 kΩ, ¼-watt resistor	271-1347
R_2(2)	1 kΩ, ¼-watt resistor	271-1321
C_1(2)	0.22 µF capacitor	272-1070
Q_1	2N2222 NPN transistor	276-2009
Q_2	2N2222 NPN transistor	276-2009
Q_3	TIP-3055 NPN power transistor	276-2020
SW_1	Momentary contact switch	275-609
SW_2	DPDT switch, 6 A	275-652
SP	Power horn, 8Ω, 25-watt	40-1440

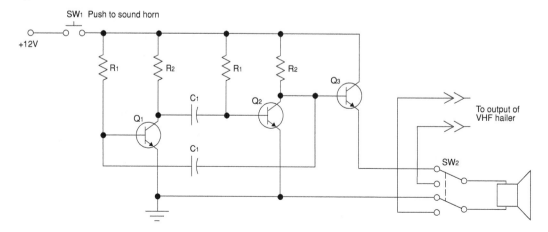

13. Refrigeration Fan Control

The efficiency of a refrigerator is affected greatly by the temperature of its condenser coil. Many small, 12 VDC boat compressors are located in warm or constricted spaces. Such condensers need fans to remove the heat from the coils.

This circuit uses a tiny thermistor, taped to the condenser tubing, to detect the need for air flow. The tape over the thermistor protects it from the direct flow of cool air, so that it measures the temperature of the coil rather than that of the moving air.

The opamp compares the voltages of two voltage dividers formed by R_1/R_T (– input) and trimpot R_2 (+ input). When the temperature of the thermistor rises above the set point, its resistance drops, the voltage at the negative input drops, and the output voltage of the inverting amplifier rises. Transistor Q boosts the opamp output current to close the relay and turn on the fan.

The temperature at which the fan comes on (the set point) is adjusted with trimpot R_2. Trimpot R_3 adjusts the gain of the amplifier and, thus, the hysteresis, or difference between turn-on and turn-off temperatures.

Components

Part	Description	RadioShack #
R_1	10 kΩ, ¼-watt resistor	271-1335
R_2	20 kΩ, 15-turn trimpot	900-8583
R_3	100 kΩ trimpot	271-284
T	Thermistor, 10 kΩ @ 25°C	271-110
Q	2N2222 NPN transistor	276-2009
K	12 V, 400 Ω, 10 A SPDT relay	275-248
741	741 operational amplifier	276-007
F	Blower fan, 12 VDC	273-243

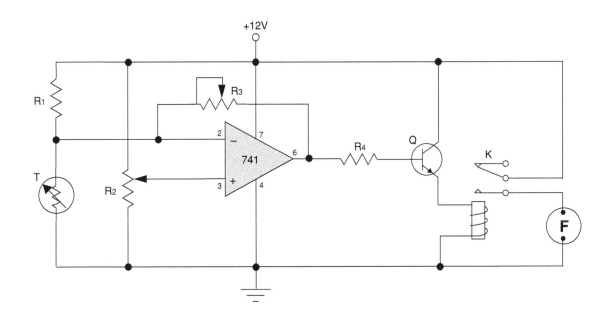

Appendices

Because boats are built and wired throughout the world we felt the least we could offer boatowners would be a listing of other wiring standards in use in the United States, Canada, and the European Union, and a table of metric conversions.

The formula for converting from Celsius to Fahrenheit degrees is awkward and difficult to compute in your head, so we thought a table of temperature conversions would be useful. Similarly, in wiring there is often need to perform power conversions from the mechanical horsepower of motors to electrical watts.

Both copper conductors and coaxial cables suffer losses as functions of length. Therefore, we have included handy tables of resistance of copper wire and losses in coaxial cables.

Although DC and AC color codes for marine wiring are discussed in the text, other wiring color codes exist, so we thought it would be useful to present them all together.

When performing electronic installation and repair, it is often necessary to identify the characteristics of components. With the trend toward miniaturization, it is increasingly difficult for manufacturers to print, and for us to read, information directly on the component. This is especially true for resistors and capacitors. Thus the manufacturers have resorted to cryptic codes involving colors and single alphanumeric characters as aids in identifying resistors and identifying capacitors.

Finally, for the mathematically inclined, we offer all of the useful electrical formulas and trigonometric tables you might need in performing electrical calculations.

Boatowner's Illustrated Electrical Handbook is based on the American Boat and Yacht Council (ABYC) *Standards and Recommended Practices for Small Craft*, a set of standards almost universally followed in the United States and increasingly referenced throughout the world. Most of the dozens of other standards in use around the world are remarkably similar, so you would not go far astray in following the ABYC recommendations. If you need to reference one of the other standards, however, here is a list of the most important ones.

United States

The United States Coast Guard: *Title 33, CFR 183.* These contain federal mandatory requirements for electrical systems on boats. Many of the Title 33 regulations are directly referenced in the ABYC standards. In no case do the two conflict. The text is available on the web at: *www.access.gpo.gov/nara/cfr/waisidx_99/33cfr183_99.html.*

National Marine Electronics Association (NMEA): *Installation Standards.* This standard is for the installation of marine electronics, primarily on large vessels. It is complementary to the ABYC recommendations, but with an emphasis on electronics. To visit NMEA on the web, go to: *www.nmea.org.*

National Fire Protection Association (NFPA): *National Electrical Code (NEC).* This is the single United States national code governing all wiring on land, including marinas. To visit NFPA on the web, go to: *www.nfpa.org.*

Canada

Transport Canada: *TP1332 E—Construction Standards for Small Vessels—Section 8 Electrical Systems.* The single, comprehensive set of standards for pleasure vessels constructed in Canada. The complete text can be accessed at: *www.tc.gc.ca/marinesafety/TP/TP1332/menu.htm.*

European Union

European Recreational Craft Directive (RCD). RCD standards are mandatory on boats constructed in European Union (EU) countries and include the following International Standards Organization (ISO) standards:

ISO10133:2000. Small Craft—Electrical systems—Extra-low-voltage DC installations.
ISO13297:2000. Small Craft—Electrical systems—AC installations.
ISO8846:1990 Small Craft—Electrical devices—Protection against ignition of surrounding flammable gas.

ISO standards can be purchased online at: *www.iso.org/iso/en/prods-services/ISOstore/store.html.*

Lloyd's Register. *Rules and Regulations for the Classification of Yachts and Small Craft, 1978.*
The Rules are used when a boat is to be built to Lloyd's Register (LR) Class rules.

BMEA (British Marine Electronics Association): *Code of Practice for Electrical and Electronic Installations in Small Craft—4th Edition.* This standard is similar to the United States *NMEA Installation Standards* and is available direct from the British Marine Federation Technical Department; tel: 01784 223634 or email: *technical@britishmarine.co.uk.*

English/Metric Conversions

Table A1 English to Metric Conversions

Multiply	English to Metric By	To Get		Multiply	Metric to English By	To Get
LENGTH						
Inches	25.4	Millimeters		Millimeters	0.0394	Inches
Inches	2.54	Centimeters		Centimeters	0.3937	Inches
Inches	0.0254	Meters		Meters	39.37	Inches
Feet	30.48	Centimeters		Centimeters	0.0328	Feet
Feet	0.3048	Meters		Meters	3.281	Feet
Yards	0.9144	Meters		Meters	1.094	Yards
Miles	1.609	Kilometers		Kilometers	0.6215	Miles
AREA						
$Inches^2$	645.16	$Millimeters^2$		$Millimeters^2$	0.00155	$Inches^2$
$Inches^2$	6.4516	$Centimeters^2$		$Centimeters^2$	0.155	$Inches^2$
$Feet^2$	929.03	$Centimeters^2$		$Centimeters^2$	0.00108	$Feet^2$
$Feet^2$	0.0929	$Meters^2$		$Meters^2$	10.764	$Feet^2$
$Yards^2$	8361.3	$Centimeters^2$		$Centimeters^2$	0.00012	$Yards^2$
$Yards^2$	0.8361	$Meters^2$		$Meters^2$	1.196	$Yards^2$
$Miles^2$	2.59	$Kilometers^2$		$Kilometers^2$	0.3861	$Miles^2$
VOLUME						
$Inches^3$	16.387	$Millimeters^3$		$Millimeters^3$	6.1×10^{-5}	$Inches^3$
$Inches^3$	16.387	$Centimeters^3$		$Centimeters^3$	0.061	$Inches^3$
$Feet^3$	0.0283	$Meters^3$		$Meters^3$	35.33	$Feet^3$
$Yards^3$	0.7646	$Meters^3$		$Meters^3$	1.308	$Yards^3$
ENERGY						
Ergs	10^{-7}	Newton-meters		Newton-meters	10^7	Ergs
Joules	1	Newton-meters		Newton-meters	1	Joules
Joules	10^7	Ergs		Ergs	10^{-7}	Joules
Joules	0.2389	Calories		Calories	4.186	Joules
Joules	0.000948	Btu		Btu	1,055	Joules
Joules	0.7376	Foot-pounds		Foot-pounds	1.356	Joules
Calories	0.00397	Btu		Btu	252	Calories
Joules/see	3.41	Btu/hr		Btu/hr	0.293	Joules/see
Btu/hr	252	Calories/hr		Calories/hr	0.00397	Btu/hr
Horsepower	746	Watts		Watts	0.00134	Horsepower
F°	0.556	C°		C°	1.8	F°
°F	0.556 (°F − 32)	°C		°C	1.8 x °C + 32	°F

Table A2 Fahrenheit Degrees to Celsius Degrees Conversion[1]

F°	C°	F°	C°	F°	C°	F°	C°	F°	C°	F°	C°
212	100	170	76.7	128	53.3	86	30.0	44	6.7	2	−16.7
211	99.4	169	76.1	127	52.8	85	29.4	43	6.1	1	−17.2
210	98.9	168	75.6	126	52.2	84	28.9	42	5.6	0	−17.8
209	98.3	167	75.0	125	51.6	83	28.3	41	5.0	−1	−18.3
208	97.8	166	74.4	124	51.1	82	27.8	40	4.4	−2	−18.9
207	97.2	165	73.9	123	50.5	81	27.2	39	3.9	−3	−19.4
206	96.7	164	73.3	122	50.0	80	26.6	38	3.3	−4	−20.0
205	96.1	163	72.8	121	49.4	79	26.1	37	2.8	−5	−20.5
204	95.6	162	72.2	120	48.8	78	25.5	36	2.2	−6	−21.1
203	95.0	161	71.7	119	48.3	77	25.0	35	1.7	−7	−21.6
202	94.4	160	71.1	118	47.7	76	24.4	34	1.1	−8	−22.2
201	93.9	159	70.6	117	47.2	75	23.9	33	0.6	−9	−22.8
200	93.3	158	70.0	116	46.6	74	23.3	32	0.0	−10	−23.3
199	92.8	157	69.4	115	46.1	73	22.8	31	−0.6	−11	−23.9
198	92.2	156	68.9	114	45.5	72	22.2	30	−1.1	−12	−24.4
197	91.7	155	68.3	113	45.0	71	21.6	29	−1.7	−13	−25.0
196	91.1	154	67.8	112	44.4	70	21.1	28	−2.2	−14	−25.5
195	90.6	153	67.2	111	43.8	69	20.5	27	−2.8	−15	−26.1
194	90.0	152	66.7	110	43.3	68	20.0	26	−3.3	−16	−26.6
193	89.4	151	66.1	109	42.7	67	19.4	25	−3.9	−17	−27.2
192	88.9	150	65.6	108	42.2	66	18.9	24	−4.4	−18	−27.8
191	88.3	149	65.0	107	41.6	65	18.3	23	−5.0	−19	−28.3
190	87.8	148	64.4	106	41.1	64	17.8	22	−5.6	−20	−28.9
189	87.2	147	63.9	105	40.5	63	17.2	21	−6.1	−21	−29.4
188	86.7	146	63.3	104	40.0	62	16.7	20	−6.7	−22	−30.0
187	86.1	145	62.8	103	39.4	61	16.1	19	−7.2	−23	−30.5
186	85.6	144	62.2	102	38.9	60	15.5	18	−7.8	−24	−31.1
185	85.0	143	61.7	101	38.3	59	15.0	17	−8.3	−25	−31.6
184	84.4	142	61.1	100	37.7	58	14.4	16	−8.9	−26	−32.2
183	83.9	141	60.6	99	37.2	57	13.9	15	−9.4	−27	−32.7
182	83.3	140	60.0	98	36.6	56	13.3	14	−10.0	−28	−33.3
181	82.8	139	59.4	97	36.1	55	12.8	13	−10.5	−29	−33.9
180	82.2	138	58.9	96	35.5	54	12.2	12	−11.1	−30	−34.4
179	81.7	137	58.3	95	35.0	53	11.7	11	−11.7	−31	−35.0
178	81.1	136	57.8	94	34.4	52	11.1	10	−12.2	−32	−35.5
177	80.6	135	57.2	93	33.9	51	10.5	9	−12.8	−33	−36.1
176	80.0	134	56.7	92	33.3	50	10.0	8	−13.3	−34	−36.6
175	79.4	133	56.1	91	32.7	49	9.4	7	−13.9	−35	−37.2
174	78.9	132	55.6	90	32.2	48	8.9	6	−14.4	−36	−37.7
173	78.3	131	55.0	89	31.6	47	8.3	5	−15.0	−37	−38.3
172	77.8	130	54.4	88	31.1	46	7.8	4	−15.5	−38	−38.9
171	77.2	129	53.9	87	30.5	45	7.2	3	−16.1	−39	−39.4

[1] $°C = (°F − 32)/1.8$

Power Conversions

Table A3 Kilowatts (kW) to Horsepower (hp) Conversion[1]

HP	kW	HP	kW	HP	kW
0.1	0.13	28	37.5	64	85.8
0.2	0.27	29	38.9	65	87.2
0.3	0.40	30	40.2	66	88.5
0.4	0.54	31	41.6	67	89.8
0.5	0.67	32	42.9	68	91.2
0.6	0.80	33	44.3	69	92.5
0.7	0.94	34	45.6	70	93.9
0.8	1.07	35	46.9	71	95.2
0.9	1.21	36	48.3	72	96.6
1	1.34	37	49.6	73	97.9
2	2.68	38	51.0	74	99.2
3	4.02	39	52.3	75	101
4	5.36	40	53.6	76	102
5	6.71	41	55.0	77	103
6	8.05	42	56.3	78	105
7	9.39	43	57.7	79	106
8	10.7	44	59.0	80	107
9	12.1	45	60.3	81	109
10	13.4	46	61.7	82	110
11	14.8	47	63.0	83	111
12	16.1	48	64.4	84	113
13	17.4	49	65.7	85	114
14	18.8	50	67.1	86	115
15	20.1	51	68.4	87	117
16	21.5	52	69.7	88	118
17	22.8	53	71.1	89	119
18	24.1	54	72.4	90	121
19	25.5	55	73.8	91	122
20	26.8	56	75.1	92	123
21	28.2	57	76.4	93	125
22	29.5	58	77.8	94	126
23	30.8	59	79.1	95	127
24	32.2	60	80.5	96	129
25	33.5	61	81.8	97	130
26	34.9	62	83.1	98	131
27	36.2	63	84.5	99	133

[1] 1 kW = 1.341 hp

Table A4 Horsepower (hp) to Kilowatts (kW) Conversion[1]

HP	kW	HP	kW	HP	kW
0.1	0.07	28	20.9	64	47.7
0.2	0.15	29	21.6	65	48.5
0.3	0.22	30	22.4	66	49.2
0.4	0.30	31	23.1	67	50.0
0.5	0.37	32	23.9	68	50.7
0.6	0.45	33	24.6	69	51.5
0.7	0.52	34	25.4	70	52.2
0.8	0.60	35	26.1	71	52.9
0.9	0.67	36	26.8	72	53.7
1	0.75	37	27.6	73	54.4
2	1.49	38	28.3	74	55.2
3	2.24	39	29.1	75	55.9
4	2.98	40	29.8	76	56.7
5	3.73	41	30.6	77	57.4
6	4.47	42	31.3	78	58.2
7	5.22	43	32.1	79	58.9
8	5.97	44	32.8	80	59.7
9	6.71	45	33.6	81	60.4
10	7.46	46	34.3	82	61.1
11	8.20	47	35.0	83	61.9
12	8.95	48	35.8	84	62.6
13	9.69	49	36.5	85	63.4
14	10.4	50	37.3	86	64.1
15	11.2	51	38.0	87	64.9
16	11.9	52	38.8	88	65.6
17	12.7	53	39.5	89	66.4
18	13.4	54	40.3	90	67.1
19	14.2	55	41.0	91	67.9
20	14.9	56	41.8	92	68.6
21	15.7	57	42.5	93	69.4
22	16.4	58	43.3	94	70.1
23	17.2	59	44.0	95	70.8
24	17.9	60	44.7	96	71.6
25	18.6	61	45.5	97	72.3
26	19.4	62	46.2	98	73.1
27	20.1	63	47.0	99	73.8

[1] 1 hp = 0.7457 kW

Resistance of Copper Wire

Table A5 Resistance of Copper Wire at 77°F (25°C)

AWG	Feet/Ohm	Ohms/1,000 Feet
0000	20,000	0.050
000	15,873	0.063
00	12,658	0.079
0	10,000	0.100
1	7,936	0.126
2	6,289	0.159
3	4,975	0.201
4	3,953	0.253
5	3,135	0.319
6	2,481	0.403
7	1,968	0.508
8	1,560	0.641
9	1,238	0.808
10	980.4	1.02
11	781.3	1.28
12	617.3	1.62
13	490.2	2.04
14	387.6	2.58
15	307.7	3.25
16	244.5	4.09
17	193.8	5.16
18	153.6	6.51
19	121.8	8.21
20	96.2	10.4
21	76.3	13.1
22	60.6	16.5
23	48.1	20.8
24	38.2	26.2
25	30.3	33.0
26	24.0	41.6
27	19.0	52.5
28	15.1	66.2
29	12.0	83.4
30	9.5	105

Table A6 Resistance of Copper Wire at 149°F (65°C)

AWG	Feet/Ohm	Ohms/1,000 Feet
0000	17,544	0.057
000	13,699	0.073
00	10,870	0.092
0	8,621	0.116
1	6,849	0.146
2	5,435	0.184
3	4,310	0.232
4	3,425	0.292
5	2,710	0.369
6	2,151	0.465
7	1,706	0.586
8	1,353	0.739
9	1,073	0.932
10	847.5	1.18
11	675.7	1.48
12	534.8	1.87
13	423.7	2.36
14	336.7	2.97
15	266.7	3.75
16	211.4	4.73
17	167.8	5.96
18	133.2	7.51
19	105.5	9.48
20	84.0	11.9
21	66.2	15.1
22	52.6	19.0
23	41.7	24.0
24	33.1	30.2
25	26.2	38.1
26	20.8	48.0
27	16.5	60.6
28	13.1	76.4
29	10.4	96.3
30	8.3	121

Losses in Coaxial Cables

Table A7 Signal Loss (Attenuation) in Decibels (dB) per 100 Feet in Coaxial Cables

Signal Frequency	RG-6	RG-8X	RG-11	Cable Type RG-58	RG-174	RG-213	RF-9913	RF-9914
1 MHz	0.2 dB	0.5 dB	0.2 dB	0.4 dB	1.9 dB	0.2 dB	0.2 dB	0.3 dB
10 MHz	0.6 dB	1.0 dB	0.4 dB	1.4 dB	3.3 dB	0.6 dB	0.4 dB	0.5 dB
50 MHz	1.4 dB	2.5 dB	1.0 dB	3.3 dB	6.6 dB	1.6 dB	0.9 dB	1.1 dB
100 MHz	2.0 dB	3.6 dB	1.6 dB	4.9 dB	8.9 dB	2.2 dB	1.4 dB	1.5 dB
200 MHz	2.8 dB	5.4 dB	2.3 dB	7.3 dB	11.9 dB	3.3 dB	1.8 dB	2.0 dB
400 MHz	4.3 dB	7.9 dB	3.5 dB	11.2 dB	17.3 dB	4.8 dB	2.6 dB	2.9 dB
700 MHz	5.6 dB	11.0 dB	4.7 dB	16.9 dB	26.0 dB	6.6 dB	3.6 dB	3.8 dB
900 MHz	6.0 dB	12.6 dB	5.4 dB	20.1 dB	27.9 dB	7.7 dB	4.2 dB	4.9 dB
1 GHz	6.1 dB	13.5 dB	5.6 dB	21.5 dB	32.0 dB	8.3 dB	4.5 dB	5.3 dB
Impedance	75 ohm	50 ohm	75 ohm	50 ohm	50 ohm	50 ohm	50 ohm	50 ohm

Table A8 Signal Loss in Decibels (dB) in Coaxial Cables

Loss in Decibels (dB)	Power Ratio	Voltage Ratio
0.0	1.000	1.000
0.5	0.891	0.944
1.0	0.794	0.891
1.5	0.708	0.841
2.0	0.631	0.794
2.5	0.562	0.750
3.0	0.501	0.708
3.5	0.447	0.668
4.0	0.398	0.631
4.5	0.355	0.596
5.0	0.316	0.562
6.0	0.251	0.501
7.0	0.200	0.447
8.0	0.158	0.398
9.0	0.126	0.355
10	0.100	0.316
20	0.010	0.100
30	0.001	0.032
40	0.0001	0.010

Table A9 Marine DC Wiring Color Code
(Adapted from ABYC Standard E-11, Tables XIV and XV)

Color	Conductor Use
Green or green with yellow stripe(s)	General DC grounding
Black or yellow	General DC negative
Red	General DC positive
Yellow with red stripe	Starter switch to solenoid
Brown with yellow stripe, or yellow	Fuse or switch to blower—If DC negative is yellow, positive must be brown with yellow stripe
Dark gray	Fuse or switch to navigation lights Tachometer sender to gauge
Brown	Generator armature to regulator Auxiliary terminal to light and regulator Fuse or switch to pumps
Orange	Ammeter to alternator or generator output and accessory fuses or switches Distribution panel to accessory switch
Purple	Ignition switch to coil and electrical instruments Distribution panel to electrical instruments
Dark blue	Fuse or switch to cabin and instrument lights
Light blue	Oil-pressure sender to gauge
Tan	Water-temperature sender to gauge
Pink	Fuel-gauge sender to gauge
Green/stripe, except G/Y	Tilt and/or trim circuits

Table A10 Marine AC Wiring Color Code
(Adapted from ABYC Standard E-11, Tables XIV and XV)

Conductor	Colors (Preferred First)
Ungrounded	Black or brown
Grounded neutral	White or light blue
Grounding	Green, green with yellow stripe
Additional ungrounded	Red, blue, orange
	Black with red stripe
	Black with blue stripe
	Black with orange stripe

Table A11 Electronic Wiring Color Code
(from the Electronic Industries Association [EIA])

Color	Conductor Use
Black	Ground, DC negative
Blue	Transistor collector, FET drain
Brown	Filament
Gray	AC main power
Green	Transistor base, diode, FET gate
Orange	Transistor base 2
Red	DC+ power supply
Violet	DC– power supply
White	B-C minus bias supply, AVC-AGC return
Yellow	Transistor emitter, FET source

Table A12 Power Transformer Color Code

Color	Conductor Use
Black	Both leads of an untapped primary
Black	Common lead of tapped primary
Black/Yellow	Tap of tapped primary
Black/Red	End of tapped primary

Table A13 Audio Transformer Color Code

Color	Conductor Use
Black	Ground
Blue	End of primary
Brown	End of primary opposite blue
Green	End of secondary
Red	B+, center tap of push-pull loop
Yellow	Center tap of secondary

Table A14 Stereo Channel Color Code

Color	Conductor Use
White	Left channel high
Blue	Left channel low
Red	Right channel high
Green	Right channel low

Useful Electrical Formulas

Direct Current (DC)

Ohm's Law

where:

V = voltage, volts
I = current, amperes (amps)
R = resistance, ohms
P = power, watts

$V = I \times R$
$\quad = P/I$
$\quad = (P \times R)^{1/2}$

$I = V/R$
$\quad = P/V$
$\quad = (P/R)^{1/2}$

$R = V/I$
$\quad = P/I^2$

$P = I^2 \times R$
$\quad = V \times I$
$\quad = V^2/R$

Resistors

In Series: $R = R_1 + R_2 + R_3 + \ldots$
In Parallel: $R = 1/(1/R_1 + 1/R_2 + 1/R_3 + \ldots)$

Capacitors

In Parallel: $C = C_1 + C_2 + C_3 + \ldots$
In Series: $C = 1/(1/C_1 + 1/C_2 + 1/C_3 + \ldots)$
Charge (coulombs) = C(farads) $\times V$

Alternating Current (AC)

Ohm's Law

where:

V = voltage, volts
I = current, amperes (amps)
Z = impedance, ohms
P = power, watts
q = phase angle

$V = I \times Z$
$\quad = P/(I \times \cos q)$
$\quad = (P \times Z/\cos q)^{1/2}$

$I = V/Z$
$\quad = P/(V \times \cos q)$
$\quad = P/(Z \times \cos q)^{1/2}$

$Z = V/I$
$\quad = P/(I^2 \times \cos q)$

$P = I^2 \times Z \times \cos q$
$\quad = V \times I \times \cos q$
$\quad = V^2 \times \cos q/Z$

Reactance

where:

X_L = reactance of an inductor, ohms
X_C = reactance of a capacitor, ohms
H = inductance, henrys
C = capacitance, farads
F = frequency, Hertz
π = 3.14

$X_L = 2\pi \times F \times H$
$X_C = 1/(2\pi \times F \times C)$

Impedance

In Series: $Z = [R^2 + (XL - XC)^2]^{1/2}$
In Parallel: $Z = R \times X/(R^2 + X^2)^{1/2}$

Power Factor, pf

pf = True power/Apparent power
$\quad = \cos\theta$
$\quad = P/(V \times I)$
$\quad = R/Z$

Resistors are generally too small to allow the imprinting of identifying information. For this reason standard resistors are coded with color bands.

Figure A1 and Table A15 demystify the color code. *Example:* What is the resistance of a resistor with brown, red, orange, and silver bands? *Answer:* 12,000 ±10% Ω.

Fig. A1 The Markings on Resistors

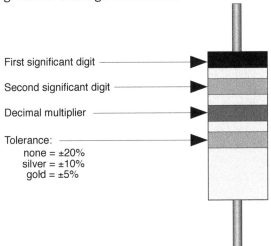

First significant digit

Second significant digit

Decimal multiplier

Tolerance:
  none = ±20%
  silver = ±10%
  gold = ±5%

Table A15 Resistor Color Codes

Band Color	Digit	Power of 10	Decimal Multiplier
Silver		10^{-2}	0.01
Gold		10^{-1}	0.1
Black	0	10^0	1
Brown	1	10^1	10
Red	2	10^2	100
Orange	3	10^3	1,000
Yellow	4	10^4	10,000
Green	5	10^5	100,000
Blue	6	10^6	1,000,000
Violet	7	10^7	10,000,000
Gray	8	10^8	100,000,000
White	9	10^9	1,000,000,000

Table A16 Standard Resistance Values in Ohms

Bold values available only in ±10% tolerance. All other values available in ±5% tolerance. Values beginning with 10, 15, 22, 33, 47, and 68 also available in ±20% tolerance.

First Band	Second Band	Gold	Black	Brown	Third Band Red	Orange	Yellow	Green	Blue
Brown	Black	1.0	10	100	1,000	10,000	100,000	1,000,000	10,000,000
Brown	**Brown**	**1.1**	**11**	**110**	**1,100**	**11,000**	**110,000**	**1,100,000**	**11,000,000**
Brown	Red	1.2	12	120	1,200	12,000	120,000	1,200,000	12,000,000
Brown	**Orange**	**1.3**	**13**	**130**	**1,300**	**13,000**	**130,000**	**1,300,000**	**13,000,000**
Brown	Green	1.5	15	150	1,500	15,000	150,000	1,500,000	15,000,000
Brown	**Blue**	**1.6**	**16**	**160**	**1,600**	**16,000**	**160,000**	**1,600,000**	**16,000,000**
Brown	Gray	1.8	18	180	1,800	18,000	180,000	1,800,000	18,000,000
Red	**Black**	**2.0**	**20**	**200**	**2,000**	**20,000**	**200,000**	**2,000,000**	**20,000,000**
Red	Red	2.2	22	220	2,200	22,000	220,000	2,200,000	22,000,000
Red	**Yellow**	**2.4**	**24**	**240**	**2,400**	**24,000**	**240,000**	**2,400,000**	
Red	Violet	2.7	27	270	2,700	27,000	270,000	2,700,000	
Orange	**Black**	**3.0**	**30**	**300**	**3,000**	**30,000**	**300,000**	**3,000,000**	
Orange	Orange	3.3	33	330	3,300	33,000	330,000	3,000,000	
Orange	**Blue**	**3.6**	**36**	**360**	**3,600**	**36,000**	**360,000**	**3,600,000**	
Orange	White	3.9	39	390	3,900	39,000	390,000	3,900,000	
Yellow	**Orange**	**4.3**	**43**	**430**	**4,300**	**43,000**	**430,000**	**4,300,000**	
Yellow	Violet	4.7	47	470	4,700	47,000	470,000	4,700,000	
Green	**Brown**	**5.1**	**51**	**510**	**5,100**	**51,000**	**510,000**	**5,100,000**	
Green	Blue	5.6	56	560	5,600	56,000	560,000	5,600,000	
Blue	**Red**	**6.2**	**62**	**620**	**6,200**	**62,000**	**620,000**	**6,200,000**	
Blue	Gray	6.8	68	680	6,800	68,000	680,000	6,800,000	
Violet	**Green**	**7.5**	**75**	**750**	**7,500**	**75,000**	**750,000**	**7,500,000**	
Gray	Red	8.2	82	820	8,200	82,000	820,000	8,200,000	
White	**Brown**	**9.1**	**91**	**910**	**9,100**	**91,000**	**910,000**	**9,100,000**	

Identifying Capacitors

Large capacitors, such as electrolytics, have their values printed plainly on them, but small disk and film capacitors usually display just two or three code numbers.

Most will have three characters, where the first two are the first and second significant digits and the third is a multiplier code. Unless a different unit is specified, the units are assumed pico (10^{-12}) farads. Table A17 shows the multipliers.

In addition there may be a fourth character (letter) indicating tolerance (see Table A18).

Finally there may be a number-letter-number code for temperature coefficient (see Table A19).

Table A20, at bottom, shows the capacitance value markings for capacitors manufactured in Europe.

Fig. A2 The Markings on Capacitors

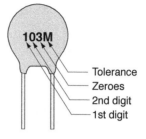

FOR VALUES ≥ 10 pF
Example: 0.01μF ±20%

103M
— Tolerance
— Zeroes
— 2nd digit
— 1st digit

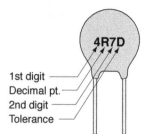

FOR VALUES < 10 pF
Example: 4.7 pF ±0.5%

4R7D
1st digit —
Decimal pt. —
2nd digit —
Tolerance —

Table A17
Capacitor Value

Digit 3	Multiplier
0	1
1	10
2	100
3	1,000
4	10,000
5	100,000
6	one
7	none
8	0.01
9	0.1

Table A18
Capacitor Tolerance

Code	Tolerance
B	±0.1 pF
C	±0.25 pF
D	±0.5 pF
E	±0.25%
F	±1%
G	±2%
H	±2.5%
J	±5%
K	±10%
M	±20%

Table A19 Capacitor Temperature Coefficients

First (letter)	Min. °C	Second (number)	Max. °C	Third (letter)	Change w/temp
Z	+10	2	+45	A	+1.0%
Y	−30	4	+65	B	±1.5%
X	−55	5	+85	C	±2.2%
−	−	6	+105	D	±3.3%
−	−	7	+125	E	±4.7%
−	−	−	−	F	±7.5%
−	−	−	−	P	±10.0%
−	−	−	−	R	±15.0%
−	−	−	−	S	±22.0%
−	−	−	−	T	+22%, −33%
−	−	−	−	U	+22%, −56%
−	−	−	−	V	+22%, −82%

Table A20 European Capacitance Value Code

pF	Code	pF	Code	pF	Code	pF	Code	μF	Code	μF	Code	μF	Code
1.0	1p0	10	10p	100	n10	1,000	1n0	0.010	10n	0.10	100n	1.0	1m0
1.2	1p2	12	12p	120	n12	1,200	1n2	0.012	12n	0.12	120n	1.2	1m2
1.5	1p3	15	15p	150	n15	1,500	1n5	0.015	15n	0.15	150n	1.5	1m3
1.8	1p8	18	18p	180	n18	1,800	1n8	0.018	18n	0.18	180n	1.8	1m8
2.2	2p2	22	22p	220	n22	2,200	2n2	0.022	22n	0.22	220n	2.2	2m2
2.7	2p7	27	27p	270	n27	2,700	2n7	0.027	27n	0.27	270n	2.7	2m7
3.3	3p3	33	33p	330	n33	3,300	3n3	0.033	33n	0.33	330n	3.3	3m3
3.9	3p9	39	39p	390	n39	3,900	3n9	0.039	39n	0.39	390n	3.9	3m9
4.7	4p7	47	47p	470	n47	4,700	4n7	0.047	47n	0.47	470n	4.7	4m7
5.6	5p6	56	56p	560	n56	5,600	5n6	0.056	56n	0.56	560n	5.6	5m6
6.8	6p8	68	68p	680	n68	6,800	6n8	0.068	68n	0.68	680n	6.8	6m8
8.2	8p2	82	82p	820	n82	8,200	8n2	0.082	82n	0.82	820n	8.2	8m2

Table A21 Values of Trigonometric Functions of a Right Triangle

Degrees	Sine (Sin)	Cosine (Cos)	Tangent (Tan)	Cosecant (Csc)	Secant (Sec)	Cotangent (Cot)	
00	0.0000	1.0000	0.0000	—	1.0000	—	90
01	0.0175	0.9998	0.0175	57.2987	1.0002	57.2900	89
02	0.0349	0.9994	0.0349	28.6537	1.0006	28.6363	88
03	0.0523	0.9986	0.0524	19.1073	1.0014	19.0811	87
04	0.0698	0.9976	0.0699	14.3356	1.0024	14.3007	86
05	0.0872	0.9962	0.0875	11.4737	1.0038	11.4301	85
06	0.1045	0.9945	0.1051	9.5668	1.0055	9.5144	84
07	0.1219	0.9925	0.1228	8.2055	1.0075	8.1443	83
08	0.1392	0.9903	0.1405	7.1853	1.0098	7.1154	82
09	0.1564	0.9877	0.1584	6.3925	1.0125	6.3138	81
10	0.1736	0.9848	0.1763	5.7588	1.0154	5.6713	80
11	0.1908	0.9816	0.1944	5.2408	1.0187	5.1446	79
12	0.2079	0.9781	0.2126	4.8097	1.0223	4.7046	78
13	0.2250	0.9744	0.2309	4.4454	1.0263	4.3315	77
14	0.2419	0.9703	0.2493	4.1336	1.0306	4.0108	76
15	0.2588	0.9659	0.2679	3.8637	1.0353	3.7321	75
16	0.2756	0.9613	0.2867	3.6280	1.0403	3.4874	74
17	0.2924	0.9563	0.3057	3.4203	1.0457	3.2709	73
18	0.3090	0.9511	0.3249	3.2361	1.0515	3.0777	72
19	0.3256	0.9455	0.3443	3.0716	1.0576	2.9042	71
20	0.3420	0.9397	0.3640	2.9238	1.0642	2.7475	70
21	0.3584	0.9336	0.3839	2.7904	1.0711	2.6051	69
22	0.3746	0.9272	0.4040	2.6695	1.0785	2.4751	68
23	0.3907	0.9205	0.4245	2.5593	1.0864	2.3559	67
24	0.4067	0.9135	0.4452	2.4586	1.0946	2.2460	66
25	0.4226	0.9063	0.4663	2.3662	1.1034	2.1445	65
26	0.4384	0.8988	0.4877	2.2812	1.1126	2.0503	64
27	0.4540	0.8910	0.5095	2.2027	1.1223	1.9626	63
28	0.4695	0.8829	0.5317	2.1301	1.1326	1.8807	62
29	0.4848	0.8746	0.5543	2.0627	1.1434	1.8040	61
30	0.5000	0.8660	0.5774	2.0000	1.1547	1.7321	60
31	0.5150	0.8572	0.6009	1.9416	1.1666	1.6643	59
32	0.5299	0.8480	0.6249	1.8871	1.1792	1.6003	58
33	0.5446	0.8387	0.6494	1.8361	1.1924	1.5399	57
34	0.5592	0.8290	0.6745	1.7883	1.2062	1.4826	56
35	0.5736	0.8192	0.7002	1.7434	1.2208	1.4281	55
36	0.5878	0.8090	0.7265	1.7013	1.2361	1.3764	54
37	0.6018	0.7986	0.7536	1.6616	1.2521	1.3270	53
38	0.6157	0.7880	0.7813	1.6243	1.2690	1.2799	52
39	0.6293	0.7771	0.8098	1.5890	1.2868	1.2349	51
40	0.6428	0.7660	0.8391	1.5557	1.3054	1.1918	50
41	0.6561	0.7547	0.8693	1.5243	1.3250	1.1504	49
42	0.6691	0.7431	0.9004	1.4945	1.3456	1.1106	48
43	0.6820	0.7314	0.9325	1.4663	1.3673	1.0724	47
44	0.6947	0.7193	0.9657	1.4396	1.3902	1.0355	46
45	0.7071	0.7071	1.0000	1.4142	1.4142	1.0000	45

	Cosine (Cos)	Sine (Sin)	Cotangent (Cot)	Secant (Sec)	Cosecant (Csc)	Tangent (Tan)	Degrees

Definitions

Right Triangle (C = 90°)

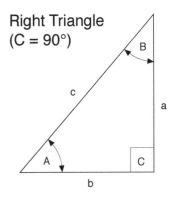

$$\sin A = a/c$$
$$\cos A = b/c$$
$$\tan A = a/b$$
$$\csc A = 1/\sin A = c/a$$
$$\sec A = 1/\cos A = c/b$$
$$\cot A = 1/\tan A = b/a$$

$$\sin B = b/c$$
$$\cos B = a/c$$
$$\tan B = b/a$$
$$\csc B = 1/\sin A = c/b$$
$$\sec B = 1/\cos A = c/a$$
$$\cot B = 1 \tan A = a/b$$

Pythagorean Theorem
$$a^2 + b^2 = c^2$$
$$c = (a^2 + b^2)^{1/2}$$

Glossary

Absorbed glass mat (AGM) battery: sealed battery in which the electrolyte is held in a fiberglass felt like a sponge.

AC grounded conductor: a current-carrying conductor that is intentionally maintained at ground potential. This is also known as the neutral conductor.

AC grounding conductor (green or green w/yellow stripe): a protective conductor, which does not normally carry current, used to connect the metallic, non-current-carrying parts of electrical equipment to the AC grounding system and engine negative terminal, or its bus, and to the shore AC grounding conductor through the shore-power cable.

Air terminal: a device at the uppermost point of the lightning protection system to dissipate the charge or start the lightning ground process.

Alternating current (AC): current that periodically reverses direction.

Alternator: a generator that produces an alternating current. In an automotive or marine alternator, the alternating current (AC) is changed to direct current (DC) by internal diodes.

Ammeter: a meter connected in series with a circuit that measures the current flowing through the circuit.

Ampere: the unit of measure for electric current that equals 1 coulomb (6.24×10^{18}) of electrons per second.

Ampere-hour: a current flow of 1 ampere for 1 hour; a measure of the electrical energy stored in a battery.

Amphoteric: capable of reacting chemically with an acid or a base. Aluminum is amphoteric, and highly susceptible to corrosion when overprotected.

Anode (galvanic mode): the electrode of an electrochemical cell with the more negative potential. The less noble metal of an electrolytic cell that tends to corrode.

Antenna: a conductor whose purpose is to transmit and/or receive radio waves.

Antenna gain: the ratio of power radiated in a desired direction to that radiated at right angles to that direction; measured in decibels (dB).

Armature: the windings in a generator that rotate.

Atom: the smallest quantity into which a chemical element can be divided and still maintain all of the qualities of that element.

Battery: a chemical apparatus that maintains a voltage between its terminals.

Battery bank: two or more storage batteries connected in series to provide higher voltage, or in parallel to provide increased capacity.

Battery charger: a device designed primarily to charge and maintain a battery, or batteries, supplying DC loads.

Battery cold cranking performance rating: the discharge load in amperes that a battery at 0°F (−17.8°C) can deliver for 30 seconds and maintain a voltage of 1.2 volts per cell or higher.

Battery isolation switch: a switch in line with the battery whose purpose is to connect or disconnect the battery.

Battery reserve capacity: the number of minutes a new fully charged battery at 80°F (26.7°C) can be continuously discharged at 25 amperes and maintain a voltage of 1.75 volts or higher per cell (10.5 volts for a 12-volt battery or 5.25 volts for a 6-volt battery).

Bleeder resistor: a resistor in the output of a power supply that removes the output voltage after the power supply is turned off.

Blocking diode: a diode that allows the charging of multiple batteries from a single source without allowing current flow between the batteries.

Bonding: the electrical connection of the exposed, metallic, non-current-carrying parts to the ground (negative) side of the direct current system.

Bonding conductor: a normally non-current-carrying conductor used to connect the non-current-carrying metal parts of direct current devices on the boat to the boat's bonding system.

Branch: a current path in a circuit.

Bulk charge: the stage of battery charging usually defined between 50% and 75 to 80% of battery capacity.

Bus bar: a heavy copper bar or strap in circuit panel boxes carrying current to all of the terminals.

Capacitance: the electrical size of a capacitor in farads. Equal to the amount of charge stored divided by the voltage across the capacitor.

Capacitor: a device that stores electrostatic charge when a voltage is applied.

Cathode: the electrode of an electrochemical cell with the more positive potential. The more noble metal of an electrochemical cell that tends not to corrode.

Cathodic bonding: the electrical interconnection of metal objects in common contact with water, to the engine negative terminal, or its bus, and to the source of cathodic protection.

Cathodic disbondment: the destruction of adhesion between a coating and its substrate by products of a cathodic reaction.

Cathodic protection: reduction or prevention of corrosion of a metal by making it cathodic by the use of sacrificial anodes or impressed currents.

Cell: the smallest unit of a battery. Also an electrochemical system consisting of an anode and a cathode immersed in an electrolyte. The anode and cathode may be separate metals or dissimilar areas on the same metal. The cell includes the external circuit that permits the flow of electrons between the anode and the cathode.

Chassis: the metal structure that supports the circuits and components of a piece of electronic equipment.

Choke: an inductor placed in series in a circuit to oppose changes in current.

Circuit: a complete electrical path from one terminal to the other of a voltage source.

Circuit breaker: an automatic switch that opens when current exceeds the specified limit.

Coaxial cable: a two-conductor cable where the center conductor is surrounded by an insulating dielectric layer, a conducting shield, and an outside insulating sheath.

Coil: turns of wire that have inductance.

Cold cranking amps (CCA): the current in amps that a battery can deliver at 0°F for 30 seconds at a voltage of 1.2 volts minimum (7.2 volts for a 12-volt battery).

Common bonding conductor: an electrical conductor, usually running fore and aft, to which all equipment bonding conductors are connected.

Conductance: a measure of the ability to carry current. The inverse of resistance.

Conductor: any material having little electrical resistance.

Conduit: a pipe, either conducting or nonconducting, in which conductors are run.

Continuity: an uninterrupted electrically conducting path.

Corrosion: the deterioration of a metal by chemical and electro-chemical reaction with its environment.

Corrosion controller: an automatic or manually operated device, in a controlled or regulated cathodic protection system, to regulate the flow of electric current for corrosion control.

Corrosion monitor: an installed hull potential meter (voltmeter) capable of measuring the voltage difference between a reference electrode and a metal hull, or cathodic bonding system, when they are immersed in the same electrolyte.

Coulomb: the unit of measurement of electrical charge. One coulomb equals 6.24×10^{18} electrons.

Couple: two dissimilar metals or alloys in electrical contact with each other that have different potentials and become anodes or cathodes when in common contact with an electrolyte. A couple may also be formed on the surface of the same metal.

Cranking performance (also referred to as marine cranking amps @ 32¡F): the discharge loads, in amperes, that a new, fully charged battery at 32°F (0°C) can continuously deliver for 30 seconds, and maintain a terminal voltage equal to or higher than 1.2 volts per cell.

Current: the flow of electrons through a material.

Current density: for corrosion purposes the current per unit area of the anodes or cathodes expressed in milliamperes per square foot.

Cycle: a complete oscillation of voltage and/or current, from plus to minus and back to plus.

DC grounded conductor: a current-carrying conductor connected to the side of the power source that is intentionally maintained at boat ground potential.

DC grounding conductor: a normally non-current-carrying conductor used to connect metallic non-current-carrying parts of direct current devices to the engine negative terminal, or its bus, for the purpose of minimizing stray-current corrosion.

Deep cycle battery: a lead-acid battery having thicker plates in order to withstand repetitive deep charge/discharge cycles.

Dezincification: a corrosion phenomenon resulting in the selective removal of zinc from copper-zinc alloys.

Dielectric: a material with high electrical resistance.

Dielectric shield: in a cathodic protection system, an electrically nonconductive material, such as a coating, or plastic sheet, that is placed between an anode and an adjacent cathode to avoid current wastage and to improve current distribution to the cathode.

Diode: a semiconductor that allows current flow in one direction but not the opposite direction.

Direct current (DC): current that flows in one direction.

Double-insulation system: an insulation system comprised of basic insulation and supplementary insulation, with the two insulations physically separated and so arranged that they are not simultaneously subjected to the same deteriorating influences (temperature, contaminants, and the like) to the same degree.

Double-pole switch: a switch having two sets of contacts, allowing two conductors to be switched simultaneously.

Drip loop: a dip in a wire or cable to interrupt the flow of water along the run.

Driving potential: voltage difference between the anode and the cathode of a couple.

Earth ground: a point that is at the same potential or voltage as the local earth.

Electrode: a conductive material, in an electrolyte, through which electrical current enters or leaves.

Electrolysis: chemical changes in a solution or electrolyte due to the passage of electric current. This term is also loosely applied to corrosion processes. However, since the term refers to solution phenomena, not to corrosion, its use to indicate corrosion should be discouraged.

Electrolyte: a liquid in which ions are capable of migrating. A liquid capable of conducting a current. Solutions of acids, bases, and salts in water are electrolytes.

Electromagnet: a magnet formed by wrapping wire around an iron core.

Electron: one of the subatomic particles with negative charge that surround the nucleus of an atom and determine its chemical properties.

Energy: the ability to do work. The unit joule equals 1 watt for 1 second.

Engine negative terminal: the point on the engine at which the negative battery cable is connected.

Equalization bus: a metallic strap, which may be installed on the interior of a boat, substantially parallel to the exterior lightning ground plate, and connected to the lightning ground plate at both ends. Secondary lightning conductors can be connected to the equalization bus. The equalization bus provides a low-resistance path to the lightning ground plate.

Glossary

Equalization charge: charging a lead-acid battery at a voltage sufficient to cause rapid gassing, the purpose being the conversion of crystalline lead sulfate on the plates back to lead and sulfuric acid.

Equipment housing: the outside shell of equipment supplied by the manufacturer of the device, or a box, shell, or enclosure provided by the equipment installer. This shell provides personnel protection from electrical hazards, burns, rotating machinery, sharp edges, and provides protection to the device from mechanical damage or weather.

Excitation: a voltage applied to the field winding of a generator in order to initiate charging.

Excitation winding: a separate, small winding in the stator of brushless alternators to initiate charging.

Farad: the unit of capacitance. The size of a capacitor is 1 farad when it stores 1 coulomb of charge with 1 volt across its terminals.

Field winding: a coil of wire used to generate a magnetic field in a generator or alternator.

Filament: the high-resistance wire in a lamp that glows white-hot to produce light.

Filter: an electrical circuit containing reactive elements that passes certain frequencies and blocks others.

Flashing a field: applying an external DC voltage momentarily to a field coil.

Float charge: the voltage that will just maintain a battery at full charge without overcharging.

Fuse: a conductive device that melts and breaks the circuit when current flow exceeds the rated amount.

Galvanic corrosion: the corrosion that occurs at the anode of a galvanic couple caused by the flow of ions (galvanic current) from the anode to the cathode through an electrolyte.

Galvanic couple: two dissimilar metals in electrical contact in an electrolyte.

Galvanic current: the electric current that flows between metals or conductive nonmetals in a galvanic couple.

Galvanic isolator: a device installed in series with the grounding (green or green w/yellow stripe) conductor of the shore-power cable to block low-voltage DC galvanic current flow, but permit the passage of alternating current normally associated with the grounding (green or green w/yellow stripe) conductor.

Galvanic series: a list of metals and alloys arranged in order of their potentials as measured in relation to a reference electrode when immersed in seawater. The table of potentials is arranged with the anodic or least noble metals at one end and the cathodic or most noble metals at the other.

Gassing: the generation of hydrogen and oxygen when a lead-acid battery is overcharged.

Generator: a machine that produces AC electricity when its coils are spun inside a magnetic field.

Giga (G): prefix meaning 10^9 or 1 billion.

Grid: one of the lead-alloy frames that conduct current to and support the active material in a lead-acid battery.

Ground: a surface or mass at the potential of the earth's surface, established at this potential by a conducting connection (intentional or accidental) with the earth, including any metal area that forms part of the wetted surface of the hull.

Grounded conductor: a current-carrying conductor that is connected to the side of the source that is intentionally maintained at ground potential.

Ground fault: an unintended leak of current to ground.

Ground fault circuit interrupter (GFCI): a device intended for the protection of personnel that functions to deenergize a circuit or portion thereof within an established period of time when a current to ground exceeds some predetermined value that is less than that required to operate the overcurrent protective device of the supply circuit. A circuit breaker that acts to interrupt current flow whenever its current limit is exceeded or a ground fault leak is detected.

Ground fault protector (GFP): a device intended to protect equipment by interrupting the electric current to the load when a fault current to ground exceeds some predetermined value that is less than that required to operate the overcurrent protection device of that supply circuit.

Grounding conductor: a conductor not normally carrying current provided to connect the exposed metal enclosures of electric equipment to ground, the primary function of which is to minimize shock hazard to personnel.

Half cell (reference electrode): one electrode in an electrochemical cell used as a reference for measuring the potentials of other metals.

Heat-shrink tubing: an insulating sleeve that shrinks dramatically when heated.

Henry (H): the unit of inductance. A 1-henry coil produces 1 volt when the rate of change of current through it is 1 ampere per second.

Hertz: frequency unit of 1 cycle per second.

Horsepower: a measure of power equaling 746 watts.

Hot: any wire or point in a circuit that is not at ground voltage.

Hull potential: the composite potential (voltage) of the hull cathodic surfaces in an electrolyte as measured against a referenced electrode.

Hydrometer: an instrument for determining the specific gravity (density) of liquids—specifically the electrolyte in a lead-acid battery.

Ignition protection: the design and construction of a device such that under design operating conditions:

- it will not ignite a flammable hydrocarbon mixture surrounding the device when an ignition source causes an internal explosion, or

- it is incapable of releasing sufficient electrical or thermal energy to ignite a hydrocarbon mixture, or

- the source of the ignition is hermetically sealed.

Impedance: the resistance to current flow in an AC circuit.

Impressed current system: a cathodic protection system that utilizes a direct current source (usually with battery) to attain the required millivolt shift in the metallic parts to be protected.

Incandescent lamp: a lamp in which the light is produced by current flow through a filament.

Inductance: measure of the back voltage produced in a coil when current is changing. Unit is the henry.

Induction motor: an AC motor where the rotor is driven by the rotating magnetic field in the stator.

Insulator: any material that is used because of its great electrical resistance.

Interference: unwanted electrical signals superimposed on the desired signal.

Inverter: an electrical device that converts DC power to AC power.

Ion: an electrically charged atom or group of atoms. A form of current flow in liquids and wet wood.

Isolation transformer: a transformer in which power is transferred from primary (input) to secondary (output) coils magnetically without any conductive path.

Isolator: a device installed in series with the grounding (green) conductor of the shore-power cable to effectively block galvanic current (direct current [DC]) flow but permit the passage of alternating current (AC) to provide a path for ground fault currents.

Kilo (k): prefix meaning 10^3 or 1,000.

Leakage resistance: the resistance (usually very high) across a device that is ideally a nonconductor.

Life cycles: the number of charge/discharge cycles a battery can withstand before it loses 50% of its capacity.

Lightning bonding conductor: a conductor intended to be used for potential equalization between metal bodies and the lightning protection system to eliminate the potential for side flashes.

Lightning ground plate (or strip): a metallic plate or strip on the hull exterior below the waterline that serves to efficiently transfer the lightning current from the system of down-conductors to the water.

Lightning protective gap (air gap): a form of lightning arrestor wherein a small air space is provided between two metallic plates, with one connected directly to the vessel grounding plate or strip, and the other to an operating electrical system, such as a radio transmitter or receiver.

Lightning protective mast: a conductive structure, or if nonconductive, equipped with a conductive means and an air terminal.

Live: having a non-zero electrical potential.

Load: any device in a circuit that dissipates power.

Load test: a battery test wherein a high current is withdrawn for a short period.

Main down-conductor: the primary lightning conductor from the top of the mast to the lightning ground. ABYC Standard E4 calls for a minimum conductivity equal to that of a 4 AWG copper conductor.

Mega (M): prefix meaning 10^6 or 1 million.

Metal oxide varistor (MOV): a semiconductor device that is normally nonconductive, but which shorts to ground when struck by a high voltage such as lightning.

Micro (μ): prefix meaning 10^{-6} or one millionth.

Milli (m): prefix meaning 10^{-3} or one thousandth.

Nano (n): prefix meaning 10^{-9} or one billionth.

Negative ion: an atom with one or more extra electrons.

Noble: the positive direction of electrode electrical potential relative to other material in the galvanic series.

Noise: an unwanted electrical signal; also known as interference.

Ohm: the unit of electrical resistance.

Ohmmeter: a device that measures electrical resistance.

Ohm s Law: the mathematical relationship between current through and voltage across an element of a circuit.

Open circuit: a break in a circuit path that prevents the flow of current.

Open-circuit potential: the potential of an electrode measured with respect to a reference electrode or another electrode when no current flows to or from it.

Overcurrent protection device: a device, such as a fuse or circuit breaker, designed to interrupt the circuit when the current flow exceeds a predetermined value.

Panelboard: an assembly of devices for the purpose of controlling and/or distributing power on a boat. It includes devices such as circuit breakers, fuses, switches, instruments, and indicators.

Parallel circuit: a circuit in which there is more than one path through which current can flow.

Parallel path: a path to ground that may be followed by a lightning strike. This path is separate from the path formed by the primary lightning conductor.

Passivation: the formation of a protective oxide film, either naturally or by chemical treatment, on certain active-passive metals like stainless steels.

pH: an expression of hydrogen-ion activity, of both acidity and alkalinity, on a scale whose values run from 0 to 14 with 7 representing neutrality.

Pico (p): prefix meaning 10^{-12} or one million millionth.

Glossary

Pigtails: external conductors that originate within an electrical component or appliance installed by their manufacturer.

Points: metal contacts designed to make and break electrical circuits.

Polarity: the sign (+ or –) of a voltage.

Polarity indicator: a device (usually a lamp) that indicates whether shore-power leads are connected properly (hot to hot, neutral to neutral) or are reversed.

Polarization: the deviation from the open-circuit potential of an electrode resulting from the passage of current, such as from anodes and impressed current systems.

Polarized system AC: a system in which the grounded and ungrounded conductors are connected in the same relation to terminals or leads on devices in the circuit.

Polarized system DC: a system in which the grounded (negative) and ungrounded (positive) conductors are connected in the same relation to terminals or leads on devices in the circuit.

Positive ion: an atom that has lost one or more electrons.

Potential difference: the force that causes electrons and other charged objects to move. Same as electromotive force and voltage.

Potentiometer: a variable resistor with a sliding contact whereby the output voltage can be varied from zero to full input voltage.

Power: the rate at which energy is used or converted. The unit, watt, equals 1 ampere through times 1 volt across.

Power supply: a voltage source, not a battery, that supplies current at a fixed voltage to a circuit.

Primary lightning conductor: the main vertical electrical path in a lightning protection system formed by a metallic mast, metallic structure, electrical conductors, or other conducting means, to a ground plate, ground strip, or a metallic hull.

Primary winding: the input winding of a transformer.

Readily accessible: capable of being reached quickly and safely for effective use under emergency conditions without the use of tools.

Rectifier diode: a high-current semiconductor device that allows current flow only in one direction.

Reference electrode: a metal and metallic-salt (e.g., a silver-silver chloride half cell) mixture in solution that will develop and maintain an accurate reference potential to which the potential of other metals immersed in the same electrolyte may be compared.

Reference potential: the voltage difference between a reference electrode and a metal when they are immersed in the same electrolyte.

Relay: an electromechanical switch in which a small input current switches a much higher output current.

Reserve capacity: the number of minutes a 12-volt battery at 80°F will deliver 25 amps before its voltage drops below 10.5 volts.

Residual magnetism: the magnetic field remaining in a core after current in the field winding ceases.

Resistance: opposition to electric current. The unit is the ohm, which equates to a voltage drop of 1 volt across a device through which 1 ampere of current is flowing.

Reverse polarity: a situation in which positive and negative conductors or terminals are reversed.

Rheostat: a variable resistor.

Ripple: AC voltage superimposed on a DC voltage.

Sacrificial anode: a less noble metal intentionally connected to form a galvanic cell with a more noble metal for the purpose of protecting the more noble metal from corroding.

Screening: sheet metal or metal screening placed around electronic equipment to shunt electrical noise to ground.

Secondary lightning conductor: a conductor used to connect potential parallel paths, such as the rigging on a sailboat, to the primary lightning conductor, or to the lightning ground plate, strip, or equalization bus.

Secondary winding: an output winding of a transformer.

Self-discharge: the gradual discharge of a battery not connected to a load due to leakage between its terminals.

Self-limiting: a device whose maximum output is restricted to a specified value by its magnetic and electrical characteristics.

Self-limiting battery charger: battery chargers in which the output remains at a value that will not damage the charger after application of a short circuit at the DC output terminals for a period of 15 days.

Separator: nonconductive material that separates the plates of a battery.

Series circuit: a circuit having only one path through which current can flow.

Shaft brush: a carbon or metalized graphite block that makes electrical contact to a rotating, or otherwise moving, shaft in order to improve electrical contact to the cathodic bonding system.

Sheath: a material used as a continuous protective covering, such as overlapping electrical tape, woven sleeving, molded rubber, molded plastic, loom, or flexible tubing, around one or more insulated conductors.

Shielding: an electrically conductive sheath or tube surrounding conductors and connected to ground in order to protect the conductors from noise.

Shore-power inlet: the fitting designed for mounting on the boat, of a reverse-service type, requiring a female connector on the shore-power cable in order to make the electrical connection.

Short circuit: a path, usually accidental, with little or no electrical resistance.

Shunt: a conductor of known resistance placed in series with a circuit to indicate current flow by measurement of the voltage drop across this conductor.

Side flash: an arc-over discharge that occurs from the lightning system to any metallic object.

Signal-to-noise ratio (SNR): the power ratio between a signal (meaningful information) and noise (meaningless).

Sine wave: the shape of a graph of voltage versus time in an AC signal. All rotary generators produce this waveform.

Slip rings: one or more continuous conducting rings that mate to shaft brushes to provide electrical contact to rotating, or otherwise moving, shafts in order to improve electrical contact to the cathodic bonding system.

Slow-blow fuse: a fuse that allows motor start-up currents in excess of its rating for a short time.

Solenoid: a relay used to switch heavy currents such as those in a starter motor.

Specific gravity: the ratio of the density of a material to the density of water. In a lead-acid battery, the specific gravity of the electrolyte is a measure of the battery's state of charge.

Spike: a high voltage peak superimposed on a DC voltage.

Stator: the stationary armature of an alternator inside of which the rotor turns.

Storage battery: a group of cells permanently electrically interconnected, and contained in a case.

Stray-current corrosion: corrosion that results when a current from a battery or other external electrical (DC) source causes a metal in contact with an electrolyte to become anodic with respect to another metal in contact with the same electrolyte.

Sulfation: the crystallization of the lead sulfate of a lead-acid battery plate, which occurs when the battery is left discharged. It hinders the battery reactions and thus reduces battery capacity.

Surge: a voltage and/or current spike.

Surge protector: a solid-state device that shunts (conducts) surges to ground.

Switch: a device used to open and close circuits.

Switchboard: an assembly of devices for the purpose of controlling and/or distributing power on a boat. It may include devices such as circuit breakers, fuses, switches, instruments, and indicators. They are generally accessible from the rear as well as from the front and are not intended to be installed in cabinets.

Terminal: a point of connection to an electrical device.

Thermistor: a solid-state device whose resistance varies strongly with temperature.

Tinning: coating a wire or terminal with solder in order to prevent corrosion or to facilitate a solder connection.

Transformer, isolation: a transformer meeting the requirements of E-11.9.1 installed in the shore-power supply circuit on a boat to electrically isolate all AC system conductors, including the AC grounding conductor (green) on the boat, from the AC system conductors of the shore-power supply.

Transformer, polarization: an isolated winding transformer, i.e., a "dry type," encapsulated lighting transformer, installed in the shore-power supply circuit on the boat to electrically isolate the normally current-carrying AC system conductors, but not the AC grounding conductor (green) from the normally current-carrying conductors of the shore-power supply.

Transient voltage surge suppressor (TVSS): a semiconductor device designed to provide protection against voltage and current spikes.

Trickle charge: a continuous low-current charge.

Trip-free circuit breaker: a resettable overcurrent protection device designed so that the means of resetting cannot override the current interrupting mechanism.

Ty-wrap: plastic strap for bundling conductors and cables.

Ungrounded conductor: a current-carrying conductor that is completely insulated from ground and connects the source of power to the utilization equipment. In direct current systems (DC), this conductor will be connected to the positive terminal of the battery. In alternating current systems (AC), this conductor will be connected to the "hot" side of the shore-power system, or to the appropriate terminal of an onboard auxiliary generator.

Volt (V): the unit of voltage or potential difference.

Voltage drop: reduction in voltage along a conductor due to the current carried and the finite resistance of the conductor.

Voltage source: a device that supplies the voltage to a circuit.

Voltmeter: device for measuring voltage or potential difference between two points of a circuit.

Watertight: so constructed that moisture will not enter the enclosure.

Watt (W): unit of measurement of power. One watt is 1 ampere through times 1 volt across.

Wavelength: the distance between identical phases of two successive waves, usually from peak to peak or from zero-crossing to zero-crossing.

Weatherproof: constructed or protected so that exposure to the weather will not interfere with successful operation.

Windings: coils of current-carrying wire in a generator, motor, or transformer.

Zone of protection: an essentially cone-shaped space below a grounded air terminal, mast, or overhead ground wire, wherein the risk of a direct lightning strike is substantially reduced.

Index

A

absorbed-glass mat (AGM) batteries, 40–41
absorption cycle, 36, 37, 59, 60, 138
ABYC. *See* American Boat and Yacht Council (ABYC)
air terminals, 77
alternating current (AC). *See also* circuits, AC
    ABYC standards, 145–46
    advantages of, 129, 130
    budget, figuring, 131–34
    color codes for conductors, 121, 126, 155, 163
    converting to DC, 123
    equivalent DC voltage, 116–17
    frequency, 116, 118
    frequency meters, 143, 248
    grounding, 120, 121, 148, 164–66
    impedance, 118, 124
    measurement of, 124–25
    Ohm's Law, 116
    phase, 50–51, 115, 116–17, 118
    polarity indicators, 149, 246
    polarity testing, 127
    power factor, 115, 118
    production of, 50–51
    rectification, 52–54
    resistance component of impedance, 124
    safety, 115, 119–20, 145
    short circuits, 120
    sources, 130
    voltage, 116–17, 124
alternators. *See also* voltage regulators
    belts, 63
    charging setups, 61–62
    DC output from, 52–54
    excite circuits, 58, 69
    galley alternator, 50
    installation, 63
    matching to load, 43, 49
    operation of, 49, 50–56
    pulley alignment, 63
    rotors and brushes, 55
    troubleshooting, 64–69
    types of, 57
alternator-type generators, 140
aluminum, 89
American Boat and Yacht Council (ABYC) standards
    batteries, 46
    bonding systems, 86
    cathodic protection, 87, 91
    galvanic isolators, 166

    ignition protection, 110–13
    Standards for Small Craft, 1
    wiring, 93, 145–46
    wiring connections, 107
ammeters, 16, 18, 19, 125, 242
ampacity, 97, 98, 145, 146, 148, 155–61
amperage rating, 97, 99
ampere-hours, 32
amperes, 5, 8–12, 131
amplifiers, 245
analog test instruments, 15, 16–18, 19, 242
anchor lights, 186, 253
antenna cable and connectors, 226–29
antennas
    installation, 223
    lightning protection systems, 77, 78
    location, 224–25
    types of, 224, 230
appliances
    AC versus DC, 130
    conservation conversions, 192
    load calculation, 38–39, 131–34, 150–53
armature-type generators, 140, 141
attenuation, 108, 226

B

backstay insulators, 224, 225, 231
batteries
    ABYC standards, 46
    battery banks, 44
    chemical reactions, 28–30
    composition of, 28–29, 30
    costs of, 42–43
    dimensions, 40
    discharge, depth of, 42–43
    discharging, 7, 27, 29, 30, 34–35
    electrical model, 31
    fully discharged, 29, 33
    galley battery, 28
    installation, 27, 46
    life cycles of, 42
    loads and, 38–39, 44
    monitoring, 27, 32–33, 250–52
    parallel connections, 7, 27, 44
    phases of, 29–30
    self-discharging, 31, 33
    series connections, 7, 27, 44
    shedding, 30, 138
    sizes, 27, 40, 42, 44
    specifications, 35
    sulfation, 30, 42
    temperature and, 31, 33, 34, 36
    troubleshooting, 64–69

    types of, 40–41, 241
    weight of, 44, 45
    winter storage, 33
battery boxes, 45
battery cables, 102
battery chargers, 123
battery charging
    absorption cycle, 36, 37, 59, 60, 138
    bulk cycle, 36, 37, 59, 60, 138
    charge controllers, 59–60, 205
    charge indicators, 19
    charging recommendations, 27, 37
    charging setups, 61–62
    chemical reaction during, 29–30
    equalization, 30, 37, 59, 60, 138
    float cycle, 36, 37, 59, 60, 138
    gassing, 30, 36, 37
    optimally fast charging, 36–37, 138
    overcharging, 30, 36, 37
    parallel connections, 7
battery eliminator, 249
battery isolation diodes, 58, 66, 68
battery selector switch, 7, 44
belts, alternator, 63
bilge, wiring in, 102, 232
bilge high-water alarm, 255
bilge pump motors, 242
blocking diodes, 199, 205
bonding conductors, 72, 73
bonding systems
    bond-and-protect principle, 86
    components of, 72–73
    controversy surrounding, 71
    purpose of, 71, 72
    stray-current corrosion, 71, 84–86
    unbond-and-isolate principle, 86
brass, 89
bronze, 89, 90
brushes, 55, 141, 143
bulk cycle, 36, 37, 59, 60, 138
buzzers, 20, 242

C

cabin light circuits, 21–24, 96
cabin light dimmer, 254
capacitors, 235–36, 240
cathodic protection, 82, 84, 86, 87–88, 91
cavitation erosion, 90
charge controllers, 59–60, 205
charge-indicator lamp, 58
circuit breakers, 205, 241
    AC, 154
    DC, 93, 103–4

Index

wind power
  average power in wind, 212–14
  choosing, 210
  energy costs, 43, 184, 210
  installation, 209, 217–19
  operation of, 211
  output estimations, 209, 211–15
  solar power and, 196
  specifications of wind machines, 216
wire
  ABYC standards, 93, 155
  ampacity, 97, 98, 146, 155–61
  color codes, 101, 121, 126, 155, 163
  construction, 97
  identification of, 93, 94, 101
  installation, 101–2, 163
  insulation, 97, 99, 155
  sizes, 97, 99, 100, 155
  voltage drop, 100
wiring diagrams, 94–96
wiring failures, 105
wiring symbols, 94, 95
wiring tools, 105

X

Xantrex inverters, 136, 137
Xantrex Link 2000-R Charge Controller, 60

Y

Y coil arrangements, 54

Z

zener diodes, 243
zinc anodes, 82, 84, 86, 87–88, 91
zinc corrosion, 80, 82
zones of protection, 75–76